THE LIFE OF
ORATOR HENLEY

THE LIFE
OF
ORATOR
HENLEY

GRAHAM MIDGLEY
FELLOW OF ST. EDMUND HALL, OXFORD

Clarendon Press · Oxford

1973

Oxford University Press, Ely House, London W.1

GLASGOW   NEW YORK   TORONTO   MELBOURNE   WELLINGTON
CAPE TOWN   IBADAN   NAIROBI   DAR ES SALAAM   LUSAKA   ADDIS ABABA
DELHI   BOMBAY   CALCUTTA   MADRAS   KARACHI   LAHORE   DACCA
KUALA LUMPUR   SINGAPORE   HONG KONG   TOKYO

PRINTED IN GREAT BRITAIN BY
WILLIAM CLOWES & SONS LIMITED,
LONDON, BECCLES AND COLCHESTER

IN MEMORIAM

W.E.M.
E.L.M.

Preface

It has been said of the remote dale in which much of this book was written, that only Yorkshiremen have heard of it and most of them don't know where it is. It might equally be said of the subject of this book that only eighteenth-century specialists have heard of Orator Henley and many of them only know him as a fleeting figure in *The Dunciad*. I am well aware that even my most gentle reader may well question the point of spending so much time and energy on attempting to re-create his life, and I find myself echoing the note of apology which one of Henley's earliest biographers John Nichols first sounded as he started his brief life in the *History of Leicestershire*. 'In delineating the life of Mr. *John Henley*, better known by the name of *Orator Henley*,' he wrote, 'we hope to be excused for endeavouring to transmit to posterity the memory of a man who deserves a place in the page of History', though I cannot, even as a 'clerical character' myself who might personally benefit, concur in the belief that I do so 'for the useful lesson these anecdotes inculcate, that an affected and *outré* singularity, such as his, rarely succeeds; and when proceeding from a clerical character, is sure to meet with the contempt it deserves.'[1] My motive has been, I hope, more objective and perhaps less lofty, than to create a moral exemplar.

I too first met Henley, fixed with a terrible permanence in Pope's couplets in *The Dunciad*:

> Imbrown'd with native bronze, lo! Henley stands,
> Tuning his voice, and balancing his hands.
> How fluent nonsense trickles from his tongue!
> How sweet the periods, neither said, nor sung!
> Still break the benches, Henley! with thy strain,
> While Sherlock, Hare, and Gibson preach in vain.
> Oh great Restorer of the good old Stage,
> Preacher at once, and Zany of thy Age!
> O worthy thou of Aegypt's wise abodes,
> A decent priest, where monkeys were the gods!

---

[1] John Nichols, *The History and Antiquities of Leicestershire*, vol. ii, pt. i, p. *259. (Hereafter referred to as Nichols, *Leicestershire*.)

But fate with butchers plac'd thy priestly stall,
Meek modern faith to murder, hack, and mawl;
And bade thee live, to crown Britannia's praise,
In Toland's, Tindal's, and in Woolston's days.   (B.III.199)

I cannot now remember the exact evening when, re-reading these
lines, I protested. Surely this could not and should not be the only
epitaph for sixty years of a human life. Behind this caricature was
a man, a man with ideas and feelings, with a family and friends as
well as enemies, with a private life as well as a public front. Was
it possible to rediscover him, to fill out the picture and add light
and shade and depth to this crude outline drawing? Isaac Disraeli's
remark that 'Pope's verse and Warburton's notes are the pickle
and the bandages for any Aegyptian mummy of dulness, who will
last as long as the pyramid that incloses him'[1] finally persuaded
me to try to unwrap the bandages on one particular mummy and
to see whether it was possible to make the shrivelled skin and dry
bones live. As the work proceeded, other reasons for this attempt
suggested themselves. Henley was no obscure little dunce only
known because he had annoyed Pope. He was a famous figure in
his day, a constant talking point in London for thirty years, a
prominent part of the day-to-day life of the metropolis. Chat in a
coffee-house, read a newspaper, visit a pamphlet shop and, sooner
or later, Orator Henley would crop up. Moreover he was involved
in so many activities—literary, religious, and political—that to
follow his career and to attempt to follow his arguments was to
see the great movements of thought and action of his time from a
novel point of view. To place Henley fully in this context would
have demanded a study requiring very extensive space and knowledge, which might well have been in danger of disintegrating
into a series of monographs on eighteenth-century thought and
history, theological, liturgical, political, literary, and journalistic,
to name but a few. Yet, to consider Henley's activity in all these
spheres without some reference to his predecessors and contemporaries, might have brought another danger of showing him as
much more isolated and eccentric in his thoughts and deeds than
in fact he was. I have tried to sketch in sufficient of the main ideas
and influences behind Henley's work to avoid this latter danger,
but 'Orator Henley' has remained, as from the beginning, my

[1] Isaac Disraeli, *The Calamities of Authors* (1812), vol. i, p. 152.

primary interest, as I attempted to follow in the footsteps of Disraeli and to rediscover in greater detail 'this worthy of literature . . . rather known traditionally than historically . . . so overwhelmed with the echoed satire of Pope, and his own extravagant conduct for many years'.[1]

The making of this book has been easier and more enjoyable through the unfailing co-operation and patience of the staffs of those libraries where I have worked, the Bodleian, the British Museum, the library of the Grand Lodge of Freemasons, the library of the Guildhall, and the Public Record Office. In the County Record Offices of Leicestershire, Middlesex, and Suffolk I received help and advice which amounted to active research on my behalf. I would like to thank my many colleagues, and especially Jeffrey Hackney, Professor Ralph Pugh, Miss Rachel Trickett, and Edward Wilson, for their various assistance and criticism and their constant encouragement, and finally to record my gratitude to Suzie and Fred for their uncomplaining companionship through the long-drawn-out labours of many years.

GRAHAM MIDGLEY

St. Edmund Hall, Oxford

[1] Ibid. i.151–2.

Contents

List of Plates

Photographs by courtesy of the Trustees of the British Museum

CHAPTER I
Childhood and Youth

IN THE CLOSING YEARS of the seventeenth century, Melton Mowbray in the county of Leicestershire was a pleasant and important town, in a quiet pastoral setting but often crowded and busy with cattle markets and fairs. Around the town flowed the river Eye, and the visitor received his first impression of prosperity and civic pride as he crossed either of the fine bridges from south or west, six-arched and seven-arched, striding the river. It was an impression confirmed as he entered the town over its well-paved and well-cleaned streets and, looking up, saw at its centre, rising above the roofs of the houses, a symbol of the town's pre-eminence and pride, its great church.

Dedicated to St. Mary, this church was one of the finest in the county, plain and elegant, battlemented around the nave and transepts and rising into its great square central tower crowned with pinnacles. Inside, large clerestory windows filled it with light, and carven angels bearing shields looked down on the nave. The local pride and wealth which built fine bridges and paved the streets had not neglected the church which, in an age when monuments were so often abandoned to dirt and decay, was remarkable for its preservation and upkeep. It was indeed a church which any town would consider an ornament and which any priest would consider an attraction to the parish, even though he might be confirmed in his decision by the £240 a year which the living was worth.[1]

It was to this town and particularly to this church that John Henley's forebears came, for the future 'preacher both and zany of his age' sprang from a family of clerics. His maternal grandfather, John Dowell, a Leicester man, educated at Christ's College, Cambridge, was instituted Vicar of Melton Mowbray on 16 September 1660, and held that living for thirty years until his death

---

[1] Nichols, *Leicestershire*, gives much detail of Melton Mowbray at this period and in the eighteenth century: vol. ii, pt. i, 'Melton Mowbray'.

on 2 October 1690.[1] 'He was', his grandson tells us, 'remarkable
for the Assiduity of his Studies, the Force of his Talents, the
Eloquence of his Pen, great Learning, and a peculiar Happiness
in Disputation, which he often publickly exerted against the
Papists, Dissenters and others as occasion offer'd.'[2] Though one
suspects that the newly established Orator was finding hereditary
sources for his own especial talents, there is independent evidence
of John Dowell's scholarship and powers of disputation. Anthony
à Wood records him as the author of *The Leviathan heretical: or the
Charge Exhibited in Parliament against Mr. Hobbes justified &c.*, published at Oxford in 1683, in which book, we are told, 'the author
saith that Oliver gaining the protectorship, was so pleased with
many of his principles laid down in the *Leviathan*, which tended to
justify and support his usurpation, that the great place of being
secretary was profer'd to him'.[3] It was generally accepted that it
was he who, in the same year, crossed swords with George
Hickes, author of *Jovian: or an Answer to Julian the Apostate*, in a
pamphlet called *The Triumph of Christianity; or, the life of Cl.Fl.Julian
the Apostate: with Remarks, contained in the Resolution of several
Queries. To which are added Reflections upon a Pamphlet called, Seasonable Remarks on the Fall of the Emperor Julian &c.*[4] Henley also
ascribed to him lives of St. Chrysostom and St. Basil.[5] The wife
of this busy and disputatious priest, Mary, had borne him a
daughter, Arabella, in 1664, destined to wed into another clerical
family and to be the mother of John Henley.

The Henleys were of ancient Devonshire stock but the family
of Henley's paternal grandfather, John, was already settled away
from that county by the seventeenth century. The boy was,
according to his grandson, educated at Lincoln School under 'the
famous Mr. J. Clarke'[6] among the Dissenters in the time of the

---

[1] The recorded fact is his burial on 5 Oct. 1690.

[2] *A Narrative*, prefaced to *Oratory Transactions No. 1* (1728), p. 1. (Hereafter referred
to as *Narrative*.)

[3] Anthony à Wood, *Athenae Oxonienses*, 3rd edition with additions, ed. Bliss (1820),
vol. iii, p. 1214. See also Wing, *Short Title Catalogue*, Entry 2056, and Term Catalogue
II.32, for June 1683, which definitely ascribes this book to John Dowell.

[4] Ibid. iv.570. See also Wing, *Short Title Catalogue*, Entry 2057, which makes this
ascription, although the Term Catalogue for May 1683 makes no reference to John
Dowell.

[5] *Narrative*, p. 1.

[6] Advertisement for 3 Aug. 1750 (Lysons 164). (Many of Henley's advertisements
appeared in newspapers which have not been preserved, but fortunately many of

Civil Wars, but conformed at the Restoration. Again one suspects Henley of further creation of hereditary talents when he adds that his grandfather was distinguished for his powers of extempore preaching and prayer which then prevailed.[1] Many years later he added to the story that his grandfather was recommended by Henry Pelham, Recorder of Lincoln, to Oliver Cromwell who, 'on hearing him preach, preferr'd him'.[2] This story of the Protector's part in the family fortunes is preserved in a curious explanation Henley later gave of his use of the initials 'J.O.C.H.' in place of his previous 'J.H.'. 'To end Enquiry,' he wrote, 'J.O.C.H. is John Oliver Cromwell Henley: I was privately baptiz'd, tho' not register'd, by that Name: not divulg'd, in fear of spoiling my Fortune: that was left to myself.'[3] The Protector's preferment, if it was indeed his, made John Henley Rector of Salmonby and Thetford in Lincolnshire, and subsequently he became Vicar of Towcester in Northamptonshire in 1662.

Here at Towcester in 1665 his son Simon was born, destined to follow his father in a clerical career. He was educated at Benet College in Cambridge and after his ordination came to Melton Mowbray as curate, signing himself curate in the Register in 1687. When John Dowell died in 1690 Simon Henley succeeded him as vicar. The oft-repeated curate–vicar's daughter romance had once more flowered and ripened, and now, established and secure, the new vicar took Arabella Dowell to wife on 8 November 1691. For more than forty years the people of Melton Mowbray and its great church were cared for by Simon Henley, 'commonly said to have been one of the best Parish Priests in England, a Pattern of Sanctity and of the Pastoral Care',[4] and Henley, writing while his father was still alive and in office, testified that 'he is so well known and approv'd in his Neighbourhood for his Learning and Piety, especially as a very able Textuary, and good Parish-Priest, that it is needless to be more particular

them are collected in a unique scrapbook of Henley press cuttings made by Daniel Lysons, now in the British Museum (*Collectanea*. B.M. 1889.e.6). Where possible I give a definite newspaper reference: otherwise I give a page reference in Lyson's *Collectanea*.) The 'Mr. J. Clarke' referred to is Mr. *Nathaniel* Clarke, schoolmaster of Lincoln Grammar School during the Civil War and the Interregnum.

[1] *Narrative*, p. 2.

[2] Advertisement for 3 Aug. 1750 (Lysons 164).   [3] Ibid.

[4] *A Catalogue of the Original Manuscripts, and Manuscript Collections, of the Late Reverend Mr. John Henley* (1759), p. 37.

on his Character.'[1] Twenty years after his father's death he still recalled with admiration his *'Erudition,* especially in ye oriental languages, not equall'd in his Time'.[2] He gave his church a silver-gilt patten and he also left behind him a manuscript of a devotional work. This manuscript Henley kept by him for many years, obviously a valued relic of a much-admired father. Fifteen years after his father's death he announced it as preparing for the press, but it was never printed. In the sale catalogue of Henley's books is the item 'A Pocket-Book of Devotions, Ejaculations, Meditations, Prayers, Hymns, Acts of Piety: and Elevation to God and Christ, Rules and Directions, daily and occasional, for Sunday Evening, Fasts, Vigils, before Easter, Preparation for the Sacrament, Method and Prayers in Sickness, for a happy Death; and for Clergymen, or Ministers . . .'. It appears that Henley had fulfilled his promise but not found a printer, for the item ends, 'Prepar'd for the Press by his Son, John Henley, M.A. Independent Minister of the Oratory; with some short Memoirs of his life and Character, 4to.—The same Book, in the Author's Hand Writing, 8vo.'.[3] Simon Henley died in his sixty-sixth year on 5 June 1731. His wife Arabella survived him a few years, dying on 17 December 1734 in her seventieth year. She was laid to rest in the tomb which contained her husband's remains and which, six years later, was to receive the body of her daughter Elizabeth.

John Henley, the subject of our story, was born the eldest child of Simon and Arabella on 3 August 1692. He had one younger brother Simon, and three sisters, Arabella, Elizabeth, and Mary. Arabella married Richard Saunders of Melton and lived there until her death in 1735; Elizabeth died unmarried on 20 March 1741; Mary married William Wright and lived to keep a grocer's shop in Melton Mowbray and had, we are told, 'a considerable gift of speech',[4] a talent—or a failing—which her more famous brother also inherited. We know little of this family and nothing of John's life at home, with that family, as a child. It must have been a comfortable household, pious and scholarly, with a father busy around his parish, studious over his books, and carefully planning for the education and future of his son. There is only

---

[1] *Narrative,* p. 2.
[2] Henley's discourse for 18 Mar. 1753 (B.M. MSS.Add. 11787).
[3] *A Catalogue of the Original Manuscripts, etc.,* item 388, p. 37.
[4] Nichols, *Leicestershire,* vol. ii, pt. i, p. ** 261.

one small glimpse afforded us of the young Henley anywhere except at his studies, a picture of a country-bred lad at play, which has the same ironic effect of contrast with his turbulent and urban future as when we read of Pope's idyllic Binfield days. 'I remember', he says in a sermon in 1727, 'when I was a Boy, that by holding a Sparrow thus upon my Finger, and chirruping to it, I taught it to fly under my Hat!'[1] There must have been other such pleasures along the banks of the Eye, in the meadows or at the fairs, but none is remembered or recorded. It is on memories of school and study, schoolmaster and scholarly achievement that Henley dwells when he remembers the past.

His first steps in learning were taken at the local Free School at Melton, one of the many small local grammar schools with their roots deep in the past, this one certainly having existed from 1347. There, under Mr. Thomas Daffye, 'a diligent and expert grammarian',[2] and Mr. Robert Trigge in the lower school, young John learnt the rudiments of Latin and Greek, and, according to his own report (for, through lack of evidence we depend upon his no doubt not disinterested account) progressed with great speed and promise. 'His Passion for Learning,' we are told, 'his Desire of Excelling others, and his unweary'd Attachment to Study, shew'd themselves in him very early and have been the Principles of his Life.'[3] In his last year of school his father removed him from Melton and sent him—not, as we shall see, without a reason—to the younger but more important school at Oakham.

Oakham School had been jointly founded with Uppingham by Robert Johnson, a Cambridge man, a philanthropist, and Archdeacon of Leicester, around 1574, and received its charter in 1587. Henley, moving there before the school buildings were restored in 1723, would have joined his new schoolmates in the Old School. There in the large hall, seated along each side of the room on a narrow gallery raised one step above the floor, the boys worked at their books and exercises under the watchful eye of the Master presiding at one end with especial charge of the Upper Side, and of the Usher, facing his superior from the other end and caring for the younger pupils. As their allotted tasks of translation and

[1] *Punchinello's Sermon* (1727), p. 12. This is admittedly a report of a sermon by Henley, or rather of two sermons conflated. It often appears to have satiric distortion, but this little aside has no satiric purpose or effect, and appears to be true reporting.
[2] *Narrative*, p. 2.   [3] Ibid.

repetition were completed, the boys came up to their masters to
say their lesson, to answer questions, and to return to their seats
for further preparation. Over this coming and going ruled the
Reverend Henry Wright, a scholar of the great Dr. Busby at
Westminster and a graduate of Christ Church, who had joined the
school in 1701, assisted at the other end of Old School by his
Usher, the Reverend Nathaniel Weston. Henley was happy there
and remembered his old mentors with admiration and affection,
crediting them with his continued progress and delight in the
ancient tongues. He remembered especially the kindness and
encouragement of Mr. Weston for 'There he was led by his
Genius to cultivate the Graces of *English* and *Latin* Poetry.'[1] His
other encourager was a more noble and splendid personage. The
Rt. Hon. Daniel Finch, Earl of Nottingham, as a trustee of the
school, had always taken more than a formal part in its administration. At that time he was engaged in building his seat at near-by
Burley-on-the-Hill and often descended upon the school, not only
to look around, but to command its scholars to special exercises.
We learn of Henley completing a 'Translation of the last Parting
of Hector and Andromache, in *Homer*, by the Command of the
Right Hon. Daniel Finch, late Earl of Nottingham . . . as a Tryal
to excell Dean Chetwood's translation of the same. A poem on the
said Great Earl of Nottingham's Motto, *Nil Conscire Sibi*, and a
Poem on the Gunpowder Plot, both by his Order.'[2] Henley tells
us that the Earl 'often declar'd his Approbation of his juvenile
Performances',[3] and he himself valued and preserved them, for
when, years later, he listed the books he had written, he included
'Scholastic and Academical Exercises in Prose and Verse, English,
Latin, Greek, Hebrew, Chaldee, from the Age of Six to Fifteen:
the Elogium of his Preceptor, the Rev. Mr. WRIGHT, Scholar
of Dr. BUSBY, and an Introduction to Logic and Philosophy,
written at Oakham School in Rutland'.[4] His studies extended and
deepened during this happy year and no doubt about its complete
veracity could prevent a biographer from including Henley's

[1] *Narrative*, p. 2.
[2] *Books written by this Author*, making up pp. i–v of Henley's *The Oratory Magazine
No. III* (1748).
[3] *Narrative*, p. 3.
[4] *Books written by this Author*. It is not clear here whether Henley means a printed
book or a manuscript. I have found no trace of either.

School Report on Henley—'It may excite the Emulation of Scholars, to let them know, that there never was Occasion to make use of Severity, or impose any Task upon him; and that his Maxim and Resolution was always to be the First of his Class, and Captain of the School.'[1]

More objective evidence of his progress and success, however, is given at the end of his year at Oakham, and Simon Henley's reason for moving his son there is made clear. In his will, Robert Johnson, the Founder, had established five exhibitions at Sidney College, St. John's, Emmanuel, and Clare Hall, Cambridge, for students of the school who 'study Divinity, were Diligent Hearers of Sermons, and skillfull in the Hebrew Greek and Lattin tongues'. A codicil altered the number of exhibitions to sixteen and made that alteration to the conditions which explains Henley's one year at the school. Preference was to be given to boys who had been 'one whole yeare at the least before their admission into the said Colleges, having been educated at Oakham or Uppingham, and are good schollers of honest conversation, and stand in need of maintenance'. It was these exhibitions which attracted to the school many able boys besides Henley, and under Wright's Mastership forty-nine pupils went up to University, eleven of them being subsequently elected to fellowships. By a strange irony, one of the unsuccessful ones was the man whose footnotes to *The Dunciad* were to add more cruelty to Pope's satirical attack on Henley—William Warburton. He was himself at the school only one year, but never rose above the lower side of the school. It would have warmed Henley's heart if he could have known that his beloved Usher Weston remembered his enemy only as 'the dullest of dull boys',[2] when he himself was among the brightest who were awarded at the end of the school year, by an examining body of the Master and senior Fellows of his chosen college, a place and an exhibition of 40s. a year.

So it was that on 15 June in the year 1709, the year which saw Pope's *Pastorals* and Samuel Johnson born into the world, John Henley was admitted Pensioner of St. John's College, Cambridge. His election had followed upon a most favourable impression

---

[1] *Narrative*, p. 3.

[2] For this and for many details on Oakham School I am indebted to W. L. Sargant's *The Book of Oakham School* (Cambridge, 1928).

made on his examiners, the Master of St. John's, Dr. Gower, and Dr. Lambert and Dr. Edmunson, Fellows,[1] to whom he had presented as further evidence of his achievements, the translations and verses he had done at the Earl of Nottingham's command.[2] Here, as at school, he found men to admire, especially his tutor the Revd. Dr. Newcombe, later to become Master, whom he considered 'a polite, learned and worthy Gentleman and an ornament of the College', and the Revd. Mr. Thomas Baker, the 'Author of the *Reflections on Learning* one of the most accomplished Scholars and one of the best Men of his Age',[3] with whom he kept on corresponding terms for some years. It was to Baker he wrote years later when he was preparing to write his Grammars, asking for advice and books, and who ended his reply to Henley with the words 'I wish they had [filled up our fellowships] whilst you were here, that we might have enjoy'd so useful a Member, and one that would have done Honour to the society.'[4] There is no reason to discount these words as Henley's enemies were later to do as 'no more than a civil compliment to a person ingaged in a learned design, who had left the college several years, and who, it is probable, Mr. BAKER never remembered there'.[5] They describe the first of the many 'might have beens' which haunt Henley's life, the memory and the frustration of which increasingly embittered him, and drove him along his ever more odd and furious way. There was no reason, indeed, why he should not, like many of his schoolmates, have gained election as a Fellow. He came up with a fine school record, impressed his tutors at the start, and considered that he always 'went through [his] Exercises with distinguishing applause'.[6] Moreover he was, in a small way, adding to his reputation that of poet and, possibly, essayist. There is a repeated tradition that in 1712, under the pen-names of Peter de Quir and Tom Tweer he wrote letters which were printed in the *Spectator*, nos. 396 and 518. The first letter from Peter de Quir is dated from St. John's College, Cambridge, and treats in a confused and over-elaborate way the art of punning in Cambridge. Its over-conscious cleverness approaches incomprehensibility, and it fully deserves Nichols's description of 'this silly letter'.

---

[1] *Narrative*, p. 3.   [2] *Books written by this Author.*
[3] *Narrative*, p. 4.   [4] Ibid., p. 7.
[5] *Grub Street Journal*, 30 Nov. 1732. (Hereafter referred to as *G.S.J.*)
[6] *Hyp Doctor*, 9 Nov. 1736.

One argument for Henley's authorship is that it foreshadows his later bantering style at its worst. The later letter is on the study of physiognomy amongst the Cambridge phizes and, though more successful in communicating a meaning, its wit is laboured and dull. Henley's most friendly biographer would not fight long to remove the doubts which still exist about his authorship.[1] His performance as a poet is not so depressing.

According to Nichols[2] the poem *On a LADY that could not help Laughing at Nothing, and another taking the Laugh from her* was written while Henley was at Cambridge, although it did not appear in print until 1719 in *The Court Miscellany No. II* when 'Printed for E. Curll' on the title-page announced Henley's early connection with that notorious master of Grub Street. As an essay in light verse it is by no means contemptible. The couplet moves easily and with variety, and the turn of phrase and idea is neat enough. It opens:

> In every Fair some reigning Talents shine,
> This Kills, and That can laugh, without Design:
> CELIA to charm requires no Art, or Toil:
> And CHLOE from no Thought creates a Smile;
> Both happy! For in all that's apt to please,
> 'Tis the first Beauty to be done with Ease.   (1–6)

He creates quite pleasantly another of those satiric portraits of women of which Pope's Belinda and the creatures of his epistle on the characters of women are the outstanding examples:

> While in the busy Round of Female Chat,
> Dear *Tea*, and dearer *Scandal* circulate;
> While at each Sip a Friend or Foe supplies,
> At Random Strokes, a careless Sacrifice;
> Soft CHLOE creams into a sudden Smile,
> That bodes no Danger, for she knows no Guile.   (22–7)

---

[1] Henley's authorship of these letters is affirmed by Nichols (*Leicestershire*, vol. ii, pt. i, p. **259) and in the *Gentleman's Magazine* for April 1780, p. 175, and May 1779, p. 256. Henley never claimed them in his lists of published writing, and they are not mentioned in the *Narrative*.

[2] Nichols, *Leicestershire*, vol. ii, pt. i, p. **259. He gives no reason for assigning it to the Cambridge period, but its subject and tone suggest more the work of an undergraduate than of a young priest seeking preferment. On the other hand, the pamphlet *A Guide to the Oratory: or, an Historical Account of the new sect of the Henley-arians* introduces the poem with the words, 'Written in the Year 1719'.

> Her roving Thought may be entirely bent
> On some new Mode, or Female Ornament,
> A *Hoop*, a *Lover*, *Monkey*, or a *Fan*,
> A What d'ye call't may in her Fancy reign:
> So, while the thinking Part is full employ'd
> On these, and many serious Points beside,
> The other are of so refin'd a Make,
> That they the easiest Turn are apt to take.   (38–45)

He indulges in burlesque imagery:

> It must be owing to pure Friendship all,
> So perfect, that 'tis grown Mechanical;
> That when the one assumes a different Air,
> Each moves alike a lovely loving Pair:
> So when two strings are struck in Unison,
> The Stroke is *double*, but the *Musick* one;
> So when the Bagpipe breaths its heaving Note,
> SAWNEY'S inchanted, and must caper to't:
> And so, *two*-harmless Bottles of March-Beer,
> In Consort *smile*, unknowing why they *fleer*.   (60–9)

He adds a turn of amorous gallantry to the mixture:

> But, oh! may this obliging Freedom prove
> A happy Omen to the Cause of Love!
> VENUS is often found to laugh aloud,
> And wanton CUPID is a simp'ring God.
> Look ever thus, ye Fair, be thus inclin'd,
> To turn your Faces to your Lovers Mind;
> And since you lavish your Kind Airs away
> In Mirth unask'd, and inoffensive Play,
> May we the same Good-nature always taste,
> And never find your Aspect overcast;
> No scornful look, no cold forbidding Frown,
> But all like VENUS, and her dimpling Son.   (70–81)

And ends the poem with a neat enough turn:

> But I restrain my eager pressing Muse,
> Who with new Fire a dying Theme persues;
> Tho' to write on without a Theme would be
> The fittest, gentle CHLOE, to thy Laugh and THEE.   (98 101)

But all was not approbation, contented studies, and belles-lettres. Even in these early years there started to assert itself that opposition to authority and that love of contention which were to grow more turbulent and outspoken until they became the dominating force in Henley's character and actions. According to his own account,

He began there to be uneasy, that the Art of Thinking regularly on all Subjects, and for all Functions, was not the prevailing Instruction: he was impatient, that Systems of all Sorts were put into his Hands, ready carv'd out for him, and that he incurr'd the Danger of losing his Interest, as well as incurring the Scandal of Heterodoxy and ill Principles, if (as his Genius led him) he freely disputed all Propositions, and call'd all Points to Account, in order to satisfy and convince his own Reason: It shock'd him, to find that he was *commanded* to believe against his Judgment, in Points of Logic, Philosophy and Metaphysicks, as well as Religion; and that a Course of the Mathematicks was the least (if any) Part of the usual academical Education. He was always impatient under these Fetters of the free-born Mind, and privately resolv'd some Time or other, to enter his Protest against any Persons being bred like a Slave, who is born an *Englishman*.[1]

Years later, in a discourse of 1753, he recalled bitterly 'St. *John's*, (ye *College* where I had ye *Stupidity* to be educated)'.[2] There is no reason to cast doubt on the sincerity of Henley's opinions as Disraeli was later to do. 'If these sentiments really were in his mind at college,' he sneered, 'he deserves at least the praise of retention: for fifteen years were suffered to pass quietly without the patriotic volcano giving even a distant rumbling of the sulphureous matter concealed beneath.'[3] They were sentiments common to many young men who encountered the authoritarian and backward-looking attitude of the Universities in this age, and are most notably echoed by Swift in his opinions of the syllabus and methods of his own University. Henley may well, for prudential reasons, have refrained from public attack while still hoping for ecclesiastical preferment, but the frequency of his return to this theme, and the evidence that his dissatisfaction was already finding expression while he was still at Cambridge, show it to be something more than the soured retrospect of a disappointed man. In a letter alleged to come from St. John's, Cambridge, though in fact a self-written letter in his own newspaper, the 'correspondent'

[1] *Narrative*, p. 3.
[2] Henley's discourse for 24 June 1753 (B.M. MSS.Add. 11790).
[3] Disraeli, *The Calamities of Authors*, i.164.

recalled how 'you . . . went through your Exercises with distinguishing Applause, (though you commonly took the least defensible Side of the Question, according to the Usual Opinion. . . .'[1] When Dr. Green, of Clare Hall, took exception to the theories of Sir Isaac Newton, Henley wrote a vindication of the scientist in 1710 and still remembered and listed it among his work thirty-eight years later.[2] He recurred to it again in another piece of self-addressed correspondence in his newspaper in 1736:

We thought you had been cured long since of this Plaguy Relish of Philosophy and Sense, by being once hinder'd of a fat Benefice for your detecting the C-----; we imagined, you had enough of it long before this, ever since you held the wrong Side of the Question at the Soph's Table, and cut up Dr. *Green* in defense of Sir *Isaac Newton*.[3]

He felt, looking back, that four years and a tolerable fortune had been employed to learn what could have been mastered to more perfection in a quarter of the time,[4] and surely had his own experience of Cambridge in mind when he described the unwholesome ideas and methods which he would avoid were he to found his own university in London:

Bigotry to a set of notions, a confin'd way of thinking, a negligence of some of the most useful and polite arts; a management by interest and party, more than an encouragement of genius and industry; a forbidding loftiness and austerity in the ruling part, which tends rather to lessen the relish of virtue, and discipline, than to promote it, and an enslaving of youth to subscriptions, tests and forms, which they neither understand, nor believe, nor approve.[5]

He did not, however, shake off his slavery nor denounce it. His love of argument he saved for official disputations and his love of a fight for taking the unorthodox side of those disputations. In the mass of criticism and satire which was later to be heaped on him, there is only one reference to any misconduct at Cambridge, an

---

[1] *Hyp Doctor*, 9 Nov. 1736.
[2] *Books written by this Author*. I have found no trace of this book among the extensive Newtoniana of the period. It was allegedly printed by J. Morphew in 1711.
[3] *Hyp Doctor*, 26 Oct. 1736.
[4] *Narrative*, p. 4.
[5] Henley's *First Sermon preached at the Opening of the Oratory*, p. 35, printed at the end of *Oratory Transactions No. 1*.

accusation of licentiousness, when the *Grub Street Journal* pretended to refrain from mentioning 'his pranks at *Cambridge*, and
elsewhere, his transactions with his own,—and with other
people's'.[1] Of such 'transactions' we know nothing, though we
are to hear more of this line of attack later. Whatever the truth
of it, neither amorous pursuits, dissatisfaction, nor poetry-
making, hindered the progress of his studies and in 1712 he
passed his exercises for his Bachelor's degree when, according to
his own account, he 'bested *Ten Examiners* & was thanked by ye
University & College for proving they were Ignoramus'.[2]

The academic foundation laid, the next step in his chosen career
was taken. Unprepared though he considered himself, he was
ordained Deacon by Dr. Wake, Bishop of Lincoln, and criticized
his University for neglect and the Bishop for carelessness in the
preparing and selecting of candidates for Holy Orders. He
accused Cambridge of 'a great Defect that tho' he was brought
up for a Clergyman, he was not instructed to preach, or pray, or
read Prayers, or speak, or catechise, or confer, or resolve a Case
of Conscience, or understand the Scriptures, or form any natural
and clear Idea of the Christian Religion'.[3] And he criticized his
Bishop because 'Examination for Orders was very short and
superficial, and by his Account of the Qualifications it is not
necessary to conform to the Christian Religion . . . but to subscribe (whether you have study'd the Matter, or believe it, or no)
to the System of the Church.'[4] Elsewhere he attacked the system
in which

If a person be design'd for holy Orders, he must, as affairs stand, be
sent to a place, where he is ty'd to certain oaths, subscriptions, Tests,
& obligations, relating to ye body, into wch. he is admitted, which he
has neither consider'd nor at present understands, & wch, perhaps,
afterwards, he can neither keep without shocking his Judgment, &
conscience, nor break, without inconvenience to his Person, fortune,
& Character

and he gives a full and sane account of the training such men
ought to receive, in scriptural and patristic theology, the teaching
of the catechism, apologetics, preaching, visiting the sick and

---

[1] *G.S.J.*, 13 May 1731.
[2] Henley's discourse for 1 Mar. 1752 (B.M. MSS.Add. 11782).
[3] *Narrative*, p. 4.   [4] Ibid., p. 10.

prisoners and the dying, and the hearing of confession.[1] So, ill prepared and ill examined, there returned to Melton Mowbray The Reverend John Henley, B.A., to learn more of his calling under his father's care and instruction, as curate at the great church of St. Mary, which had towered over him through these years of childhood and school and University.

[1] *A Proposition for a New Institute of ye Sciences, School Learning & ye Classicks* (B.M. MSS.Add. 19925).

CHAPTER II

A Rural Interlude

RURAL AND QUIET though the outward setting was, these years of Henley's return to Melton Mowbray were not to be years of bucolic calm or stagnation. It was obvious from the start that the quiet round and moderate ease of a country curacy were insufficient for him. Impossible for him the forty years of calm service and piety which were to be his father's history, for the fierce energy and industry which drove him on even to his closing years were already stirring in him, forcing him to find outlet after outlet for a restless mind and growing ambitions. Looking back on these years, he admitted that even here he had formed a resolution to improve in books and conversation as soon as possible in London.[1] Meanwhile there was much to do, testing his strength and preparing his forces before the attack on the City where every ambitious young man, sooner or later in this London-centred age, had to try his chance.

The routine work of a curate occupied plenty of his time. There are, in the list of his manuscript remains, four quarto volumes of sermons which he preached at Melton and the preaching of many occasional sermons found him other pulpits and a wider reputation, Assize sermons at Leicester before Mr. Dodd and Mr. Justice Prat being remembered by him as incidents of honorific distinction which he needed and sought.[2] But it was in the school of his native town, where he himself had learned his first lessons, that he found a possibly more absorbing occupation. He was at heart a teacher, always seeking to instruct, always dissatisfied with those who would instruct him, always seeking some new platform from which he could impart knowledge and demonstrate a superior method of instruction to those who had taught before. His Oratory, his *Hyp Doctor*, his schemes for private universities— all these sprang from this strong urge, and his first limited field for experiment was at his old school. He was asked by the trustees of the school to assist there as soon as he returned home, and in

[1] *Narrative*, p. 11.   [2] Ibid.

1716 was appointed Master, a position he held until he left for London in 1720. He claimed to have raised the school in these few years from a declining to a flourishing condition and to have attracted an increased number of scholars.[1] Remembering too what he considered the faults and irrationality of his Cambridge teachers and teaching, he began reforms at home, reforms which a modern educationalist would surely approve. He opposed the teaching of grammar without a reasoned explanation of its working, a drilling of paradigms in a vacuum without showing at the same time the language at work in lines and metres. He realized the impossibility of good teaching when boys of unequal capacities were crowded into one class—the perfectly normal and accepted method in small grammar schools—and, in an age when the rod and the birch were the badges of office of the usher, he opposed the use of punishment and force to shape the understanding.[2] On the positive side his innovations seem to have been part of an effort to encourage individual thought and personal expression in his scholars. Instead of the formal construing and answering of catechisms of set questions, he introduced a method whereby each boy could 'learn and give an Account of his Studies, without the Necessity of consulting others, or of being examined by particular questions'.[3] It is here too that we hear for the first time of Henley's interest in the art of elocution and oratory, for it was among his young boys at Melton that the future 'Orator', the future 'Restorer of Ancient Eloquence' worked on his ideas, giving elocution lessons and, both morning and afternoon, supervising public speaking of passages from the classics and the delivery of orations.[4] It was no doubt a very proud schoolmaster as well as author who sat in the school hall on 16 May 1720 and heard the best scholar pronounce an oration of his Master's composition before Bishop White Kennet and the clergy assembled there for the episcopal visitation. It must have been a no less gratified author who received a copy of the printed version of the oration which was published later that year. Why a London publisher should consider it worth while to print a Latin visitational oration delivered so far from the capital is difficult to guess, but print he did. Of all Henley's published works, this is

[1] *Narrative*, p. 5.
[2] *A Dissertation on Nonsense*, p. 12, in *Oratory Transactions No. II*.
[3] *Narrative*, p. 5.   [4] Ibid.

perhaps the most elegantly produced, a wide-margined quarto on very decent paper, in large type, and adorned with a headpiece and decorated initial. One wonders how many of the London public were tempted by the title-page to buy a copy:

Oratio habita in Schola Meltoniensi,
Ad Comitia Cleri, Calata, Maii 16, 1720
Per Alumnum istius ludi primarium.
Auctore Johanne Henley, A.M. Gymnasii Praefecto.
Londini: Venundantur a J. ROBERTS, in vico vulgo vocato
Warwick Lane; & a J. PEMBERTON sub Insignia Cervis
& Solis, e regione Ecclesiae Sti. Dunstani, Fleetstreet.[1]

Perhaps the Henley of a few years hence was glad if few had been sold, for the beliefs and sentiments so elegantly latinized are oddly at variance with the future rebel's war-cries, and his satirical enemies might have gleefully compared the aspiring and hopeful young cleric praising and defending the Establishment on which his preferment depended, and the later schismatic rebel attacking the Establishment which had disappointed and frustrated him.

Henley's courtship of the Muses during these years was not confined to cultivation of the ancient tongues nor the cadences of prose. His poetic talent had only as yet tried its wings with light satirical verses but now, like all true aspirants to poetic fame, he turned to epic, albeit a minor epic, and in 1714 was printed his one sizeable poem, *The History of Queen Esther. A Poem in Four Books*, a second edition appearing in 1715. Henley was later to state, in a controversy with Christopher Smart, that the poem was written when he was fifteen years old,[2] but it is more than likely that, so long after the event, Henley had become confused or, like his enemy Pope, tended to pre-date his early successes and emphasize his creative precociousness. It is far more likely that the date of composition is nearer the date of its publication, the fruit of his leisure hours at Melton and of reading in his father's library there.

The poem of nearly 1,000 lines is presented with fitting serious-ness and apparatus. Following the dedication to Thomas Bennett of Welby in Leicestershire, who was patron of his father's living, comes a lengthy section on the conduct of the poem, carefully

[1] The British Museum possesses a copy, which is the only one I know.
[2] Advertisement for 4 July 1752 (Lysons 174).

setting out the argument of each book, a learned Preface and finally, after the poem, a six-page index. The Preface clearly demonstrates the amount of thought and reading which had gone into the preparation of the poem. A thorough reading of Hyde's *History of the Religion of the Ancient Persians* enabled him to discuss learnedly the date of the Book of Esther, the problem of the name Ahasuerus, the details of sun-worship, and to sprinkle his writing impressively with quotations in Greek, Hebrew, Persian, and Samaritan. He had also considered carefully his source material and the possible methods of handling it. He considered the story 'the most beautiful in Scripture history for Poetical Improvement' because the grandeur of its settings, the splendour of its events, and the variety of characters offered a fine field for elaboration in descriptive and dramatic enlargement. He was influenced in his tone and language by another version which persuaded him not to admire and to do otherwise—Joshua Barnes's Greek paraphrase, on which he wrote, 'His was so ill a Model that I could not reconcile my self to any Thoughts of Copying him. His Fancy is too Wild for a Paraphrast; and his Language, however Poetical, is too Luxuriant. His Management is full of Weaknesses, very often Trivial, and Improper: and not seldom void of Sense.' Henley's concern for the control of Fancy, the moderation of language, the decorum of presentation, are all respectably Augustan, as is his own stress on construction and transition, his avowed attempt 'to prevent any Abruptness or Gap in the Narration, to make the Transitions Full, Easy and Regular, and contribute to the Embellishment of the Poem'. He desires that his poem be not judged 'upon any other Rules, than such as are immediately Proper to a Profest Paraphrase; I mean, its Correspondence with the Original, the Justness of the Sentiments, and Propriety of the Expression'. By 'paraphrase' here he obviously means the freest form of re-telling the original tale, maintaining the narrative outline, the characters and events, but by no means maintaining a relation with the words of the source, however free that relationship. Henley's poem is a piece of original narrative-verse composition and as such it can be judged, not at all to its shame. The narrative is conducted in a clear and unobstructed way, using its four books for the large division of material, often gaining good suspense and never becoming dull. Compared with many of the unread epics of the century it is not a mean attempt.

Conscious of the unusual seriousness of that attempt in a time of social verse, the young poet opens, as Milton had done, with an invocation to the Holy Spirit:

> While *Fancy* leads her Gayer Sons astray,
> In Fabl'd Scenes, and a Romantick Way;
> While Lower Themes confine the Noble Fire,
> Debase the Song, and prostitute the Lyre;
> Thou, Sov'reign Muse, who tun'st the Orbs on High,
> Where Thou, and Harmony, are all the Joy,
> To whose Blest Ear each Poet Angel plays,
> And Consecrates thy Musick to thy Praise;
> Bear me, O bear me to those Sacred Plains,
> Where Awful Truth in Genuine Beauty reigns.   (I.1–10)

But although the sentiment is Miltonic the language is not, and despite a scattering of Miltonisms here and there—'The Monumental Equippage of War', 'from Heav'n he ruin'd down', 'nor obvious Winds defeat them as they fly'—the chief influence on the poem, the poet one is most often reminded of in so many ways, is not Milton but the man Henley considered 'the best English poet'[1]—Dryden, especially the mature Dryden of *The Fables*. Like Dryden he seizes on the descriptive possibilities of his source and the richness and colour of the scene of Ahasuerus' feast in Book I is reminiscent of such writing in, say, *The Flower and the Leaf* or *Cymon and Iphigenia*:

> The Higher Guests approach a Room of State,
> Where Tissu'd Couches all around were set,
> Labour'd with Art; O'er Iv'ry Tables thrown,
> Embroider'd Carpets fell in Folds adown.
> The Bow'rs and Gardens of the Court were near,
> And open Lights indulg'd the breathing Air.
> Pillars of Marble bore a Silken Sky,
> While Cords of Purple and fine Linnen tye
> In Silver Rings, the Azure Canopy.
> Distinct with Diamond Stars the Blue was seen,
> And Earth, and Seas, were feign'd in Em'rald Green;
> A Globe of Gold, ray'd with a pointed Crown,
> Form'd in the midst almost a real Sun.   (I.153–65)

---

[1] Henley's discourse for 8 Apr. 1750 (B.M. MSS.Add. 11777).

He can, like Dryden, tighten and pack his couplet to good effect in character portraits and didactic comment, as in these lines on Esther:

> Receiv'd the Sun-shine and the Storms of Fate,
> Severely Fortunate, and Humbly Great:
> She all the Arts of Speech compleatly knew,
> And, what was more, the Arts of *Silence* too.   (II.164–7)

and has inherited the Chaucerian-Dryden trick of the sharp couplet to end, with almost shocking speed and brevity, a planned act:

> Xerxes the Prudent Overture approv'd,
> Proclaim'd the Fact, and Vashti was remov'd.   (II.95–6)

Like Dryden, too, he delights in seizing the opportunities which his story affords for contemporary reference, whether the short aside about the young harp-player at the feast:

> Pupil to *Locrus*, a *Memphitic* Sage;
> For *Memphis* was the *Cambridge* of That Age.   (I.227–8)

or the more extended reference to the Queen:

> *Cyrus*, whose Virtues none can justly sing,
> The Perfect Model of a Finish'd King:
> Whom ANNE alone is destin'd to excel,
> In Living, Ruling, and in Conqu'ring well;
> With such well-temper'd Wrath her Sword's employ'd,
> The Vanquish'd thinks he's on the Victor Side:
> Heav'n leaves his Bolts in her Deputed Hand,
> And knows She'll deal them with a God's Command.   (II.121–8)

The portrait of Haman, the first Minister, achieves some of its vitality from this contemporary relevance of details, a fore-shadowing of the later attacks on Walpole and Bufo and their kind, which were to come from the Tory satirists:

> The Reins of State were left in *Haman's* Hand,
> And all his God could see, was his Command.
> To the great Idol all the Palace bow'd,
> And Kings were Happy that could gain a Nod.
> For him a Fry of craving Bards would tire,
> With many a painful Thumb the drudging Lyre.

For him the Curious oft would plod the Sky,
And each new World was *Haman*'s Property.
Himself in Constellation sparkled there,
And *Haman* hung with Honour in a Star.
He was the Muse invok'd by ev'ry Pen,
Of the Projecting, Reas'ning, Chyming Train:
Dub'd by his Heighth of Favour with the King,
A Critick, Poet, Sage, and ev'ry Thing.
They that aspir'd to gain the Fav'rite Side,
Caress'd his Vanity, and sooth'd his Pride.
For Honour was the Quarry he pursu'd,
And Grandeur was his First, his only Good.
To compass these no Engine he would spare,
But all was Virtue, if it center'd there:
Would, as the Juncture ask'd, Embrace or Kill,
Hug you to Death, or Stab you with a Smile.
All the wild Lengths of Noble Mischief run,
And leave no shining Wickedness unknown.
Demurely o'er the Publick Ruins move,
And Colour ev'ry Step with Publick love.   (III.134–59)

Such extensive quotation seems justified by the rarity of this piece, and because it has undoubted quality which needs demonstration. Henley handles his couplet with confidence, to drive on his narrative or to sharpen an epigram; he enriches the poem not only with description but with a steady flow of imagery and epic simile; and he disposes his narrative material well. It is an interesting fact that later satirical attacks on Henley, which knew no limits in searching the past for material, hardly ever used *Esther* as a rod to beat him with. Apart from a very late attack by Christopher Smart, only one couplet in all the mass of calumny refers to the poem, a couplet in a doggerel attack in the *Grub Street Journal*:

And all the Town will own, I'll lay a tester,
That this Epistle's better than *Queen Esther*.[1]

It was rather, Henley asserted, 'approv'd by the Town, and well receiv'd',[2] and the pamphlet *A Guide to the Oratory*, which appears to have Henley's authority, adds another reason for its being read with interest, that

---

[1] *G.S.J.*, 16 Sept. 1731.   [2] *Narrative*, p. 7.

The Town would have it, that this Poem was wrote in Compliment to
Queen ANNE, and that the Author had drawn in a lively Manner a
reigning Dutchess at Court in the following Lines,

> A Rebel Pride it was deform'd the Dame,
> And left a Blemish on her Virgin Fame.
> Deep in her Heart the Pois'nous Rancour spread,
> And on each Infant Seed of Vertue fed.
> In wild Ambition all her Passions meet,
> And every Thing is Good if it be Great.[1]

More independent evidence that he had made some reputation as
a poet was his inclusion in 1720 in Giles Jacob's *An Historical
Account of the Lives and Writings of our most considerable English Poets*.
His entry is mainly a digest of the biography in the *Narrative*
prefaced to the first *Oratory Transactions*, and the only criticism is
'This Gentleman has published an Excellent Poem upon the
Scripture History of Esther, in Four Books.'[2] It only runs in all
to twenty-five lines—exactly the same as the entry for George
Herbert which immediately follows Henley. Almost a century
later Isaac Disraeli permitted himself the praise: 'The versification
is musical, the imagination is lively, and the narrative is never
tedious.'[3] But this was not enough to rescue Henley's work from
the forgotten minor poems of an age of minor poets. I have found
only one note of interest in a lonely voice in that echoing-dome
of lonely voices, *Notes and Queries*, expressing 'some surprise that
the production is so entirely forgotten' and believing that 'the
unhappy celebrity of the author might impart to it, one would
think, a certain degree of interest, independently of the erudition
displayed, and the poetical ability by which the work is undoubtedly characterised.'[4] Any reader who, like this correspondent,
troubles to dig out the book from its few hiding-places might
well agree, and regret that Henley's energies were diverted from
poetry. But diverted they were, and almost immediately. He
himself said, in his public letter to Pope:

I was once poetically addicted, and had I *persever'd in the Sin*, or had
been inspir'd with *your Muses*, a fantastical *Imagination*, a *very vain Head*,
and a *consummately evil Heart* . . . could by this Time have surpassed you:

[1] *A Guide to the Oratory etc.*, p. 4.   [2] p. 72.
[3] Disraeli, *The Calamities of Authors*, i.156.
[4] *Notes and Queries*, 21 July 1855, p. 45.

but universal Learning, and more generous Principles and Habits, have naturally made me the Object of a meritorious Aversion in Knaves and Coxcombs.[1]

It was the first seductive beckoning of that 'Universal Learning' which now led Henley into another scheme on which he could expend his energy and indulge his hopes of fame, a scheme destined, however, to bring nothing but regret on his part and recurrent contempt from his opponents. Sometime early in 1719 he conceived the idea of producing a Universal Grammar, moved once more by the conviction that previous teachers of grammar had been obscure and tedious and that he was sent to bring new light and simplicity into the study of languages. He wrote:

The only Bar to this Sort of Study is, That it is dry and tiresome, by the needless Length of Grammars, and the Multiplicity of Rules and Examples. I have in this Attempt, the first of this kind, endeavour'd to clear those Obstructions, and to lay down a short, clear and full Institution of the Grammatical Principles of each Tongue; without clogging it with a Number of Definitions, that may be known at once from the Common Latin Grammars; or with an Explication of Words, that do properly belong to a Lexicon, or a Dictionary to explain.[2]

In later years he suggested another reason for embarking on this work (and, incidentally, indulging as with *Esther* in a pre-dating of his early literary productions). A close study of the Bible had, he claimed, always been the foundation of his plan and 'It was with a View to the Philological learning of it, that I began to compile those Grammars of the Tongues which you reflect upon, at the Age of Eleven, and finished them before I was nineteen . . .'[3] Whatever may have been the predominant motive behind this ambitious, not to say foolhardy undertaking, he laboured under many disadvantages which combined to ensure its failure. Firstly, he was short of books. He had his father's library in the vicarage and no doubt his own old books from school and Cambridge, and he wrote to his old tutors at college, Thomas Baker and Francis Hutchinson, asking for advice and the loan of books, but all these were insufficient for the task. His protest is an interesting one,

---

[1] *Why how now, Gossip POPE?* (1736), p. 16.
[2] Preface to *A Grammar of the Spanish Tongue* (1719), p. ii.
[3] *Hyp Doctor*, 23 Dec. 1735.

suggesting as it does a solution which was slowly to be realized
by the founding of many provincial libraries later in the century.

Here I must take Leave to deplore the want of Books, under which
Men of Enquiry commonly labour; except in London, and the Two
Universities. It is extreamly to be wish'd, that this Disadvantage was
made up by those, who only can and ought to be the Friends of Learning, in every County of this Kingdom, by a well-furnish't Library,
establish'd on a safe Foot; or by any useful Project to that Purpose.[1]

The second difficulty he alleged, and which must have been in
some degree a real one, was his distance from his printers in
London and the difficulty of ensuring proof corrections. Roberts
and Pemberton, publishers with whom he was to have a continued association, had undertaken to print his work, and the
young provincial was no doubt delighted, but when the attacks
on his performance intensified, it was to the errors of the press
and the perversity of printers that he constantly recurred. He
first voiced the complaint while the Grammars were still coming
out: 'The Reader is desir'd to correct with his Pen any Literal
Errata (as there are but few, and of a smaller Nature) that he finds
uncorrected in these Grammars: The Author's great Distance
from the Press, not allowing that nice Exactness he desir'd in the
Impression.'[2] Some years later he repeated his criticism of 'the
Press, a fantastical Machine, which no Writer can command;
those of my Grammars formerly publish'd, are due to the same
Quarter, and were very much occasion'd by my great Distance
then from London',[3] and he attacked his printer, Samuel Palmer,
for failing to print errata he had supplied.[4] There is, no doubt,
much truth in Henley's blaming of his printer and the press, but
it is also true that the tools are being blamed by a poor workman.
For the third great difficulty preventing success was, in fact,
Henley's ignorance of many of the tongues he presumed to teach,
an ignorance exaggerated in later attacks but which, even allowing
for this satiric distortion, nevertheless existed. He certainly knew
his Latin and Greek and had studied Hebrew from his schooldays,
but there is no evidence that he had more than the smattering of

---

[1] Preface to *A Grammar of the Latin Tongue* (1720), p. xii.
[2] Note at the end of the *Errata* which closes *A Grammar of the French Tongue*.
[3] Preface to *Oratory Transactions No. 1*, p. iv.
[4] *Why how now, Gossip POPE?*, p. 6.

modern languages which enabled him to read in them, or even that he knew even that much of some of the other languages in his series: there is, rather, as we shall see, positive evidence to the contrary both in his method of working and his results.

Undeterred by any difficulty or misgiving, Henley launched into the task with enthusiasm and an industry which surprise in these more leisurely days of scholarship and writing, but which were perhaps not so phenomenal in the days of professional hacks and the frantic production-line of Grub Street. If Henley gained nothing else by his Grammars, he proved his right of immediate acceptance into that dubious fraternity when the time was ripe. In August 1719 the first volume of the series was offered to the public at a shilling. Its title-page announced the plan:

The Compleat Linguist, Or, An Universal Grammar of all the Considerable Tongues in Being. In a Shorter, Clearer, & more Instructive Method than is extant. Collected from the most Approv'd Hands. To be published Monthly, one distinct Grammar each Month, till the whole is perfected: with a Preface to every Grammar, relating to each Tongue. Numb. I For the Month of August, 1719. Being A Grammar of the *Spanish* Tongue.

While he was still working at Melton, he managed to keep up his promised production. September saw the Italian Grammar, October the French, November the Greek, with a doubling of price to two shillings. In February of the new year came the Latin Grammar which had taken two months to bring out, and then longer delays started to occur, the Grammar of the Hebrew tongue not appearing until May 1720. Henley left Melton for London in the course of the next year and doubtless the demands of other literary and ecclesiastical work diverted his attention and curtailed the time he could devote to the universalizing of the Universal Grammar. It is in years rather than in months that the next instalments appear, in 1721 *A Grammar of the Chaldee Tongue, as it is in the Old and New Testament; the Rabbins Talmud, Targumin, &c*, in 1722 *A Grammar of the Arabic Tongue*, and in 1723 *A Grammar of the Syriac Tongue*. Three years passed before in 1726, no. X of the series was published, *An Introduction to an English Grammar*, and in its Preface he announced the abandonment of further instalments. He would *not* now be publishing grammars of Ethiopic, Coptic, Persic, Samaritan, Armenian, Turkish, Chinese,

Damillian or Malarabic, Malayan, Indian, Sclavonic, Teutonic, Hibernian, British, Gothic, Runic or Islandic. Even his English Grammar was not the complete work he had hoped to write, conflating what he had planned as several grammars into a dissertation on the descent and relationship of English to other Germanic languages, and providing a twenty-six-page Old English Grammar. 'The necessary Delays of the Press, on so nice a Subject, join'd with the Urgency of other Affairs' were held responsible. He still promised a full English Grammar, but this seems never to have appeared.[1] Life had by that time become too full and hectic even for Henley to fit in the dull plodding of grammar writing.

From every recorded comment it would appear that the Grammars were a total failure. We cannot discover their sales, although Samuel Paterson the bookseller, who knew the trade well and knew Henley personally, told Nichols in a letter in 1794 'none of his Works ever sold in my time—the name of *Henley* was sufficient to make them to be thrown aside—not even his *Grammars*, which of late years have been in some request, on account of their scarcity, when *complete*.'[2] On the other hand one wonders why the booksellers, whose motive was hardly disinterested service to scholarship, continued to publish them over a period of seven years. The *Grub Street Journal* repeatedly beat Henley over the head with them. In an essay on Impudence a correspondent wrote: '"Tis by the power of this happy Faculty that your Members, Mr. Bavius, quote Authors they never saw; translate books they can't read; and write *Grammars* of languages they don't understand. O HENLY! thou eldest Son of Effrontery! how shall thy fame be transmitted to after-ages, as it deserves?'[3] The question was asked 'Whether all the Felons that have been hang'd at

---

[1] Arthur G. Kennedy in *A Bibliography of Writings on the English Language from the beginning of Printing to the end of 1922* (Cambridge and New Haven, 1927) records as item 5476 'Henley, John. On the English tongue, London 1731 (Ichikawa's Cat.)'. In the *Catalogue of the library of Sanki Ichikawa, Professor of English Philology at Tokyo, Pt. I* (Tokyo, 1924, privately printed), the item 'Henley, John. On the English Tongue, London 1731' is marked with an asterisk, indicating that the book was burnt to ashes in the fire which ravaged the University in 1924, so any check on the accuracy of this description is impossible. Neither the British Museum nor the Bodleian has a copy, and no other major library appears to possess one.
[2] Letter dated 18 Nov. 1794, printed in Nichols, *Literary Anecdotes of the Eighteenth Century*, vol. viii, pp. 483–4.
[3] *G.S.J.*, 11 Mar. 1731.

Tyburn for five years past, were not honester and handsomer men, juster in Action and Speech, and better GRAMMARIANS, than the BULL BEEF ORATOR?'[1] An article pleading for the further study of the Scots and Welsh languages ended, 'It would have been a great encouragement to this, if your great Linguist, Mr. HENLEY, had been pleased to publish a Grammar of it: for I am satisfied he is as well skilled in Welsh, as in most of the languages, of which he has hithertoo published Grammars.'[2] Later comments are few, for, as Paterson says, the Grammars fell into complete obscurity into which only a few collectors of rarities penetrated. Out of the obscurity only two later notices appear. Bosworth in 1823 wrote off the *Introduction to an English Grammar* as 'a very short and imperfect Saxon Grammar. . . . The Grammar . . . is a very imperfect abstract of Hickes,'[3] and in 1885 another scholar, Richard Wülker, was briefer but more ruthless. He merely commented on the English Grammar—'Wertlose Schrift'.[4]

Is it possible to do anything more than join Henley's contemporaries' chorus of abuse, and include all the Grammars in that unequivocal Teutonic condemnation? We may take it that in the Latin and Greek Grammars and possibly in the Hebrew, he was working in languages he knew well and producing correct instruction in no way in advance of the many grammars and primers already available. In his Grammars of the modern languages he was on less familiar ground, and indulging, often carelessly, often ignorantly, in the typical Grub Street activity of compilation and digest from easily accessible sources. Thanks to a contributor to the *Grub Street Journal*, who for once gave detailed evidence as well as general abuse, we are put on the track and can follow Henley's often wandering footsteps.[5] He reports how,

Soon after they were published, going to see a friend, I observed a book lying upon his table, with some marginal notes of his writing. These were upon *Henley's Italian*, and *French* Grammars. And seeing such words as these, *Unheard of Impudence!—This is a most ignorant, and impudent fellow.—Monstrous!—Was there ever such Ignorance! &c.* I asked my

---

[1] *G.S.J.*, 25 Mar. 1731. [2] *G.S.J.*, 6 May 1731.

[3] J. Bosworth, *The Elements of Anglo-Saxon Grammar* (1823), Preface, p. xxix.

[4] Richard Wülker, *Grundriss zur Geschichte der angelsächsischen Litteratur* (Leipzig, 1885).

[5] *G.S.J.*, 13 May 1731. The letter is anonymous, but Henley suspected the writer to be Samuel Palmer, the printer of the Grammars.

friend what he meant by all this? he told me he had just look'd into
those two *Grammars*, not doubting but (however *useless* they were) the
man *understood* the *languages*, of which he wrote *Grammars*: but finding,
to his astonishment, that the case was quite otherwise, he could not
forbear expressing his *just indignation* in the manner I saw: he said he
had mark'd the places; desired me to look over them, and judge
whether he had not reason. I cast my eye upon the passages; and, lifting
up my hands, declared myself as much amazed as he could be. What!
(exclaim'd we both) for a fellow to *write Grammars* of *Languages* Which
he *knows nothing of*! This exceeds all the prodigies of *Impudence* that ever
any age produced.

The evidence then presented is, alas, sufficient to justify this
display of melodramatic outrage. Henley, the Italian grammarian,
is shown to be ignorant of the difference between *questo* and *quello*;
to confuse singular and plural nouns; not to know the difference
between *loro* the conjunctive and *loro* the possessive. And the
source of these mistakes is shown to be the incomprehending use
of the older grammar from which he is copying. One example
re-creates the harassed and time-pressed author at work:

P. 18. '*Date melo*, send it to us.' *Date melo* is not SEND it to US, but
GIVE it to ME. One may, without much sagacity, discover what gave
birth to this Translation. In the grammar, he transcribed from, there
are, undoubtedly, the following words: *Date melo*, give it to me;
Mandate celo, send it to us. He, thinking one of the examples sufficient
for his purpose, took the *Italian* of the first, and the *English* of the
second, by a slip of his eye passing over what was between.

The same source of confusion is demonstrated in his use of
Boyer's *The Compleat French Master*, the source of his French
labours. Here again he is shown to be ignorant of singulars and
plurals, of different tenses, and 'Among the irregular verbs he
makes wild work of it.' One example of his confusion in transcription must suffice.

P. 23. 'Nouns expressing a thing *divided*, or, *some*; N. *du pain*, some
bread. G. *du*, *de pain*. D. *Au*, *a du pain.—De la viande*, &c—*De l'argent*,
&c. *de l'Herbe*, &c.' Does he mean it thus, G. *Du de pain*, of some
bread? Or thus, *du pain*, or *de pain*, of some bread? One it must be, and
both are false. For as to the former, *du de* is not *French*: as to the latter,
it cannot be said *du pain* or *de pain*; because it is *de pain* only. *Du pain* is
of the bread not *of Bread*, or *of some bread*. The same is to be said, *mutatis
mutandis*, of his D. *au*, *a du pain*. And the whole is applicable to the other

three examples: in all which he manifests a most deep and fundamental ignorance. The thing happen'd thus. Mr. *Boyer*, from whom Mr. Henley transcrib'd, joins together *le pain*, the bread, and *du pain*, some bread, in the nominative case. And then proceeds; Gen. *du pain*, of *or* from the bread, *de pain* of bread &c. so in the other instances. Our *compleat linguist*, not knowing the difference, and studying brevity, leaves out *le pain* entirely; and then proceeds with his *du*, *de*, *au*, *a du*, as aforesaid: which makes a compleat Bevüe of the whole.

A similar confusion is shown in his rehandling of Boyer's rules on the conjunctive mood. Small wonder that Boyer, infuriated by Henley's misuse of his work and even more by Henley's criticisms of it, permitted himself this outburst in the Preface to the eighth edition of his Grammar:

'Tis no Wonder, if with an Assurance peculiar to *Sciolists*, he takes upon him to censure what he does not understand. Neither am I surprized, if, writing *Post-Haste*, he charges his Over-sights, as Errors upon me, and in particular, makes me say what I never did, in Relation to *Etymology*. As to his Criticisms about *Dipth-thongs* and *Accents*, he only betrays his absolute Ignorance of the True *French* Pronunciation & Prosody, which, it seems, this *Compleat Linguist* would pretend to settle by the Standard of the *Latin*. A pedantick Ridicule, rather fit to divert, than provoke one's Spleen!

The point on these two Grammars seems made firmly enough for us to accept without much misgiving the *Grub Street Journal*'s conclusion—'His other Grammars if well look'd into, would undoubtedly yield us as fruitful a crop of animadversions: but this may serve for a sample at present.' The reader may well feel that the sample is already too large, but, in tracing a life so distorted and misrepresented, part of the task is to strive to present a fair judgement and not to refuse to hear evidence. In this case Henley's enemies were right, and we may feel no regrets, as we do with *Esther*, that the Grammars fell into complete neglect and disappeared, except where a few survivors lie gathering dust in the great libraries of the world.[1]

---

[1] These survivors are catalogued by R. C. Alston in *A Bibliography of the English Language from the Invention of Printing to the Year 1800*, vol. ii, Entry 148 (Bradford, 1967), and they are all reprinted by him in one volume (Scolar Press, Menston, 1970). The following are the chief sources from which, as the *Grub Street Journal* quite rightly alleged, Henley had borrowed heavily:
Spanish: the grammar in John Stevens's *New Dictionary Spanish and English* (1706).

The time had arrived however when the narrow compass of
Melton Mowbray confined his opportunities and ambitions too
severely, and he put into practice that resolution he had formed
years ago to come up to London. Contact with his London
publishers must have whetted his appetite, and the hundred miles
between Melton and the capital stood in the way of much more
than accurate proof-reading. Accordingly in 1720 he warned the
parish and the school trustees to begin a choice of a new curate
and schoolmaster. He himself claimed that his leaving was
'against the Inclination of his Neighbours, and his School, which
was now as from his first Entrance upon it, still advancing. And
his Method being established and approv'd, one of his own
Scholars was appointed to succeed him.'[1] This pupil was the
Revd. John Browne who took over his duties in 1721. The
picture of a much-regretted departure of a valued and successful
local figure is, of course, Henley's, but there are more than vague
suggestions of some scandal in the background of the picture,
and of motives not entirely reputable.

In its desire to find every possible avenue for attack on Henley,
the *Grub Street Journal*, in the early '30s, continually returned to
this scandal. Quoting Henley's own comment in the *Narrative* on
his departure from Melton—'But it was not for a second rustication that he left *the fields and the swains*'—the *Journal* suggested that
'the period would run better, the fields, the swains, and the
nymphs'.[2] In other words, that Henley's rural interlude had
ended with getting into trouble with some local lady and that his
departure was a wise and perhaps necessary flight 'to avoid', as a
nineteenth-century comment on the incident puts it, 'the scandalous embarrassments of illicit love'.[3] The *Journal's* innuendoes are
general, accusing Henley of promiscuity in his sexual life. In a
long and ingenious comparison of him to a plant, the point is
made:

Italian: Giovanni Torriano's *The Italian Revis'd* (1673) and Thomas Uvedale's *Italian
    Grammar* (1711).
French: the grammars of Guy Miege (1687) and Abel Boyer (1694).
Hebrew: the grammars of William Robertson (1653) and Johann Buxtorf (1656).
Chaldee: the grammar of John Leusden (1686).
Old English: the *Thesaurus* of George Hickes and the grammar of Elizabeth Elstob
    (1715).
    [1] *Narrative*, p. 12.   [2] *G.S.J.*, 24 June 1731.
    [3] J. W. Newman, *The Lounger's Commonplace Book*, 3rd ed. 1805, p. 137.

But what is so evidently levelled against Mr. H--- is the conclusion of this Definition, that it has *a power of propagating itself by seed*. Here, his character is evidently drawn, it being generally thought, that his abilities this way have been very great; and that, by his great talents of *Elocution* and *Action* he has frequently *sowed* the proper *seed* of an Orator in *private Gardens*, long before he opened his *publick Nursery* in Lincoln's Inn *Fields*.[1]

The following week saw the indecent prophecy that 'if he keep himself from being *hen* peck'd, all the world must own he is the finest *Cock* in England.'[2] When Henley failed to produce a promised oration on a recently hanged criminal, Sarah Malcomb, but instead spoke against Bishops' Courts, the *Journal* suggested why:

> 'Gainst these, 'tis sayed, which to thy fame I tell,
> Substantial cause inflamed thy righteous zeal:
> For Bishops courts, by way of commutation,
> Demand too much for jobs of fornication.[3]

When a report came in of a girl possessed of a devil in Melton Mowbray, the *Journal* could not resist the Rabelaisian comment: '*It is pity* the conjuring Doctor *who came from* Melton Mowbray, *is not in that neighbourhood at this time: tho' some think, he is better at* putting the Devil in, than *at casting him* out.'[4] There had been similar attacks in early years. In a pamphlet of 1726, William Wood had told Henley, 'I have a *due* Value for you, and therefore have several Times vindicated your cause in Relation to your private Character, which, I think, is a Thing too tender to be touched. Hundreds can prove the Truth of this.'[5] The accusation became a little more dangerously circumstantial in an anonymous pamphlet published the following year when, having disposed of Henley to the fate of Judas, the writer added, 'Think seriously on your Predecessor, *Simon Magus*, and his Fate; on *Simon Magus*, I say, whose Crimes and yours as they are not much unlike, (for as he had his Helena, so you it seems your Tolsona)'.[6] The vague general scandal has narrowed to a specific case, and the lady in the

---

[1] *G.S.J.*, 15 Apr. 1731.   [2] *G.S.J.*, 22 Apr. 1731.
[3] *G.S.J.*, 22 Mar. 1732.   [4] *G.S.J.*, 26 Oct. 1732.
[5] William Wood, *The Dueling Orator delineated* (1726), p. 10.
[6] Anon., *A Letter to the Celebrated Orator in Newport Market, With a Word or two to his admirers and followers* (1727), p. 11.

case revealed, allegedly a Mrs. Tolson. It is to Henley himself that
we are ironically enough indebted for further details which add
substance to the charge. Between 1726 and 1727 there developed
a violent quarrel between Henley and the eccentric theologian
William Whiston, a quarrel we shall later have cause to examine
in greater detail, but an immediate cause of this quarrel was
Whiston's publishing, in self-defence, a series of Henley's letters
to him. We have no copies of Whiston's letters, but Henley's
denials make quite clear the details of his accusations, and the
particularity of those details and Henley's tone lead us to agree
with Whiston that 'he did not deny it; but rather by the Tenor of
his Answers, acknowledged it to be true'.[1] In a letter dated
3 November Henley wrote:

Tho' you have no Concern with me, or Right to Catechize my Character,
yet I sink so much beside my self as to inform you, that no Scandal
forced me to leave *Melton*; but I gave warning voluntarily, against the
express desire of the whole Neighbourhood. . . . I was, on leaving
Melton, recommended to some of the Greatest Men in Town by the
most considerable Persons about *Melton*, Clergy and Laiety; under
their hands; by about 30 Letters: which would not have been, had any
Scandal there, had Weight with them.

In your story of Mrs. *Colson* [Tolson] you are misinform'd; and in
your Reflections on that and me, you are invidious and malicious, not
impartial and charitable. . . . As to Particulars, these are false Facts
amongst others: That she followed me to *London*: That she ever
separated from her Husband, that I know: that I ever had an ill Correspondence with her [here Henley had blotted out 'Unless a frequent
access be so call'd'] That she ever pass'd for my Wife, or I for her
Husband: That any Debt of hers was ever demanded of me, directly
or indirectly: That I ever kept her in Lodgings: That I ever knew of
any Debts of that Kind: That I ever had what you charge me with by
her: (and you could not be authentickly assur'd of that in a married
Person, where the Husband was within the four Seas, by authentick
Law:) That she ever, that I know, lodg'd in *Gray's-Inn*: These are false
in particular every one of them. And I could give you *one Demonstration*,
that you ought to suspect your Information of the whole Affair. I never
liv'd with any Woman till I married; nor promised to pay any Debts of
hers . . .[2]

---

[1] *Mr. Henley's Letters and Advertisements which concern Mr. Whiston. Published by Mr.
Whiston, together with a few Notes* (1727), p. 23.
[2] Ibid., p. 15.

Certainly Henley does not deny that he knew Mrs. Tolson or that he was on easy visiting terms with her. He never really denies that he had her as his mistress, simply that he never lived with her, never had a child by her, never had any dealings with her after he came to London. We shall perhaps never be able to discover the whole truth behind the violence of accusation and self-defence, but there are more than tentative grounds for suspicion that not only ambition and a desire to use his talent sped the young curate from Melton, and that substantial rumours accompanied him as well as those thirty letters of introduction in his pocket.

And so, in November 1721, with those letters for the future and, for present needs 'an honest 400£ of my own' which, if he had it, he must have saved from his stipend and his publishers' fees, he arrived in London, the only place for ambition to thrive, there 'to display his bright Parts on this grand Theatre of the Western World'.[1] Here were pulpits, publishers, patrons—and prelates. It was here he must put his foot upon the ladder of preferment and start the climb, perhaps, as Disraeli put it, 'with the aerial perspective lighted by a visionary mitre'.[2]

---

[1] *Historical Register*, vol. xi, no. xliii (1726), p. 240.
[2] Disraeli, *The Calamities of Authors*, i.165.

CHAPTER III

The Ladder of Preferment

1720–1726

THE CLERICAL SCENE of the eighteenth century was in one way exactly the reverse of that in our own. There were too many ordained priests and too little for them to do, or, more accurately, too few livings and appointments which provided any degree of security or anything approaching a living wage. Annually the Universities produced another generation of clerks and annually the bishops laid their hands on a large proportion of them, producing another batch of priests and deacons all jostling for preferment in an already overcrowded market-place. The young cleric of high birth, large fortune, or good connections, moved easily into a living and often advanced with surprising speed to higher office and honours, but for those without any of these advantages, the struggle was indeed a hard one. For these men, as Professor Norman Sykes said,

the operation of the unreformed ecclesiastical administration presented the appearance of a game of chance, in which the dice were biassed heavily against their condition. Denied the advantages of birth and influence which opened to the privileged minority an easy way to promotion, their entrance into the profession of Orders partook in truth of the nature of a lottery; and of a lottery in which the number of blanks was alarmingly high, and the proportion of small prizes higher.[1]

Despite this, the number of those who would cast their ticket into the lottery was high, and scores of these unattached and unsupported clerics converged on London where there seemed more chance of giving the wheel a helping twist, and where at least a man could keep the wolf from the shepherd's door by preaching occasional sermons, reading prayers, labouring as a hack-writer or even, for the first half of the century, running a trade in Fleet marriages.[2]

It was not, then, as a lone adventurer that Henley arrived in

---

[1] Norman Sykes, *Church and State in England in the XVIIIth Century* (1934), p. 189.
[2] That is until 1754, when this practice was stopped by Lord Hardwicke's Marriage Act.

London and took up residence in Millman Street, beyond Bedford Row. His life during this period is of interest, not only in itself, but as a detailed example of the typical patterns which, both in success and failure, Swift ironically presents in his *Essay on the Fates of Clergymen.* A real-life example which may be compared with Henley's is that of Benjamin Hoadly, who left a Cambridge fellowship in 1701 and came up to London. For ten years he held, though neither happily nor very successfully, a lectureship at St. Mildred, Poultry, in the City, but meanwhile sufficiently impressed the Dean and Chapter of St. Paul's to be appointed by them to the Rectory of St. Peter Poor in Broad Street. A living assured, he now struck out for further preferment by entering the political arena with a series of sermons defending Whig ideas, again with success, for the Whig House of Commons in 1710 recommended the Queen to bestow some dignity in the Church on him for his eminent service to Church and State. He had to wait until the fall of Oxford and Bolingbroke before that promise was fulfilled, but meanwhile becoming chaplain to the Duke of Bedford and thereby qualified to hold another living in plurality, he could afford to bide his time at his new country benefice of Streatham until Whig hands crowned him with the mitre of Bangor, subsequently promoting him to the see of Hereford, to Salisbury, and finally to the rich prize of Winchester. Lectureship, chaplaincy, political involvement, and country living—all these were parts of Henley's story, but a story which unlike Hoadly's led nowhere, a story of efforts continually frustrated, through his own faults, the perversity of patrons, the wrong fall of the dice, a story not to end with the office and work of a bishop, but with a venture far less splendid, and in many ways far more exciting.

He did not, as we have seen, arrive unarmed with testimonials and letters of introduction, nor was he without patronage. As soon as he was settled in town, he found employment, humble no doubt, but a sufficient base from which to mount his attack. He became assistant preacher at St. John's Chapel near Bedford Square, to Dr. Burscough (who was later to become Bishop of Limerick in 1725) and also Reader at St. George the Martyr, Queen Square. At these churches and in many others he found what he needed—a pulpit before a large and no doubt influential congregation, where he could display his talents and make a name for himself in the city. According to his own account, he 'preach'd

more Charity-Sermons about Town, was more numerously followed and raised more for the poor Children at those Sermons
than any other Preacher, however dignify'd, or distinguish'd'.[1]
Nor were charity sermons his only speciality. In 1729 he preached
again a sermon on the Truth of the Christian Religion which—in
what must have been a proud and hopeful moment for him—he
had preached before the Lord Mayor of London, Sir G. Conyers,
in St. Paul's, appointed to the task by the Lord Bishop of London.[2]
Towards the end of his life he recalled many such occasions of
success and promise, long since disappointed. 'I preach'd at St.
George's, Hanover Square', he remembers, 'before the Late Rt.
Hon. Lord Carpenter, who invited me to dine with him &c.',[3]
which he later expands:

I mention'd my Preaching, at St. George's, Hanover-Square, before the
late Ld. Carpenter; he took me in his Coach, introduc'd me to Court,
and to Sir R.W. I preach'd at the New Church in the Strand, where the
Charity-Trustees by Mr. Hall, Draper, sent me a Letter of Thanks, for
the great Appearance and Collection, beyond that when the late B. of
L's Tutor, Bp. of C. was in the Pulpit; I preach'd at St. Martin's Tabernacle, for Dr. Trapp, at St. James's Church, for Dr. Clarke, at Queen-
Square Chapel, before the late E. of Harborough, &c.[4]

Meanwhile Henley managed to climb one more recognized
rung on the ladder when, by an instrument dated 24 March 1722,[5]
he was appointed a chaplain to Robert, first Viscount Molesworth,
an appointment which brought more practical benefits than his
chaplain's scarf. Such an office, which hardly ever required him to
fulfil any spiritual duties for his patron, gave him the legal title
to hold benefices in plurality, as well as the encouragement of a
man of power whose influence and connections could speed the
aspiring young cleric on his way. The competition for such an
appointment was great and it can be no mean testimonial to
Henley's talents and perseverance that only two years after his
arrival in London he gained one of the coveted prizes. The
following year saw everything progressing to plan, when he was
instituted Rector of Chelmondiston, a Crown living in the county
of Suffolk worth, according to Henley, £80 a year, though

---

[1] *Narrative*, p. 12.   [2] Advertisement for 1 Nov. 1729 (Lysons 39).
[3] Advertisement for 26 Sept. 1755 (Lysons 196).
[4] Advertisement for 3 Oct. 1755 (Lysons 196).
[5] The instrument is printed in full in the *Narrative*, p. 13.

Bacon's *Liber Regis* puts it at £120. The patron who preferred him to this living was one whom he always remembered as his most generous benefactor, Thomas Parker, Earl of Macclesfield, who was Lord Chancellor from 12 May 1718 to 4 June 1725. Henley may have already formed some acquaintance with him through local connections before he left Melton, but it is certain that he strengthened that acquaintance and obtained the Earl's favour through his literary endeavours during this period. Henley's translation of *Vertot's Miscellanies* was printed in 1723, though no doubt completed earlier, and is dedicated to the noble Earl in a fulsome letter which refers in its closing lines to an earlier and promising meeting: 'But I ought not to press too long upon your Lordship. I would only crave Your Permission to repeat those sincere and ardent Wishes, which I had some time since the Honour to pay Your Lordship; that you may be ever Happy and Glorious.' By the end of the year the prize had been won, and Henley began his collection of translations of Pliny's Epistles with a dedicatory letter dated 15 November 1723, actually written from the Rectory of Chelmondiston, the solid evidence of his patron's generosity:

I beg leave to make this second Approach to Your Lordship, with one of the noblest Remains of Antiquity, now first appearing in an *English* Habit: As I paid an Offering of Zeal and Respect to Your Lordship in a former Work, This I would set up as a Monument of Gratitude to my first Maecenas. . . . To conclude, my Lord, tho' I shall always acknowledge the Strongest Obligations to yr. Lordship. yet give me leave to declare, both to your self, and the whole World, that whatever is in the Power of your Lordship to give, can never equal the *Manner of your giving it.*

The following year, on 2 September, he penned the dedicatory letter to his translation of Montfaucon's *The Antiquities of Italy*, fearing that

The fresh Trouble I take the Boldness to give your Lordship in this repeated humble Offering, might justly be constru'd an Exercise of your Patience . . . I have no other Method of expressing the constant Attachment, and the Personal Veneration I bear to your Lordship: besides the Tie I am under to pay every mark of respect that lies in my narrow Compass to your Lordship, who by the growing Obligations, and kind Assurances, I have receiv'd from you, are the greatest Friend I have yet experienc'd in Life . . . it is happy, that since the wise Administration, of which your Lordship is at the Head, by the profound

Tranquility it has establish'd among Us, has almost put it out of Our Power to merit of the Publick, in a Political Light . . . I would, with a decent Boldness, in the name of all the younger Candidates for a Place in the Temple of Honour; of those who may be capable of distinguishing themselves for the CHURCH, the STATE, and the REPUBLIC of LETTERS, humbly tell your Lordship, that their main Refuge is You . . . 'Tis from You they hope to see . . . The Majesty of the Pen retriev'd, and the PULPIT recover'd to the Life, the Dignity, the Lustre of *Athenian* Eloquence and Action . . .

This gratefulness to Macclesfield was no mere formality, for it remained with Henley throughout his life[1] and no doubt further favours might have been forthcoming from a patron in whose hands lay so much direct and indirect power of preferment. But Macclesfield resigned the seals of office on 4 June 1725, when Henley most needed his influential support. He later expressed his belief that 'had he lived in Power, nothing could have obstructed my direct Advancement to the highest Honours',[2] and this is not entirely improbable. The loss of Macclesfield at this stage in Henley's career is yet another of those perverse tricks of fortune which so often frustrated his just hopes. His other patrons were to prove broken reeds, none of them strong enough to lean on, and one, indeed, destined to pierce his hand.

Meanwhile, his chaplaincy and his country living achieved, he set out to gain what he most wanted, a London pulpit and ultimately a London benefice which he could now legally hold in plurality. The pleasant riverside setting of Chelmondiston did not often tempt him from London. He was certainly in residence during the month of his induction but after that he gave £20 a year to a neighbouring clergyman, William Herne, to take services for him and to baptize, marry, and bury. He himself obtained a dispensation to be only in residence on a single annual visit in the summer, when, we are told, he 'was always received with an equal Welcome of Joy and Affection by his Parishioners'.[3]

[1] An advertisement 'To the Young Gentlemen of the Law' for December 1743 (Lysons 122) refers to it.

[2] *Why how now, Gossip POPE?*, p. 6.

[3] This information on his activities at Chelmondiston comes from *A Guide to the Oratory etc.*, pp. 11–12. The records of Chelmondiston church before 1725 were stolen and burnt. The church itself was destroyed by enemy action in 1944. The Bishop's Transcripts (Ipswich and East Suffolk Record Office 50/2/6B.1723; FF 528/1724; 50/2/7.1725) record the baptisms, burials, and marriages, and the signature of the curate.

But his real interest and his real efforts were in London. An appointment as lecturer to a City church was the thing he sought, where he might display his talents and gifts of elocution and attract further notice from influential patrons. Such positions were recognized and coveted steps towards further promotion, being often the first stage in careers which were crowned with honour. Archbishop Sharp had held the Friday lecture at St. Lawrence, Jewry, where on Tuesdays, Tillotson had lectured, and Hoadly, Blackhall, Gibson, Atterbury, and Newton were among those who, starting as City lecturers, finished as bishops. The first available lectureship was at the church of St. George the Martyr, Queen Square, where he was already known as an occasional preacher, but according to his own version of events, '[he] would have stood . . . had the Trustees elected.'[1] The choice of lecturer lay with the vestry, and such elections were the most unpredictable and precarious, 'being subject to so many various humours, and depending altogether upon the goodwill and pleasure of so many different persons'.[2] On 30 November 1725 Dr. Lucas was elected to fill the place, and Henley turned his attention to the lectureship at the neighbouring Bloomsbury Chapel where he was also an occasional preacher. A contributor to the *Gentleman's Magazine* gives this version of the affair:

. . . about this time [he] was an unsuccessful candidate for a lectureship at one of the neighbouring chapels. The Lectureship becoming vacant, Mr. Henley as a candidate, among others, preached a probation sermon, but his action gave great offence. Conscious, perhaps, of his own superiority, and vexed at his ill-judging auditory, he preach'd a second sermon, setting forth that action was an essential part of Oratory, for in those humbler days, no city cheese-monger presumed to contend for *voice* and *action* in a preacher. However, all would not do: he was rejected.[3]

A later account adds much picturesque detail, the source of which is unstated, but which has the authentic Henleian ring:

Henley, in early life, had been a candidate for the lectureship of Bloomsbury parish, but was rejected by the congregation, because he threw

[1] Letter to Whiston dated 3 Nov., in *Mr. Henley's Letters and Advertisements which concern Mr. Whiston etc.*, p. 15.
[2] Life of Dr. Thomas Newton, in *The Lives of Dr. Edward Pocock, Dr. Zachary Pearce, Dr. Thomas Newton & the Rev. Philip Skelton* (1816), vol. ii, p. 117.
[3] *Gentleman's Magazine*, April 1786, vol. lvi, p. 294.

himself about too much in the pulpit. Rushing into a room where the principal parishioners were assembled, he thus addressed them— 'Blockheads! are you qualified to judge of the degree of action necessary for a preacher of God's word? Were you able to read, or had you sufficient sense, you sorry knaves, to understand the renowned orator of antiquity, he would tell you, almost the only requisite of a public speaker was action! action! action! but I despise and defy you— *provoco ad populum*—the public shall decide between us.' He therefore published his 'sermon', to show their ill-taste in rejecting him.[1]

If the rest of this anecdote be true, it appears that this rejection rankled with Henley for many years afterwards, for

when he held forth in Clare-Market, if one of his Bloomsbury friends came into the room, he could not resist the opportunity of having a fling at him. With a triumphant look at the crowds by whom he was surrounded, he would fix his eye upon him and exclaim, 'You see, sir, all mankind are not of your opinion. There are, you perceive, a few sensible people in the world, who consider me not wholly unqualified for the office I have undertaken.'[2]

The only mystery in the whole story is connected with that 'second sermon, setting forth that action was an essential part of oratory' and its eventual publication 'to show their ill-taste in rejecting him'. There is, indeed, among Henley's published sermons, one which appears to fit the case—*The HISTORY And Advantages of divine Revelation with the Honour, that is due to the Word of GOD; especially in regard to the most PERFECT MANNER of delivering it, form'd on the Antient Laws of SPEAKING and AC-TION*, in which he stresses the necessity for a variety of voice, deportment, and volume, and a reflection of the various passions in the preacher's conduct and gesture. This certainly sounds to be his defence against the charge of throwing himself about too much in the pulpit. The trouble is that the sermon is dated Sunday, 15 November 1724, which is too early for the Bloomsbury Chapel sermon, and that it was preached 'in the CHURCH of St. George the Martyr' where he did not stand for election. It may be that the facts and the chronology of this thinly documented affair are confused: it may be equally true that Henley—a practised re-user of sermons—used for this sermon of self-defence at Bloomsbury

---

[1] *Fly Leaves: or Scraps and Sketches*, published by John Miller (1855), pp. 92–3.
[2] Ibid., p. 93.

a previously preached St. George's sermon on his favourite topic, which he then published after the Bloomsbury débâcle. Without further evidence we cannot be certain: the one certainty is that he failed to be elected to the Bloomsbury lectureship. Shortly after this, according to Henley, he 'was desired to take a City Lecture, and soon gave it up'.[1] His stress here is on 'desired' as opposed to his seeking election. This appointment was at St. Mary Abchurch, in November 1725, when it was announced that 'Mr. Henley is made Choice of to be one of the constant Preachers of the said lecture',[2] and he held it together with his Suffolk living until he threw aside all his offices in the great gesture of fury and frustration which ends this period of his life. But this is to anticipate. There was much more to fill his days and nights besides sermons, country living, and City lecture, though all intimately connected with that urge to advancement which here, as at Melton, produced amazing activity and industry.

Some of his publications have already been mentioned, but those few titles give sparse indication of the extent of Henley's involvement in what at best may be called literary activity, and at its worst Grub Street hack-writing. Henley always repudiated with indignation 'the Fling, that I wrote for Booksellers ... I might take an honest Chance to augment my Pocket like others, by writing, or an Oratory, but never did absolutely depend on either, nor *was necessitated* to that.'[3] The sort of 'Fling' he is furious about is typified by a *Grub Street Journal* attack, which tells how '... he unfortunately fell into the hands of the Booksellers, who rode him off his legs: with whom however he was even, by frequently causing them to make use of their own against their will. In short, he threw them so often, that not one of them would venture on his back any more.'[4] There is more truth in the attacks than in Henley's indignant repudiation. It is as a denizen of Grub Street during these years, in the hands of some of its chief controllers, that Henley produced book after book in a way which forms an interesting personal example of this phenomenon of eighteenth-century literary production-line methods. Even before he came to town, there is ominous foreboding in the names

[1] Letter to Whiston dated 3 Nov., in *Mr. Henley's Letters and Advertisements which concern Mr. Whiston etc.*, pp. 15–16.
[2] Advertisement for 26 Nov. 1725 (Lysons 6).
[3] *Why how now, Gossip POPE?*, pp. 7–8.   [4] *G.S.J.*, 9 Nov. 1732.

of the three booksellers who undertook the publication of his
Esther—'A. Bettesworth, E. Curll, J. Pemberton'. We do not
know how Henley first formed a connection with Edmund Curll,
the most notorious operator in Grub Street, but once it was formed,
he remained very much in his employ or in that of other booksellers who worked closely with Curll, found grouped in various
permutations and sharing the copyright on many title-pages.

The setting in Henley's house in Millman Street might not have
been the traditional garret, but the type of book he produced and,
when we can detect it, the method of production, form illumina-
ting examples of Grub Street at work and the sort of demand the
Grub Street hack-masters existed to satisfy—translation, compilation, and unscholarly editions. It was in 1721 with an 'edition'
that Henley started his London career as a writer—*The Works of
the Most Noble John Sheffield, late Duke of Buckingham. Published, by
his Grace, in his Life Time*, with the name of E. Curll boldly on the
title-page. It seems more than likely that Henley's part in this
volume was mainly confined to the writing of the dedication, for
the Advertisement announces that these pieces had already been
corrected for the press by Sheffield himself and handed over to
Gildon for printing in 1721. Little more editorial work was called
for and, as Henley's reputation to date was as a poet, Curll asked
him for a poetic dedication to the Duke of Argyll, which was
forthcoming:

> Sheffield's Illustrious Muse attends your smile,
> And aims like all her Sex, to please Argyll:
> To you her Lute she variously Strings,
> Of Wisdom, Valour, Wit, and Love she Sings;
> Yet still directing to one point of View,
> She owns the Height of Ev'ry Theme in You.
> Was I possess'd of her Superior Fire,
> Strongly I'd paint the *Hero* I admire;
> First in the hardy Science of the Field,
> And in each softer Art compleatly skill'd:
> For ev'ry Grace by kind *Minerva* turn'd,
> That e'er the Senate, Court, or Camp adorn'd.
> One, whom the Brightest Virtues recommend,
> Truth to his Prince, his country, and his Friend;
> But Prose and Pedantry by Vein controul,
> Long it has been my *Duty* to be Dull.

Th'Augustan Age of Wit, alas! is fled,
O! where shall we supply the *mighty Dead*?
Once more ye great distinguish'd Shades arise,
To captivate our Hearts, and bless our Eyes!
Provok'd Apollo Frowns upon our Sins,
And punishes the Land with *Harlequins.*
Unbounded Avarice, and Lust of Sway,
Engross our Schemes, and chase the Muse away.
ARGYLL, to Thee we Look; do Thou restore
The Antient Genius to its rightful Power;
When HENDELL Plays, the Music is Divine,
O! May her Sister-Arts the Consort join!
May *Poetry* advance her Genuine Strain,
And *Classic* Oratory live again;
May Tragedy exert a govern'd Rage,
And *Nature* shine afresh upon the Stage.
These may the Polish'd *Languages* attend,
And Beauteous *English* find a Standard Friend.
This will new Laurels in thy Garland weave,
And Triumph to Great SHEFFIELD'S MANES give.

The accepted reward for a poetic dedication was not, however, forthcoming, and years later Henley bitterly recalled this approach to Argyll 'who generously gave him oo'.[1]

As yet he was not under great pressure from the booksellers, and in the following year was only asked to complete a translation of Vertot's *A Critical History of the Establishment of the Bretons among the Gauls.* Volume I had been completed by an unknown hand and Henley was only responsible for the second volume. Even so, his share was a book of 243 pages, and one hopes that such labour was better rewarded by the dedicatee, the Rt. Hon. Sir Peter King, Lord Chief Justice of the Common Pleas, than it had been by the noble Duke.

Meanwhile his powers of rhetorical prose were allowed a public performance with the printing of his *Apotheosis. A Funeral Oration; Sacred to the Memory of The Most Noble John, Duke of Marlborough. As it was Spoken on the Day of his Interment. Form'd upon the Manner of the Antients.* Marlborough had died on 16 June 1722 and been given a most spectacular state funeral in the Abbey. Where this particular oration was delivered—if the references to

---

[1] *Books written by this Author* in *The Oratory Magazine No. III,* pp. i–v.

the scene of 'this Assembly, no less Mournful, than it is August' are anything more than a conventional or even disingenuous fiction—we do not know. For thirty-five pages Henley maintains a hugely inflated style, heavy with classical and mythological references, with a contrived rhythmic regularity and figured paragraph endings. He manages to survey Marlborough's birth and family, his marriage and progeny, his warlike prowess, his temporary disgrace and return to favour and righteous rewards. It is a thoroughly Whig performance, and there is no doubt about where Henley is looking for favour, as he manages to encompass most of the Establishment in the amazing climax of adulation:

Look with Pleasing Awe upon a MONARCH, that alone deserves to be UNIVERSAL: that alone can blend the Extremes of Love and Terror. A PRINCE, who looks and moves the Hero, who cleft his Foe under the Standard of our Great Leader, and chas'd away his IN-GLORIOUS RIVAL; A PRINCESS, enrich'd with a Soul and Form, equally Celestial; A ROYAL STEM, that prolongs our Hope, and ensures the Spring of our Joy Eternal. A MINISTRY that will establish us Happy in spight of ourselves, and may claim in Merit the Rank of Sovreigns: A BENCH OF FATHERS, that justly unite the Service of HEAVEN AND THEIR KING; a SENATE, that is truly *British*: AN ARMY, Faithful and Intrepid; and A PEOPLE, however tempted, too Discerning, Honest, and Brave, to forfeit a Vow'd Obedience, betray an Indulgent Master, and Sacrifice a Free-born Country. These Images of Consolation relieve a present Pain, and cut off a future Anguish; while PARKER is the Lov'd Oracle of the Pitying GODS, and BOYLE commands the Master-Spring of Empire: While HOLLES leads the Royal Circle: TOWNSHEND and CARTERET Adorn the Orb of State; Superior Beings in the Form of A TALBOT, A TRIM-MEL, A GIBSON, are ANGELS OF THE CHURCHES: While They, with THE LOYAL College of the Mitre, confirm the Vow, grace the Altar, guard the Temple, and bless the Sacrifice; while PRAT and KING direct the Voice, the Sword, the Scale of Justice; and Tenacious Virtue preserves the DARLING Figure of a WALPOLE.

Finally the glorified Marlborough enters Heaven 'where CAESAR and the great NASSAU expect (long, very long, may they expect) the Greater GEORGE'. No devoted party writer could have thrown in his lot more completely, or strained every nerve and sinew to flatter and persuade a favour. Later in life Henley said that this piece was 'publish'd in Consequence of an irrevocable

Stipulation with a *B-----*, who broke it',[1] and again 'the Oration on the late Duke of Marlborough, besides other Matters, was the *Pledge*.'[2] His Bishop is Gibson, Bishop of London, a man of power working closely with Walpole in an alliance which, it has been said, 'settled itself to the exploitation of the land of promise and to the establishment of a virtual Whig monopoly of episcopal preferment'.[3] Henley's preferment was made conditional on his support of the Ministry, and *Apotheosis* was his side of the bargain. Gibson's side was never fulfilled. Indeed Henley's only gain seems to have been the obtaining of an entrée to Walpole, on the far lower and more inglorious level of a spy and informer.

The year 1723 sees the real start of Henley's Grub Street labour, ranging over translation, compilation, and even anti-quarian transcription. The latter was the small task, which no doubt brought him in a guinea, of transcribing and translating 'the Greek, Hebrew and Aetheopic Inscriptions on the Monuments of the two wives of Sir Samuel Morland . . . publish'd in the Antiquities of that Abbey'.[4] In the work to which he refers— *The Antiquities of St. Peter's, or the Abbey-Church of Westminster* —and of which Curll was a part-publisher, his entry covers only two pages, and a much more substantial work appeared in the March of this year, *An Historical and Chronological Treatise of the Anointing and Coronation of the Kings and queens of France, from Clovis I to the Present King; And of all the Sovereign Princes of Europe. To which is added, an Exact Relation of the Ceremony of the Coronation of Louis XV. By M. Menin, Counsellor of the Parliament of Metz. Faithfully done from the Original French.* There is no indication on the title-page nor on any of the 333 ensuing pages of Henley's being the translator, but in his frequent lists of his printed works he never omits it, and there seems little reason to doubt the truth of a claim few wanted to disallow. He openly claimed the credit, however, when he returned to translate another work of the author he had worked on the previous year, Vertot. The title-page of *Vertot's Miscellanies* announces 'Done from the Original French, in the Memoirs of Literature of the Academy, Printed at *Paris*, by John Henley, M.A.'. It is a curious collection of pieces by Vertot, on the origins of the French race, the Salic

---

[1] Ibid. [2] *Hyp Doctor*, 20 Jan. 1741.
[3] Norman Sykes, op. cit., pp. 35–6. [4] *Books written by this Author.*

Law, the Holy Vial of Rheims, and ancient French oaths, and adds, for good measure, Mabillon's article on the burial places of the French kings, and Vaillant on the nativity of Christ discovered from ancient medals, providing a good example of the type of Digest production which was perhaps more the staple product of Grub Street than the more publicized obscenities and libels. In the short Preface, Henley reflects on the lack of an Academy in England, echoing the sentiments of Swift and many great men of his age,

That it is a Disadvantage and a Discredit to us in England, that we are destitute of an Establishment like this of the French Academy. The Genius and Qualifications of our Countrymen, I believe, will hardly be question'd, or even brought into a comparison with those of the French, by any but a Frenchman: and was the Encouragement of the Court, and the Countenance of great Men equal, the British Sense would conquer them again as easily, as the British Valour has done before. Our Tongue would rise to a superior Degree of Perfection, and we might improve much higher, in Arts and Sciences, in Letters and Politeness.

The year's toil was completed with an openly confessed digest directed at a reading public which was unable or unwilling to read at large, and which the Grub Street of every age struggles to supply. This was a *History of Sweden from the Most Early and Authentick Accounts of that Kingdom, to the Erecting of it into an Absolute Monarchy, and the Establishment of the Reformation. Containing A view of the most remarkable Turns of State, Commotions, Conspiracies, and principal Events, during that Period, by J. Henley, M.A.* Henley exactly describes the work in his Preface—'a Short and Naked Series of Facts, without Remark or Embellishment'— admitting that there are larger and better works on the subject but that 'a Mignature of it has appear'd to be wanting'. For lazy readers, who still wished to know something of Sweden's history, the gap was now filled, and Henley tells his dedicatee, Lord Carteret, that with encouragement he would produce a more worthy work on the subject.

It was a promise he would have had little time to fulfil, for 1724 saw him still heroically at work adding volumes great in bulk if not in value to his list of published works. Translation still took up much of his time, and considerable labour must have been required to produce the two large volumes—one of 491 pages, the other of 428—of *A new Treatise of the Art of Thinking; or a Compleat System of Reflections, concerning the Conduct and Improvement of the Mind. Illustrated with Variety of Characters and Examples drawn from the Ordinary Occurrences of Life. Written in French by Mr. Crousaz, Professor of Philosophy and Mathematics in the Academy of Laussanne. Done into English.*[1] For this work he took no credit and one only hopes that a decent down-payment compensated for this anonymity's failure to increase his literary reputation. The title-page of the other work of translation this year gave him his due credit—*Pliny's Epistles and Panegyricks. Translated by several hands. With the Life of Pliny. By Mr. Henley. In two volumes.*[2] This work admirably illustrates that other method of Grub Street production, the team effort, where the bookseller assembled a small stable of hacks and appointed a ring-master to control and consolidate their work. Henley was chosen as ring-master over some eleven contributors —not counting some of Addison's translations lifted from the *Tatler*—and he describes the method of this edition in his Preface. 'Each hand is to answer for the part that belongs to him, and no single person is concern'd in the work of another, or in the Design or Discharge of the whole.' Despite the help, and sometimes because of the delinquency of his contributors, his labour in 'the Design and Discharge of the whole' could have been no mean one. If the ascription of translations to the other contributors is correct, Henley was responsible for 323 epistles, besides having to complete some which his contributors failed to finish, and providing the prefatory Life. For this little work of thirty pages Henley had obviously done his homework, and consulted the Pliny authorities and critics, displaying an impressive knowledge of manuscripts and printed sources, and even evidence that he had done some collation of them. But in such works one must be wary, as is so conclusively demonstrated by the last one of this year, *The Works of the Honourable Sr. Philip Sidney, Knt. In Prose and Verse. In Three*

---

[1] There is no indication on the title-page nor in the body of the work of Henley being the translator. The ascription of this work to him rests on his own lists of printed works in *Books written and Publish'd by the Rev. John Henley* (1724).

[2] I have decided to deal with this as a work of 1724. The title-page has 'MDCCXXIV' although the following page states 'Printed in the Year MDCCXXIII'. Henley's dedication is dated 15 Nov. 1723, and it seems possible that the work was intended for publication that year but was for some reason delayed until 1724. The *Monthly Catalogue* announces the work in July 1724.

*Volumes. Containing I The Countess of Pembroke's Arcadia II The
Defense of Poesy III Astrophel and Stella IV The Remedy of Love;
Sonnets &c. V The Lady of May. A Masque VI The Life of the
Author.*[1] Curll and his associates were the booksellers responsible
for the publishing, though how much editing responsibility was
Henley's is difficult to determine. He appears to have done little
more than take over the text of the last edition which had been in
1674. What he did in writing the Life is more certain, for here we
are given a fine opportunity to look over the shoulder of a Grub
Street writer and see him, pressed for time and lacking first-hand
knowledge, busily at work stealing and compiling. Open on his
desk are Fulke Greville's Life of 1652, the Life of Sidney prefacing
the 1662 edition, and Anthony à Wood's entry on Sidney in
Athenae Oxonienses. His eye moves from one to the other as he
copies out verbatim here a piece, there a piece, sometimes omitting
the odd word, shuffling the pieces a little, until a jigsaw of stolen
pieces is fitted together. One can follow his tracks from line to
line, to discover that there is not one original word in the whole
piece. How many of his colleagues, slaving away at ignorant
piecework, must have acquired a similar expertise in literary
plundering, and how little we can condemn them, considering the
economic pressure under which they worked.

Certainly the pressure on Henley does not seem to have relaxed,
for in the February of 1725, again under Curll's distant super-
vision, appeared *The Antiquities of Italy. Being the Travels of the
Learned and Reverend Bernard de Montfaucon from Paris through Italy,
in the years 1698 and 1699. . . . Made English from the Paris Edition
of the Latin Original. . . . The Second Edition, Revis'd throughout; with
Large Improvements and Corrections, communicated by the Author to the
Editor JOHN HENLEY, M.A.* This work had been on Henley's
desk for some time, and it would appear that his method was to
keep various assignments going at once, turning his attention
from one to another, until a fiercer demand forced him to finish

---

[1] Here again there is no indication in the work of Henley's responsibility. He
includes in his *Books written and Publish'd by the Rev. John Henley,* 'The Works of Sir
Philip Sidney in II vol. octavo publish'd in the Year 1724'. There is some confusion
over the date, MDCCXXV being the date on the title-page, but the three volumes
are dated MDCCXXV, MDCCXXIV, MDCCXXIV respectively. There is, however, only one edition of Sidney in either of these years, and Curll's involvement
makes this almost certainly Henley's work.

one for the printer. As early as June 1723 we know that he was proposing this translation of Montfaucon, for we have a letter from him to Montfaucon written at that date from Gray's Inn, outlining his editorial policy and the extent of his own responsibility. 'So that in fitting out this *Second* Edition of it,' he writes, 'I set myself to correct the Mistakes, supply the Defects, and give a better Turn and Polish to the Expression . . . preserving, in the meantime, a great Part of the first Edition, where all was right and the Perfection and Beauty of the Work was not impair'd, as it stood before.'[1] Montfaucon replied in the September, addressing his letter to 'eruditissimo clarissimoque Viro, D. Johanni Henleio', giving Henley a list of errata and new readings, and bidding his new editor 'Farewell, and proceed as you have begun, to adorn the Commonwealth of Letters.' It was a testimonial Henley valued greatly, for he often in later years referred to it and used it in self-defence against his attackers. An examination of Henley's work in this edition bears out his claims. At times he re-wrote or re-translated, at times he used the previous translation word for word, at times with the smallest stylistic alterations. It was exactly the sort of work he could keep moving alongside his other tasks.

By 1725 Henley, as we have seen, was becoming more and more involved in clerical labours, preaching around the city and exerting himself in quest of the coveted lectureship. In August he preached for the benefit of fifty poor children at St. Catherine's by the Tower, in September a collection sermon at St. James's in Duke Place, and a charity sermon at St. Dunstan's, Stepney, while in October he preached yet another at St. John's, Wapping.[2] His literary works become fewer. Only one more commission was completed and his involvement here was no more than to pen a poetical dedication to another of Curll's productions, *Miscellanies in Verse and Prose. Written by the Right Honourable Joseph Addison, Esq.* This is a typical Curll book, made up of old productions, separately dated and paginated, sewn up with a few new translations from Addison's Latin poems and offered at 3*s.* as a new book. Henley's dedication, dated from Gray's Inn, 29 October 1724, aims high both in style and the patron aimed at:

---

[1] Printed as part of the prefatory material in this edition.
[2] Advertisements for these are collected in Lysons, p. 6.

To
The Right Honourable
The
Lord Walpole.

My Lord,

I

Indulge this Off-ring, nor the Vow disown;
A WALPOLE still should guard an ADDISON.
To change the Altar, would offend his Shade;
Profane his Urn, and *violate the Dead.*
This darling Son of universal Fame,
Justly attends the leading Patriot Name:
Both in one Orb, as Kindred Stars agree:
Both in the glorious Cause of *Sense and Liberty.*

II

Here mingled Themes delight the searching Eye,
And *bind a Sheaf of various Poesy*:
Now Grave, the Muse in solemn Measure treads;
Now Gay, to sportive Plains the Fancy leads;
Sometimes, *O Nature*! shews thy hidden Pow'rs,
Th'Aërial *Force*, the *Healing Skill* explores;
Then paints the *Terrors* of the *Final Doom,*
Tremendous Images of Wrath to come;
Here *sliding* o'er the *frosted Wave* she's seen
There casts the *byas'd Globe* upon the Green;
Pigmies are *Heroes* at her strong Command,
And a *new Race* lives from the *Carver's Hand*;
Well-chosen Colours the *great Antients* draw,
And *Peace* is *spoke* to *Europe* by NASSAU;
Graces Divine, to soothing Musick brings,
And with *Apollo's* Charm, *Apollo's* Art he sings.

III

But he, alas! the *wond'rous he*, is gone:
When shall we view a second ADDISON?
Where's the bright *Genius* in the Womb of Time,
To emulate his Force, his Heights to climb?
A WALPOLE might in ev'ry Form have shin'd;
But for a *larger Sphere* was he design'd:
The Help, the Guide, the Guardian of *Mankind.*
   Our other Hope! *Thou*, to one Mark aspire,
The Talents and the Virtues of thy Sire:

Since *Albion*, with Repose his Counsels bless,
Let the FINE ARTS compleat the Train of *Peace*:
Auspicious on each *growing Merit* smile,
And bid *successful Letters* grace your Isle:
So shall the conscious Globe to *her* submit
The Universal Monarchy of Wit:
So shall our *Science*, like our *Arms*, advance,
And win the *fairest Laurel* from the *Brow* of *France*.

Except for occasional ugly distortions of word order, the piece is a competent exercise in the high style of panegyric, and no more fulsome than many of its kind. Henley could no doubt have produced many more such effusions had not other tasks distracted and finally banished his Muse. It was to be his last published poem, but not his last association with Walpole. The conjunction of this address on the First Minister's merits, and Curll's name on the title-page brings us to another of Henley's activities during these years, slightly mysterious and certainly disreputable.

Though some of the details have been distorted through the fog of scandalous gossip which always surrounds Henley, there is no doubt that he became involved in what could euphemistically be called Secret Service work or, more honestly, the work of an informer. Walpole's payments for Secret Service were large, and the system of controlling the press, discovering and punishing seditious libels, though involving such great officials as the Secretaries of State, the Attorney General, and his emissaries the Messengers, depended ultimately on a huge body of men willing to supply information for money and favour. Among these Curll must certainly be numbered and he, besides introducing Henley to the labours and rewards of Grub Street, also involved him in what now appears a completely despicable method of currying favour and protection from the great. This work of Henley's was not unknown to his enemies, who continually brought it up to his discredit. The note to Henley's portrait in *The Dunciad* enshrines his enemies' version: 'He came to town and after having for some years been a writer for Booksellers, he had an ambition to be so for Ministers of state . . . however he offered the service of his pen, in one morning, to two great men of opinions and interests directly opposite, by both of whom being rejected. . . .'[1]

[1] *Dunciad*, Book iii (1729), note to line 195. The note to the 1751 edition omits 'in one morning'.

The *Grub Street Journal* often repeated the accusation, as in its proposed subject for a disputation, 'Whether a man, who has offer'd the service of his pen to two opposite parties, at the same time, can be truly sincere to either',[1] or in its interpretation of the figures in the notorious print 'The Art and Mystery of Printing Emblematically display'd', 'That of Janus in the second shows him, either according to a former *transaction* of his, of which there is an account in Dunciad Book III.'[2] Henley's defences are interesting examples of equivocation, denying details but never referring to the substance of the attacks, rejecting the accusations of trying to run with hare and hounds, but never denying that he was running. 'I never was rejected by either,' he writes, referring to Walpole and Pulteney, 'never offered the Service of my Pen to Mr. *P.* nor even attended him, never was near his Door or his Person, I have no personal Disrespect to him; but *both these honourable Gentlemen* know this *respectively* to be Fact.'[3] From the evidence available, Henley made no approaches to anyone except Walpole. It was with the Administration and its episcopal right arm, Gibson, that he had cast his lot, and the climax of *Apotheosis* and the dedication to the Addison Miscellanies are further proof of this. It is true that he 'never was rejected by either', firstly because he had made no approaches to the Opposition and secondly because—although he always refrains from actually stating this— he was accepted by Walpole, not only to send written information but even to be granted the occasional audience.

It is a curious phenomenon of eighteenth-century administration, and one hardly credible to us, that the Prime Minister and the Lord Chancellor should have had time or inclination to deal personally with such petty matters or such people as Curll and Henley, yet they obviously considered this an important part of maintaining the King's Peace and the stability of his Government. A letter from Curll to Walpole, dated 2 March 1724, establishes the situation, showing the sort of information he and Henley were especially equipped to supply, and the sort of reward expected for such information. It also shows why Henley was necessary for Curll in this work, as the public go-between with an as yet clear reputation, whereas Curll, already a public scandal and too fre-

---

[1] *G.S.J.*, 15 Dec. 1737.   [2] *G.S.J.*, 30 Oct. 1732.
[3] *Why how now, Gossip POPE?*, p. 6.

quently in trouble with the authorities, had to work behind the scenes:

Hond. Sir,

Yesterday Mr. Henley and myself were eye-witnesses of a letter, under Mrs. Manley's own hand, intimating that a fifth volume of The Atlantic had been for some time printed off, and lies ready for publication: the design of which, in her own words is, 'to give an account of a sovereign and his ministers who are endeavouring to overturn the constitution which their pretence is to protect; to examine the defects and vices of some men who take a delight to impose upon the world by the pretence of public good, whilst their true design is only to gratify and advance themselves.'

This, Sir, is the laudable tenour of this libel which is (but shall be in your power only to suppress) ready for the intended mischief upon the rising of the Parliament.

Mr. Henley called on me this morning, to acquaint me that your Honour had appointed Wednesday morning next for your final determination relating to these kind of services.

As your Honour was formerly pleased to promise me your friendship, I now hope to feel the effects of it for what I can, without vanity, call my unwearied diligence to serve the Government, having in a manner left off my business for that purpose.

Mr. Goode told me that I might depend upon having some provision made for me, and that he had named something in the Post-office to your Honour for my purpose. And I hope that, either in that or some of the many others over which your Honour presides, I shall be thought on.

Just upon Lord Townshend's going to Hanover, I receiv'd his Lordship's instructions, at any rate to get out of the custody of Mr. Layer's Clerk, Stewart, some papers then intended to be privately dispersed. This I effected, and am ready to deliver them up to your Honour. Mr. Cracherode and Mr. Buckley called on me to see them, but had not their end; my design being strictly to observe the trust reposed by his Lordship in me, who ordered me, when he gave me the above instructions, to attend your Honour for whatever money I should have occasion for.

Now, Sir, as I have not intruded upon your important minutes, neither can I pester your levy with an Irish assurance, I humbly hope for your present favour for my past expences, and what Mr. Henley and myself have now under your consideration, since we shall either desist or proceed according to your determination. I am, honoured Sir, your ever devoted and most obliged humble Servant,

E. CURLL.

P.S. Lord Townshend assured me he would recommend me to your Honour for some provision in the Civil List. In the Stamp-Office I can be serviceable.

On the Wednesday appointed, Henley must have had his interview with Walpole and he then wrote to confirm another appointment at the end of the week, emphasizing a little more subtly than Curll his hopes of reward, and making very clear his importance as the public agent in these cloak-and-dagger negotiations:

Hond. Sir,

I will attend you on Friday for your final determination. My intentions are both honourable and sincere; and I doubt not but from you they will meet with a suitable return. This affair has been very expensive, which I hope will be considered when I wait upon you; and, as to any former matters, Mr. C. tells me he has always made good what he proposed: and the reason of his not attending upon you oftener was from your own commands to him to go to Lord Townshend when he had any thing to offer.

As you please to determine on Friday, I shall either desist from or pursue my enquiries of this kind. It not being at all proper for Mr. C. to appear in person on these occasions, all will be transacted by *me only*.

As I expect your Honour's favour, believe me to be, upon all occasions, your Honour's most devoted servant,

J. HENLEY.

As to Mr. Higgons's and Mrs. Manley's affair, I have some original letters under both their hands.[1]

There is evidence that Curll, despite public disgrace in the pillory and in prison, continued to aid the Government with information against printers and booksellers. There is some evidence to show that Henley himself possibly continued in this work, and his being employed to write a pro-Government paper in 1730[2] would indicate that his abilities and his political soundness were still fresh in the minds of men who governed and censored the press and its productions.

[1] These two letters, together with two more of Curll's to Walpole and Lord Townshend, and a reply from Townshend dated 29 Sept. 1728, are printed in the *Gentleman's Magazine*, March 1798, vol. lxviii, pt. i, pp. 190–1. They were sent in by M. Green who wrote that they were 'communicated to me by a respectable friend'. Another letter from Curll, dated 6 Sept. 1728, expressing willingness to give such information against printers and booksellers, is preserved in the P.R.O. (S.P. Domestic 36/8/113).

[2] See Chapter VII, part iii, below, for the story of the *Hyp Doctor*.

And what of the rewards of all this industry, the midnight oil spent in translating and compiling, the many sermons preached from as many pulpits, the low shifts of spying and informing, the exciting personal interviews with the Great Man himself? Henley was expending his physical and nervous energy for more than the odd few guineas in booksellers' fees, vestry gifts, or informer's rewards. He hoped for favour from the great men in whose hands were concentrated so many good gifts. He wore his chaplain's scarf; he had his country living in Suffolk; he had his lectureship at St. Mary's Abchurch. He wanted more. He wanted a London living, and who knew what honours then lay before him? It still seemed, in 1725, that such things were not idle dreams: the following year was to see those dream visions of rectories and mitres fade away.

His first and fruitful patron, as we have seen, was the then Lord Chancellor, the Earl of Macclesfield, through whose favour he was instituted Rector of Chelmondiston, and whom he always remembered and spoke of with gratitude. But as, in later years, he remembers his kind patron, he remembers always the misfortune of him not living on in power, and the perfidiousness of the man on whom he chose to set his future hopes. Macclesfield, he records, in words which must have been the summary of many a hopeful day-dream, gave him for his dedication of the Pliny 'an hundred guineas with his own hand and a Living, and promised to make him Preacher of the Savoy, King's Chaplain, Dean and Bishop; from all which he was insidiously debarr'd by a P–––––'.[1] Many years afterwards, in October 1747, he voiced the same grievance:

Had I not been debarr'd that Ecclesiastical Preferment which was my Right, by a wrong-headed envious **, I had, before this Time, been, what I never aim'd at, in a Chair, where I would have given 5000£ out of the revenue for the Good of the Nation, prov'd myself the best that ever sate in it, and done more Service at a Pinch than Russians and Prussians &c.[2]

The same story of promise and the same prelatical villain recur the following month:

[1] *Books written by this Author.*
[2] Advertisement for 17 Oct. 1747 (Lysons 150).

a late bright and learned Lord Chancellor honour'd me with his peculiar Favour, promis'd to introduce me gradually to the highest Dignities: his Chaplains gave me Testimonials; my Intent was a Pulpit in Town, at the utmost of 250 £. a Year: a Bishop irrevocably stipulated that I should have my Intention: the Ministers the like, all in the name of the Crown, as its Agents.[1]

The Prelate in the case has already entered the story, Gibson, Bishop of London from 1723, and already an active supporter of the Whigs in his previous see of Lincoln. While there he had himself been a pamphleteer of no very dignified status, agreeing to write a pamphlet in 1721 defending Government action over plague precaution. His enemies had sneered that 'this is a very mean work that he submits to for his hopes of London',[2] but his hopes nevertheless were fulfilled, and, enthroned at the time when Walpole was finally entrenched in power, he wielded, through Walpole, tremendous influence on Church appointments. It was on such a man that Henley, bereft of his former patron, centred his hopes.

The fullest version of Henley's side of the story is in a letter published in the *St. James's Evening Post* on 26 October 1732:

. . . I waited some years on a certain PRELATE with a Sollicitation of a Pulpit in Town, signifying my Resolution to cultivate and exercise the Talent of Preaching, which God had given me in the most compleat and public Manner. His Answer was, 'That I might be of Use, but before he could do for me, he must have a PLEDGE of my Attachment to the Government.' I was an entire Stranger to Politics, but gave him that PLEDGE. A Pledge demanded, given, and accepted for a Consideration, is a Contract for that Consideration; the Hinge of my Interest and Fortune very much turned upon it: It was the year 1721–2, a tender Crisis, and doubtless, he made a Job of it to the Government. When I applied for the Consideration, he shifted me off; had he any possible Exception to my intellectual or moral Qualifications, (tho' nothing can be more immoral, or sooner make the World Atheists, than a Perfidious Prelate,) he should, before he drew me in, have told me, that if he met with any such Exception, he would not do what I sollicited: and that he would take Time to examine. This would have been fair: He assigned no Exception at all during a whole Year, 'till I

---

[1] Advertisement for 7 Nov. 1747 ibid.
[2] Norman Sykes, op. cit., p. 59.

had sacrificed my Interest to him, on his own Demand; and it is easy to frame Exceptions, if a Person be inclined to break his Word.[1]

Whatever may be the accuracy or reliability of the details, one thing is clear and certain: Henley had been given definite hopes of preferment by Gibson who, for some reason, repudiated him when he pressed his claim. The reason is uncertain, though various suggestions were made and we may make our own conjectures. Henley himself believed that jealousy was at the root of this change of heart. 'My judgment is,' he wrote, 'he and his clergy even envied me in the pulpit, and were jealous of my advancement, timorous that at court there might be a patron or patroness of learning, and apprehensive that I might outstrip them there',[2] a belief which had been earlier expressed in the *Narrative* where he alleges that 'This Popularity, with his enterprizing Spirit, and introducing regular Action into the Pulpit, were the true Causes, why some obstructed his rising in Town, from Envy, Jealousy, and a Disrelish of those who are not qualified to be compleat Spaniels.'[3] At the opposite extreme was the scandalous suggestion made by an enemy—the first instance of a repeated and not unfounded accusation—that he was 'obstreperously noisy and facetious over a Cup', and that 'by an early Misapplication of his Time, and a boisterous Exercise of *uncommon Talents* among Publicans and Sinners, [he] fell into such Disrepute as to be *rusticated* by the learned *Londono* to his *Cure*, which rather than obey and quite his riotous Excesses, he abdicated.'[4] It is likely that this was a small part of the truth and that many other reasons influenced Gibson. Henley's eccentricity in the pulpit was already a subject of discussion and his violent behaviour over the Bloomsbury lectureship could not have gone unnoticed. There is evidence that he was called before his Bishop and his preaching habits and reputation questioned. Henley

---

[1] *St. James's Evening Post*, 26 Oct. 1732, and quoted in *G.S.J.*, 16 Nov. 1732. In *G.S.J.*, 16 Nov. 1732, it is discussed in a long letter from 'Ecclesiasticus', who doubts its origin and takes it to be a *G.S.J.* forgery. In *Fog's Journal*, 4 Nov. 1732, Henley himself published an advertisement claiming it to be a forgery. But it is there in the *St. James's Evening Post*: it has the tone of Henley: and it is difficult to see what was to be gained in the fight against Henley by forging such a latter. I treat it as genuine, though there must remain some element of doubt.

[2] *St. James's Evening Post*, 26 Oct. 1732.

[3] *Narrative*, p. 12.

[4] Anon., *A Comparison between Orator H——— and Orator P———-* (n.d.), pp. 4–5.

recorded 'That "I *called myself* the R*estorer of Ancient Eloquence*" was expressly disproved, before the Bishop of the Diocese by two Church-wardens, personally, who confess'd and declared, that they and others gave me that Title, to multiply Auditors at Charity-Sermons.'[1] Possibly rumours of his alleged amorous adventures at Melton and the continuing pursuit of Mrs. Tolson reached the ears of his superiors, together with the reports on his love of the pleasures as well as the labours of the town. A mysterious remark by Henley in the closing years of his life, that 'As I was always known to be an Advocate for the Ladies, I lost, in their Behalf, one Chance for an Archbishoprick...'[2] suggests that there might be some element of truth in such a conjecture. Certainly Henley believed that he had been spied upon and his activities reported. He later spoke of some person unknown as 'ye gossip of *ye* Diocese who was ye Newsgatherer to ye late Bishop of *London*; *Spy* and *Informant* General', and believed that 'all a clergyman's conversation was carried home and recorded at Fulham in a Book of Remembrance.'[3] Add to this the undoubted fact that Henley, despite his own high opinion of his talents, was but one small voice amidst a crowd of suppliants, and Gibson could not have felt that he was destroying the Church's other hope in refusing Henley's request. For refusal seems to have been the extent of Gibson's actions except in one reference to active interference, when Henley alleges that Gibson 'drove his coach and four, *Jehu-like*, at Eleven at night, to ye late Lord Chancellor *Macclesfield*, to hinder a person's being made Preacher of ye Savoy, King's Chaplain, Dean and Bishop, against his word, & all Justice'.[4] Henley's enemies would insist that he was banished from London for ill behaviour, but in the absence of any evidence beyond their assertions, it seems more likely that the Bishop, suspicious of Henley's dependability and devout sobriety, suggested that as he already had his country living, he could be perfectly useful and contented there. It would be a way out of the situation which any bishop, harassed by petitioners, would be glad to seize, and it is the one which Henley himself

---

[1] *Why how now, Gossip POPE?*, p. 7.
[2] Advertisement for 6 Oct. 1752 (Lysons 175).
[3] Sermon for 10 Sept. 1749 (B.M. MSS.Add. 11776).
[4] Sermon for 13 July 1750 (B.M. MSS.Add. 11778).

related, denying that he was ever *required* to take up residence there:

For there was no Objection to his being toss'd into a Country Benefice by the Way of the Sea, as far as *Galilee* of the *Gentiles* (like a Pendulum, swinging one Way as far as the other) . . . But when he press'd his Desire, and Promise from a great Man of being fixed in Town, it pass'd in the Negative. He took the People too much from their Parish-Churches; and as he was not so proper for a *London* Divine (in the *Speech*, not the *Sentiments* of one who had engaged to place him there,) he was very welcome, notwithstanding all Difficulties, to be a *rural Pastor*.[1]

Nothing could have been less welcome to Henley, and his reactions, immediate and long-term, were angry and violent.

He was never to forgive Gibson. The memory of his desertion continually rankled him and found expression not only in Henley's uninterrupted attacks on all Gibson's subsequent theological and ecclesiastical activities, but in repeated asides in discussions on completely different subjects, as when he thanked friends 'for that kindness, which a promising Bishop never shewed me'[2] or promised to drop one of his schemes 'as soon as a certain Prelate shall do Right to his Promise'.[3] And in his newspaper advertisements he frequently burst out against his 'one Original capital Enemy'[4] and the 'Tools of a holy Tyrant'.[5] In 1740, exhorting a well-settled divine to vote for the Government, he let slip this personal aside:

I'll tell you a Secret, Doctor, I was once debarr'd from entering a *fat Pasture* in the Church, by the Keeper of a *great Turnpike* on the *narrow Way* to the *Holy Land*, who had been endowed there by this Ministry, purely because I was too good a Friend to his own Patrons to come into those Doctrines and Practices of his that undermine and sap the Ground on which they stand who raised him, and leave a back door for him to desert them, and their enemies to come in upon them.[6]

---

[1] *Narrative*, p. 13.
[2] Advertisement for 4 Jan. 1744, in the *Daily Advertiser*.
[3] *Hyp Doctor*, 23 Nov. 1736.
[4] Advertisement letter, 3 Aug. 1743 (Lysons 117).
[5] Advertisement letter, Dec. 1743 (Lysons 122).
[6] *Hyp Doctor*, 8 July 1740.

He gave over one of the last numbers of the *Hyp Doctor* to a furious open letter to Gibson, signed 'John Guess' and, so many years after the event, recalled once more the hope and the dashed promises:

... you ordained me, said I might be very useful in Town, and in the Year 1722, demanding of me a public Pledge of my Attachment to the Administration at my setting out in what you called a *sore Time*, by which I must, as I then said, lose and surrender all my Power and Interest to your Hands, the Consideration expressly mentioned being a *Pulpit in Town*, you promised, *I should have my Intention*; this I often demanded, and whether you gave or obtained it for me, is pretty evident.

You shewed no Cause, nor could, to be an equivalent to the Loss. One of your Principles and Elevation, (tho' you was lower once and may be again) was above that ...

This is fact, neither saucy nor scandalous; it is hard that the Subsistence of a Clergyman, who is, what you never was, a *Free-holder born* of *Great Britain*, descended of three Ancestors, some of the most *renown'd Parish Priests* in Christendom, and by his Education and the Canons, cannot turn himself to another Method of subsisting, must be at the arbitrary Mercy and precarious Word, of such as you, Sir.[1]

His hatred was undiminished when Gibson died in September 1748, and, on the Sunday following, Henley no doubt enjoyed his own eloquence even more than usual, as he preached 'St. Peter's Funeral Sermon on Judas Iscariot: that Preachers ought to rebuke Sins, of Dead and Living: Judas's Name, Sop, Satan, Bag, treacherous Kiss: Sects he made: And who to come after him: in English'.[2] At the end of the week in which speculation about the next Bishop of London must have been rife, he promised to discuss from his pulpit the 'Time &c. of appointing the next Alexander the Coppersmith'.[3] The thought of what he had lost financially became an obsession with him. The living he had been promised was worth £250 a year and in later years, when illness and the struggle to make a living made the memory more bitter, he claimed this as the beginning of a debt owed to him by his betrayers: 'This founds the Claim of a Debt, which I can prove by all the Evidence of which such Transactions are capable,

---

[1] *Hyp Doctor*, 20 Jan. 1741.
[2] Advertisement for a sermon on 18 Sept. 1748 (Lysons 154).
[3] Advertisement for a sermon on 25 Sept. 1748 ibid.

or no Contract of Faith can subsist . . .',[1] and through the following years he published statements of accounts owing, including 'Principal and Interest, besides Damages of several sorts',[2] calculated by some mathematical system peculiarly his own! By the end of 1747 he claimed that £6,600 were owed to him: by the end of 1748, £10,008: by the end of 1749 the amount only increased to £10,015, and he had obviously lost real interest or the ability to add up in the following three years when the demands of £10,021, £100,025, and £10,038 were published.

Such were the future regrets and recriminations: for the present, decisions had to be made. The prize of a city living and all the honours which might have followed were now definitely and—whilst Gibson remained in power—irrevocably cut off. The country life of Melton Mowbray had proved intolerably restricting to his ambitions and his energies, and he knew that he could never endure the life of the quiet Suffolk Rectory which was the only permanent outlet for him now. It was not, as he said, 'for a second rustication that he left the fields and swains', and if rustication was all the Establishment offered, he would find his own way to fame and prosperity. He resigned the living of Chelmondiston towards the end of 1725, his successor being instituted there on 12 January 1726,[3] and he gave up his lectureship at St. Mary Abchurch. Relieved now of all encumbrances and responsibilities, he was free to shape what course he could. The course he took was a strange and violent one, but his anger and disappointment were violent too. The months of forced literary labour, the hopeful dedications, the eager preaching of sermons, the spying and informing, the encouraging promises of the great —all these had brought him only the prospect of vegetating as a country rector. Now he would rely on himself and make something personal, something independent of patronage and establishment. The next thirty years of his life are the tumultuous story of the thing he made, which perhaps gave him more fame than any City living would have done, and brought him the one title he was ever to have, Orator Henley.

[1] Advertisement for 7 Nov. 1747 (Lysons 150).
[2] *Books written by this Author.*
[3] P.R.O. Institution Book, Series C. vol I, pt. ii, page 257 verso.

CHAPTER IV

The Foundation and Plan of the Oratory

A PIECE OF COFFEE-HOUSE GOSSIP about Henley was being retailed in 1727 that he had 'told a certain Bishop, *If they would not Provide for you, you would go over to the Church of Rome*'.[1] The gossip doubted the full truth of the story, and so must we. Of all possible places of refuge for him, Rome could never have been one. Nevertheless, the main threat of separation was true. After the events of 1725, Henley, realizing that further advancement in the Church of England was barred to him, decided to break away from that church in which his father and both his grandfathers had served so long and faithfully, to shape a career where he alone was master of his fate.

For all the violence of the step he proposed, his first actions were circumspect and cautious. He had no wish to rush from an unhopeful to a hopeless situation and he was, as Disraeli said, 'prudent before he was patriotic'.[2] This prudence led him to write for very necessary advice to the Reverend William Whiston, and thereby to involve himself in his first spectacular public controversy. Whiston was, like Henley, a Leicestershire man, a son of the manse and a graduate of Cambridge. Like Henley, too, he had held a Suffolk living until his reputation as an astronomer and mathematician led to his election to Newton's Chair in Cambridge in 1703. Unfortunately he was not content with his mathematical and experimental work, and entered into theological inquiries, reaching conclusions which persuaded the Cambridge Heads of Houses that he was a heretic of the seed of Arius. For his Arianism he was deprived of his Professorship, banished the University and, in 1710, moved to London where he continued to study and publish. Convocation voted for his prosecution as a heretic but the proceedings never terminated, and Whiston continued his eccentric course for many years, lecturing on comets and eclipses in halls and coffee houses, running a small farm near

---

[1] Anon., *A Letter to the celebrated Orator of Newport Market. etc.*, p. 10.
[2] Disraeli, *The Calamities of Authors*, i.165.

Newmarket and, towards the end of his life, showing his scale model of the Temple of Jerusalem to what audiences he could gather. Despite his eccentricity of manner which increased with the years, he was a man of honesty and integrity, declaring his opinions with straightforward simplicity, no matter how powerful or dignified his victim, and maintaining his beliefs and their consequences through a long life of struggle and difficulty. 'Whiston belonged,' wrote Leslie Stephen, 'to a familiar type as a man of very acute but ill-balanced intellect. His learning was great, however fanciful his theories.'[1] It was a type very like Henley, and this, together with his history, must have persuaded Henley that in him he would find sympathy and advice. He accordingly wrote to Whiston:

Reverend SIR,

I would beg the Favour of you to resolve me, 1. What Power the University has, or in Fact exercises, on Church of *England* Priests, openly separating from that Church? 2. What Processes and Censures Ecclesiastical, and Civil Penalties He incurs by it? 3. What are the most proper Defences to each, especially Prohibitions, and Civil or Ecclesiastical Pleas. I ask pardon for this Trouble: and would intreat your Opinion of each Head; taking some time, if you please, to digest it. I am, with my most humble Service to Mr. *Barker*,

Reverend SIR,
Your most Humble Servant,
J. HENLEY.

Especially on the Head of, 1. Degredation or Privation of Orders. 2. Excommunication.

Please to direct to me at *Millman-Street*, below *Bedford Row*.[2]

Whiston's reply has not been preserved in their published correspondence, and we do not know how far he confirmed Henley in his intentions or calmed his fears. Henley certainly went ahead with his plans, and though for the rest of his life he was vilified and attacked, no attempt was ever made by the ecclesiastical authorities to deprive or excommunicate him, perhaps because his views were not easy to define, perhaps because in many ways they were held secretly in high quarters, perhaps because authority simply did not think him worth worrying about so seriously.

[1] Entry for Whiston in the *D.N.B.*
[2] *Mr. Henley's Letters and Advertisements which concern Mr. Whiston etc.*, pp. 3–4.

It is clear, however, that it was not only for this assurance that he chose Whiston as his adviser. He was also at work putting together some scheme of ideas and doctrine on which to build his breakaway church, and it is apparent that he felt he had the framework for it in Whiston's previous writings. The foundation and plan of the Oratory did not spring entirely from Henley's head. The seeds of it are to be found in Whiston, though, admittedly, that unknowing father did not recognize and angrily rejected his offspring. About this time we find Henley re-reading Whiston's works. He sent him a note 'to enquire whether the liturgy of the Apostolical Constitutions could be had by itself', and wrote twice to buy or borrow books:

Reverend SIR,
    If you have any of Mr. *Brocklesby's* Christian Theist (Gospel Theism:) I should be proud to know whether they be dispos'd of, and if so, on what Terms. I would desire the Favour of one of your Books to the Bishop of L. on the Doxologies; and the Argument about the Dissenters Baptism. The Bearer will pay for them.

I am SIR,
Your most Humble Servant,
J. HENLEY.

If not, you would oblige me with the use of *B*'s Book one Month, or inform me where I can reasonably procure it.[1]

He sent a later note with his servant to

Ask Mr. *Whiston*, as to his *Essay towards restoring the Text of the Old Testament*, whether there be any thing in it defending the Constitutions? I have his two Pamphlets, and his *Clement* . . . Ask what else he has in Defence of the Constitutions, and the Price. Bring a Catalogue of his Books.[2]

With these books as his guides, Henley started to clarify his ideas and also, it must be added, to justify his own position. His ability to select those parts of Whiston's work which suited his purposes and justified what he wanted to believe, and to reject those parts which were unpalatable, was to arouse the fury of Whiston as both an unscholarly and a dishonest proceeding.

It was not Whiston's most famous Arian heresies which interested Henley, so much as what may be called his 'Primitivism', his belief that the Church of his day had deviated grossly from the

---

[1] Ibid., p. 5.   [2] Ibid., p. 5.

intentions of Christ and the practice of the primitive Church, and must attempt to rediscover those ideas and reshape her practices. This desire led him early in his career to accept the *Apostolical Constitutions* of Clement as a genuine apostolic production and a record of the beliefs, practice, and worship of the Apostolic Church, second in authority only to the New Testament. From these two sprang his beliefs. In a single-page pamphlet of 1712 he suggested that societies be formed to seek 'that Faith which was once delivered to the Saints', to seek into the true history of baptism, to reject doctrines not known by the Apostles, to discover a true apostolic order and discipline, and to reinstate the *Apostolical Constitutions*. In the same year he produced *Primitive Infant Baptism Reviv'd, or, An Account of the Doctrine and Practice of the two First Centuries, concerning the Baptism of Infants*, in which he asserted that the baptism of instructed catechumens and not infants was the primitive custom, that total immersion and not sprinkling was the only valid means, and that confirmation and baptism ought to be one rite. These ideas were developed in a fuller discussion in 1714 in *An Argument to Prove that either all Persons Solemnly, tho' irregularly set apart for the Ministry, are Real Clergy-men, and all their Ministerial Acts are Valid; or else there are now no Real Clergy-Men, or Christians in the World*. If, he argued, we consider things 'in the Rigor of the Law of Christ', then there are no valid clergymen for they have not been freely elected, they are made under rules and take ordination vows unknown to the Apostles; there is no valid Eucharist such as the primitive Church knew; there is really no Church, as valid orders, baptism, and Eucharist have disappeared. But such rigorous conclusions are contrary to the equity and goodness of God, and if men had acted ignorantly but with an honest mind, there is a possibility and a need for restoration, most of all in Rome, the most corrupt, but also in the Anglican Church, where the secular power's nominating of bishops and the lack of apostolic discipline among the clergy remove her from the true nature of Christ's Church. So, if our own ordinations, practice, and discipline are irregular, the non-episcopal churches overseas and the English Protestant Dissenters are only irregular in a *different* way, a *different* deficiency. The time had come to cease bickering and recrimination, and for all churches to reform themselves towards 'the pure and undefiled Religion of our Lord and Saviour'.

It was upon such arguments that Henley pondered, and produced the body of belief and ideas on which the Oratory was first founded and his own position justified. The years were to see many changes in Henley's theology,[1] an increase in eccentricity and violence, but its early shape, as presented to the first congregations at the Oratory, owes its main lines to Whiston.

The appeal of the Oratory was to the primitive Church—'the Oratory, which is raised on the principles of the Reformation, and refers all christian enquiries to the rule of the first ages',[2]— and this Henley defined as the

most antient, of the earliest use in the church of God: that is, the Old and New Testament, and the first writers after them . . . where our scripture is obscure, or dubious, the primitive writers are the best explainers of it . . . and there is not a profession in Christendom, which does not hold something that is not in the New Testament, and which it takes from the nearest times of antiquity to it.[3]

He agreed with the Church of England in accepting as this primitive period the first four Councils of the Church, though he asserted that the Church of England 'differs in practice from her own principle'. He followed Whiston closely in accusing all the churches of their deviation from the primitive pattern in their canon of Scripture, the matter and form of the sacraments, the coercive powers and the property-holding of the Church, the practice of infant baptism and the teaching of the necessity of baptism for salvation.[4] On these grounds he justified his breaking away into independence: 'I think the modern churches grossly erroneous, and I therefore divide; and I think he only that separates from the primitive church is guilty of schism. And whom hath God made a judge between us, to determine the controversy?'[5] His past acceptance of Anglican orders and his present position were reconciled because 'When I subscrib'd to the Church of *England*, I did it as far as I thought her Primitive; I am still the same; and I now dissent from her, only as she dissents from her self, and the Primitive Church.'[6] Similarly he seized on

[1] See Chapter VII, part ii, below.
[2] *The Appeal of the Oratory to the First Ages of Christianity* (1727), p. v.
[3] *A Homily on the following Liturgy*, pp. 46–8, in *The Appeal of the Oratory etc.*
[4] *The First Sermon etc.*, pp. 30–2, in *Oratory Transactions No. 1*.
[5] *A Homily on the following Liturgy*, p. 60, in *The Appeal of the Oratory etc.*
[6] Henley, *Milk for Babes etc.* (1729), p. 49.

and elaborated another of Whiston's main ideas, to justify his new position and ministerial validity—namely, that there were no real clergymen in existence and no true episcopal authority. He denied the succession of Apostolic power and any evidence of its being handed down: 'There ought to have been an exact Register kept of the express Powers given in Ordination by the Apostles to their immediate Deputies, and so on to this Day, to make good a personal Claim of Right from the Apostles.' Such a register did not exist and to admit that 'Men uninspir'd, and frail as ourselves, would exercise their Power' was repugnant to reason, the rights and liberties of Englishmen, and the laws of Nature.[1] Moreover, in England the lack was made doubly sure by the inadequate formula used in the consecration of Archbishop Parker, 'so that the distinction of clergy and laiety, the independence of the church on the state, the indelible character, the apostolical succession, all clerical pretensions whatever, are O O'.[2] In this sad case, the best must be used no matter how imperfect that best might be, and it is interesting that Henley's definition of the best curiously describes his own position.

We affirm we have no such apostolic Clergy, the Church of England herself neither affirms we have, nor thinks it essential: We assert the same . . . [But he is nearer who] has publick Authority, and what is call'd episcopal Ordination, and adheres to the Doctrine and Worship of the apostolick Age and the primitive Church.[3]

So far Whiston's ideas had been essential for the justification of his schism, his continuing right to minister and his independence of the bishops. He had seized them eagerly, but there was another side to Whiston's Primitivism and belief in the *Apostolical Constitutions* which was anathema to Henley and which he repudiated as eagerly. This was Whiston's insistence that the code of behaviour and discipline contained in those same *Constitutions* should again be observed and enforced. Henley, glad to have argued off episcopal authority, was loath to bow beneath another, and his arguments on this point caused the breach and the violent quarrel which ended his association with Whiston.

He used a variety of arguments to rebut Whiston, not all of

---

[1] *A Defence of the Oratory*, p. 28, in *Oratory Transactions No. 1*.

[2] Footnote to Rubric 3 of *The Primitive Eucharist* in *The Appeal of the Oratory etc.* p. 119.

[3] *A Defence of the Oratory*, p. 36, in *Oratory Transactions No. 1*.

them sound, not all of them honest, but all presented with a vehemence which betrayed his concern. He now doubted the total veracity of the *Apostolical Constitutions*: 'I have not that Attachment to them you have: and I don't know whether your Copy of them be faithful from that of *Clement*: till when, yours are not all to me Apostolical: and I judge what are so, to my self';[1] and again: 'I believe what you call DISCIPLINE, which is Force in Religion, is so far from being Primitive, that it is against the Gospel, and borders, in this Realm, on High Treason. I shall ask Counsel about that; and I don't allow all the Constitutions to be *Clement's*.'[2] He also denied that they could be applied in any way to the clergy of the day because 'only Men Apostolically Ordain'd can be bound by Apostolical Laws',[3] and he had already, with Whiston, accepted that no such men existed. Moreover 'they bind only the Baptiz'd, the Faithful', and Henley claimed that he had only recently been validly baptized and therefore any sins and misdemeanours of his past could not be judged or disciplined by non-applicable laws. The only laws he was willing to receive were those which 'I entertain freely and will not suffer the Imposition of them, in any respect, or Degree, whatever; for I own no Judge in Spirituals, but God only, and those who are set over me, by Lawful Authority, to administer and execute by my own free consent the just Laws of my Country.'[4] This controversy over discipline and the Apostolic laws had, in fact, a very specific and not a purely theoretical urgency. Whiston had by 1726 decided that Henley was not only unscholarly and unscrupulous in his handling of ideas: he was convinced that his life was scandalous and that he ought to be exposed. As we have seen, he only published Henley's letters to him and so the accusations have to be inferred from Henley's defensive replies, but they were obviously to do with his alleged misbehaviour at Melton and possibly that obstreperousness in taverns reported from other unfriendly sources. Whatever they were, they quickly reduced what had been an academic correspondence to a furious row, picturesque in its violence and worthy of recounting here, at the expense of violating strict chronological narrative. We must move forward to the first year of the Oratory's existence to round off the

---

[1] *Mr. Henley's Letters and Advertisements which concern Mr. Whiston etc.*, p. 12.
[2] Ibid., p. 16.   [3] Ibid., p. 16.
[4] This and the subsequent details and letters are all from the above source.

story of Henley's first encounter with Whiston, and to see the first indication of a side of Henley's character which was to become more pronounced as attack and vilification embittered him—his furious temper and equally furious language.

Whiston started the row in his eccentrically straightforward way, by delivering his letter of accusations publicly in the Oratory. His own account of the scene runs thus:

Upon the Lord's-Day, *Octob.* 22, in the Evening, about six-a-Clock, I went to Mr. *Henley's* Oratory; and having sat on the Outside for about half an Hour; where he could neither see me nor I him; but I could hear him very well: I waited till all was over, and he had given the Blessing: when, the inner Door being opened, I went in; and with a Letter in my Hand, went up towards the Pulpit, and desired the Congregation to take notice, that I brought a letter for Mr. *Henley.* When I came towards the upper End, I delivered it to one that seemed to be his Clerk, for him: he being himself gone into the Vestry.

Henley read the letter and exploded in wrath, called a coach and rushed to Whiston's lodgings demanding to see him. Whiston, perhaps wisely, refused, and his friend Mr. Barker negotiated at the side of the coach, successfully persuading Henley to write instead. The letter arrived by Porter, Henley's last furious thoughts scribbled on the cover: 'To Mr. *William Whiston.* I give you warning not to enter my Room at *Newport-Market* at your Peril. *J. Henley.* Return the 4s. you took from my Servant, for the 2d. Volume of what you call Records.' Inside was more fury:

SIR, Your base and villainous Libel against me; full of Lyes, Mis-informations, Misconstructions, &c. With that rash and fanatical Entrance into the Oratory, (to disturb my Assembly,) founded on the Apostles Laws; which Mr. *Whiston* has no more Right to execute than I have; shall speedily be Answered, and your Insolence be Chastis'd.

I deny absolutely every particular in your old trump'd-up Story, and it will never hurt me. I will sift your Writings to see whether all those be not Romance, Inconsistency, Forgery, put on ill Evidence: I will let the World know your Integrity from your own Works. You have no Concern with me; and I both contemn and defy you. Tho' you have no Right to demand it, you will have a Reply in three Weeks: (other Studies intervening.) And I will engage in the Upshot, that your private Character, and the Prevarication of your Works, that Hypocrisy, Malice, Frenzy, Slander, Selfishness, but without Success, and all your Saint-like Picture shall be more hurtful to your own Name Writings, and Schemes for ever, than all you vilely project against him, who has as much Resolution, Labour, and perhaps Knowledge of you as you of your self.

J. HENLEY.

N.B. The Gentlemen only said when you came in, That was *Mad Whiston*. Have a Care of stealing Eclipses from *Halley*; and other things from *Brockelsby: &c.*

Henley could not hold off the promised three weeks and, by one o'clock, managed to complete a long letter of self-explanation dispatched by footboy and sealed with many seals, in which Whiston was addressed as 'Traytour to the Civil Government . . . Publick Enemy . . . Stupid Man and uncharitable . . . Beware and Repent. . . . Have a Care, and Remember J. HENLEY.' A week later a porter arrived and, delivering a verbal message 'That he was willing to meet me anywhere', handed over another long account and defence of Henley's life, continuing with further threats to expose Whiston, and concluding:

I say no more at present: but Mr. Whiston, who is an Aggressor upon me, may Repent of his Base and Vile, Unchristian, Ungenteel, and Unscholar-like Step. He may wish he had never been so great a Reviler, and so absurd a Wretch. He shall find my Spirit superior to all such Attempts; and that my Fortune in Life SHALL crush all such Opposition. JOHN HENLEY.

Whiston noted that Henley had declared himself ready to answer for the truth of these accusations before a Bishop's Court and he accordingly tried to bring him before the Bishop, without success. He recalls the attempt in his *Memoirs*:

'Tis now about 20 Years ago that I wrote to the Bishop of *London*, to call the Presbyters, Deacons, and Principal of the Laiety of the Diocese together, in the Way of Primitive Christian Discipline, and to summon withal before them Mr. *Henley* the Orator; whose vile History I knew so well, that I offered to come and *Tell it to the Church*, according to our Saviour's Rule, Matth.xviii.17. In order to his Vindication of himself, or Conviction, and Exclusion from the Christian Society: Of which true Ecclesiastical Discipline knows nothing. The Answer returned me from the Bishop by Dr. Nathaniel Marshal was this, 'that since no Canon (now in force) enabled him so to proceed, he could do nothing.'[1]

The Bishop must have been glad to find a simple legal excuse for not becoming involved in controversy with two such eccentric stragglers from his flock, and Whiston let the matter drop while Henley became absorbed in other work and other controversies. Nevertheless, to the end of his life he never forgave Whiston or forgot his attacks. He took every opportunity to gibe at him in his adverts and orations as the 'Coney-Skin Prophet',[2] as 'Mthr. Wh---ton, the ingenious Rival of Mthr. Shipton',[3] and as one 'scarcely qualify'd for an Urinal-Prophet'.[4] One wonders, too, whether Henley was not the author of the report in *Fog's Journal* for 1 February 1735—'N.B. Mr. Whiston's desire to be assistant to the Oratory is refused.' It would have been the ultimate triumph.

We have broken the chronology of our story to complete the episode of Whiston, and must retrace our steps. The decision to separate from the Church had been made, its possible consequences explored, and some working out of the shape of things to come had been completed. Now the step must be taken; but how was it to be done? Henley's solution was simple, neat, and legally useful. He was already a figure of enough interest in the town for the newspapers to report his action, even if not entirely accurately or certainly. On 23 April 1726 the *London Journal* announced: 'The Rev. Mr. Henley, Restorer of the Ancient Elocution in the Pulpit, having resigned his Preferment in the Church of England, on Tuesday last took the Oaths required by Law to qualify himself for a Baptist Preacher.' *Mist's Journal*, on 1 May, retorted with 'It has been said of late, and published in some News Papers, that the Reverend Mr. Henley qualified himself for a Baptist Teacher, whereas we are assured the said Report is false and groundless.' The truth lies somewhere between both assertion and denial. Henley did *not* qualify himself as a Baptist preacher, but used his scruples over infant baptism as the ground for registering himself as a Dissenter from the Church of England, as required by the

---

[1] William Whiston, *Memoirs of the Life & Writings of Mr. William Whiston* (1749), pp. 251–2.
[2] *Hyp Doctor*, 8 Aug. 1732.
[3] Advertisement for 16 Mar. 1750 (Lysons 162).
[4] *Hyp Doctor*, 19 Aug. 1735.

Toleration Act, which laid down the conditions under which corporate dissent from the Established Church was allowed and under which the Dissenters were allowed to meet together for public worship. The meeting-house had to be registered at the Archdeacon's Court, and all meetings in such places had to be held behind unlocked doors. In registering himself and his meeting-house in this way, Henley accepted the slight restrictions, in exchange for the much more important legal status granted. It was a legal status he often asserted and appealed to when the assault on the Oratory, both verbal and physical, grew fierce. Even now, he was apprehensive about the certainty of his position, and we find him writing to Dr. Thomas Brett, the Non-Juror and liturgiologist, very shortly after his registration, to obtain advice on safeguarding his new venture against possible new attacks:

> Millman Street, beyond Bedford Row
> May 25. 1726.

Reverend Sir,
>   I have dissented, on ye Act of Toleration, from ye Church of England, and design to revive, as far as I can, ye Primitive Church, as you have recommended it, in your Liturgies.
>   I would beg of you to inform me, how I may cover my self from ye Law in ye Conduct of ye affair, as to prayers & preaching; your Information in þs point, to make me safe in my Scheme, wd. be a real favour to,

> Reverend Sir,
> Your Admirer, &
> most humble Servant
> J. Henley.

I mean, especially as to ye Bp of L———, in ye Spiritual and Temporal Courts, ye Convocation, privy-council, parliament, &c. to prevent incurring Suspension or being Silenc'd, in my Congregation. I will send you my plan, if you will order where & wd. desire yr. Encouragement in town. I have tickets for a year, or longer.
> To. The Reverend Dr. Brett
>   at Spring-Grove,
>   near Ashford in Kent.[1]

For the purposes of registration, he must by this time have

---

[1] Bodleian MS. Eng.Th.c29, ff. 143–4.

found the home for his new independence, the place where at last he might put his newly gathered ideas into practice and achieve that fame which the temples of orthodoxy had denied him. The first Oratory—for so it was named from the first days—was situated in Newport Market, one of the busy meat markets of London. Hostile reporters, intent on exaggerating the meanness of the undertaking, describe is as 'a wooden booth, built over the shambles in Newport Market'[1] and 'over the Market-House, up in the highest Loft'.[2] But the meanness and unfitness of the place have been misrepresented. The room was a large room at the top of the Market House, which had a long history of use as a meeting-house or chapel. As early as 1693 a Huguenot congregation had moved in from St. Giles-in-the-Fields, fitted it out with benches, and worshipped there until 1700, and, as other such congregations succeeded each other up to 1705, it became known locally as 'the French Church'. Another Dissenter, Jos. Harrington, used it as a meeting-house from 1714 to 1716, so that when Henley moved in, it had a long-standing connection with dissenting worship and was, in fact, still furnished with the benches, a Communion table, and a pulpit.[3] The only alterations which we definitely know to have been made by Henley were firstly to control and charge for admission. These were described by an enemy who found the place 'much more like a Theatre than a place of Worship: For first of all, when we come up, there is a Bar much after the manner as in a Play-House: Secondly a hatch spiked: And Thirdly, a man to take Money'.[4] He also added 'Two Rostras' to accommodate the performers at the Disputations, of which we shall soon hear more.[5] Beyond this we know little of the appearance of the first Oratory and it seems true to say that Henley took it over as he found it, without much adaptation, considering it only a temporary resting place. The first service was held there on Sunday 10 July 1726, after there had been a week's delay occasioned, it was suggested, by the slow printing of the service books for the Oratory liturgy.[6]

[1] T. Wright, *England under the House of Hanover* (1848), vol. i, p. 104.

[2] Anon., *A Letter to the Reverend Mr. John Henley, M.A. concerning his Novel Project: wherein his Design is fully exposed* (1726), p. 10.

[3] *Milk for Babes etc.*, p. 29.

[4] *A letter to the Reverend Mr. John Henley etc.*, p. 9.

[5] Advertisement for 3 June 1727 (Lysons 13).

[6] *Historical Register*, vol. xi, no. xliii (1726), p. 243.

An advertisement as early as 23 April 1727, in *Mist's Journal*, announced plans for a removal to what is significantly called 'a design'd Oratory (Measures towards which are now taking)'. Either the accumulation of necessary funds or the size of the necessary alterations took some time, and no move was made for another two years, although word of it had spread around the town. 'But certain it is', ran an anonymous pamphlet of this time, 'that the Orator has taken a House in *Lincoln's Inn-Fields*, and is going to remove there from *Newport Market* in a very short Time, for fear the Butchers should scare him, as the *Sacheveralitish* Mob did Dr. *Burges*.'[1] The last meeting advertised for the Newport Market Oratory was on 15 February 1729, and for the following Sunday Henley's congregation was bidden to the Oratory in Lincoln's Inn Fields, being more accurately directed the following week to 'the corner near Clare-Market'. In this second Oratory, Henley worked for the rest of his life, and there, for the next twenty-seven years, the curious, the devoted, and the riotous came to hear him. The house in Newport Market, vacated by Henley, continued to be used as a meeting-house until 1744, and even had its share of the sort of riotous disturbance which accompanied Henley to his new home.[2]

Fortunately we can form a much clearer picture of this permanent Oratory and of its exact whereabouts in Lincoln's Inn Fields. Nichols describes it as 'at the Corner of Lincoln's Inn Fields, near Clare Market', and further directions appear in a number of Henley's advertisements. We can, I think, accept Leigh Hunt's consideration of the evidence, and agree with his conclusion:

Some describe his Oratory as being in the Market, others in Duke Street, which is the street going out of the western side of Lincoln's Inn Square through the archway. Another writer says it was the old theatre of Sir William Davenant, in Gibson's Tennis Court . . . and which is said to have been in Vere Street. . . . We take Henley's Oratory to have been the old theatre, with a passage to it from the Market, from Vere Street, and from Duke Street.[3]

---

[1] Anon., *The Case between the Proprietors of Newspapers and the Coffee-men of London and Westminster fairly stated* (n.d.), p. 14.

[2] A riot is reported there in July 1738, after a sermon by a lapsed Roman priest. See the *Craftsman*, 6 July 1738.

[3] Leigh Hunt, *The Town: its memorable characters and events* (1848), ed. A. Dobson (1907), p. 290.

Having found one's way through the passage, one reached the front door which Henley was later to alter so that only one person could push through at a time. This helped his doorkeeper to control the crowds, and was also Henley's response to his congregation's complaints of cold draughts in the Oratory itself.[1] Inside one was faced with a considerable flight of steps[2] at the top of which was the pay-box, rather like a modern theatre pay-box, with a small window and the cashier behind. The stairs allowed ten people at a time to stand waiting to pay and so the entry into the Oratory could be controlled until, on such days as that happened, the place was full. Once having mounted the stairs and paid the entry fee, one entered the Oratory itself, described by Nichols as 'larger and more commodious' than the first establishment. Certainly contemporary prints bear out this description, and also agree very closely in the depiction of its layout and fittings. It was a lofty room, well lit by large windows, between which was constructed the pulpit, its architectural pre-eminence truly reflecting its importance in the scheme of things. This was 'Henley's gilt tub', as Pope immortalized it. The tub was in fact a large two-decker, the clerk's desk below, Henley's imposing pulpit covered with velvet and gold fleurs-de-lis above, the whole edifice topped with a large sounding board. One print shows the hanging behind embroidered with the initials 'I.R.', but this, I think, can be dismissed as a satirical invention implying that 'James Rex' is the more likely meaning than 'Jesus Rex'. To the left of the pulpit stood the altar, rather tucked away, but which was nevertheless to gain as much notoriety for a time as the pulpit. Pope mentions it in the same note as the tub—'He had also a fair altar, and over it this extraordinary inscription, *The Primitive Eucharist.*'[3] The whole of this end of the Oratory, containing pulpit, altar, and the passage to the vestry, was railed off by what might have seemed a Communion rail, were it not for the savage-looking spikes with which it was armed. Those spikes, as we shall shortly see, were most necessary, for they often served as a real line of defence rather than as a symbolic separation of the sanctuary. In front of this spiked rail, the congregation was accommodated with differing degrees of comfort and vision

[1] Advertisement for 1 Feb. 1746 (Lysons 142).
[2] Nichols, *Leicestershire*, vol. ii, pt. i, p. 260.
[3] *Dunciad*, Book ii, l.2, footnote.

according to the entry fee they had paid. The Oratory was not laid out with pews and aisles as a church, but had an enclosed area at the front where seats were provided. Around this was a large area for that part of the congregation which could only afford standing space, while a gallery along one wall provided more standing space with a better view, and perhaps a better position for interrupting and heckling. In such a form the Oratory continued throughout its history, with very little alteration. A handsome clock, presented to Henley by his congregation, was fixed up in 1732,[1] and now and again Henley ploughed back some of his profits into repairs and maintenance. The Oratory was painted and beautified within and without in 1732,[2] and was closed for the whole month of August in 1749 for repairs.[3] In 1743 there was talk of a new Oratory and Henley appealed for subscribers to the building fund, but obviously support was not forthcoming and Henley continued to orate from the same pulpit in the same Oratory almost to the day of his death.

It is not easy to decide with any certainty what size or what type of congregation gathered here. The proprietor, for obvious reasons, may be suspected of exaggerating the size and respectability of his assemblies, whilst his enemies were only too eager to report a sparse and ever-diminishing attendance of disreputables. Certainly at its opening and in the first few years of its existence, the venture prospered. Even a hostile reporter admitted that 'At its first establishment it was amazingly crowded, and money flowed in upon him apace; and between whiles it languished and drooped', and again, 'The Doctor being such a Person as I have describ'd him, it may be wonder'd that his Oratory should be so prodigiously frequented.'[4] An account of 1726 recorded that at the opening service, 'the *Natural Curiosity* of all Men, was raised to a prodigious Degree: The Institutor got a numerous Auditory, and consequently Large Contributions; and the Crowd about the Oratory was so great on Sunday the 24th of *July*, that some Persons in Chairs were forc'd back.'[5] Henley had to publish a request for people not to crowd the steps of the Oratory,[6] and

---

[1] *Daily Journal*, quoted in *G.S.J.*, 17 July 1732.   [2] Ibid.
[3] Advertisements for 29 July and 30 Aug. 1749 (Lysons 159).
[4] Anon., *The History of the Robin Hood Society* (1764), p. 137.
[5] *Historical Register*, vol. xi, no. xliii (1726), p. 252.
[6] Advertisement in *Mist's Journal*, 15 Oct. 1726.

three years later the confluence of sedan chairs into the narrow approaches of the place was still giving trouble, Henley asking those who were travelling in chairs to arrive early, to avoid the pedestrian crowds.[1] Throughout the years of its existence Henley asserted the continuing popularity of the Oratory. In 1737 he claimed that 'there ever was a crowded Audience';[2] in 1752 we find him thanking 'the Humane, and, for the Season, numerous Congregation of the Oratory-Chapel, on Sunday last';[3] and as late as 1755 he published his thanks 'to my worthy Friends, who made so numerous and agreeable an Appearance at my Congregation, the last Lords Day'.[4] Throughout these same years his enemies report how sickly and faint the enterprise becomes, and how near demise the deserted Orator is. The truth lies between these extremes. The first novelty brought great crowds, but as the years went by and the novelty became an accepted and familiar thing in the London scene, a smaller but steady attendance continued, now and again swollen to the old size when some new eccentricity or excitingly dangerous topic aroused the interest of the town. Certainly, without any other source of income, Henley managed to keep going, to maintain the fabric of his establishment, and to cut some sort of figure in London. To the end he was never without a servant, could pay three or four staff in the Oratory, and often graced the social table and shared a convivial bottle. We have figures for his takings from 14 August 1743 to 30 December 1744, noted in his own hand on a collection of his advertisements, and these add up to £196 1s. 0d. for seventy-one performances.[5] At times he had very thin congregations, with only 10s. 6d., 12s., or 19s. taken at the cash-box, but other weeks fetched in £7. 10s. 0d. or £5. 14s. 6d. The figures show wide fluctuation with a steady taking of about £2, and from these one can roughly work out an attendance varying from 9 to 125, the general attendance being in the region of 50, with a definite falling off in the summer months. In the later years he could assert 'I . . . have subscribers; took, from the first, sometimes 5s. at other 25£. They who do not come, 'tis their loss: I forbid 70 in 100 from

[1] Advertisement for 25 Oct. 1729 (Lysons 39).
[2] *Hyp Doctor*, 10 May 1737.
[3] Advertisement for 29 May 1752 (Lysons 173).
[4] Advertisement for 27 June 1755 (Lysons 194).
[5] Collected by Lysons in *Collectanea*, pp. 117–36.

coming.'[1] Certainly with such takings, and the income from his book sales and fees for private teaching, he was richer than he would have been in his country living, and nearly as well off as if he had gained the coveted City church.

A similar uncertainty surrounds the type of person who came to hear Henley. His enemies present him as surrounded by a rude mob of butchers and meat-porters, turbulent and vociferous in their approval or abuse, and by the general lower levels of trades-men and apprentices. Nichols unquestioningly continues this version. 'The audience,' he records, 'was generally composed of the lower ranks.'[2] Henley, on the other hand, makes more impressive claims of the quality and rank he addressed, that 'Some of the Greatest Persons in Church and State, have been frequent Auditors at the ORATORY,'[3] and that 'the greatest, most polite and learned Persons are frequently present'.[4] He records, as late as 1752, 'The distinguish'd Satisfaction I had the happiness to give on the three Sundays last past, to numerous genteel Congre-gations, (encreasing this Summer, when others have dwindled or disappeared) and to the Ladies, in particular, who did me the Honour to be present'.[5] Sometimes he does it with the attractive *naïveté* of one advertisement for an oration—'N.B. a Duchess liked this',[6] and sometimes with more detail—'on the late Lord V. Gage's dying a *, as I hear, his Advice to his Children, his Introduction of me to the late Prince and Princess (now Dowager) of Wales, on their Marriage; late Lady Gage, late Duchess of Norfolk, and late Duke of Norfolk's honouring the Oratory with their Presence'.[7] He claimed to have drawn others distinguished by achievement as well as rank. Pope, he asserts, heard him, and 'The late Lord Bolingbroke heard in the Oratory this proposition in his Patriot King, that to remedy Errors, Absurdities or Grievances, the Subject of them is to be call'd back to its first Principles.'[8] Nearly twenty years after the event, he recalls another famous visitor, 'for on Jan. 3rd., 1738, in my Oratory, Mon. Voltaire, who perhaps now may forget it, told me that my Plan

[1] Advertisement for 27 Mar. 1752 (Lysons 172).
[2] Nichols, *Leicestershire*, vol. ii, pt. i, p. 260.
[3] *Milk for Babes etc.*, p. 45.   [4] *Narrative*, p. 47.
[5] Advertisement for 29 Sept. 1752 (Lysons 175).
[6] Advertisement in the *Daily Advertiser*, 3 Sept. 1743.
[7] Advertisement for 24 Jan. 1755 (Lysons 191).
[8] Advertisement for 1 Nov. 1754 (Lysons 189).

might be encourag'd by the King of France if I propos'd it as an improvement on the French Academy; I am sorry I overlook'd that Hint.'[1] There is something a little sad in that 'who perhaps now may forget it'! Voltaire was certainly in England at that time and, with his interest in the English religious scene, its sects, and worship, might well have made a curious excursion to the Oratory. He certainly did not remember either it or Henley well enough to mention them in his account of his English journey. Again the truth seems to lie somewhere between these two extremes. The backbone of Henley's congregation was the lower- and middle-class tradesman, often liberally sprinkled with the butchers of Newport and Clare Markets, enlivened now and again by visitors from Oxford and Cambridge or by rowdy gangs of young lawyers from the Temple, and graced by more illustrious visitors who came to see and hear for themselves this much talked-of celebrity. 'It became the fashion', a later writer tells us, 'for ladies and gentlemen, to make parties to hear his lectures.'[2] His perform-ances had that spice of scandal and low life which, as with the sleazy speak-easies or Wapping public houses nowadays, has always had a romantic attraction for the *beau monde* wondering how to finish an evening, and it would seem most likely that their visits to the Oratory were motivated by little more than curiosity and a desire for amusement. Whatever the motive, Henley wel-comed such visitors. At the best they added tone to the Oratory; at the least they paid their entry fee.

This entry fee and the pay-box require further attention, if only because they became one of the main targets in the satirical assault on Henley. The principle of Henley's system can be defended, and it is difficult to see how he could have found a different way of applying that principle. The churches of the Establishment had their endowments and tithes to support their priests: the gather-ings of Dissenters in their meeting-houses were able, from the very regularity of their meetings and the steadiness of their congregations, to support their ministers and their conventicles from their faithful contributions, the burden often being eased by their ministers working in other employment and preaching for little or nothing. Henley had no endowments nor tithes,

---

[1] Advertisement for 7 Nov. 1747 (Lysons 150). The date "1738" in this advertise-ment is an obvious error for "1728"

[2] *The Lounger's Commonplace Book*, p. 141.

depending entirely on the income of the Oratory for his livelihood: his congregation varied in size and composition. It was often with the easy certainty of the Established Church in mind that he declared his system as more defensible than Church revenues and the methods of obtaining them.

> ... the great Expences in all Incidents, [he writes,] besides the Time and Labour, always employ'd in this most extensive and toilsome Undertaking, all lying upon himself, this Way of supporting it is necessary: the Clergy will demand and prosecute for their Pay, whether they deserve it, or no: his return for his Pains and Endeavours to Merit is precarious, accidental, and at the Mercy of all Mankind; tho' as his Method is free from Compulsion, it is absolutely Primitive.[1]

It was hypocritical of the Church to pretend that, apart from forced tithe-gathering, no charges were made in her churches. 'What', he asked, 'is the Price of an Informer's Oath, or of the Diversion of seeing the Tombs in *Westminster Abbey*; or taking a *Seat extempore* in any Chapel, or Church in Town; otherwise, how must a Chapel, especially such as are unprovided for by a Parish, be supported?'[2] He hammered home his point with other examples. It is no more unlawful to 'tip a Verger, or Pew-keeper, a Smack of *Simon Magus*; or commute Sixpence for your Spurs. The Church Revenues are Good, (I wish those of some Clergymen were better,) yet one Example of Industry may be pardon'd in a Christian Country, without laying him at the Mercy of Knights of *the Post*.'[3] What difference is there, he demands, between his system and the custom of renting pews? 'Let those that would have a Seat there at any Subject, rent it, or pay, as at Somerset-Chapel, and other Churches, else let them budge, and not offer to stand on the Owner's Ground without his leave, let they be taken up for Street Robbers.'[4] This legal standing of his Oratory and his legal proprietorship of it were often invoked to establish his right to say who should enter and on what conditions. He also needed to control the influx of 'pay-at-the-door' congregation lest the regular seat-renters be crowded out. Over and above all these reasons, there was the simple fact that he had as much right to take money as men in other professions, and perhaps did more to earn it. 'As to taking money,' he asserted towards the end of his career, 'I do not know the Man, that does not, if he can . . . he

---

[1] *Narrative*, p. 17.   [2] *Milk for Babes etc.*, p. 33.   [3] Ibid., p. 47.
[4] Advertisement for 14 Dec. 1728 (Lysons 27).

that takes no Money can pay none; and what will become of the Government, the World? Physicians, Lawyers, and Divines, take Thousands of Guineas, I am educated to the Principles of all, and do more for 6*d*. than any of them for 600£.'[1]

He took his money in two ways. One could climb the stairs and pay at the cash-desk, one shilling being the normal entry charge, entitling the visitor to a seat if one was still available, otherwise to join the crowd in the standing area, where a certain number were also admitted free. Henley puts the number at fifty, and mentions this to prove his non-mercenary motives, although the other motive of ensuring a minimum congregation for his orations cannot be discounted. When he started the Friday orations in October 1728, and their topical and burlesque content promised to be a more popular draw than the Sunday services, he took the opportunity to raise his charge, 1*s*. 6*d*. being asked for the first seats and 1*s*. for the second. Occasionally, throughout the years, he put the prices up for very special occasions, promising always to advertise such alterations in the press.[2] Those who desired to become regular attenders at the Oratory could buy the equivalent of a season ticket in the form of a special Oratory Medal. Henley had these struck at the very start of the undertaking, showing a star rising to the meridian, with the motto 'Ad Summa' and below it 'Inveniam viam, aut faciam'. The medals, in gold, silver, and bath metal, were sold at various prices and carried various rights. A single printed sheet, undated, records these for us[3]

	MEDAL	PERPETUAL WITH PRAEMIUM, WITHOUT,		YEARLY
in the fore-seats	Gold (for 3 persons)	15 guineas	12½	3
	Silver (for 2 persons)	10 guineas	8	2
	Bath	5 guineas	2	12/–
in the back seats	To be a perpetual renter without a medal	3 guineas	2	12/–

[1] Henley, *Second St. Paul in Equity Hall etc.* (1755), p. 26.
[2] Advertisements for 23 and 30 Nov. 1728 (Lysons 27); 26 Sept. 1730 (Lysons 47).
[3] The only copy I have seen is Bodleian Vet.A4.e.2167.

The medals were separately numbered, were non-transferable, and a deposit was paid on the gold ones. It might well be asked whether any of these medals were ever purchased, or whether they belong to one of those wish-fulfilment fantasies we often suspect in Henley's publicity. The evidence shows that there was a steady trade. The first impression of medals was taken up, and in May 1728 the public was informed that 'A new and beautiful Impression of the Medals of the Oratory, as demanded, is now finished, and is there to be distributed,'[1] and again in August 1753, 'A new Beautiful Impression of the Oratory Medals is struck, each entitling to Advantages above Double the Purchase.'[2] The availability of medals was advertised in such detail as to indicate a going concern—'N.B. The Medal whose Number was mention'd in a Letter dated Nov. 18th. is parted with; any other is at the Person's Service'[3]—and there survive three fragments in Henley's handwriting to record definite purchases, as well as to reveal another of Henley's methods of encouraging sales—the annexing of the copyright of his published works to a medal. On the flyleaf of a copy of *The Original of Pain and Evil* he noted: 'Mr. Atkinson bought of me a Medal of ye Oratory call'd perpetual for himself and family, every Sunday, during his Life, preserving and shewing ye same, or having value recd. in ye copy right of this lecture. Ye medal to be forfeited, if others us'd it, & ye Copy right also.'[4] Similar transactions are noted on the verso of the title-page of a copy of *The Pangs of Expiring Penitents*—

Mr. Richardson bought of me a medal of ye oratory, call'd Perpetual, that is, for Every Sunday, for himself and Family, while he liv'd, preserving and shewing ye same having value received in ye Copyright of this Sermon, with Liberty to dedicate it ye Medal to be forfeited if others us'd it and ye Copyright also, and he, his heirs, Exec, admsts or offspring to pay me or mine for my Medal.[5]

A similar note in a copy of *Deism defeated and Christianity defended* records that a certain Mr. Wilson entered into the same agreement.[6] It would be interesting to know whether the income from

---

[1] Advertisement in the *London Journal*, 18 May 1728.
[2] Advertisement for 24 Aug. 1753 (Lysons 189).
[3] Advertisement for 27 Nov. 1731 (Lysons 59).
[4] Henley, *The Original of Pain and Evil*, B.M. Copy 4374.c.17.
[5] Henley, *The Pangs of Expiring Penitents*, B.M. Copy 4477.c.44.
[6] Henley, *Deism Defeated and Christianity defended*, B.M. Copy 4015.c.21.

the copyright of any of these publications ever reached the 15 guineas paid for the medal. One suspects that Messrs. Atkinson, Richardson, Wilson, and their families continued to enjoy permanent entry to the Oratory throughout their lives. Henley kept a sharp eye open for any abuses of his system of medals, and a rebuke of one such offender was publicly proclaimed in the *Daily Advertiser*. A certain Crawford had presumed to sell his medal, claiming that it was his own, and Henley angrily denied this right. He might allow temporary transfers if the new owner behaved well, but he insisted on his sole right to determine the use of his own property.[1] Mainly on this assured capital from the sale of medals and from the very fluctuating takings at the cash-desk, the Oratory subsisted, sometimes helped along by gifts and even legacies such as the one Henley acknowledged in a funeral service on 'a lady who bequeath'd a Legacy above two Years conceal'd from us; in her political Principles, attach'd to the Non-Jurors; in her Religious, to that Godlike Conformity with Reason and Virtue which is our Religion; and many years of this Congregation.'[2] A satisfied listener to his four lectures on 'The Bishops no Right to their Estates' presented him with 10 guineas, and he gallantly acknowledged another gift of half a guinea apiece from four ladies for four of his lectures—'an Angel is 10s. but 6d. more from four fine Women makes them more than Angels'.[3] 'Subsisted' must be the word. There is no evidence that Henley made a fortune, though, as we have said, he made a better living than many a vicar. Considering the labour involved, the payments he had to make in rent, repairs, and decorations, we must accept his own assessment that "One Time with another, little is got by an Oratory: it is no Object of Envy.'[4]

In the closing years of the Oratory it becomes plain that Henley was indeed no object of envy, and that the labour and the uncertainty of income were both worrying him. He began to suggest new methods of financing his undertaking, all of them with the aim of giving him a fixed, steady income, helped and backed by the investment of sympathizers' money. He was, in fact, trying to float the Oratory as a company, as well as acquiring capital. The

[1] Letter in the *Daily Advertiser*, 16 June 1744.
[2] Advertisement in the *Daily Advertiser*, 26 May 1744.
[3] Advertisement for 28 Dec. 1753 (Lysons 184).
[4] Advertisement for 1 Feb. 1746 (Lysons 142).

first full proposal of this kind came in 1747, although he stated that he had proposed such a plan as long ago as the Newport Market days and annually since.

These earlier proposals to which he refers occurred in the late '20s and the late '30s and are, because of the scanty documentation, shrouded in mystery. It is difficult to say exactly what Henley was up to, and equally difficult to be certain how far these schemes ever got beyond the proposal stage. The first scheme, for some sort of Commercial or Trade Society, is aired in March 1728—'On Wednesday, at Six, the Academy will have a Discourse on the History of Money; to oblige a Society of Trade now enlarging, into which one of each business may enter.'[1] In the following week, Henley expounded his plans more fully— 'On Wednesday at Six, will be a Discourse on the Plan of a new Society of Trade, and the landed and money'd Interest.'[2] The proposals for this 'select Society now subscribing' could be inspected at the Oratory and promised 'a Platform beneficial to each Subscriber'.[3] Whatever these proposals were, interest was sufficiently aroused for Henley to continue his invitations for subscribers to join. In January 1730 he recorded that 'The Advantageous Society continues for Subscribers in Course of Seniority',[4] and in April was still informing potential members that 'They who would subscribe for the Advantages annex'd to the Society are to do it in the Vestry, Mondays and Thursdays, at 12 o'clock, before the end of May, or they forfeit the said Advantages.'[5] That he was obliged to extend his closure date is clear from a further invitation in August 1730 to medal-holders of the Oratory to become members—'N.B. Those who have Bath-metal Medals of the Oratory, and would enter the Society, are desir'd to meet on Wednesday next, at the usual Place, at eight in the Evening, and the Silver on September nine.'[6] It appears that there were indeed subscribers and that the Society existed. A published sermon of 1729 bears on its title page 'Publish'd at the Desire of the Commercial Society of the Oratory',[7]

[1] Advertisement for 9 Mar. 1728 (Lysons 19).
[2] Advertisement for 16 Mar. 1728 (ibid.)
[3] Advertisement for 13 Apr. 1728 in *Mist's Journal*.
[4] Advertisement for 24 Jan. 1730 (Lysons 41).
[5] Advertisement for 26 Apr. 1729 (Lysons 31).
[6] Advertisement for 15 Aug. 1730 (Lysons 45).
[7] Henley, *The Conflicts of the Death-bed etc.* (1729), title-page.

and subscriptions were still being taken in August 1731. It is impossible to be so certain about what the Society actually did for its members. In a pamphlet of 1729, Henley describes the Society as 'A COMMERCIAL SOCIETY . . . in which, the First of any Profession who enters it, has the First Business of that Profession, according to the Terms, with other Advantages',[1] which suggests that it was a kind of mutual trade society in which the varied representatives of each trade pledged to put their work and purchases in other trades in the hands of their fellow members—an open organization of the unspoken benefits which are often alleged against modern freemasonry or rotary clubs. In default of further evidence, the 'other Advantages' are not clear. One thing is clear however: the subscriptions paid for obtaining the benefit of mutual trade were in Henley's hands, and the Society, whatever else it did, provided a little capital in addition to current income. After 1731 a silence descends and we hear no more of the Commercial Society until, in 1736, it reappears with proposals to extend its activities. Henley announced that 'The Commercial Society of the Oratory is to meet once a Week, to consider of a Method for a Bank and half-yearly dividend,'[2] and the aims of this venture are more explicitly set out towards the end of the following year:

The opening of the Books of *Transfer* and Dividend of the Money'd and Trading BANK will be advertis'd, and daily Attendance given; it is calculated on the most fair and unexceptionable Footing, to produce to each Person submitted to subscribe, a greater Premium, on less as well as greater Sums, than in other Funds, and a speedier Receipt; the Undertaking being calculated to supply the defects, rectify the Abuses, and improve on the Advantages of all others.[3]

It is difficult to see how Henley could promise higher returns on invested capital than any other of the funds, unless in fact he hoped that door receipts at the Oratory would be large enough to pay the dividends and leave him something to live on, whilst he himself had the capital from subscribers to live on or reinvest. After this the silence is complete and the society is never referred to again. We can be fairly certain that, dubious as some of these proposals seem, no scandal occurred and no fraud was alleged.

---

[1] *Milk for Babes etc.*, advertisement at the end of the pamphlet.
[2] *Hyp Doctor*, 10 Aug. 1737.   [3] *Hyp Doctor*, 4 Oct. 1737.

The papers and the pamphlet writers would never have let slip such an opportunity for exposure and recrimination.

The 1747 scheme is at least less devious than these earlier plans for raising capital. Henley suggested that

for one Year's Experiment fifty Persons (I one of them) advance me Five Guineas each, 250 guineas, and they shall take the whole Income, all the Offertory to the Mount of Piety, by their own Receiver, to their own Banker, for a quarterly Dividend. The Place will hold above double the Sum. I will pay Rent, Taxes, Repairs, Wear and Tear, Candles, Advertisements, Books, Servants (except their Receivers) &c. which be above 100£ a year; and I will drudge more for them than for myself in composing and performing the Orations, or they themselves shall be the Orators, within the Rules: I shall not take 150£ a Year to live upon, except my Dividend; which Gentlemen should encourage rather than envy: since worse Orators than I am, (all Orators, good or bad, we be Brethren) get many Thousands a Year for nothing or worse than nothing.[1]

The scheme never got farther than the proposal stage, and potential investors no doubt saw that the amount of their dividend was less certain than Henley's income and upkeep allowance—albeit the size of this was no more than we saw him making in 1743/4. It was certainty rather than increase of income he longed for, and seven years later he came up with a new subscription scheme with this as its aim.

First, that 50 Gentlemen frequenting this or a new Oratory to be subscrib'd for, shall be Copartners; at present, each advancing half a Guinea a Quarter, for one or two Years Experiment, the Body to come Gratis, and receive all above 5£ that I take (the Place will hold at one Time near the rate of 12£) to give to such Poor as they know, or as they please: and the Copy-Rights of all the Performances, and other Advantages . . .[2]

This scheme also remained only a suggestion and joined the rest of the hopeless attempts of these later years to establish the Oratory on a firmer financial footing. One other might be mentioned, to show Henley's ingenious invention clothing the same motive in a different dress, this time appealing to the patrons of down-and-out men of letters to allow him to train and provide a platform for

[1] Advertisement for 2 Apr. 1747 (Lysons 147).
[2] Advertisement for 3 May 1754 (Lysons 187).

their protégés—as well as providing him with an assured lump sum and providing performances he had not to labour over!

There are, in Circumstances of Disadvantage, Learned and Ingenious Gentlemen, Authors, Clergymen, Artists, Professors &c. who might be Gainers by Preaching, Speaking, Lecturing, or Disputing, in the Chapel or Academy of the Oratory, whether by Lincoln's Inn Fields, or elsewhere: One Method might be to prevail on 10 or 20 of their Friends, to advance, each, Half a Guinea, or a Crown, and take the income of the Performance: I will assist them: Teach them to think, distinguish, define, reason, demonstrate, to dispute, conclude self-evidently, chuse and manage Questions and Subjects; frame Composition, speak Extempore, universal Rhetorick, Principles of Wit, and Science, in one: on the most perfect Plan ever form'd.[1]

All this ingenuity proved in vain. To the end he had to depend on his own labours and the fluctuating takings of the cash-desk and the sale of medals, labouring almost to his death-day to keep his Oratory in the public eye and attract an audience as uncertain in temper as in size.

To ensure that this potential audience should never forget the existence of the Oratory and should be persuaded that a journey to Clare Market would be worth the labour, Henley developed a technique of advertising and publicity which employed all the tricks used by the persuasive art, from the beginning until now, playing upon the curiosity, the snobbery, the love of the scandalous, the fear of not being in with the latest thing. He used the 'puff' in all its varieties, producing 'news items' of the proceedings, the great crowds attending, the polite and distinguished visitors among the audience, writing 'letters' from delighted and highly instructed members of the congregation, and printing unsolicited testimonials to the spiritual and intellectual pre-eminence of the Oratory and its presiding master. Each week he announced to the town the subjects for the week's assemblies and in these advertisements developed his own unique methods. At first they were quite sober and straightforward announcements of the subjects to be dealt with, as in this example for 3 September 1726:

Tomorrow the Oratory in Newport-Market begins at half an Hour after Ten in the Morning, and at Five in the Evening, exactly: The

---

[1] Advertisement for 5 Apr. 1754 (Lysons 186).

Morning Subject is, the natural Happiness of Religion: The Theological Lecture is, Textuary Divinity, or the Study of the Scriptures: the Academical Lecture, on Wednesday next at 5 in the Evening, is the first on Logick, of the Art of Thinking.

But as the years passed by, the tone became more colloquial, the prose more broken and allusive, until a typical Henleian advertisement is this one for 26 June 1742:

> Is the Queen of Spain dead? Room for Cuckolds.
> At the ORATORY,
> The Corner of Lincoln's Inn Fields, near Clare-Market, Tomorrow, in the Evening, at half an Hour after Six, after the Exhortation and Prayers, the Lecture will be on the Adventures of Peter and his man Paul, celebrated this Week; a German Court; the Intrigues of Count Polten and Baron Compellum to bite the Country; an Italian Count; Cardinal Gibbi risen from the Dead, and his Singing-Bird promoted to the Cage at Windsor; a Cock's Challenge to a Cock-pit Lady; the Irish and English Register, a Match; Ladies invited to a Sale of precious Stones; the King of P. in second Mourning; the Report of a Pop-gun in White-powder; the Mulberry-Garden Silk-worms turn'd to Butterflies: Amphibious Animals in the Com---ns; Miracles in St. S---'s Chapel; a Shrine to a heavy-bottom'd Sinner, or the Dutch Skipper will not skip; the State a Tumbler; Westminster People good, good; the grand Prior of Fulham, &c. . . .

They can become even more eccentric and gibberish than this with odd interjections of 'ha ha ha', 'hei-day', 'sob and hiccup' or 'oh my poor spectacle case', and one might well conclude— as Henley's enemies and many subsequent commentators did— that his undoubted eccentricity developed into lunacy as the years went by. The truth was quite otherwise. The tone and obscurity of these advertisements were a calculated effort at mystification, to stimulate curiosity and to draw the crowds to hear just what Henley could possibly make of the promised rigmarole. He succeeded, through them, in keeping his name always on the lips of the London public. Horace Walpole, a good indicator of the gossip of the day, does not fail to mention to his correspondents such items as 'orator Henley preached t'other day on the Tarinity',[1] and 'Sir Charles Windham is got into Henley's advertisements; you know he declaims upon all subjects within the news-

---

[1] Horace Walpole to Mann, 18 June 1744. The Yale edition of the correspondence, ed. Lewis, Smith, and Lam, vol. xviii, p. 465.

papers and the bills of mortality: today is given out a discourse on consecrating heathen temples at Ranelagh.'[1] Any increase in incoherence and oddity in these advertisements was, if anything, not a sign of growing mental confusion, but of an increasing desperation in his efforts to attract an audience. Henley himself was quite clear and specific in his explanations of his advertising technique and, if his enemies had read him carefully, they might have attacked him for cunning, but never for the feeble-mindedness a contemporary satirist detected: 'When silly people read such an advertisement, they say, See, what a mad Preamble is here.'[2] In 1753 Henley gave this explanation of his methods in a published ' letter':

My Lord, the Censors of our Advertisements continue their Blunders, and blame them for their Beauties: when they ought to be incomprehensible, Abracadabra, Jargon, Chimaera; to have Riddles; and we only the Key; be incog, Masquerade; Feints, Amusements: be foreign, and we to naturalize them: Cryptical, as Logick and Dr. Watts required: have their Arcana, Secrets, Mysteries, as Courts, Cities, Professions have:- and be Masonry, Cabals, Rosycrucian Lore, Alchymist, the Technic, the Profound: in a World of Conjuration; and are no more bound to say all, than every Lady * to shew all. J.H.[3]

He later played a variation on the same explanation.

I have written Advertisements as seemingly incoherent as possible, especially the last, and exemplify'd the Connexion in the Oratory Chapel; Your Lp. approving it made me a Promise: on my Simile, of an Image confus'd on a Plane, and rectify'd by a Lens and objects inverted in the Eye, but seen erect; I can mathematically demonstrate all my Advertisements, but am not bound to give Brains to their Censors, or divulge my Art. J.H.[4]

The manuscript sermons which survive indeed show him carefully listing the items of his advertisements as the headings for the planning of his discourses. So, week by week, he whetted the appetite of the town with a menu of obscurity and inconsequential items, tempting his readers to come along and hear him wonderfully clear the obscurity and 'regulate the Trans-

---

[1] Horace Walpole to C. H. Williams, 7 July 1744. Yale edition, ed. Lewis and Smith, vol. xxx, p. 56.
[2] Peter Farmer, A New Model for the Rebuilding of Masonry (1730), p. v.
[3] Advertisement for 2 Mar. 1753 (Lysons 179).
[4] Advertisement for 16 Feb. 1753 (Lysons 178).

position of the Subjects'.[1] There in his pulpit he would stand, he promised, and 'obey you in making from the Chaos of an advertisement a New Creation'.[2]

It is to these many new creations we must now turn, to try to discover what exactly went on at the Oratory, what the audiences drawn by these advertisements actually heard, when they had climbed the stairs, paid their shilling, or shown their medals, and assembled around the velvet-adorned pulpit of the Orator.

[1] Advertisement for 21 Sept. 1753 (Lysons 183).
[2] Advertisement for 17 May 1754 (Lysons 187).

CHAPTER V

The Proceedings of the Oratory

THE PROCEEDINGS OF THE ORATORY were shaped partly by the belief in a truly primitive Church which Henley took over from Whiston, and which affected the content of much of his early preaching and his Oratory liturgy, but the variety and scope of Henley's activities cannot be explained without adding his equally deep belief in the universal applicability of the faith, to which no subject, knowledge, or event, academic, social, or political, was irrelevant or incapable of being included within the great scheme. His *Plan of the Oratory* announced 'This is an ecclesiastical institution; but, since the holy Bible and theology cannot be understood without the other arts and sciences, it will also take in, on a religious footing, an academy of the sciences and languages: the whole design being calculated to the utmost elegance and perfection...[1] Ten years later he gave a similar explanation of his intentions, answering a supposed inquiry from a noble Lord:

The ORATORY is, my Lord, a Social Institution of an Universal extent, calculated to supply the Defects and improve on the Advantages of all others, Antient or Modern, Domestick or Foreign, in the Theory and Practice of Sciences, Arts, Languages, Genius, Literature, Commerce and Politicks, for the utmost Perfection, Efficacy and Success, ordinary and occasional, of all the Laudable and desirable Ends of Communities, Families and Individuals, the greatest Glory of God, and the most compleat Felicity of Mankind.[2]

In the year before his death he had not changed this description of his aims:

Therefore I thought it my Duty to form a Method of Instruction, more excellent, and perfect, than others, to exalt the Powers which God has given us, to the greatest Height, by comprehending all Objects of useful Knowledge and Practice, in the most compleat Manner: and not

---

[1] *Oratory Transactions No. 1*, p. i.   [2] *Hyp Doctor*, 10 May 1737.

confine the Subjects of Preaching to the narrow Custom and dull Repetition of the Generality of Preachers and Sermonisers.[1]

On these ideas he preached the first sermon at the Oratory on Sunday, 13 July 1726, taking as his text 'That which hath not been told them, shall they see, and that which they have not heard, shall they consider' (Isaiah 52:15), and claiming that Isaiah's description of the new religion of the Messiah as singular and astonishing, might well be applied to the Oratory. The Oratory rang with the rhetoric of the peroration:

In short, to be primitive, is the beauty of religion; to be just, elegant, extensive, is the crown of knowledge.

This only is our plan.

To free the mind from darkness and fetters, that more than Egyptian bondage, the slavery of the understanding.

To oppose a tyranny over the body, is the natural bent of an English spirit; and shall the free born soul, the immortal part, be a vassal. Assert your selves, my fellow christians: In learning and religion, see with your own eyes, think with your own judgments: What is more beautiful than truth? What is dearer than Liberty?

On this Basis, let our structure rise: if there be any lustre in the same, the honour of our native country; any allurement in surpassing former or present times; if there be any thing advantageous or pleasing in universal knowledge; any thing great or awful in the primitive church; let all conspire to recommend our attempt; Suffer me once to congratulate with you the first rise of a design which contributes to all of them.

In this affair, we appeal from ignorance to politeness, from modern delusion to antient christianity, from the adversaries of learning, to you, whom we would make the patrons and protectors of it.

Let the dignity, the worth of the undertaking be some atonement for the imperfections of those, who embark in it. Let the design engage your judgment, and let the execution of it be the object of your humanity.[2]

The execution of the design did, in the first years, clearly reflect the twofold but interrelated programme of religion and education. For the first two years there was a service with sermon and sometimes a celebration of the liturgy, at 10.30 on Sunday mornings, and a theological lecture at 3.0 p.m. At 5.0 p.m. on Wednesdays, the company gathered for an Academical Oration. There is nothing out of the ordinary about either his subjects or his

[1] *Second St. Paul etc.*, p. 6.   [2] *Oratory Transactions No. 1*, p. 40.

tone, both the devotional subjects of the sermons and the theological subjects of the lectures appearing perfectly orthodox. At
the Wednesday discourses he held forth on Homer, Horace,
Ovid, and the joys of poetry. He delivered a large number of
talks on the art and practice of elocution, and did not neglect
the sciences in his talks on natural philosophy, astronomy, and
astrology. General studies of the idea of history completed his
course. In 1727 the story is much the same, although the theological discourses become more polemical and he more often
rides his hobby horses—the true primitive Church, holy orders, the
authority of Scripture—and examines the work and ideas of other
theologians. The academic discourses continue their scheme of
popular education with lectures on the genius of Lee, the true
nature of the sublime, pastoral poetry, and the character and
morals of Shakespeare. Some lectures began to take on a more
political tinge, but still fairly general and historical, such as the
lecture showing 'that France may be relied on by a Protestant
power against the Emperor', or discussing 'the British Senate,
its Rise, Advance, Dignity, the talent of a good Senator, parallell'd
with those of Rome and Athens &c.'. In 1728 changes started
to appear. The sermon subjects remained serious, although he
showed a new fondness for discussing more curious minutiae in
scriptural stories. The academic discourses continued to instruct,
but a new type of subject, more topical, curious, and possibly
controversial was advertised—'On Wednesday the Subject will be
a general History and Explanation of what no Person could ever
understand': 'On Wednesday will be a dissertation on the World;
Insides and Outsides; the Gallery of Humour; the Force of Nature;
a Review of Masks, Machines, Bridles, Packsaddles, and Theatrical
Habits, with an Essay on the wonderful Blessing and Mystery of
Parish-Jobbing': 'On Wednesday, in Respect of My Lord
Mayor's Show, will be a sober Enquiry into the History and
Adventures of Whittington and his Cat.' More important was the
addition, from 12 October, of a further performance on Fridays,
given over to commentary on the affairs of the times, political and
social, presented with humour, burlesque, and doubtless a touch
of scandal. The popular feature was 'The Chimes of the Times',
a collection of the week's events or newspaper reports of them,
with a satirical commentary. These appear to have been a medley
of what is now so familiar to us in such journalism as *Private Eye*

or Saturday television satire, but were startlingly new and successful in an age when newspapers consisted of either uncommented
news items or solid essays. This type of Friday performance was
ultimately to become the main offering of the Oratory but, until
1741, the Sunday sermons and lectures and the Wednesday academical discourse continued, with the addition of a Monday performance for a few weeks in 1729/30, until, on Henley's own
admission, the preparation of so much in one week proved too
much for him.[1] While the sermons and argumentative divinity of
the Sunday gatherings continued unchanged, the weekday
performances on both Wednesdays and Fridays took on more and
more burlesque and satirical comment on contemporary affairs, as
the advertisements for some of them clearly show:

On Friday, something odd; after each, the Travesty of the Universe.
(26 July 1729)

On Wednesday, the Oration will be on the Skits of the Fashions, or a
live Gallery of Family Pictures in all Ages; Ruffs, Muffs, Puffs manifold;
Shoes, Wedding-Shoes, two Shoes, Slop-Shoes, Heels, Clocks, &c. &c.
(27 Sept. 1729)

On Monday will be an Oration on the Ministers and Favourites of
Princes, from Gaveston to Villiers. (13 Feb. 1730)

The Wednesday's Oration will be on the World toss'd at Tennis, or a
Lesson for a King, displaying the Views of England, France, Italy,
Spain, Holland, Germany, in a new Light. (16 May 1730)

On Wednesday, at half an hour after six, occasion'd by the speedy
meeting of the Parliament, will be a new Dissertation on the Idea of a
compleat Member of Parliament, General, and Ambassador. (16 Jan.
1731)

By 1741 this change in the Oratory's interests had become complete and was reflected in the pattern of the performances. There
is now no evidence for a regular Sunday-morning service and
sermon, nor for the Wednesday academical or Friday burlesque
performances. All had been combined into a strange miscellaneous
affair taking place at 6.0 or 6.30 on Sunday evenings. This began
with a brief preliminary of exhortation and prayer which he
progressively made shorter 'to make way for a greater Variety
in the Lecture',[2] and which were, though prayers, equally

[1] Advertisement for 30 Aug. 1729 (Lysons 37).
[2] Advertisement for 8 Feb. 1751 (Lysons 161).

political comment and criticism. When, for instance, he led a general confession of sins, he confessed the faults 'of all orders amongst us, especially ye orders of archbishops and bishops—their flocks have err'd and stray'd like lost sheep—and they—in sheep's clothing—have been ravening wolves—they have set their Affection indeed, as to Things *above*, on advancements and Translations—from Bangor to Salisbury—& Lincoln to London—'.[1] He petitioned God to 'Give our superiors Grace not to walk disorderly—in ye Mall or on any side of it; not to be Busy-bodies or Balancers of Power; not to be ye Gossips and Go-betweens of Europe . . . not wander about from House to House, from ye House of Stuart to ye House of Austria', or, with heavy irony, he prayed him to 'Grant, that it may no longer be thought a great Marvel if thou givest our Bishops thy Grace'.[2] After these opening prayers, Henley indulged in a quite unclassifiable variety of comment on contemporary affairs, ecclesiastical, political, literary, or merely scandals and notorious events of the Town. A typical evening's oration was such as the one advertised for 10 October, 1741:

after a new Exhortation, Lesson and Prayers, Political and Martial, the Lecture will be on Mother Church in Good Humour, or the Sunday's Entertainment; the Convocation-House made a Necessary House, tho' unlawful; the Roads from Hanover, the Prophetic Parson, and Omens on this, the Coronation-Day; the new Art of War and Peace, the Neutrality, Barrier, Balance, and Treaties; a new Miracle, Peace at Vienna, France former Mistress of the Empire, a curious Memoir; a glorious Footing at the Scheme for the Bishops to buy the late Earl of Oxford's Library, and then Questions, the Divine's, Physicians, Lawyer's, Gentleman's etc.

So for the next fourteen years Henley continued in this way, 'Preaching', as he put it, 'on the world as it is, serious or ridiculous',[3] and presenting each Sunday a 'lecture spiritualising things present and things to come,[4] ranging from attacks on the Episcopacy to the conduct of the Battle of Dettingen, from the building of a new London Bridge to the shooting of deserters from the Highland regiments, touching on dangerous subjects

---

[1] Prayers for 12 Sept. 1742, in BM. MSS.Add. 19919.
[2] Prayers for 10 Jan. 1748, in B.M. MSS.Add. 11774.
[3] Advertisement for 19 Nov. 1743 (Lysons 121).
[4] Advertisement for 30 July 1743 (Lysons 117).

with a brazenness which must have been a large part of the Oratory's attraction. There was a smell of sedition about such advertisements as 'Dissertation on the Stuarts, that Great, but seemingly unhappy family', 'An Argument on an anti-National W*r', 'New Discourse on the Folly of a Minister of State's being a Tool of a B**', and his orations on the '45 rebellion proved, as we shall later see, too dangerous for the government to ignore. Despite a temporary attempt at good behaviour, Henley proved incorrigible, and continued his risky course to the close of his life, when he loved to present himself as the one true Patriot, recalling the glories and the strength of Old England in a degenerate age. He gave more time to theological argument, stating and defending and explaining his beliefs which had changed so much since the days of Primitivism and near-orthodoxy, to become the 'Rationalism' which he claimed to be the basis of all the Oratory activity, the justification of his involvement in all the affairs of the world and the mind, and the justification, too, of all those affairs being right subjects for a preacher.

Such was the predominant pattern of the Orator's sermons and lectures, on which, when occasion called, he made variations. He frequently gave commemorative sermons, sometimes on the great and famous, sometimes on neighbours and faithful members of his congregation. And he continued to give charity sermons as in the early London days of hopeful busyness. On such occasions there was no entry fee, and the collection went to a variety of good causes:

For the Relief of an indigent Scholar, a CLERGYMAN'S Son, of St. Mary's Hall in Oxford, reduced to Misfortunes. (23 Jan. 1731)
... for a reduc'd Tradesman, turn'd out of his habitation, with a wife and four Children. (10 Jan. 1731)
for the Relief of an ingenious Gentleman reduced to Misfortunes, and oppress'd with bodily Infirmities, as well as Age. He was the Translator of Philip de Comines, and Signor Veneroni's Italian Grammar ... (3 Oct. 1730)
For THE LATE POOR SUFFERERS BY FIRE in Lincoln's Inn Fields. (19 June 1731)
for the Inhabitants of TIVERTON in Devon ... 2000 Persons have been reduced to deplorable Circumstances by the late FIRE. N.B. What the Charitable will be pleased to give at this lecture shall be faithfully communicated to the said poor Sufferers. (1 Oct. 1732)

The strain of preparing these sermons and lectures, in addition to other labours which he now and again took on himself, proved at times too much for him, and he had to cancel and postpone performances, informing his potential congregation in the press. In the summer months, when attendance was at its lowest, he sometimes closed the Oratory for a few weeks 'for a Tour into the Country';[1] or he pleaded urgent business to explain a temporary absence from the pulpit—'The Burlesque Wednesday's discourses of the Oratory are discontinued for some time, on an obligation which the Rev. Mr. Henley has entered into';[2] or 'My Judgment and Assistance being call'd for lately, on a Point of Ecclesiastical Law and Revenue, by a Gentleman, was a necessary Avocation from the Oratory Chapel on Sunday last.'[3] Sometimes he merely pleaded 'indisposition' which his enemies were quick to explain as the result of the previous evening's conviviality. But the general steadiness of production and performance, without assistance or substitutes, is impressive. Week after week he completed and delivered something new, to shock and scandalize the orthodox and delight the rest, not only by this new all-inclusiveness which took all human activity as a valid subject for preaching, but also by the language and style of his delivery.

Before the Oratory was conceived and established, Henley's reputation for a very personal manner of elocution and action had caused the title of 'Restorer of Antient Eloquence' to be conferred upon him. In a sermon of 1725 his ideas on how to revive the spirit of preaching had been enunciated, calling for a preacher completely involved in the delivery of his message, rather than an elegant reader glued to his written text. All a man's faculties should be involved in his delivery, voice and body matching and emphasizing the variations in subject, 'even to a line of the countenance'. The various passions dealt with should be reflected in the varying pronunciation and gesture, avoiding always levity, excess, affectation, indecency, and impropriety, and aiming always at a natural, easy, lively, graceful, harmonious and solemn style.[4] These were the first theories in the application of which he

---

[1] Advertisement for 26 July 1746 (Lysons 144), as also advertisements for 24 July 1742 (Lysons 112) and 3 July 1731 (Lysons 55).
[2] Advertisement for 13 Jan. 1732 (Lysons 61).
[3] Advertisement for 22 May 1752 (Lysons 173).
[4] Henley, *The History and Advantages of divine Revelation* (1725), pp. 14–17.

promised 'to recover the spirit of the antient preachers and assert
the honour of the English pulpit. . . . to banish for ever from this
island, the Gothic manner, the mere still life, the lethargy of
preaching'.[1] The aim was indeed a laudable and a necessary one.
'The Gothic manner' of seventeenth-century preaching, learned,
text-dissecting, figured and complex in its turns and intellectual
wit, was falling out of use and favour and being replaced by the
'mere still life, the lethargy of preaching', produced by what he
later described as 'the phlegmatic Sermon-vampers and sleepy
letter-mongers of our Ingenious Age'.[2] He was not a lone pioneer
in this attempt to reform and enliven pulpit eloquence, and many
treatises on the content, composition, and delivery of homilies
appeared throughout the century. Typical was such a work as
John Edwards's *The Preacher*, published, in its three volumes,
between 1705 and 1707, which put forward many of the ideas
which Henley was later to discuss. Edwards regretted that 'scarce
one is left that dares stir in a Pulpit, that dares Preach with any
Warmth and Vigour. But they study to be Cold and Frozen,
and unconcerned.'[3] He could not approve 'Pulpit-Men who stand
Moveless in that place, as if they were tyed to the *Stake*: a Sign
that Preaching is a *Martyrdom* to them'.[4] This was nevertheless
to prove the prevalent style of those clearly reasoned and too
frequently dull discourses which better expressed the rational and
latitudinarian faith which spread as the century progressed. Even
so faithful a Churchman as Dr. Johnson later admitted

that the established clergy in general did not preach plain enough; and
that polished periods and glittering sentences flew over the heads of the
common people without any impression on their hearts. Something
might be necessary, he observed, to excite the affections of the common
people, who were sunk into languor and lethargy, and therefore he
supposed that the new concomitants of methodism might probably
produce so desirable an effect.[5]

In many ways, Henley's basic methods of expressive gesture and
voice modulation were neither new nor shocking. They spring
ultimately from the classical writers on eloquence and rhetoric,

[1] *The First Sermon at the Oratory*, p. 33, in *Oratory Transactions No. 1*.
[2] Sermon for 8 Apr. 1750 (B.M. MSS.Add. 11777).
[3] Vol. i, pp. 193–4.
[4] Vol. i, p. 184.
[5] Boswell, *Life of Johnson*, ed. G. B. Hill, revised and enlarged by L. F. Powell
(1934), vol. ii, p. 123.

and Edwards himself, in the eminently orthodox *The Preacher*, advocated '*Elevation of their Voices*, and the *fitting Gesture of their Bodies*'[1] together with the rule 'that the Voice ought to be conformable to the Subject that is treated of'.[2] Rather it was Henley's uninhibited and increasingly eccentric application of these ideas which produced sensational and theatrical excesses, and outraged the eighteenth-century sense of religious and pulpit decorum. If we have found *The Preacher* agreeing with many of Henley's theories, it was also strangely prophetic in its description of the errors into which preachers might fall through lack of moderation. Edwards might almost be listing the accusations soon to be hurled at Henley:

... nothing that is Light and Vain must be heard or seen from the Pulpit. (vol. i, p. 197)

... to be blustering and obstreperous, to be clamorous and boisterous, is none of his Character. (vol. i, p. 198)

... to use no immoderate Movings and Shiftings of the Body, no Antick Postures, no Mimical Gestures and Grimaces, and not to Over-Act in the Pulpit. (vol. i, p. 200)

Buffoon or *Mimick*, *Scaramuchio* or *Zany*, are no good Titles or Epithets for a Preacher. (vol. i, p. 201)

In years to come, they were all epithets and titles which, with some justification, were to be bestowed on Henley as he increasingly outraged his generation, but in the first years of the Oratory his sermons were by no means despicable attempts to unite something of the rhetoric, cadence, and imagery of the old school with a new simplicity and directness of language.

A sermon on the text, 'His Confidence shall be rooted out of his Tabernacle, and it shall bring him to the King of Terrors' (Job, 18:14) provides good examples of his rhetorical and highly figurative style, which we must imagine reinforced by his gesture and expression:

In Sickness, the former Gaiety of the Spirit is alter'd; and the Interests and Pleasures of past Life lose their Relish. The Soul begins already to put on the Shroud, before the Tabernacle is dissolv'd, and lays aside the light Garment of vain Desire; she counts the slow Moments by the Pauses of Meditation, and reckons the falling Sands by her Prayers; her

---

[1] Vol. i, p. 180.   [2] Vol. i, p. 199.

Cloathing of Flesh sits troublesome upon her, and sorrowful is her Habitation; her Sun declines in Darkness, a Midnight Curtain veils over the glittering Scenes of the World, and she sees *a Hand upon the Wall* taking down the Ornaments, and pointing to the Coffin alone in Secret. . . . The Senses are languid and unactive, all the Daughters of Musick ceasing to the Ear, the Eye bereav'd of its Lustre, wan and motionless, like a Glass cover'd with Dew, or the Aspect of the Sky, overcast with angry Clouds, the Forerunners of the Tempest of God: the Limbs benumb'd and inanimate; or betraying the Tumults within; the Spirit trembling on the Brink of its Flight, as a tired Eagle on a Precipice, forc'd to stretch across an Ocean for Safety; the Mind a Blank, its Images all fading, like departing Shadows.[1]

A similar highly emotional rhetoric fills his sermon on *The Pangs of Expiring Penitents*, as he contemplates the uncertain acceptability of death-bed repentances when

. . . the Wrath is gone forth from the heavenly Presence, not to be recall'd, and no Mediator stands in the Gap, to avert the Judgment; the Sword of Fire is even now consuming; the insensible Heart is bruis'd with the Rod of Chastisement, which was not made the broken Sacrifice of a timely Contrition. . . . He turns away from Prayer, because that gives him a Prospect of Heaven, to make his Anguish more intolerable. God is his Enemy, he will not have Mercy, none, none is able to redeem, or to deliver him from his Hand; his very Visage is a Copy of inward Pangs; Horror and Amazement unalterable, and his Departure is only endur'd as a Change of Place, hardly of his Condition.[2]

And lest it might appear that only the darker of the four Last Things inspired him, here, as a last example of his eloquence, is his description of the joys of heaven:

This *Sion* will have the Glory of God: He that made the Eye, shall he not see? He that fram'd the Sun, that beautify'd the Lilly and the Rose, that cause'd the Ruby and the Diamond to sparkle, that gave the Stars their shining, that sow'd the Coral Groves and Pearl in the Sea, that burnishes the Fruits of the Earth, and paints the mix'd Veins of it with glowing Metals; what is his Splendor? What his Glory? Ascend from the Effect to the Cause, and trace the consummate Light which none can approach, even in the very Glimmer of his Works, that are opening the Dusk to a Noon Day. Here the Sun is scorching, the Moon variable;

---

[1] *The Conflicts of the death-bed etc.*, pp. 9–12.
[2] *The Pangs of Expiring Penitents*, pp. 3 and 26.

without Annoyance or Alteration, the Light of Heaven is that of a Jasper, attending the immutable State of the joyous Mansion.[1]

In addition to this rhetorical and rhapsodic element, his sermons reflect his belief that all aspects of human life and thought, the things and actions of daily life, the facts of history and the discoveries of science, are as much the material of gospel preaching as the great general concepts of theology. At its best this belief produced startling but thought-provoking novelty in looking at familiar things and discovering significant relationships: at its worst it resulted in an incongruous hotchpotch of scraps of information forced together in a strained and often ludicrous way, as he searched his Concordances and his library for material, and exercised little judgment in the use of what he found. *The Butchers' Lecture* of 1729 offers a good example of this latter type of performance. Addressed to a congregation of butchers, its aim was

to display the religious History and Use of the Butcher's Calling; to observe what Considerations offer in Scripture, and learning, to the advantage of it, by the particular notice taken of what relates to it in the Bible, and other Authors . . . to vindicate it from Objections commonly urg'd; and to plan the Theology of this Vocation.

To this end he sought out scriptural texts; he invoked the microscope to show that even a vegetarian diet involved the killing and eating of millions of living creatures; he quoted Milton to show by the skin-coats of Adam and Eve that killing of creatures existed from the start; Homer, Aesop, and Horace were quoted; Wolsey was cited to show what great men have sprung from the trade; and he could even indulge in such odd items of 'proof' as 'It is plain, that this Calling is esteem'd by the Law, and the Constitution, because the whole of both is preserv'd in writing, upon the Skins of Cattle.' A more successful but equally typical example of this style is a sermon of the following year, *The Lord, He is God; or the Atheist Tormented by Sure Prognosticks of HELL FIRE*. This is a scriptural-geographical-scientific examination of the nature of the Fires of Hell, ranging far and wide in its search for materials, from Sodom to the subterranean caves of Hekla and Stromboli, from Nadab and Abiram to the phenomenon of hot springs. His

[1] *Sion in Perfect Beauty: or the Heaven of Heavens* (1730), p. 10.

scientific knowledge confirmed the truth of the fate of Sodom, for 'The Plains of this Region were fill'd with Bitumen: the Fire of Heaven falling on these Veins, soon communicated their Heat to the whole Territory, consum'd all Things, and form'd the lake Asphaltites, or the Dead Sea.' Hot springs and volcanoes were brought as proof of the central fire of the earth which an act of God could release in an instant, plunging His creation into the Final Fire, and on this thought his rhetoric was brought to bear, producing something of the school of Donne, in its curiousness and its rhythms:

But this may afford a distinct Lesson; it is no powerful Charm to fasten our Desires to this Planet we tread upon, to reflect, that the inward Regions of it are call'd Hell, and that we daily lie upon Beds and walk over Caverns of Fire. That our Minutes and Hours do not consume more speedily, than the World in which we delight is ever wasting by its secret Fever; that we do, in a Literal Sense, pass over the Kiln; the Shell of the Furnace; the Wicked, like the Grass on the House-top, to Day is, and To-morrow is cast into the Oven beneath: that all the Force of the Seas will be unavailing to oppose this working Power, since it will sometime dissolve all the Frame, and leave no Sea upon it; that our darling Earth is not so solid a Thing as we imagine, it is a hollow Fire-Ball, whose Power has not yet penetrated to the Surface: that will sometime afford us the Trial of an Escape to our Heavenly Country, as by Fire, and is a Doctrine in the mean Time of Virtue, and Religious Circumspection.

There was, however, something more to his theory of preaching than expressive elocution and universal scope, which was to move more and more to the forefront until it became the chief explanation of all his later performances. This was the use of wit, ridicule, burlesque, as he variously called it. As this became the main reason for later attacks on Henley's preaching, some effort must be made to understand Henley's version of his method and motives, before judging him through his enemies' eyes. In 1729 he announced:

To burlesque Error, Vice, and Folly is part of my Religious Persuasion, as a Teacher, in my Place of Worship; it is doing Honour to Religion; the Prophet Elijah ridicul'd or Burlesqu'd Baal's Priests; and I think myself bound in Conscience to use what Wit God has given me, as a Teacher, to gain some that Way, as well as Argument and Learning, to be all things to all Men. St. Paul, 2 Cor. 15. quotes a verse from a Comedy. J.H.[1]

In the same year in a published answer to his enemies, he claimed that 'Burlesque Teaching is founded, like all Teaching, on the Bible, and is therefore Part of religious Worship, if Teaching in General be a Part of Religion.' Burlesque included comment on the times, witty turns of phrase, scorn, sarcasm, and irony, strong language, exclamation, and quotation, the last of which he supported by quoting Herbert's

> A verse may find him, who a Sermon flies,
> And turn delight into a Sacrifice.

and he defended laughter as a legitimate weapon of the preacher.[2] Throughout his life he defended his belief that laughter in church was not profane but fitting, that a joke could make a point as well as a syllogism, and that satire and the language of abuse could strike at sinners as powerfully and religiously as solemn remonstration. He was not ashamed to advertise 'More Learning and Wit for 18d. in an Hour, than in a B*p's stale Imposture for 2 Millions a Year',[3] or that his lecture would be 'enliven'd with Strokes of Humour, Variety, Novelty, Rational Entertainment and Delight, beyond what is met with in any Assemblies or Authors; the Wit unborrow'd, without Mimickry, or Imitation, original'.[4] It was this cheerfulness and vivacity which he continually stressed, comparing it always with the dull stodge and gloomy propriety of the general run of accepted preachers—'A New Discourse on Pulpit Craft, or the In-dignity of Preaching, in Proof, that a cheerful Preacher of good Tidings of great Joy is God's and Christ's Preacher, and that a sorry sad Preacher like our Pope John of S* Hall, is the Devil's Chaplain',[5] or again, with a typical example of his own burlesque,

Since many Pulpits are appointed to administer Spiritual Opium to their Hearers, and preach the People to a Lethargy, there may, surely, be tolerated, one Pulpit to *awaken them*, to prevent the Enemy *sowing Tares, while they sleep*; that every Body may not be obliged to say,

---

[1] Advertisement for 1 Feb. 1729 (Lysons 29).
[2] *Milk for Babes*, pp. 36–42.
[3] Advertisement for 14 July 1744, in the *Daily Advertiser*.
[4] Advertisement for 15 May 1747 (Lysons 147).
[5] Advertisement for 23 Feb. 1745 (Lysons 137).

behold, it is all a Dream: was there One Oratory to a Thousand Dormitories it might be very *Reasonable*.[1]

In the year before he died, in a full-scale defence of his beliefs and methods, he defiantly repeated his creed: 'Alacrity, or a cheerful Spirit, is an Article of it in Life and Doctrine; to mix the pleasant with the Serious, so far from Buffoonery, that it is a Duty. . . . The Bible is full of Joy, Instances of Derision and Mirth, —what some Fools call Burlesque and Buffoonery.'[2]

Henley might well have quoted another authority besides the Biblical for his use of Derision and Mirth, an authority widely read and highly influential in so many areas of thought in his time—Anthony Ashley Cooper, the third Earl of Shaftesbury. In his *Characteristics* he had claimed Ridicule to be a legitimate way to discover truth, for 'Truth, 'tis supposed, may bear all lights; and one of those principal lights, or natural mediums, by which things are to be viewed, in order to a thorough recognition, is ridicule itself, or that manner of proof by which we discern whatever is liable to just raillery in any subject.'[3] This probing application of ridicule, to find what is truly serious and what is in itself ridiculous, must be made without fear in all fields of thought, for, he insisted, 'if we fear to apply this rule in anything, what security can we have against the imposture of formality in all things?'[4] Religion, therefore, was not to be protected from such testing, for 'provided we treat religion with good manners, we can never use too much good-humour, or examine it with too much freedom and familiarity. For, if it be genuine and sincere, it will not only stand the proof, but thrive and gain advantage from hence; if it be spurious, or mixed with any imposture, it will be detected and exposed.'[5] In the third volume of the *Characteristics* which appeared in 1711 as the *Miscellaneous Reflections*, Shaftesbury suggests that his earlier ideas had fallen on fruitful ground. He writes:

The burlesque divinity grows mightily in vogue. And the cried-up answers to heterodox discourses are generally such as are written in

---

[1] Henley, *The Victorious Strike for Old England etc.* (1748), p. 29.

[2] *Second St. Paul etc.*, p. 12.

[3] *Characteristics of Men, Manners, Opinions, Times*, ed. J. M. Robertson and Stanley Grean (Bobbs-Merrill Co. Inc., 1964), p. 44.

[4] Ibid., p. 11.

[5] Ibid., p. 24.

drollery or with resemblance of the facetious and humorous language of conversation.

Joy to the reverend authors who can afford to be thus gay, and condescend to correct us in this lay-wit. The advances they make in behalf of piety and manners by such a popular style are doubtless found upon experience to be very considerable. As these reformers are nicely qualified to hit the air of breeding and gentility, they will in time, no doubt, refine their manner and improve this jocular method, to the edification of the polite world, who have been so long seduced by the way of raillery and wit. They may do wonders by their comic muse, and may thus, perhaps, find means to laugh gentlemen into their religion who have unfortunately been laughed out of it. For what reason is there to suppose that orthodoxy should not be able to laugh as agreeably, and with as much refinedness, as heresy or infidelity?[1]

This might well be a description of Henley's method, but for one important difference—it refers to written controversy, to pamphlets, dialogues, and discourses. It was Henley's innovation to bring such methods to the ears and not just the minds of his audience, to make burlesque divinity mount the pulpit steps, and to rouse laughter in a way which even Shaftesbury might not have considered a right way to truth. Certainly a Shaftesbury-admiring generation steadfastly refused to accept Henley and continued to regard his orations as shocking profanity. One of the 'Fools', whom Henley castigates, reported a sermon he had heard, in these words: 'He held forth indeed, about three Hours, but the same bombastic Cant, the same stupid Joaks, and the same sudden prophane Transitions from the Language of the Gospel to the Dialect of Newgate were repeated twenty Times over,'[2] As the years passed and Henley's subjects became more and more political and contemporary, the irony and ridicule, the strong language and the jokes, became more congruous to a generation well versed in social and political satire. 'Sedition' rather than 'Profanity', 'Improper' rather than 'Ungodly' became the words of attack. But whatever the subject and whatever the response, Henley saw all his work, early or late, as a piece, applying constantly his ideas of universality of scope, liveliness of elocution, and the use of the various instruments of laughter, believing that only thus was he faithful to his idea of God and the duty of

[1] Ibid., vol. ii, pp. 337–8.   [2] *Punchinello's Sermon*, p. 6.

the rational man, to strive towards 'Conformity to the Divine Attributes, one of which is *Omniscience*'.[1]

With this delivery of the Oratorian Word, Henley administered the Oratorian Sacrament, that Primitive Eucharist emblazoned above the fair altar which stood beside his pulpit. 'All this passed', as Pope sneeringly wrote, 'in the same room; where sometimes he broke jests, and sometimes that bread which he called the Primitive Eucharist.'[2] It was an unworthy sneer, springing from ignorance and prejudice. Henley's ideas may have been wrong, his scholarship faulty, but there is no evidence at all to show any insincerity of motive or any irreverence in performance.

A possible reform of the liturgy had been one of the questions discussed in the early negotiations with Whiston who, in 1711, had published as Volume ii of his *Primitive Christianity Reviv'd*, *The Constitutions of the Holy Apostles by Clement*, containing as its Eighth Book, a Liturgy which he hoped might provide a model for reform. He moved with a caution, however, which was not to mark Henley's future decisions, and when he published in 1713 *The Liturgy of the Church of England Reduc'd nearer to the Primitive Standard*, his alterations to the established liturgy were slight, only expanding the Prayer for the Church Militant with prayers for the saints and the faithful departed, and joining the Prayer of Oblation to the Consecration Prayer. It was, in a way, a forerunner of the 1928 revision, and he offered it similarly as an interim rite 'to provide a good, tho' imperfect Form of Christian Worship, for sincere and pious Persons in the mean time, till those more Sacred and Apostolical Remains can be fully examined into, received and put into Practice by them'.[3] A more influential and more widely used liturgy appeared five years later in *A Communion office, taken partly from the Primitive Liturgies and partly from the first English Reformed Common Prayer Book*. This was the liturgy celebrated by the 'usagers' among the non-Jurors, and based on the theory of the primitive so dear to Whiston and Henley—'And since the *New Testament* has given no Form for the Principal Part of the Christian Worship, the safest way is to be govern'd by the Practice of the Ancient Church: Those early times were the best judges of Apostolical Precedent and Tradi-

[1] *The Victorious Stroke for Old England*, p. 22.
[2] *Dunciad* (1729), Book iii, l. 195, footnote.
[3] Preface to the work.

tion. . . .' It made more drastic changes than those in Whiston's liturgy, replacing the Ten Commandments with a single Kyrie and a summary of the Law, adding at the placing of the Elements a prayer for acceptance abridged from the liturgy of St. Basil, recalling in the words of Institution 'the most signal instances of the Divine Providence and Bounty . . . paraphrastically taken from St. James's Liturgy', following the words of Institution with a Prayer of Oblation and Invocation from the *Apostolical Constitutions*, and placing the prayer for the whole state of Christ's Church after the consecration and oblation, using much the same words as those of the reformed English liturgy. This was a much bolder revision, which no doubt formed a more persuasive model for Henley as he moved towards his decision to make a more complete use of the liturgy from the *Apostolical Constitutions*. It shows, at least, that Henley's liturgy, far from being an eccentric oddity, was very much in line with the more advanced liturgical thinking of his time, and that he gave quite serious thought to liturgical problems before he produced a specific form.

His rejection of the Prayer Book rite was based on ideas which would find wide acceptance in our own days of liturgical reform, firstly that it suffers from Calvinistic influence, and secondly that a rite so different from the ancient form is an obstacle to oecumenical advance—

The present communion office of the church of England, which entirely departs from it [i.e. the primitive shape of the liturgy] was alter'd from a model of this kind by parliament without a convocation, to please Calvin and his friends at a political juncture; whereas the keeping or restoring this form would be most likely to gain over both the dissenters and the Roman Catholicks; for all would chuse a primitive method, were all convinc'd which was that method: and accordingly this agreement with the antient church has been, and is the wish of the most learned and serious men ever since the reformation.[1]

The names he gave of some of these learned and serious men indicate the scope of his preparatory reading—'Dr. Hammond in his Practical Catechism: Dr. Wake, Archbp. of Canterbury: Mr. Strype in his Life of Archbp. Whitgift: Mr. Thorndike: Bishop Taylor: Bishop Forbes of Scotland: Dr. Grabe: Gerard John Dossius: Renandot in his collection of old liturgies'. His readings

---

[1] *A Homily on the Primitive Eucharist*, p. 109, in *The Appeal of the Oratory etc.*

here, and his study of these old liturgies—he mentions those of
Clement, James, Mark, Chrysostom, Basil, Nestorius, and Severus,
and the Gothic, Gallican, Ethiopic, and Mazarabic rites—led him
to establish a basic shape of the liturgy, reflecting the pattern of
Christ's actions at the Last Supper, when he took bread, blessed,
gave thanks, communicated, and commanded a continuance.
This shape he outlined as:

1. the eucharistic thanksgiving.
2. the oblation of the elements.
3. the invocation for the descent of the Holy Ghost to make
   the elements the body and blood of Christ.
4. prayer for the whole Church.
5. prayer for a worthy partaking of the sacrament.
6. pardon of sin.
7. humble access.
8. ἄγια αγιοις.
9. distribution.

The nearer the liturgy approached this shape, the nearer it
approached the action of the Lord and the primitive Church.
As for the matter of the sacrament, unleavened bread was to be
used as Christ did at his Passover meal and as the Church in
general did, and the mixed chalice was to be used, which was a
Jewish custom, supported by Old Testament types, New Testament texts, and the practice of the early liturgies. As for the
language of the liturgy, this too had to be as primitive as possible.
His seventh rubric before the liturgy commanded 'Let not the
language of the first liturgies be vary'd but in scripture expressions'
so 'that all people may have the satisfaction of praying to God,
as near as possible, in the way in which the first believers prayed
to him'.[1]

With these principles to guide him, Henley chose as his model
the liturgy in the Eighth Book of the *Apostolical Constitutions*
of Clement. In accepting this as ancient and apostolic Henley
was wrong, but we must beware of too much hindsight in our
judgement of him. In the early eighteenth century, scholarship
had not removed the question of their authenticity completely

[1] *A Homily on the following Liturgy*, p. 50, in *The Appeal of the Oratory etc.*

from the area of responsible discussion, although learned voices had expressed grave doubts. Of these Henley was not unaware, and he acknowledged the disagreement about their authorship. Nevertheless, he made his decision: 'I therefore, on the most clear and universal historical demonstration, receive the constitutions, as an exact account, in substance, of the thoughts and customs, the worship and discipline of the primitive church.'[1] He was not entirely wrong if by 'in substance' he meant 'in general outline' as opposed to 'verbatim authenticity'. Though the document he used had nothing to do with Clement or the Apostles, and was a compilation made by a notorious forger no earlier than the fourth century, and though the liturgy as recorded was unlikely ever to have been celebrated, yet it still has some value. It is the earliest entire liturgy unchanged since the fourth century and, though its phrasing and devotional language are the work of the forger, in its general form it is in agreement with more fragmentary but unimpeachable evidence. To believe that in its general form he had the shape of the primitive liturgy was not entirely wrong: in believing that the very words spoke from that primitive past, Henley erred.

For this is, in fact, what his Primitive Eucharist shows he believed. It is a very close adaptation of the Clementine liturgy, altered here and there where the early conditions no longer applied, and the wording changed where the original was too prolix or expressed ideas Henley could not accept. Beginning his own version after the original's Kiss of Peace and the Deacon's proclamation, he followed the structure of his original exactly in its divisions of Thanksgiving, Institution, Oblation, Invocation to the Holy Spirit, Prayer for the whole Church, Prayer of Access, Communion, post-communion Thanksgiving, and the Benediction. His verbal alterations were mainly in drastic reductions of the impossibly lengthy prayers of the original, and in general his recensions are skilful and sensible. The lengthy Eucharistic Thanksgiving was greatly concentrated, as he removed puffy verbiage. One such example typifies his method. At one point in this Thanksgiving, the original reads:

Thou madest water to drink, and for ablution; and the vital air, for respiration, and for the transmission of the sound of the voice, by

[1] Ibid., p. 55.

means of the tongue striking the air, so as by reception to perceive the speech lighting upon it. Thou madest fire for a consolation in darkness, and for relief of necessity that we might thereby be warmed and enlightened.[1]

This little physics lecture to the Almighty is removed and replaced simply by 'the fire, the air, the water, are thy servants'. He similarly removed a long section where God is given a tedious résumé of Old Testament history from Adam to Joshua; and throughout there are numerous minor excisions of references to such things as 'bishops, presbyters, deacons, subdeacons, readers, singers, virgins, widows, laiety', or of such prayers as 'for all the army, that they may be peacably disposed towards us', where the conditions or persons no longer applied to the eighteenth century or, more particularly, the Oratory. Despite all these reductions, Henley's liturgy is too wordy, and it is known that in use it was further cut down. But once this has been admitted, there is nothing in it which justifies the scorn and scandalized outrage of his opponents. Though his original was of questionable worth and his liturgical scholarship not extensive, he produced a liturgy which pursued to extremes that desire to rediscover the primitive shape and prayers of the Eucharist, which motivated all this post-1662 liturgical activity, but which other liturgists approached with more caution.[2] It was printed in 1726 in time for the opening of the Oratory, appearing in true Prayer Book solemnity complete with black-letter type and rubrics correctly printed in red. An improved version, from which Henley had removed certain anomalies, was printed in 1727 in *The Appeal of the Oratory to the First Ages of Christianity* and it was also bound in with the *Oratory Transactions Number 1* of 1728. These books were on sale at the Oratory and certain booksellers, so that, for an outlay of one shilling, the devout attender could follow closely the celebration of this Primitive Eucharist.

[1] Quotations from the Clementine liturgy are taken from *The Liturgy of the Eighth Book of the Apostolic Constitutions*, tr. R. H. Cresswell (1900).

[2] The liturgical experiments of the seventeenth and eighteenth centuries, from Edward Stephens's *The Liturgy of the Ancients Represented* (1696), together with Whiston's and Henley's liturgies and the non-juring forms of 1718 and later, form too intricate and detailed a subject to be dealt with more extensively in such a study as this. The reader who wishes to examine the subject more closely is referred to W. Jardine Grisbrooke's excellent monograph, *Anglican Liturgies of the Seventeenth and Eighteenth Centuries* (S.P.C.K. 1958), where the texts of these liturgies are printed along with detailed commentary.

It is curious that, while we have frequent eye-witness accounts of Henley's preaching, we have no such evidence of how he celebrated the Eucharist, not even satirical descriptions where some facts may be discerned through the distortion. From the rubrics with which he prefaced and ended his liturgy we can surmise a little. The altar stood, as we have seen, at the side of the Oratory, and near it were conveniently placed the unleavened bread and the water and the wine. After the dismissal of non-communicants, Henley moved to the altar. The fourth rubric raises interesting doubts—'Let the use of the sign of the cross, the splendid vestment, and other primitive ceremonies, in this, and all public devotions, be recommended only, not imposed.' No one could impose on Henley who was his own Ordinary. Why include this rubric unless it described the practice of the Oratory itself? And what was this garment described in a phrase taken over from his original as 'the splendid vestment'? Was it the eucharistic chasuble or the much-favoured cope of Anglican ceremonial? We cannot be certain. The use of the chasuble out-side Rome would be most unusual at this period, and yet certain accusations of Popery levelled against Henley might suggest that he used this ancient Mass vestment. Disraeli had obviously gathered some such information to lead him to write that the manner of celebration 'was restoring the decorations and the mummery of the Mass.'[1] All we can say is that Henley appears to have doffed his usual preaching gown and, vested in either cope or chasuble, approached the altar to place on it, at the opening of the service, the alms, the bread, wine, and water 'in decent order'. As with the placing of the offertory, so with the whole conduct of the rite, he commands with St. Paul, 'Let all things be done decently and in order.' This applied especially to action and word. 'Let the action be solemn, devout, and awful, suited to the highest act of devotion, that can be paid by man to God the Father, thro' Jesus Christ, in the Holy Spirit,' and 'Let the reading of the liturgy be always performed according to the laws of speaking and action, established in the Oratory, founded on a just impression in the mind and heart of the reader, and a ready command and memory of the whole service. The voice and gesture varying, as the thing required.' So the service

---

[1] Disraeli, *The Calamities of Authors*, i.172.

proceeded to the Communion of the people who sat before the altar, the men sitting separately from the women, and during the Communion, the 32nd Psalm or the great *Hallel* consisting of Psalms 113 to 118 was sung, to commemorate the hymn sung at the end of the Passover supper. The remaining elements were removed to the vestry immediately after the Communion and before the final thanksgiving and blessing. There is no hint in all this of anything eccentric or irreverent. The whole impression is one of solemnity, order, and formal ceremonial, and this impression seems confirmed by the fact that there are surprisingly few references to the liturgy amidst the mass of satire on his other activities.

One other reason, however, may be that the Primitive Eucharist was only a minor feature of Oratorian activities in that period when the religious services were predominant, and before the political and educational orations moved more to the fore and ultimately took over. In the early years the sacrament was celebrated monthly[1] and also on great Feast Days, when Henley gave special information in his advertisements:

On Whitsunday the Primitive Eucharist will be celebrated.   (6 May 1727)

The Holy Eucharist will then also be celebrated, according to the Institution of Christ, and the Rites of the Primitive Church and Fathers, And the English Homilies.   (1 July 1727)

On Wednesday, Christmas Day, will be Prayers, Exposition, Sacrament and Sermon, Morning and Evening.   (21 Dec. 1728)

Henley never advertised the monthly sacraments in the newspapers, so no conclusion can be drawn from the advertisements' silence on that score. No advertisements for special celebrations appeared after 1728. The last newspaper reference to the liturgy was in an advertisement for 4 September 1731—'N.B. Some Foreigners having desir'd a Translation of the Liturgy into French, for the view of the Churches abroad, it is now translating', and this indication that it was still a part of the Oratory is confirmed by a mention in a long 'Improv'd Plan of the Oratory' in the *Hyp Doctor* of 15 October 1734, that the Eucharist is celebrated at least once a month. After this there is complete silence and it would appear that, after the early period when

---

[1] Advertisement for 2 Sept. 1727 (Lysons 15).

set morning and evening services,[1] observing of fasts and feasts, and predominantly religious subjects formed the pattern of the Oratory, the liturgy, together with much else of religious practice, fell out of use. Certainly, by 1741, with the one Sunday evening meeting given over to political and contemporary themes and comment, and with Henley's theological position markedly changed, it would be difficult to conceive of the Primitive Eucharist still being celebrated.

Such, then, were the specifically religious proceedings of the Oratory, but the universal nature of this undertaking demanded a scheme 'comprehending', as we have seen, 'all objects of useful Knowledge and Practice, in the most Compleat Manner', and Henley would have rejected any description of his work which excluded the educational plans which constantly supplemented the religious. In the year before his death, in retrospective mood, Henley noted that 'From 1726 the Oratory was always advertised to be an Academy on the Week Days, only',[2] and it is interesting that, before the Oratory actually opened, the first Henley-inspired advertisement in *Mist's Journal* for 14 May 1726 concentrated on this academic side of the undertaking—'We hear the Reverend Mr. Henley is for erecting an Academy for teaching and propagating Oratory, Languages, &c. upon the following Plan or Scheme, the Usefulness of which to Professions or Sciences, we shall leave to others to judge, without offering our own private Opinion.' A contemporary comment indicates that it was these Oratory proposals which interested the Town before the horrid truth became clear, that because of the early advertisements' stress on the academic aims, 'many Persons were inclined to entertain a favourable opinion of it' until they realized 'that under Colour of an ACADEMY, he intended to set up an ORATORY, or in plain *English*, a NEW SECT'.[3] There was, in fact, no such subtle deceit in Henley's plan for, from the first full proposals and in all his subsequent policy statements, he presented the religious and educational activities of the Oratory as equal and interdependent. Together, also, they sprang from sources of frustration in his past. A furious disappointment about preferment led him to force his own way to an eminent pulpit and a

---

[1] Henley wrote three services for morning use and one for evening use. They are printed, with the Eucharist, in *The Appeal of the Oratory etc.*

[2] Advertisement for 1 Nov. 1755 (Lysons 197).

[3] *The Political State of Great Britain* (1726), vol. xxxiii, p. 175.

name: a deep dissatisfaction with what he considered the out-of-date syllabus and time-wasting methods of school and University education persuaded him that there was much to do in this field, and that he was the man to do it. In a small way, as schoolmaster at Melton, he had started to experiment and innovate: now, freed from trustees and tradition, he could realize his ambition more completely. In his first sermon at the Oratory he referred to his academic proposals with a flourish: 'Its design is no less than that of an universal school of science and letters, in theory and practice, for instruction, exercise, and accomplishment, in all parts of them', and, with no less a flourish, to the true significance of his own endeavours:

Full oft, has an English academy been delineated, long has it been desir'd, here the actual foundation of it shall be attempted. And what has requir'd the spirit of a distinguishing monarch, and a whole realm to commence abroad, shall here, on the single impulse of a private mind, be push'd into being at least, and with the divine blessing, and the smiles of our superiors, executed.[1]

A fuller scheme, explaining most of his motives and giving more details of his practical proposals, was published at the same time as the sermon:

Its general design is, 1. To supply the want of an University, or universal school in this capital, for the equal benefit of persons of all ranks, professions, circumstances, and capacities; to rectify the defects, remove the pedantry and prejudices, and improve on the advantages of all the usual methods of education, and institutions, common, scholastic, or academical; domestic or foreign: to give the readiest institute to the three learned faculties, and the service of church and state, as well as all useful and polite functions: to celebrate all scholastic and academical exercises, orations, declamations, disputations, conferences: communication of letters of correspondence with great men, and learned bodies; as also of observations, discoveries, improvements, and experiments; courses and praxes in the arts and sciences, for knowledge, business or accomplishment; and meetings of the most eminent persons in all liberal professions and faculties: to lay a scheme for the best encouragement of men of merit, parts and learning, to form an amicable society on the most polite principles; and promote the justest turn of free impartial thinking on all occasions, in order to retrieve and exalt the genius of Britain.

[1] *The First Sermon at the Oratory*, p. 37, in *Oratory Transactions No. 1*.

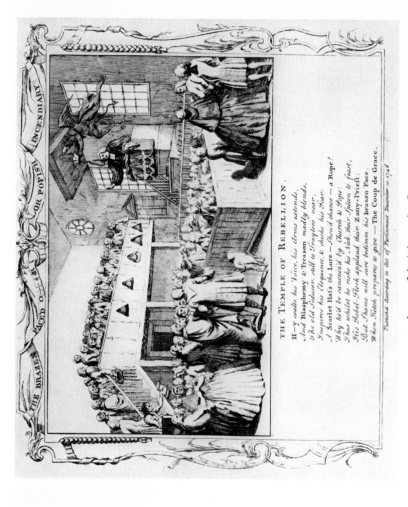

I. A peaceful night at the Oratory

In particular, it is more especially design'd, 2. To lay a foundation for the long desir'd English Academy; to give, by just degrees, a standard to the English tongue; to clear, regulate, ascertain, and digest the English history: to revive an ancient Athenian and Roman school of Philosophy, rhetorick and elocution; which last is reckon'd among the Artes perditae: and to afford the best and readiest lights on all curious or occasional topicks.[1]

The plan was, to say the least, ambitious, and the ambition not at all despicable. The vision of this academy, the ideal of this widely available education, urged Henley on throughout his life, finding its expression in many schemes and proposals, the details of which we can accurately describe, but the practical fulfilment and effect of which it is impossible to assess with any certainty. The beginning, at least, was modest. 'For this end, at first, once a week, there will be a reading on some learned or polite subject, form'd on the most natural deduction, to compleat a course of human knowledge, in the most just and regular method &c.'[2] This reading formed the Academical Orations given every Wednesday evening, and we have already looked briefly at some of the historical, literary, and scientific topics upon which Henley discoursed. By the end of 1728, however, sober and orthodox subjects such as the nature and art of satire, drama and pastoral poetry, logic or the art of thinking, history and principles of English law, the history of the English tongue, the history of money, had started to give way to more burlesque and satirical commentaries on current affairs, and the academic work of the Oratory shifted to lectures now given on Mondays. Throughout 1729 and 1730, Henley continued to fulfil his educational promises and the titles of some of these Monday evening talks demonstrate the range of popular education offered:

On mastering the English History.

The History of the Navy, and Sir Francis Drake.

The History and Principles of Natural Philosophy: with the Ancient & Modern Hypothesis.

The School of the Heart, or the Talent of Touching the Passions.

To the memory of Sir I. Newton, giving a more Concise Idea of the State and Progress of the Mathematicks than is extant.

The Painter's Praise, and Sir G. Kneller.

[1] *The Plan of the Oratory*, p. iii, in *Oratory Transactions No. 1.*   [2] Ibid., p. iv.

But through pressure of work and possibly the greater popularity of the more exciting burlesque commentaries, these Monday lectures disappeared also from the advertised life of the Oratory. It was becoming too difficult to maintain the originally proposed programme on a full public scale, and the educational work which Henley valued so, but which did not attract such crowds, suffered even before the more specifically religious activities were also overcome by the increasingly political and satirical emphasis of the Oratory. It was a mark of Henley's concern that, although he made no effort to revive and reinstate the religious services and liturgy, he invented a new scheme whereby the educational plan could proceed alongside the rest of the Oratory performance, without interfering with the valuable evening hours of popular orations.

This scheme was the invention of the Gentleman's Own University, the story of which we can trace with some degree of certainty from 1736 to 1749, though we can be less certain of the truth of the story. Of all Henley's activities, that of the Gentleman's Own University presents the greatest problem of deciding how much was fact and how much wish-fulfilment fantasy. Henley, in his own advertisements and journalism, is our only witness: nowhere can we find an independent account by a scholar of his University which might help us to check our facts. All we can do is to hear Henley's account and attempt to remove the more obvious exaggerations and unlikelihoods. It was on the evening of 4 July 1736 that he made his first proposals for the 'Gentleman's Proper University', informing his hearers that 'Courses of Lectures for particular Gentlemen begin on Monday at Eleven in the Musaeum of the Oratory, to excel in Debates, Pleadings, and such parts of universal Knowledge, Theoretic and Practical, as others will not, or dare not teach, avoiding all Objections of Time, Expence, and other Inconveniences.'[1] In the following week, at the request of certain gentlemen, he published more detailed proposals which indicated more clearly that the major departure of this from previous schemes was in its private rather than public method of teaching, based on tutorials and seminars rather than on the general public lecture:

[1] Advertisement for 3 July 1736, in the *Daily Gazette*.

Whereas there are many and great Complaints of, and Objections to, the present Methods of Instruction. . . . It is therefore proposed, that each Morning at half after Ten, to Twelve O'clock; or Hours appointed by Gentlemen, in the Oratory, or in the Musaeum contiguous to it, publickly or privately, jointly or singly, such Gentlemen as would most effectually attain the desirable Ends aforesaid, may be most naturally and fully form'd by distinct Lectures or Courses of them, demonstratively, at less than a fiftieth Part of the Time and Expence, consum'd in other Methods, in certain Universities, Academies, and other Places of Education, or Ways of Acquirement, by me, and such learn'd and skillful Assistants, as, when a Subscription to that end is perfected, shall receive better Encouragement from me than from any other Quarter: and I attend at those Hours there for this Purpose.[1]

In this and the following year, Henley elaborated the details of the syllabus. The first simple outline became more complex and ultimately becomes quite unbelievable. A first prospectus offered 'Logic, rhetorick, debate, also a course of University learning Academical, Political, Theological, and this in a set number of Lectures' and also 'A course of Natural Philosophy to any particular Gentlemen in a set number of Lectures and direct the books proper to be consulted . . .'. The following week saw this elaborated to include 'Theology, Politicks, Belles Lettres, or the Humanities and Philology, Greek, Latin and Hebrew Tongue, Diction, Law, Rational Moral Natural and Technical History, Arts of Publick speaking, Debating, Pleading and the Grammar of Wit'.[2] A month later the syllabus had grown so much that it had to be set forth under main headings within which was a fantastic variety of subdivisions. The prospective student could chose from 'I. Occult Knowledge. II. Polemical. III. Interdicted. IV. Intelligential. V. Aulic. VI. Ministerial. VII. Beau-monde. VIII. Proprietary i.e. land and property. IX. Parliamentary. X. Fiscal. XI. Ecclesiastical', and the reader of the *Hyp Doctor* could often examine the details of the complex offerings of each course or institute, be it in Composition, Theology, Political Science, or Philology.[3] It becomes in the end impossible to believe that Henley ever gave or could have given instruction in all he offered. Perhaps safe in the knowledge that no one would demand the course he offered

---

[1] Advertisement for 8 July 1736, in the *Daily Gazette*.
[2] *Hyp Doctor*, 13 July 1736.
[3] Such syllabus details will be found in the *Hyp Doctor* for 23 and 30 Nov., 14 and 21 Dec. 1736; 4 and 11 Jan., 10 May 1737.

—especially if he asked a prohibitive fee—he enjoyed the inventive thrill of offering a course for the 'Bibliothecarian' with an astounding range of bibliography, textual criticism, and library organization, or including, among a list of 215 possible subjects, such oddities as 'No. 184. Art of an Attic or Roman Night, call'd Deipposophy', or 'No. 199. Metallurgic, Typography, Gnomonic, Scenography, Isorropic, Biastic, Thereutic, Ixeutic, Halieutic, Cynegetic, etc. of the Antients and Moderns'.

Combined with this increasing incredibility of syllabus was a parallel development in the scale of fees.[1] The early plans might have attracted eager seekers after knowledge: the later fees were so high that one cannot believe even the richest ignoramus would pay them. The first proposal was a version of the subscription method much loved by Henley to obtain an immediate capital sum and an assured income. Each of his first fifty gentlemen students enrolling for a course of fifty-two lectures was to advance 10 guineas and, after ten lectures, a sum to be agreed for each lecture. For this sum the student could choose his course of study and the special sections of it, and was also given an Oratory silver medal (a gold if he deposited 20 guineas) which entitled him to free entry to all other Oratory activities. Certain special courses carried higher fees. Such 'Extraordinary Articles' as 'the Art of tracing the Devotionals and Practical Theology of the Age,—of Occult Philosophy, of Eminence for the greatest Employs, Views, and Professions; of Disputing, Debating &c. in public Assemblies' required an advance of not less than 100 guineas. A twenty-five hour Composition course was advertised at 100 guineas, a twenty-hour course on the Occult and Interdicted Knowedge cost the same, and for a similar large advance only ten hours of instruction on Debating and Disputing were offered. The 'Bibliothecarian' aspirant advanced 99 guineas for his hundred hours of varied lectures, while a better bargain was a mere 12 guineas for twelve hours of instruction 'to master any language whatsoever'. One can only hope that misprints were responsible for offering another course at 'M Guineas' and a course of 'Academical Literature for Ladies of Quality and Condition' in fifty hours at 'XM guineas'. Henley attended at the Oratory on weekdays at 11.0 and 6.0 o'clock, delivering his instruction, often

[1] The proposals are abstracted from the *Hyp Doctor* for 13 and 20 July, 24 Aug., 23 Nov., 21 and 28 Dec. 1736.

extempore, for an hour or sometimes two hours to the students, singly or in groups, prescribing reading for them, producing special courses by request for certain gentlemen such as a 'Course of Private Institutes on the Principles of Language and Philology,'[1] and exhibiting the progress of his elocution and rhetoric pupils by allowing them to display their accomplishments at the public proceedings of the Oratory.[2]

When Henley's own puffs are our only evidence, it is impossible to say what reality lay behind the claims of growth and success. We are told that the University grew with 'great Encouragement of several Gentlemen',[3] that there was a steady increase in the number of applications making it necessary for him to attend at the Oratory on Sundays to enroll pupils,[4] and that 'the Persons concerned in this Proper University are principally young noble-men, Gentlemen, Artists, Merchants and Members of Parliament.'[5] The sessions of the University were advertised as carrying on throughout 1736 and 1737. In 1741 we still hear that 'Institutes are daily here' and in addition to the daily 'Institutes for Gentlemen on the Principles of Universal Learning', courses in Anatomy and Experiments were being prepared;[6] but an advertisement for 2 January 1742 presents us with what seems more like a glimpse of the true facts. Gone are the complex schemes of advances and terms of 10 to 100 guineas: gone are the special arrangements for gentlemen. We read that 'Daily is held the Gentlemen's University for 1*s*. 6*d*. each at 10 in the Morning in private Institutes',[7] and this advertisement was repeated throughout 1742 and 1743, when a new table and chairs for the institutes were finished 'in the brightest manner[8]—an unspectacular but solid piece of evidence that something really did take place. The truth seems to be that behind the extravagant puffs of large numbers and genteel clientele, behind the fantastically elaborate syllabus and outrageously hopeful suggestions for fees, Henley did carry on a steady trade in popular education at a reasonable fee, and found, most probably amongst the apprentices and tradesmen, men deprived of formal education and eager for knowledge. The

[1] *Hyp Doctor*, 22 Mar. 1737.   [2] *Hyp Doctor*, 8 Mar. 1737.
[3] Advertisement for 23 July 1736, in the *Daily Gazette*.
[4] Advertisement for 13 Aug. 1736, in the *Daily Gazette*.
[5] *Hyp Doctor*, 24 Aug. 1736.
[6] Advertisement for 17 Oct. 1741 (Lysons 109).
[7] Advertisement for 1 Jan. 1743 (Lysons 114).
[8] Advertisement for 17 Dec. 1743, in the *Daily Gazette*.

general growth of debating societies and study groups in this period is evidence of this demand, as is also the establishment of a rival academy in 1742. An establishment calling itself the London University was set up in Exeter Change and advertised in much the same terms as Henley's. The charge was one shilling a meeting and promises were made of the engagement of a complete set of masters and the building of new schools by mid-summer. Henley attacked it furiously as 'the Wapping University set up by a broken Gazeteer, and Professor Teague teaching Arts and Sciences in his Mother Tongue',[1] and rejoiced when it closed by announcing that 'The Wapping University is buried at Execution Dock.'[2] His own University is buried in silence after 1743, no references to it appearing in any of his advertisements, and we cannot be certain how long he continued to digest and popularize knowledge for the group around his special table. In 1747 he came forward with new proposals, reminiscent of the first optimistic plans, but these strike one as unrealistic as the many other proposals for capital-raising which appeared in these later years.

I propose to 120 Gentlemen 52 Week-Days Institutes, one each Week, an Annual Course, or, perhaps, more each Week at half an Hour after Six, or at Seven in the Evening, at Two Guineas each the whole Course; One Guinea advanced, and the other at the 27th Institute: in the general Principles and Connexion of Universal Learning, Arts and Sciences: and at the end of each Institute, a Lesson in the Grammar of Universal Wit, for the Readiest, Brightest, Happiest Command and Application of Good Sense and Learning on all Occasions, never taught before: with Examples on each Head.[3]

There is something brave as well as sad in Henley's persisting in these grandiose proposals when, in reality, if his educational work still continued at all, he was most likely only gathering his 1s. 6d.s from the few who came, ignorant and eager for information, to hear such potted histories and popular digests which the few remaining manuscripts of his academical orations suggest were the basic fare offered.[4]

---

[1] Advertisement for 12 June 1742 (Lysons 112).
[2] Advertisement for 26 June 1742 (ibid.)
[3] Advertisement for 28 Feb. 1747 (Lysons 146).
[4] Examples of these lectures are contained in B.M. MSS.Add. 19,925.

There remains another activity at the Oratory to consider, differing from the others in one outstanding feature—that other voices than Henley's were heard in its pursuit, heard, that is, officially and with permission, for many other voices, as we shall discover, were heard over the years, uninvited and unwelcome. This activity consisted of conferences and disputations which were part of the Oratory proceedings from the start, and for which Henley laid down rules in an early plan.[1] The conferences took place after every lecture and sermon and their subject was to be one arising from the topic of the previous discourse, the aim being 'to search the truth of one single proposition, by a mutual free communication of sentiments in an amicable manner'. The participants, never more than twelve in number, sat at a table, with the rest of the congregation as silent audience. The theme was proposed, its terms agreed and explained, and discussion followed under the very strict rules of procedure enforced by the Moderator, the aim being not 'contention for victory, decision or malice, but truth only'. Each member of the conference expressed his views and opinions which were examined and debated, queries, doubts and difficulties being resolved or minuted for further discussion. Over all this debate presided the Moderator, whose power it was to limit the time of speakers and 'to see, that the proposition be stated, the precise meaning of each word clear'd, to call for, and minute down, the opinions, queries, reasonings &c of those who confer: recapitulate the force or sum of the arguments alleg'd, execute the laws of the conference, . . . assisting at it, with the rest'. It is quite clear that, even when he allowed other voices in his Oratory, Henley made sure that his would not be drowned and that his word would be the last. The disputation differed from the conference in that only two debaters took part, with Henley again as the Moderator. The debaters stood in the special rostra while Henley, having descended from the pulpit, sat in judgement in the reading desk below it.[2] The subject for disputation had been advertised and the debaters came prepared to dispute under the same strict rules, the question being stated, the respondent proposing his thesis, the opponent arguing in

[1] These rules, on which this account is based, are contained in *The Laws of the Conferences of the Oratory* and *The Laws for the Disputations of the Oratory*, and are printed in *Oratory Transactions No. 1*.

[2] Advertisement for 3 June 1727 (Lysons 13) and for 17 June 1727, in the *London Journal*.

reply. Then, after a review by the Moderator, the opponent proposed his thesis, the respondent argued against it, the Moderator
again reviewed the argument to date, and the respondent was
here allowed the last word in his 'conclusive Address to the
Moderator, the Opponent, and the Auditors'. The last were
required to keep strict order and silence on pain of forfeiting their
places, although there is evidence—not, admittedly, friendly—to
show that their performance often failed to live up to the ideal
plan Henley described, and that a growing tendency for the
auditory to keep anything but the desired silence and strict order
was responsible for the ultimate abandonment of these disputations. The conferences are never advertised, but a note that
'they who take Seats are free to the Sunday Evening's Conferences
and Disputations'[1] suggests that they were a regular feature and
still continuing in 1735. The disputations continued to be advertised until 1742, and they covered a curious variety of religious,
political, and general topics—'That Motion is essential to Matter';[2] 'a gentleman will be ready to dispute on Gormogonism';[3]
'on the uninterrupted Succession';[4] 'Whether the 39 articles be
defensible'[5] (only twenty could have been covered, for the
following week the last nineteen were set down for discussion);
'Whether Law and Prejudice apart, the Story of the Nativity,
be true';[6] 'Whether the Morality of the Sermon on the Mount
be as superb as it is boasted';[7] 'on the Cheat of a Foreign Land
War to enrich some on Pretence of helping Austria, the Dutch
&c.';[8] 'a Deist the only Christian';[9] 'Whether an Act of Parliament may not be against Law, and the Remedy'.[10] Sometimes,
especially in the early years, the disputant was known and advertised, such as Mr. Marcus, a converted Jew, who disputed on the
Messiah, and whether the Jews were bound to believe in Christ.[11]
We hear of Augustin Poyntz disputing with Henley on whether

[1] Advertisement for 25 July 1730 (Lysons 45).
[2] Advertisement for 17 Feb. 1728 (Lysons 19).
[3] Advertisement for 13 June 1730 (Lysons 45).
[4] Advertisement for 29 Aug. 1730 (Lysons 47).
[5] Advertisement for 28 Nov. 1741 (Lysons 110).
[6] Advertisement for 19 Dec. 1741 (ibid.).
[7] Advertisement for 30 Jan. 1742 (Lysons 111).
[8] Advertisement for 20 Feb. 1742 (ibid.).
[9] Advertisement for 11 Dec. 1742 (Lysons 114).
[10] Advertisement for 8 Jan. 1743 (ibid.).
[11] Advertisement for 18 Nov. 1727 (Lysons 17).

the marriage of cousins-german be lawful,[1] of three Quaker men and one woman disputing whether Quaker women have a Gospel-call to preach,[2] and of a reverend clergyman who came 80 miles from the country to take part.[3] Anonymous gentlemen and others hiding behind such names as 'Generosus', 'Philalethes', and 'Philanthropos' are reported as sustaining 'learned and Nervous Arguments'. Often eminent men were challenged to appear in disputation to defend their case and to confute Henley's position, though there is no evidence to show that any of them took up the challenge and prevented the proposed disputation from being anything but a victorious monologue by Henley. By the late '30s, however, there are signs that all is not well. In a *Hyp Doctor* report of 1 February 1737, of the last disputation held, there is the note that 'only the Argumentative Part of the Subject is to be spoken to, by such only, as shall be advertised, and no others shall be then answered',[4] and at the end of the same year he saw fit to reprint at length in the *Hyp Doctor* the original laws for the disputations of the Oratory with their stress on orderly procedure.[5] Things appear not to have improved for, in 1742, he advertised: 'Then Questions not for Public Disputation (which shall never be permitted here in promiscuous Congregation, but particular ones only)';[6] and in the following week, 'Note. No public Disputations are allowed, nor speaking to the Preacher.'[7] The suspicion that these disputations were degenerating into noisy arguments, and that audience participation was spreading beyond the rostra, is confirmed by the repeated warnings given in advertisements throughout 1742 and 1743 on the penalties for interruption, noise, and misbehaviour. After this we only find offered 'An Argument (no other speaking or Questions answered)' and for the rest of the Oratory's existence there is complete silence about disputations. Henley had apparently decided, as the Oratory entered into the stormier waters of its later years, that the early vision of seeking the truth through free discussion was no longer attainable. Comment, question, and interruption came fast enough without any

[1] *Hyp Doctor*, 1 Oct. 1734.   [2] *Hyp Doctor*, 22 July 1735.
[3] *Hyp Doctor*, 24 Feb. 1736.   [4] *Hyp Doctor*, 1 Feb. 1737.
[5] *Hyp Doctor*, 20 Dec. 1737.
[6] Advertisement for 20 Mar. 1742 (Lysons 111).
[7] Advertisement for 27 Mar. 1742 (ibid.).

encouragement, and it was safer that one voice only, and that voice the Orator's, should discourse, expound, and argue.

Such, then, was the busy life of the Oratory throughout the thirty years of its existence, a continuous activity of services and sermons, discourses and disputations, lectures and a variety of educational endeavour, all of them borne on the shoulders of Henley himself with very little help from others. His days and much of his nights must have been given over to performing in the Oratory or preparing for those performances. Whatever else might be said of him, no one could deny the energy and the industry and the perseverance of the man. Whatever money he made at the Oratory he most certainly earned, and the boast he put into the mouth of the supposed author of the *Narrative* in 1728 was one he could have made with even more justification at the end of his career:

But that he should have the Assurance to frame a Plan, which no Mortal ever thought of; that he should singly execute what would sprain a Dozen modern Doctors of the Tribe of *Issachar*; that he should have Success against all Opposition; challenge his Adversaries to fair Disputations, without any Offering to dispute with him; write, read and study Twelve Hours a Day, and yet appear as untouched by the Yoke, as if he never wore it; compose Three Dissertations each Week, on all Subjects, however uncommon, treated in all Lights and Manners by himself, without Assistance, as some would detract from him; teach in one Year, what Schools and Universities teach in Five; offer to learn —to speak and to read; not to be terrify'd by Cabals, or Menaces, or Insults, or the grave Nonsense of one, or the frothy Satyr of another; that he should still proceed, and mature this bold Scheme, and put the Ch––– and all that, in Danger;

This man must be a — a — a — a — &c. A Complication of all the Names that were ever furnish'd by the *splendida Bilis*: He can have no good Disposition, he DOES ALL for Lucre, while some DO NO-THING for it.[1]

The chronicle of all this activity has been made in as unbiased a way as possible, casting doubt now and again on the factual existence or realized performance of some of it, but on the whole accepting for its material Henley's proposals and claims. It is time now to turn over the Oratory medal and see the other side,

[1] *Narrative*, p. 15.

the image presented by the host of enemies and mockers who assaulted Henley and his works year in, year out. Perhaps somewhere between the ideal image and the distortion, the truth may be detected.

CHAPTER VI

The Assault on the Oratory

THE FIRST ORATORY in Newport Market had hardly opened its doors before the attack started, and Henley and his performances became the talk of the town. A member of that first congregation on 3 July 1726 saw fit to publish his shocked reactions, and establish the tone and some of the lines of attack taken by all Henley's detractors through the next three decades.

The whole Performance on *July* 3 [he wrote] both Morning and Afternoon was ridiculous: The Reader's Performance excepted, who for the Lesson chosen *1 John ii* when the Apostle speaks of the Antichrists which should start up in these latter Days; for there was a dull Clark, and an over-active theatrical Preacher. This produced a sneering and laughing. And to say no more, the Place was more like a Theatre than a place of worship.[1]

The suitably named newspaper the *Censor* took up the attack the following month by publishing a letter from another shocked eye-witness who had rushed straight from the Oratory to his desk to record his own feelings and the opinions of the town:

Dear Sir, I do not question but you have heard of the *Oratorians,* a Sect newly set up by one Mr. *Henley,* who assumes the name of *Orator.* The several Advertisements he has publish'd cannot surely have escap'd your Notice; which, with the general Discourse of the Town concerning him, has occasion'd my making a very scrutinous Enquiry of the Man's Character, and particularly the Doctrines he exhibits; both which I find so disagreeable to my own Sentiments and Manner of Thinking, as well as to the Thoughts and Opinions of a great many well-dispos'd Minds of my Acquaintance. . . . The Notions of the Populace concerning him are various: Is he crazy, say some? Others cry him up as a Man of good Sense and Parts: Many call him a *Papist,* or, what is worse, an *Independent,* and of no Religion at all; and not a few of that abominable Sect call'd *Socinians.* For my part I think him a very mercenary Man, a mere Simonist! and withal an imitator of a Mountebank; I say, an Imitator of that despicable Animal, for he can

[1] *A Letter to the Rev. Mr. John Henley etc.,* p. 19.

never pretend to come up to him either in Pronunciation or Gesture; but I cannot allow Mr. *Henley* to be an Orator, no, nor a Mountebank. It is certain that he has many Followers, and even some of note. . . . I had the Curiosity last Week to hear him Preach, and repeat his Lectures, as he calls them, and was so fir'd with Zeal at the Impudence of the Man, that I could scarce forbear discovering my Indignation against him, and acting the Censor's Part in the Assembly.[1]

Many others could not, even at this early stage, forbear discovering their indignation, and their vehemence is surprising when, as far as we can discover, Henley's orations were as yet not excessively unorthodox in content or manner. The reasons for attack are various. Henley is a heretic or at least a sectarian; he is profane and ribald; impudent in his pretensions; theatrical in his gestures; mercenary in his motives. Very few voices were raised publicly in his defence. A gentleman signing himself Tim Shallow rebuked the *Craftsman* for publishing a letter attacking one of Henley's lectures on Horace, asserting that this was a misrepresentation and misreporting of what was in fact an 'ingenious entertainment';[2] and the *Censor* had the fairness to print a communication from 'a gentleman who was pleas'd to call himself an *Henleyarian*' who had written to say

That, among others, the *Censor* had writ against the famous Orator, who, instead of being censur'd, deserv'd the Admiration of the whole World, for his Parts and Goodness: That it was nothing but Envy made People speak against him, because he gets more money than other Preachers, for, tho' the least Place in any of his Pews is paid for no less than one Shilling, yet there are Hundreds at a Time, who are oblig'd, much to their Sorrow, to go back for want of Room.[3]

These were but straws against the wind. The weather for the most part was set foul and never shifted from that quarter. The *Historical Register* for 1726, recognizing Henley already as a necessary figure to chronicle as part of the times, embodied the hostility which subsequent history was to endorse and embellish. In the midst of its inaccurate and destructive report of his doings it asserted:

The Place Mr. *Henley* pitch'd upon for his Oratory, is very remarkable, and befitting his Noble Institution; being a sort of *Wooden Booth*, built

---

[1] *Censor*, 10 Aug. 1726.   [2] *Craftsman*, 2 Jan. 1727.
[3] *Censor*, 16 Nov. 1726.

over the Shambles in *Newport Market*, near *Leicester* Fields, formerly used for a temporary Meeting-House for a *Calvinistical* Congregation: So that the *British* World may expect excellent Fruit from latent *Arianism*, grafted upon a *Geneva* Stock![1]

Wrong as the *Register* may have been in its doctrinal pedigree, it prophesied truly of the continued interest of the British World in the fruits of the Oratory, an interest intent on proving the fruit rotten or more actively trying to destroy the tree.

The sources and methods of the attack are various, and many of them, in print or action, are available or chronicled. The enemies are sometimes known—as Whiston, or Pope, or Smart—or they are anonymous outraged gentlemen eager to defend the Church, the Universities, Decency, and Reverence. But in addition to this mass of open assault and avowed opponents, Henley continually complained of more insidious undermining of his reputation and the machinations of secret enemies against him. The cats-paws of these secret enemies may have seemed wretched enough—'a French Quack in Orange Street, an Apothecary who has been fined £100 on the Gin-Act and Mad Browne, who has taken the Benefit of the Insolvent Debtors' Act, and came to Mr. Henley to ask Charity',[2] or 'one A. O. Anonymous [who] has, with some other of his Gang, us'd his weak Endeavours to misrepresent and defame me in scurrilous, inhumane verses and reflections, incog, that is, robbing and ponyarding with a vizard and a dark lanthorn'.[3] But Henley repeatedly asserted that they were the tools of an eminent foe, above all his old enemy Gibson, Bishop of London. In 1737 he wrote:

I can authentically prove that a perfidious Pr———e has said, that *he had rather answer me clandestinely than openly, and that he lik'd what expos'd me,* AND I can prove, that he sent Advertisements with Money to revile me. . . . I exhort all rational and brave Minds to concur as one Man for Liberty, wherewith Christ has made us free, and I will, at any Crisis, head them with Resolution and success, tho' at the mouth of a Cannon, or what is worse, the Conscience of such a Pr———e.[4]

In the same year, using his favourite nickname for Gibson, he repeated his accusation and defiance—

---

[1] *Historical Register* (for 1726), vol. xi, no. xliii, p. 242.
[2] Advertisement for 5 Nov. 1737, in the *London Post.*
[3] *London Daily Post*, 5 Nov. 1737.   [4] Ibid.

The Means and Agents used by Dr. Codex being apparently calculated
to mob and assassinate Mr. H. for unmasking his pernicious Principles,
makes himself the Author of the like on all his Rank, Clergy, Ministers,
their Families and People. See Genesis 9. But he has to do with a man
that will, on proper occasion, Preach, Talk, Dispute, Write and fight
him for the Governement.[1]

This conviction that Gibson was behind so much of the persecution was almost obsessive. Years later he recalled together Gibson's
first alleged betrayal of preferment promises and his continued
underground attack. He was betrayed

originally, by the Implements and Tools of One, who first gave Occasion to it, by cruel perfidious Usage of the Author, which alarmed him
to examine, whether his Principles might not be like his Actions; and
who since, declar'd, to some, that disputed in the Oratory, that he
would take other Methods, than Disputing, more private Methods:
This has been done, by all clandestine Artifices of traversing the
Author, of conveying Whispers, Accusations, Calumnies, and private
letters to Ministers of State . . .[2]

Whatever the part played by Gibson or other great enemies in
all this, it seems clear that when we consider the mass of published and open attack, fair and unfair, which brought Henley
under continuous nervous strain, and produced increasing
frustration and fury, we must also take into our consideration
this equally continuous but more insidious persecution which
made him feel a man spied upon, misrepresented, and misreported,
the subject of false rumours and scandals, and whenever possible
thwarted in his attempts to communicate his ideas and beliefs.
In 1731 the authors of the *Grub Street Journal* openly admitted
that they had 'spoken to Mr. WESTON to take his trumpery

---

[1] *London Daily Post*, 19 Dec. 1737.
[2] *Sermon II*, p. 39, in *The Oratory Magazine no. III.* Henley's suspicions are not
entirely unfounded, although the extent of Gibson's activities against him might not
have been so great as he thought. There exists a letter of 8 Sept. 1726 from Gibson
to Lord Townshend, informing him that the Oratory was not barred on its outer
doors, but effectively guarded at its inner door, and therefore possibly in violation
of the Toleration Act. He expressed a dread that 'if Henley were able to carry his
point in the metropolis of the Kingdom', there might be too soon 'a Henley in
every diocese'. He suggested that the Oratory was supported by 'persons who meant
ill to the constitution of the Church', and asserted that the Toleration Act would
become 'the abhorrence of the clergy and the cry of "the danger of the Church"
be revived' if Henley's activities were not curbed. (Correspondence of the First
Lord Hardwicke, B.M. Add.MS. 36136, No. 63.)

down in short-hand, to be printed at length, in order to convince his few remaining auditors of their folly',[1] and this activity of what Henley calls 'sermon-trappers' was still going on years later. In 1748 he complained of allegations in a paper which was being handed about town containing extracts from his sermons with destructive comments, and defended himself on many grounds, including accusing the reporter of being too drunk to understand him.[2] An advertisement of 1751—one of a stream of such—captures the feeling of plot and counterplot and unsavoury back-street politics, involving incidents we cannot understand and people we shall never identify, which weave this web of contention:

What Wretches its Enemies are, take this Specimen (besides a late most scandalous Case): Two or three of them were sharping Confederates in a Lie, Cheat, Compound Robbery, Perjury, Forgery, Sacrilege, and the most unnatural Cannibalism to their own Countrymen and Religion: by a false Administration, false Sale of near 3000£ Stocks, Fraud and Plunder on the Dead, and Executors, stifling a Will: a Warrant was out to take one, who absconds: while another inflames a Coffee-House Cabal (the old Bite) against me. As to the Moorfields Ribband-Weaver, he is warp'd, and I'll thrum him.[3]

With all this plotting and scandal below the surface, and with all the open assault which we are about to explore, little wonder that Henley's words on the degeneracy of the times should sound with intense personal feeling:

We are fallen into the dregs of an age when scandal is mechanical, and overflows all ranks of men like a deluge: when the most innocent, and best deserving are obnoxious to be represented as the most criminal and worthless, by artful malice, and popular falsehood, when the keen darts of obloquy are yet more sharpen'd by the CRAFT of men lying in wait to deceive, by the rage and views of party, by the rancour of resentment, and the fury of passion, by study'd rumours, and cunning suggestions, by treacherous whispers, insidious hints, and perfidious insinuations; when a reported or a written piece of ill-fame clandestinely convey'd, and unmerited, will suddenly and almost irretrievably poison the hearts, engross the conversation, and settle the aversion of the unknowing and the undetermin'd, much more of the prepossess'd

[1] G.S.J., 24 June 1731.
[2] The Victorious Stroke for Old England, p. 8.
[3] Advertisement for 28 June 1751 (Lysons 169).

2. Reynard turn'd parson

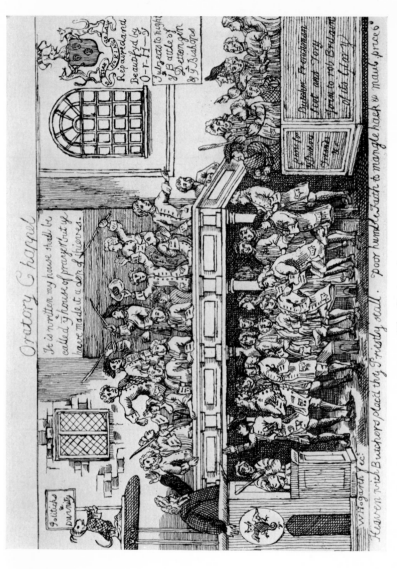

3. The Oratory in uproar

and the partial, ready to believe the worst, when none knew the motive, the circumstance, the persons, the quarter, from whence the scandal issu'd . . .[1]

He might well, as he preached, have been thinking how such 'artful malice and popular falsehood' had resulted in something far from secret and insidious—the first official action against him of the Government's censorship machinery, and of the time when enemies had engineered his presentation by a Grand Jury of the City and Liberty of Westminster.

On 8 February 1728, the town read in the newspapers that 'Thursday Morning Mr. John Henley was taken into Custody of one of his Majesty's Messengers, by Virtue of a Warrant from the Lord Viscount Townshend, Secretary of State; and he has been bound over to appear at the King's-Bench Bar at Westminster.'[2] The *Craftsman* gave the additional information that his offence was 'his Advertisement in the Daily Post of Wednesday last'.[3] The Government censors had obviously seen grounds for suspecting that seditious libel was afoot and the usual machinery of issuing a warrant for the arrest of the offender pending investigation had been put in motion. Henley did not, however, suffer the law's delays which so often ruined the livelihood of such offenders even when no penalty was ultimately imposed. On 9 February, the day after his arrest, Mr. Cracherode wrote to Charles Delafaye, the Secret Service man involved in the case, to say that he had inquired into the question of bail for John Henley, Clerk, of St. Andrews, Holborn, and approved it. Joseph Booth, a corn chandler of Russell Street, Bloomsbury, and Simon Henley, an apothecary of Holborn both stood bail £100 apiece, and Henley was released.[4] Returning home after his short stay in custody, he immediately set pen to paper and dispatched a letter in humble tones to Lord Townshend:

My Lord,
            My Bail is approv'd, & certify'd by Mr. Cracherode, & I humbly beg that your Lordship would do me ye honour to appoint what Hour this afternoon or Evening I may have ye Favour to attend your Lordship with my Bail.

---

[1] Henley, *The Sermon that shou'd have been preach'd before the Societies for the Reformation of manners* (1732), p. 9.
[2] *London Journal*, 8 Feb. 1728.   [3] *Craftsman*, 10 Feb. 1728.
[4] P.R.O., S.P. Domestic 36/5/100.

> I am, My Lord,
> Your Lordship's
> Most Faithful, &
> Most Dutifull Servant,
> J. Henley.[1]

One presumes that at that interview he not only discussed his bail but personally explained his innocence, as he did publicly in his next advertisement for the Oratory, 'N.B. The short Expressions of a late Advertisement in the Daily Post have created a wrong Interpretation of its meaning',[2] for in the next piece of evidence in his case it appears that Lord Townshend had received him favourably. On 11 June 1728, Henley wrote to the Duke of Newcastle:

> May it please your Grace,
>   I humbly ask your Graces pardon, if I surprize you with ye freedom I now take in begging one kind Word from your Grace to my Lord Townshend, in that ye Encouragement his Lordship has given me to hope my Appearance this next term shall be discharg'd, may take effect?
>   Your Graces Protection of Liberty, & the Happy Day of his Majesty's Accession, will, I hope, plead my Excuse for this Application.
> I am,
> My Lord
> Your Grace's
> Most Devoted, &
> Most faithful Servant,
> J. Henley.[3]

Either the humble application had its effect or that desired effect might have come anyway without Henley's intervention. The necessary fright and warning had been given, and Henley knew he was now being watched. When, on Thursday 28 November, on the last day of term, 'several Persons appeared in the Court of King's Bench upon their Recognizances, for Printing and Publishing Seditious Libels, and for other Misdemeanours', we read that in this end-of-term clearing-up, 'Mr. Orator Henley appeared upon his Recognizances, and was discharged.'[4] This

---

[1] P.R.O., S.P. Domestic 36/5/101. The letter is unaddressed.
[2] Advertisement for 17 Feb. 1728 (Lyson 19).
[3] P.R.O., S.P. Domestic 36/7/23.
[4] Advertisement for 30 Nov. 1728 (Lysons 27).

incident was closed with little more than inconvenience suffered, but Henley had only a few months' respite, before, from another quarter, another attack was mounted.

The Presentation by the Grand Jury of the County of Middlesex, in January 1729, was the climax, according to Henley, of a conspiracy headed by 'That Able Divine, Eminent Lawyer, and Honest Politician, Mr. H——s, and his Disciples',[1] and although our only witness, Henley himself, is necessarily an interested party, it certainly appears that underhand and questionable means had been used to find a pretext and ensure a case against him. Mr. H——s had first set spies to work who were then to act as informers to the Jury.

A Tall and a little Man [wrote Henley] came in Masquerade-Habits, to the ORATORY; by the Negligence of my Servants, while I was in the *Rostra*, without my Knowledge, or Consent, a Tall and a Little Man inform'd, upon Oath, against it, about Masquerading: Mr. *Huggins*, with one *Hopkins*, said to be of the *Fleet*, and Others, and a Letter-Carrier, (who was the Chief Informer, and being a Man of Letters, an able Judge of the ORATORY,) manag'd this Presentment.

One of the accusations, as we shall see, turned very much on this presence of people in masquerade at the Oratory, and Henley denied that there were ever more than two, and these two, he asserted, were playing the double role of planted evidence and informers—'Two came, and no more, perhaps they were the Informers; who sent them? And why?' Clearly it was the chief plotter, 'Mr. H——s, who though one of my Judges, acted as a Sollicitor, and as a private Justice in this Matter'. He not only planted the informers, but interfered in the proper conduct of the Jury's proceedings and 'swore these witnesses, not before the Court, but in another Place, where the Court was not sitting'. The Jury does not appear to have been too certain or happy about the situation. 'Some, who own'd they could not present me, on their personal Knowledge, said they were influenc'd to take the Information of Two Witnesses . . . some were told it was their Duty to present; that some averr'd, they were drawn in; that many of them, after signing it, declar'd, this could not affect the Doctor.' For all this uncertainty and unwillingness,

---

[1] *Milk for Babes*, the title-page. All Henley's other allegations on this affair come from this pamphlet.

with Henley not allowed to be heard and to defend himself, and without inquiring further than the allegations of the witnesses, the Grand Jury found a true bill against Henley and signed a Presentment on 9 January 1729. The court, after due consideration, ordered the Presentment to be printed and published in one or more of the public newspapers, and, on 18 January it duly appeared:

Whereas the Act made in the first Year of the Reign of King William and Queen Mary, for exempting their Majesties Protestant Subjects dissenting from the Church of England from the Penalties of Certain Laws, was wisely designed as an Indulgence for the tender and scrupulous Consciences of such Dissenters, and as a Means to unite all the Protestant Subjects in Interest and Affection. And whereas it is notorious that John Henley, Clerk, in Priest's Orders, according to the Form of the Church of England, did about three Years since hire a large Room over the Market-House in Newport-Market, within this City and Liberty of Westminster, and cause the said Room to be registered in the Court of the Archdeacon of Middlesex (pursuant to the said Act of Toleration) as a Place for Religious Worship to be performed therein by him the said John Henley, who pretended to dissent from the Church of England on Account of Infant Baptism (although that had been the least of his Exercises, nor are his Audiences of that Persuasion) and by his Advertisements in the publick News Papers, invited all Persons to come thither and take Seats for Twelve Pence apiece, promising them Diversions under the Titles of *Voluntaries, Chimes of the Times, Roundelays, College Bobs, Madrigals and Operas, &c.* And whereas it appears to us by Information upon Oath, that the said John Henley, notwithstanding his profess'd Dissention and Separation from the Church of England, has usually appear'd in the Habit worn by Priests of the Church of England, and in that Habit has for several Months past, upon one or more Days in the Week, made use of the said Room for purposes very different from those of Religious Worship; and that he has there discoursed on several Subjects of Burlesque and Ridicule; and therein, and in his Comments upon the publick News Papers, and in his weekly Advertisements, has uttered several indecent, libertine and obscene Expressions, and made many base and malicious Reflections upon the Established Churches of England and Scotland, upon the Convocation, and almost all Orders and Degrees of Men; and upon particular Persons by Name, and even those of the highest Rank. And whereas it appears to us more particularly by Information upon Oath, that he the said John Henley did on the 12th. Day of December last, cause to be published in the Daily Post an Advertisement, giving

Notice that on the Evening of the next Day he would pronounce *King Lear's Oration in an Apology for Madness*, on which Evening he did in the said Room, (called by him the Oratory) in the Habit of a Clergyman of the Church of England, repeat a Speech out of the Tragedy of King Lear, acting in such Manner and with such Gestures as are practised in the Theatres. And that the said John Henley did on the Seventeenth Day of the same Month cause to be published in the said Daily Post another Advertisement, inviting such as went the following Evening to the Ball in the Hay-Market, to come first to his said Room in their Habits and Masques for Twelve Pence apiece; and that according to such Invitation, several Persons so dress'd and masqu'd did then and there appear, and were admitted upon their paying the said Monies for their Seats.

We the Grand Jury for the City and Liberty of Westminster, conceiving that this Behaviour of the said John Henley is contrary to the Intention of the said Act of Toleration, and tends to bring a Disrepute upon the Indulgence so charitably granted to truly scrupulous Dissenters, that it gives great Offence to all serious Christians, is an Outrage upon civil Society, and of dangerous Consequence to the State, and particularly, that the said Assemblies by him held as aforesaid, are unlawful ones, his said Room not being licens'd for Plays, Interludes, or Masquerades, do present the said John Henley, and his Accomplices and Assistants to us unknown, as guilty of unlawful Assemblies, Routs and Riots, committed the 13th. Day of December last, and on the 18th. Day of the said Month of December, and on the first Day of this Instant January, by him and his Assistants, being so unlawfully assembled for the unlawful Purposes aforesaid, to the Number of Fifty on each of the said Days and Times, against the Peace of our Sovereign Lord the King, his Crown and Dignity; and pray this Court to cause proper Proceedings to be had in order to bring to Punishment the said John Henley and his Accomplices by due Course of Law. Dated this Ninth Day of January 1728–9.

Wm. Pickering,

Stephen Whitaker,	Samuel Hatton,
Thomas Powell,	Thomas Henwood,
Matthew Raynold,	Thomas Daniel,
Richard Cobbett,	John Ellis,
Ja. Whitfield,	Robert Bowie,
Rob. Aunger,	John Wilkins,
John Richardson,	Charles Benn,
Michael Hanet,	Samuel Margat,
James Hall,	James Gibson,
Benjamin Timbrell,	Thomas Webb.

The justices appear to have thought that the publication of the Presentment was severe enough action to take, a way of bringing Henley's goings-on into public disrepute and possibly deterring future visitors to the Oratory. There is no record of any further proceedings and, after the publication, the newspapers for 1729 are silent about the matter.[1] Not so Henley. On the same day as the publication of the Presentment he informed his readers that 'My Answer to the Westminster Presentment is in the Press, which will clearly vindicate me from the Infamy design'd me by it in every Article.'[2] It was not in fact until August that his answer was published, with the title *Milk for Babes: or a Hornbook for That Able Divine, Eminent Lawyer, and Honest Politician, Mr. H———s, and his Disciples: by way of Answer to his Godly and Conscientious* SCRUPLES *relating to the* ORATORY, in which he answered the accusations head by head, and exposed the unsavoury and suspicious nature of the participants and the methods which he alleged had led up to the Presentment. After this, he never returned to the fray. Perhaps he was not entirely sorry about the affair, if there is any truth in a report in the *London Evening Post* for 23/5 January in 1729: 'We hear that the Reputation of Mr. Henley's Discourses and the Number of his Assemblies is encreas'd by the late Bug-bear, designed only in pure Malice, by Artful Lies and Calumnies, to thin his Oratory.'

No sooner had Henley escaped from or beaten down one attacker, than another sprang up to take his place. When Government censorship and Grand Jury had been safely overcome, a vicious and persistent literary enemy took their place. In 1730 the first copy of the *Grub Street Journal* was offered to the town and for the next seven years was to prosecute its avowed intention of extending the destruction of Dulness and Dunces initiated in Pope's *Dunciad*. In prose and verse it ran with great dispute through all

---

[1] The Presentment was printed in the *Weekly Journal or the British Gazetteer* for 18 Jan. 1729, and in *Applebee's Original Weekly Journal* for the same day. A fairly extensive search among surviving records of the Westminster Sessions and the Middlesex Sessions confirms the opinion expressed by W. J. Hardy and W. Le Hardy in their *Middlesex County Records, Reports* (1928), pp. 64–5, that 'The action of the court thereon is somewhat remarkable, as there is no record that they ordered the arrest of Henley and his friends, but they ordered that the presentment "be printed and published in one or more of the public newspapers".' The original order has not survived.

[2] Advertisement for 18 Jan. 1729 (Lysons 29).

the realms of nonsense, were they literary shoddiness, news-reporters' inaccuracy, medical quackery, or political chicanery. Purporting to emanate from a Society of Dunces resident in Grub Street, it ironically welcomed to the Club all true aspirants to Dulness, to inscribe them in the great roll of Dunces which Pope had started to compile. Small wonder that Henley, who had appeared prominently in that original, should soon receive its unwelcome attention. In the 62nd number on 11 March 1731, came the first attack in an essay on Impudence, with Henley figuring as the one great example, and from then onwards he was a regular victim. From 1731 to 1734 hardly a month went by without some note or verse mocking and insulting him, and many a month he received a weekly stab. From 1735 onwards, for some reason, he escaped more lightly though he was never quite forgotten, and after too long a gap in the offensive the *Journal* regretted 'Having too long neglected our learned Brother the *Puffing* Orator' and returned to the task. This steady outpouring of mockery and distortion must have been a sore and irritating thorn in Henley's flesh, as he waited, Thursday by Thursday, to read the new scandal, and prepare his replies for his own paper, the *Hyp Doctor*[1], which appeared each following Tuesday. No side of his many activities escaped attention, and his past as well as his present was raked over for scandal. As grammarian, poet, Grub Street hack, preacher, heretic, he was presented as a demented Dunce and upstart ignoramus. A typical verse satire continues Pope's line of attack, and even echoes it:

> 'Tis not the Champion's voice, or limbs or mien,
> That makes him terrible, when heard or seen,
> But 'tis the sacred place, in which he stands,
> Alternate brandishing his holy hands;
> The shining Altar, and the gilded Tub,
> That hoarsely loud resounds with mystic dub:
> These strike at once my wand'ring eyes and ears,
> And fill my mind with superstitious fears.[2]

and there are many more examples of this very general and all-inclusive satire. In doggerel:

> If for writing profanely, or lewdly, or nonsense,
> With no regard to truth, to honour, or conscience;

[1] For a full discussion of the *Hyp Doctor*, see Chapter VII, pt. iii, below.
[2] *G.S.J.*, 13 Apr. 1732.

If for opening a shop of Oratory pragmatical,
To rail at all bishops in English ungrammatical;
To draw an assembly of wise-acres, from many,
Who have lost their religion, or never had any:
If for pirating copies, or title pages new-vamping,
And the first sole edition with third or fourth stamping;
With long-winded puff and fallacious advertisement,
On the public imposing a general excitement. . . .[1]

In prose:

The butchers of Newport-market had more courage; which soon almost entirely extinguished the remainder of his, they being as hard riders as the booksellers. But hoping to meet with a more civilized sort of them, he removed to a new Stable near Clare-Market; where he had recourse to a Quack DOCTOR; who, instead of repairing his broken constitution, has rendered him quite incapable of local motion. So that there he stands, moving only his head and fore-feet, with great variety of action; and is shown twice a week to all comers for sixpence apiece. And indeed, it must be owned, that the sight for once is worth the money: for tho' he is a battered, spavined, foundered, glandered, broken-winded horse; yet he has a bold, undaunted look, and appears as MILTON describes SATAN, *Majestic though in ruin.*[2]

Or in parody:

This day is published,
A new operatical, Comical, Farcical Entertainment in Grotesque Characters; entitled, the BULL-BEEF ORATOR; or REYNARD turn'd PARSON; with the Comical *Monkey-tricks* of his *Man* AMEN Clark and *Cashier* to the *Oratory—Ingredere ut proficias—*All in, all in—*Inveniam locum aut faciam—*Pray *Gentlemen.* sit close—*Silence! When the* Fox *preaches let the* GEESE *look to themselves—*PRIESTS *of all* RELI-GIONS *are the same.*—DRYDEN for that. Hen––y and *Reynard* piss in a Quill—the Difference where? In Stock only—Hen—y's trans-actions at 10*s.*—if you'll credit the Papers; *Reynard's* no *Church Bubble,* no *rising Stock—*Not to be bought in *Change Alley—*or *Lincoln's Inn Fields—*but at the *White Hart* over-against Devereux Court without Temple-Bar, at the modest price of 6*d.* Which will be a perpetual Ticket all the year round.
    N.B. The *Picture* is very like the MAN.
            With *brazen Front* and *Ignorance,*
                I *preach*—I *pray*—I *cant*
            'Tis not your SOULS that I regard,
                Your CASH is all I want.[3]

---

[1] *G.S.J.*, 27 Dec. 1733.   [2] *G.S.J.*, 9 Nov. 1732.   [3] *G.S.J.*, 8 July 1731.

When all else failed to inspire the invention of the Grub Street satirists, Henley's advertisements and puffs were a constant stand-by. As we have seen, Henley developed this common form of exciting public curiosity to a fine art, keeping his name always on the lips of the town, and the *Journal* grudgingly acknowledged this:

The first, from the length of time in which he has exercised the art, and from the number and nature of his *puffs*, justly deserves the title of PUFFERUS PRIMUS. It is now many years since he first endeavoured to preach, and write, and *puff* himself into preferment. But failing of success, he set up a new institution about nine years ago, which he has endeavoured to support chiefly by advertising and *puffing*. During which whole time, there has not passed a week in which he has not published several recommendations of himself and his labours: either exhibiting a bill of fare, or boasting of the number and quality of his guests, or challenging and defying his adversaries, &c. And so great has been the number and variety of his *puffs*, that if they were collected together, they would make a pretty large pamphlet; in which the whole art of *puffing* would be exemplify'd in all its branches.[1]

Upon this plentiful supply the *Journal* exercised a great variety of destructive tactics. A favourite method was to analyse their grammar and logic with a pedantic—and often unfair—exactness, to expose their illogical and illiterate nonsense, often failing to see that this very incoherence and unintelligibility was a conscious part of Henley's curiosity-arousing technique. Sometimes the Grub Street Muse was let loose to versify Henley's advertisements when, with a very few additions and alterations to the original (always shown in italic type) the oddity of the original was rendered ridiculous by the jingle. A typical example of this form of attack is the versification of his advertisement for 17 July 1731, transformed overnight by a Grub Street poet into rhythms reminiscent of Swift's long-lined *Mrs. Harris's Earnest Petition*:

Since I am thought by some persons considerable enough
To be made a constant subject of the most malicious dirty *stuff*
In Papers weekly employ'd and levell'd against me,
And Oratory, and carried to that extent, that my family,

[1] *G.S.J.*, 19 June 1735.

My circumstances, and even my deceas'd Father
Have not been spar'd; I hereby give notice *the rather*
To those Murderers of all decency, as well as honesty, and sense,
That I can and always could, live handsomely without my *own pence*;
That no Author of those Slanders dares personally make use
Of such expressions to me of *obloquy and abuse,*
And therefore he is Anonymous, which is unfair;
(*Tho' I do this ev'ry week my self with a HYP-DOCTOR'S air*)
That my Oratory is now, and has been in this place,
Upon a better footing, (tho' I'm in somewhat worse case,)
Both as to the yearly Subscription, and the Audiences *grinning,*
One time with another, than it has been from the beginning:
That, was I dispos'd that way, the law would not suffer
The Preacher of any Congregation to be so singled out for *a Puffer*
And that I will, by God's blessing *upon my Elocution,*
Always endeavour, with the utmost spirit and resolution,
To deserve the continued encouragement of the Town,
In spite of the tribe of Levi, Issacher, I mean, the Gown.[1]

The common form of puff beginning 'we hear that. . . .'' brought
Henley new nick-names, 'Mr. ORATOR-WE-HEAR' and
'Mr. Auditor Henley' for 'We, *according to* Mr. Orator's *Grammar,
is a Person of the Singular number, who is always his own* Auditor.'[2]
Week after week a 'puff count' was published by the *Journal,*
sometimes as unadorned statistics, sometimes with picturesque
variations—'Hyp-o-crit-orical advertisements';[3] '*Five* puffs *of*
Foggy March wind *blown from the Oratory*';[4] or, when the number
dropped, 'Mr. ORATOR, though as much puff'd up as ever,
could not, by reason of a cold, puff out so well this month';[5]
or as a 'Bill of Hyp-oratorical mortality for the year 1732', when
a recount and summing-up was made:

Hyp-puffs, 60. Oratorical ditto, 62. In all 122—Hyp advertisements, 65.
Oratorial ditto, 83. In all 148. Sum total of puffs and advertisements,
270—500 males more than females were baptiz'd this year: 48 females
more than males were buried; and 26 more advertisements than puffs
were born: but all these, both puffs and advertisements, died immediately after birth, having in vain cried out for help; and had nothing
Christian, at their first appearance, or exit, neither baptism, nor burial.[6]

[1] *G.S.J.*, 8 July 1731.   [2] *G.S.J.*, 9 Mar. 1732.
[3] *G.S.J.*, 11 May 1732.   [4] *G.S.J.*, 8 May 1735.
[5] *G.S.J.*, 8 Mar. 1733.   [6] *G.S.J.*, 18 Jan. 1733.

So it went on, week after week for years, missing no chance or trick of ridicule and scandal, of enrolling Henley with every other quack or crook, of paralleling his writings with the lowest forms of sub-literature. Little wonder that when the *Journal* ended its career at the end of 1737, to be replaced but briefly by the *Literary Courier of Grub Street*, Henley should exult over the expired enemy:

All the Grub Street Journal's Hyp Oratorical Puffs and eight years of conscious Scandal to themselves against the Oratory, puff'd by the Soul of Pope, Whiston, Codex, and all pretended enemies of the Oratory, could not make it puff on, or breathe, beyond this Day: it is in hopes of a better Resurrection, which is a mistake after Death and Damnation.[1]

The *Grub Street Journal* in its wide-ranging search for lines of attack, was a microcosm of the greater satirical world which left no aspect of the Oratory's plan and proceedings unexamined or unscathed. A great body of pamphlets and parodies, newspaper reports and burlesques survived to enable us to see, through hostile eyes, those many activities which, until now, we have seen mainly through Henley's, to discover a critical version of the Henleian ideal image.

A mixture of mockery and outraged righteousness informed the attacks on the Oratorian ministry of the Sacrament and the Word, although, as we have said, the scarcity of any detailed comment on the Primitive Liturgy and its celebration is remarkable in an otherwise abundant field. Most of it comes from the very early days during the first Oratory in Newport Market, and most of it concentrates on the weaknesses in Henley's liturgical scholarship, with little laughter or satire and much scandalized piety. 'This Liturgy', reports the *Historical Register* in 1726, 'is chiefly a Rhapsody of the *Clementine* Constitutions, reviv'd and trump'd up some Years ago by the profess'd *Arian*, Mr. *Whiston*, but exploded long before, as a spurious Interpolation',[2] while someone purporting to be a Quaker, Ezekiel Hopewell, wrote to *Mist's Journal* in the same year that

verily some other Person shou'd be employ'd about it, who might approve himself a Workman that need not be ashamed, and not such a bungling Cobbler of Liturgies and Forms of Prayer . . . There be, that

---

[1] Quoted in the *Literary Courier of Grub Street*, no. 1, 5 Jan. 1738.
[2] *Historical Register* (for 1726), vol. xi, no. xliii, p. 243.

say, his Knowledge is very shallow, and that he boasteth of those Things that he understandeth not, and that his *compendious apostolical Thanksgiving* (which consisteth of 14 pages) is very ignorantly and unfaithfully translated . . . the Reasoning, and Sense, and English of his Liturgy, are all very bad . . .[1]

Another letter-writer to the *Censor* sniffed Arianism in the Liturgy's prayers, doxologies, and forms of address to the Second Person—

The Orator in his *Liturgy* has kept nothing of our own, in which our Saviour is made equal with *God the Father*; and tho' he begins one of his Prayers thus: *O our Eternal Saviour, the King of Gods*, (a very odd, if not extravagent, Expression) who alone art Almighty, and *the Lord, the God of all Beings, &c.*, yet it plainly appears that the whole Prayer is directed to God the Father; not but he directs some of his Prayers to Jesus Christ, and to the Holy Ghost, but they are of the same Nature as that which is directed thus, *the Angel which redeem'd us from all Evil, bless us*. This is something like the Distinction Popery makes in the worship of God, the Angels and the Saints. I hope some Clergyman will examine the said Liturgy, and give us their Opinion of it.[2]

The fullest attempt to satisfy that closing wish was by the anonymous writer, whether reverend or not we do not know, of *A Letter to the Reverend Mr. John Henley, M.A. concerning his Novel Project: wherein his Design is fully exposed*, where the liturgy is attacked for its prolixity and tediousness and unnecessary tampering with the accepted Anglican rite. All this is very quiet, serious, and scholarly, with its talk of authenticity of source, orthodoxy of doctrine, and weaknesses of style, and quite unlike the shriller and more extreme tone which informed the mass of Henleian satire. There is surprisingly little comment on his action at the altar compared with the amount of abuse of his action in the

---

[1] *Mist's Journal*, 23 July 1726.

[2] *Censor*, 10 Aug. 1726. In September 1726 one eminent clergyman, Bishop Gibson, had privately given his opinion, in his letter to Lord Townshend (see above, p. 129, n. 2) of Henley's 'mangling the Book of Common Prayer and setting up new liturgies and rubrics against it', and Lord Townshend consulted the Attorney-General on the subject. Sir Philip Yorke replied that he could find no law in the Act of Uniformity or the Act of Toleration against the composition of new prayers and liturgies, and advised the Ministry not to undertake 'a prosecution without any prospect of success, the event of which might rather encourage than restrain the mischief it was intended to suppress'. (Correspondence of the First Lord Hardwicke, B.M. Add.MS. 36136, No. 64.)

pulpit. Only one writer accused him of desecrating 'the *Eucharist*, by celebrating it in an unheard of Manner, thereby exposing it to the Derision of the Profane, who desire nothing more than to see the most sacred Things in Religion turn'd into Jest!' (though this piece of evidence is somewhat invalidated when its author admitted 'we never were in your Oratory'!).[1] The ever-at-hand accusation of Popery is revived, because 'His lamenting the Disuse of *the ancient Forms of celebrating the Sacrifice of the Altar*, or in plain *English, the Mass*, strongly savour of *Popery*: Nor can anybody doubt of this, who looks upon his *Rubricks*, which like those of the *Roman Catholic* Liturgies, are printed in Red Characters.'[2] Again, there is something suspiciously desperate in the etymological ignorance which dare use a red letter as an argument for Popery. Either Henley's liturgy aroused little interest or his critics were too uninformed to criticize it—or, its performance was neither impious nor undevout. The positive evidence would seem to point to this last conclusion.

Far otherwise was the torrent of abuse hurled at the 'gilded Tub', the Orator, the Restorer of Ancient Eloquence. His theories on gesture and expression, his belief that all subjects and sciences were relevant to religious preaching, his ideas on the use of laughter, wit, and burlesque as teaching and corrective methods—all these were distorted and exaggerated to create a scarecrow picture of an impious zany and mountebank, exhibiting himself to the delight of a shabby and illiterate audience. Typical is this account by an anonymous reporter:

. . . he set up a public *Stage* in the *Shambles*; mounted it, and hung up the shameless Flag of Defiance against the Law, against Virtue and Decency, while he impiously mock'd his God, and ridicul'd the Religion of his Country, together with the whole *Druidical* Order. He drew the Dregs of the Multitude after him by his Ribaldry, and cracking obscene Jokes, like a *Jack Pudding* in *Bartholemew* Fair, at the same Time that he was clad in the venerable Vestments of the sacred Order, and with the volume of Salvation in his Hand; while his dirty Auditory, crying *Smoke the Parson*, rung Peals of *Marrow-Bones and Cleavers* to their Orator's Praise.[3]

---

[1] *A Letter to the celebrated Orator etc.*, pp. 4–5.
[2] *Historical Register* (for 1726), vol. xi, no. xliii, p. 246.
[3] *A Comparison between Orator H———— and Orator P——— etc.*, p. 5.

The same sneers at his congregation fill the *Grub Street Journal*'s
picture of him in action, when

> ... from Gilt Tub, sublime in Masquerade,
> TULLY reviv'd the unknown God display'd;
> Clare-Butchers, mix'd with Saints of Drury-Lane,
> Astonish'd heard the learned, lofty strain;
> Which like the theme, th'*Athenian God* unknown
> Still left, but manifested plain his own.[1]

It was especially his use of jokes and satire and word play in the
pulpit which scandalized those critics who equated seriousness
with solemnity, and who separated topics strictly into 'religious'
and 'non-religious'. As we have seen, the religious content of
Henley's discourses diminished as the years went by and they
became more and more critical and burlesque commentaries on
current affairs; but the earlier mixture of sacred and profane,
in both topic and language, aroused such wrath as:

Is not the most consummate Impudence exerted in all his words,
actions and gestures, and diffused over his whole person?... his
unparallell'd profanation of sacred things, by his monstrous jumble of
divinity and buffoonery, of a Church and a Farce-House, of a Bartholemew-fair Booth, and a Sacrament; his Church of England gown in a
Meeting-house tub.[2]

A more balanced account later in the century nevertheless made
the same accusation:

The Doctor was indeed a Composition of Inconsistency and Singularity. He wanted not Sense or Learning, but perverted both to the
most unworthy Purposes. He understood the Principles of Religion
very well; but his chief Delight was in making it appear ridiculous, by
the ludicrous Light in which he view'd it himself, and represented it to
others. . . . But though the Doctor understood Religion tolerably well,
and could, when he thought proper, compare the different Sects, and
exhibit their various Excellencies in a striking and picturesque Manner,
yet he was more disposed to cull out their several Defects and Imperfections, so as to make them all appear mere human Inventions, and the
Creatures which interested Priests and artful Knaves had dressed up,
to impose on, and frighten the Vulgar. His chief Talent lay in Buffoonery, and making the most amiable Things appear mere Monsters and
hideous Caricatures. Thus Religion was vilified, her Ministers traduc'd,

---

[1] *G.S.J.*, 15 Apr. 1731.   [2] *G.S.J.*, 13 May, 1731.

Morality laugh'd at, Merit treated as mere Non-entity, and the greatest Characters in the Kingdom taken to Pieces and anatomised with all the Licentiousness imaginable every *Sunday*, when the Ollio of Scandal and Nonsense was serv'd up to the Public.[1]

Two examples of these performances so struck two of his auditory that they recorded them years after the experience had shocked them. The earlier recorder wrote:

Some of those Lay-subjects were very full of Ribaldry: Once, having advertis'd that the following *Wednesday* he intended to make an Oration on *Marriage*, he drew after him a considerable Number of *Ladies* and *Gentlemen*, chiefly *Butchers Daughters* and *'Prentices* out of the City, and a *few Sneerers*; when he had that prodigious Presence of Brass, without changing Countenance, to tell the Ladies, '*That he was afraid that oftentimes, as well as now, they came to* CHURCH *in Hopes to get Husbands, rather than be* INSTRUCTED *by a Preacher.*' But he intreated of them, '*not to set their Affections too much upon* THINGS *that were* BELOW'.[2]

Years later a correspondent in the *Gentleman's Magazine* told Mr. Urban of a similar experience:

Orator Henley appeared to me a master of a good voice and a forcible elocution. His address to the Deity was at first awful, and seemingly devout; but it degenerated into an indecent buffoonery. After expatiating on the several sects who would certainly be damned, he seriously invoked the Deity to *un-dam* the Dutch; a long string of gross impiety to introduce that wretched bastard of a pun: it seemed to please the marrowbonians, who gave their testimony of applause. I think in the lecture he undertook to prove the petticoat as educible from Scripture, by quoting the passage where the mother of Samuel is said to have made him a *little* coat, ergo, a *petti*coat . . .[3]

To make such impiety worse, it was delivered with a voice and gesture which gave equal offence. Henley's use of hands, arms, and expression to emphasize his points inevitably placed him with actors and mountebanks. The *Grub Street Journal* ironically could not understand why Henley should figure in a poem on bombast actors, 'unless', as it added in a footnote, 'it were to call him a farcical zany, and twit him for learning the action of the ancients

---

[1] *A History of the Robin Hood Society* (London, 1764), pp. 135–6.
[2] William Ayre, *Memoirs of the Life and Writings of Alexander Pope* (1745), vol. i, p. 279.
[3] *Gentleman's Magazine*, vol. lvii, pt. 2, p. 875.

from a modern player. For, by the four next lines, it is plain, the author thinks him a miserable actor, and that he ought, as such, to be rank'd with Jack-puddings, or Bartholemew-fair puffers . . ."[1] More circumstantial and with the note of authenticity about it, is the recollection of an eye-witness at the Oratory who told how

About the usual hour of the Orator's entering the public scene of action, a trap-door gave way behind the pulpit, as if forced open by some invisible hand; and at one large leap the Orator jumped to the desk, where he at once fell to work . . . but to come to his oration, which turned on the important subject of Education antient and modern, I had entertained hopes of meeting with something curious at least, if not just, on the great theme he had made choice of; though, instead of it, I heard nothing but a few common sentiments, phrases, and notions, beat into the audience with hands, arms, legs, and head, as if people's understandings were to be courted and knocked down with blows, and gesture and grimace were to plead and atone for all other deficiencies.[2]

Inevitably the sprightly poets of the *Grub Street Journal* fell eagerly on this most promising subject, as indeed had their master Pope. There are dozens of examples which could be quoted to amplify his *Dunciad* portrait, but three will suffice to add a few small details to our picture of Henley in the pulpit, and the twisting of that picture to ludicrous ends.

> Say, envious GRUBS, why thus is H----y blam'd;
> For *Elocution* and for *Action* fam'd?
> You see, he daily challenges his Foes:
> None dares the Champion face to face oppose.
> Nor wonder, since his voice, and limbs, and mien
> Are terrible to all, when heard, or seen.
> While ancient *Elocution* he restores,
> *Action* reviv'd inforces what he roars.
> And should his lungs, or voice, or visage fail,
> His brawny brandish'd arm must needs prevail.
> Triumphant he would end the whole dispute,
> And with one knock-down argument confute.[3]

---

[1] *G.S.J.*, 1 Mar. 1733.
[2] Quoted from the *Weekly Journal* in J. P. Malcom's *Anecdotes of the Manners and Customs of London during the Eighteenth Century* (1808), p. 238.
[3] *G.S.J.*, 30 Mar. 1732.

H--l-y the rostrum mounts, displays his hand—
Settles his scarf—and well adjusts his band—
With front elate surveys the pious dames—
Then—challenges them all,—t'oppose his themes.[1]

and finally some stanzas from a long poem in which the street-
ballad rhythms add force to the satire, which now includes in
Henley's repertoire the notorious nasal twang of the dissenting
Aeolist, as well as the roar and the bombast:

Clare-market then from every stall
    Shall send her butchers forth;
And each blue frock of Leaden-hall
    Adore thy gifted worth.

But sacred subjects lay aside,
    O Harlequin Divine:
Nor in burlesquing Scripture pride,
    With thy unhallow'd whine.

What tho' Non-Cons their barns still keep
    And through the vocal nose
Do tune their gentle flocks asleep,
    With opiated prose?

Thy Nonsense-tub gives more offence
    To all well-judging men:
Where greasy butchers snore for pence,
    And bull-dogs snarl *Amen*.[2]

The last stanza introduces another favourite satirical topic.
Not only did his Nonsense-tub and his performance in it give
offence: people actually paid to hear this nonsense, and this
brought down more obloquy and scandal upon his 'canting
trade'. Canting was bad enough: to make a trade of it was
impious baseness.

We have already examined the financial arrangements of the
Oratory and tried to show, as objectively as possible, their
necessity and, from Henley's point of view, reasonableness. It
was only too easy for his attackers to ignore all such explanation
and defence, and present financial gain as the central and lowest
motive of all Henley's undertakings. 'People boldly affirm',
wrote William Wood in 1726, 'that the Want of Money, or some
such Affair, not the promotion of *Literature*, and the *Primitive*

[1] *G.S.J.*, 9 Sept. 1731.   [2] *G.S.J.*, 20 Oct. 1737.

Christianity, is the *Real Original* Cause of his *Institution*',[1] and from this very first year of the Oratory's existence, this accusation was to sound again and again. That same year an open *Letter to the Rev. Mr. John Henley* repeated the charge with outraged righteousness. The writer concluded,

Upon the Whole, whoever knows any Thing of the Matter may with half an Eye see through your Design, and view at once that Money is the God whom you worship, that this your Religion is calculated for Gain, to corrupt the Principles of Mankind, and to impose upon the World . . . we must give One Shilling to the Door-Keeper, for the Seats were personal Property. A very fine Story indeed! and such a one, that is not to be parralleled, that we should pay a Shilling before we can worship GOD![2]

The following year a hypocritical note of pious concern was added to the chorus of protest. 'Is the Gain of some hundreds of Pounds', Henley is asked, 'together with the Applauses of the worst part of Mankind, your usual Auditors, (and what though some of them be in Red Ribbons?) an Equivalent for the loss of your Immortal Soul!'[3] while another pamphleteer asserted that 'his only End must be with a mercenary View, viz. Money, and heartily wishing it may not tend to utter destruction both of his Character and Soul; to render the one Infamous and the other liable to the Divine Wrath and Vengeance.'[4] Once this idea was rooted, any word or deed however trivial was scrutinized to find the underlying lust for lucre. One such example incidentally adds a curiously vivid detail to our knowledge of Henley's action in the pulpit, for

. . . he is observ'd, when he speaks, to move his right Hand partly open'd, and his Fingers bending downwards in a Posture of one that is striving to grasp at a Heap of Money, which extraordinary Gesture of this famous Orator, shews how far his Principles, whatever they be, are influenc'd by that Beloved Mamon. They say, that being ask'd by his Sexton what he should say of his Religion to those who ask'd the Question of him? His answer was, the *High-Church*. But one who pretends to know him, tells me, that his Answer would have been

---

[1] *The Dueling Orator delineated*, p. 25.

[2] *A Letter to the Rev. Mr. John Henley*, pp. 19 and 9.

[3] *A Letter to the celebrated Orator etc.*, p. 7.

[4] Anon., *The Art of Speaking in Publick: or an Essay on the Action of an Orator* (1727), the Introduction.

more proper, had he said he was of any Religion where there was money to be got; High Church and Low Church being all one to him.[1]

It was not only the fact that money was taken which upset Henley's critics: it was the way in which it was taken. An offertory plate or a charity box in church were decent because they were customary: a pay-box and cashier at the door were monstrous, and the sordid transaction at the top of the Oratory stairs was often the subject for demonstrating the Oratory at its worst. A shocked visitor there reported how

At the door I was accosted by a man, whose face I charitably supposed might be an emblem of his devotion, it being so exceedingly red and carbuncled. He demanded of me a shilling; upon which I asked him, whether that was the lowest price: to which he answered, Yes, to gentlemen. Then, said I, I'll not come in at all, and turned my back upon him: but he immediately pulling me by the sleeve, cryed, Come, give me your tester: which I did, and found myself the first person that had been admitted. But I was soon followed by a large number, most of which, as I judged by the continual disputes at the door, were admitted on the same terms or for nothing: and who seemed to be chiefly printers, book-sellers or authors.[2]

On a later occasion similar disputes echoed through the Oratory when, for an Elogium on Freemasonry, the price had been raised to 2s. and the relief doorkeeper, an old woman, vainly attempted to silence the outraged regular customers by explaining 'that it was an *Elogium*, not an *Oration*, which only subscription-tickets gave a right to hear: and that therefore nought but current coin would be received that night'.[3] Even when there was no charge at the door, as on Good Fridays, the money was collected within-doors from the full freely admitted congregation in, it was alleged, the same uncouth manner:

> The dialogues, and *new oration* ended,
> To ask their charity AMEN attended.
> Some drop a sixpence each; AMEN cried so,
> But many drop a half-penny—Poh! Poh!
> With bolder metal now soon cover'd o'er,
> The Modest silver coin appears no more:
> But shows an emblem, in half empty plate,
> Of Oratorial pocket, phyz, and pate.[4]

---

[1] *Censor*, 10 Aug. 1726. [2] *G.S.J.*, 10 May 1733.
[3] *G.S.J.*, 19 July 1733. [4] *G.S.J.*, 29 Mar. 1733.

There were, it seemed, no words bad enough to condemn this mercenary prostitution of religion, no villains evil enough with whom to compare the Orator. When a malefactor Shelton was hanged at Tyburn in 1732, the *Grub Street Journal* seized the opportunity of publishing his 'farewell poem', wherein the dying man blamed Henley's preaching for leading him from the strait and narrow way, and proclaimed that, even in his terrible degradation, he had never sunk to Henley's low contrivances to make money:

> Ne'er, like Quack Doctor, had the face or conscience
> To make fools pay for hearing of my nonsense:
> By false advertisements and lying puff,
> Drawn to attend my incoherent stuff:
> Nor with vamp'd title-page have ever sold,
> For pamphlet new, sad trumpery, vile, and old.
> I scorn'd such *Oratorical Transactions*,
> Poor, paltry, pilfering, pick-pocket actions.
> Unequal Lot! that I sublime should hang:
> Thou still sublime in gilded tub harangue.[1]

Shelton draws our attention to one of the activities of the Oratory which we have hitherto neglected, but which Henley's enemies never did—the printing and sale of Oratory publications. The printing of the *Primitive Liturgy* in 1726 and its revised versions in 1727 and 1728 were only the first of many special Oratory books and pamphlets. *Oratory Transactions* and *Oratory Magazines*, sermons and special tracts were printed and distributed at the pamphlet shops and at the Oratory itself.[2] A never-ending flow of advertisements and puffs announced their appearance, their favourable reception, and wonderful influence, the necessity of purchasing quickly as supplies dwindled in the face of a surprising demand, and the appearance of new impressions, revised and corrected, when the first impression had been snatched up. Henley's enemies found many aspects of these publications fruitful subjects for attack, and not only the alleged nonsense and worthlessness of their content. They made a careful scrutiny of these works of

PUFFERUS HYP-ORATORICUS, whose offering consisted of *Oratory* Transactions, lately anabaptized, *Books of the Oratory, proper for*

---

[1] *G.S.J.*, 19 Oct. 1732.
[2] A list of Henley's publications is given in the Appendix.

Gentlemen and Ladies to take into the Country; a load of *Academical Lectures*, so heavy, that they broke the back of poor MAC EWEN his bookseller: *Hyp Doctors* as innumerable as unintelligible; *Orations, Lectures, Sermons, Expositions, Postills* &c in manuscript; all *new*, and such as the like to them were never delivered in any pulpit in Britain.[1]

One such bibliographically inclined critic wrote to expose Henley's publishing methods, in a letter to the *Grub Street Journal* showing the amount of time and labour which went into the preparing of sticks to beat Henley. The critic had purchased a copy of *A LECTURE ON HIGH FITS OF ZEAL, or Miss CADIERE'S Raptures. In which &c. II The Third Edition of Miscellaneous Tracts on Various Subjects of History, Polemical Divinity Education and Rhetorick. By J Henley, M.A. Institutor of the Oratory*, and revealed the scandal exposed by his inspection of his purchase.

When I came to examine my purchase, [he reported,] I found I had been bit: for this THIRD EDITION is not more applicable to any part, than to the whole. For after the *Lecture on high fits* &c. containing only 11 pages, follows a spare leaf, *Miscellaneous Tracts on several subjects: the third Edition*. Which *Miscellaneous Tracts* were printed in 1728, under the title of *Oratory Transactions*, No. 1, with which edition, the pretended Third Edition appears evidently to be the same, retaining the same typographical errors, the same distances between the words etc. so that unless there has been so great a demand for these *Miscellaneous Tracts* as to keep the letter standing these 4 years, this edition is neither a *third*, nor even a *second*.[2]

It is quite clear what Henley was up to. When advertisement and puff failed to sell one of the Oratory works, he added something new, bound it up with unsold sheets of an older production, altered the title-page to mislead possessors of the old book, and added details of a new edition to give the impression of great popularity and sales. A bibliographical examination of the Oratory publications, which is outside the scope of this narrative, would reveal an interesting picture of the less reputable side of eighteenth-century publishing and the untrustworthy evidence of title-pages. The *Grub Street Journal* had no doubts. It cast a quizzical eye on every 'New Impression' advertised and, when Henley announced that only 210 copies were left from an impression of several thousands of one work, noted how it 'has succeeded wonderfully according to this account: we may

[1] *G.S.J.*, 12 Apr. 1733. [2] *G.S.J.*, 24 Feb. 1732.

therefore soon expect a *fourth-first* edition'.[1] More practical
attempts were also made to prevent the sale of Henley's works.
He complained that 'Endeavours having been used to make the
Books of the Oratory deny'd at some Shops, they are, if not there,
to be had at the Oratory.'[2] and 'if any Arts be us'd to hinder the
circulating of these, or any Books of the ORATORY, by refusing
or decrying them', he had them on sale.[3] Such a boycott might
well have been the result of hostile influences. On the other
hand it might equally have been the wise decision of canny booksellers unwilling to take on a load they would never sell. Even
the bitterest of Henley's critics never suggested that he made a
fortune from his publications. It was enough to show his motives
and methods to be mercenary and crooked, and also to exult
over his failure to make money or keep up the deception.

In the same way, those critics who denounced the shilling
entry fee as impious and scandalous, could at the same time
demonstrate Henley's insignificance by reporting how few
shillings he actually took. Henley's own announcements of large
and genteel congregations were counterpointed by reports of
sparse and disreputable auditors. Throughout its campaign
against him, the *Grub Street Journal* alleged that 'the Auditors
are reduced to a very small number',[4] that 'many of his Auditors
I hear . . . have entirely left his meeting: and that the few who
still resort thither, are under much shame and confusion of face',[5]
and that 'Mr. Orator's quondam Auditors, whom he now calls
his enemies, have indeed cryed Quarter: insomuch, that, (to
immitate his burlesque manner) not a quarter of a quarter of a
hundred will come once a quarter, to see and hear learning
hang'd, drawn and quartered.'[6] Estimates of ten, twenty, and
twenty-five were given for the numbers at the Oratory, and the
Journal was not slow to take the credit for this decline:

> A stranger asks a large-paunch'd butcher, Pray,
> Are you so full on any other day?
> —Yes—once we were; but ever since a scrub
> Has writ a weekly paper—What! The Grub?
> —Yes, Grub—of papers all the very scum:
> All but some neighbours are asham'd to come.[7]

[1] *G.S.J.*, 1 June 1732.   [2] Advertisement for 4 Oct. 1729 (Lysons 37).
[3] *The Sermon that shou'd have been preach'd etc.*, title-page.
[4] *G.S.J.*, 1 July 1731.   [5] *G.S.J.*, 22 July 1731.
[6] *G.S.J.*, 13 Jan., 1732.   [7] *G.S.J.*, 29 Mar. 1733.

The 'large-paunch'd butcher' is a stock figure in these attacks on the type of congregation, and the rattling of cleavers and marrowbones echoes through them. Here is the antithesis of Henley's picture of an influential and elegant gathering of the Town, graced by men of letters and men of power, and we have suggested that the truth lies between the two. Many types were drawn to him by many motives, and they were types and motives to be found in all walks of society. A writer later in the century admits this social variety, while insisting on a common disreputable motivation. To him it was no wonder that the Oratory congregation was often numerous and attracted men from all social levels:

Novelties will always attract, Scandal has Charms for many Appetites; and an unrestrain'd Licentiousness of railing against Religion and Government, will always draw vast Numbers of Infidels and Libertines to hear their Patron and Advocate sounding the Trumpet of Sedition. Not but that others of a different Cast attended the Oratory: Some came to laugh *with* the Orator, and some to laugh *at* him: Some, to unbend their Minds, and forget the rigid Rules of Morality they had just before heard in our Places of public Worship; and some to confirm themselves in Infidelity and Impiety, and enable themselves to become Disputants.[1]

If Henley's enemies were right, no man of any self-respect would have dreamed of becoming a disputant, far less had an ambition to be one, for they show the disputations of the Oratory, represented by Henley as one more method in his search for truth and instruction, in a far different and more lurid light. How different is Henley's ideal definition of a disputation, 'to search the truth of one single proposition, by a mutual free communication of sentiments in an amicable manner', from the rigged and empty displays of nonsense and ill-manners which they are alleged really to have been. No genuine and serious disputants were said ever to have appeared to help Henley in the search for truth, although he claimed otherwise. Addressing Pope, he wrote,

You tell the World, that I was for putting Questions and *none would dispute with me*: Professors of most Parts of Literature, many Clergymen, Students from both the Universities, Poets, Counsellors, Physicians, Dissenters of all Sorts, *Romish* Priests, *Carmelites*, *Jesuits*,

---

[1] *The History of the Robin Hood Society*, p. 137.

Dominicans, Benedictines, Gentlemen of all Ranks, ingenious Artists, have maintain'd publick Disputations there, very frequently.[1]

He thundered defiance in advertisement after advertisement, challenging bishops and scholars to break a lance with him, but there is no record in his own announcements or in other records of any eminent opponent ever taking up his gauntlet. He himself took this as a sign of his unchallengeable rightness and invincible position: his enemies explained that no one of any worth and respect would so demean himself:

> Undaunted chief, GOLIATH'S second, hail!
> Inpenetrable clad in native mail.
> Who, if a blush by chance thy phyz inflam'd,
> Woud'st of thy very blushing be ashamed.
> Securely you your challenges may sound,
> And bid defiance to the champions round:
> Safe without rival you may mount the stage;
> For what knight errant durst with you ingage?
> What mortal shot-free can expect to pass,
> From slugs of lead, and blunderbuss of brass?[2]

and again, in an imaginary conversation in the Oratory:

> A taylor asks, For what's that desk that's lock'd there?
> —For him that dares dispute it with the Doctor.
> —Dispute! Tho' challeng'd oft, none dares dispute:
> None e'er had confidence to do't.[3]

There is one story retailed by Disraeli of an evening when con-testants did appear. He tells us,

Once HENLEY offered to admit of a disputation, and that he would impartially determine the merits of the context. It happened that HENLEY this time was overmatched: for two Oxonians, supported by a strong party to awe his 'marrow-boners', as the butchers were called, said to be in the Orator's pay, entered the list; the one to defend the *ignorance*, the other the *impudence*, of the Restorer of Eloquence himself. HENLEY found the rivals!—As there was a door behind the rostrum, which led to his house, the Orator silently dropped out, postponing the award to some happier day.[4]

---

[1] *Why how now, Gossip POPE?*, p. 12.
[2] *G.S.J.*, 4 Oct. 1733.   [3] *G.S.J.*, 29 Mar. 1733.
[4] Disraeli, *The Calamities of Authors*, i.179.

It was to avoid such possible defeat at the hands of able opponents that Henley, according to his enemies, carefully chose his 'Disputants' and fixed matters as he wished them to be. The *Grub Street Journal* alleged 'that what he calls a *Disputation*, is his giving a poor fellow a shilling to come to his Oratory, and to produce upon some very foolish *Question*, two or three foolish arguments, which Mr. ORATOR is beforehand prepared to answer',[1] and it was not alone in making this accusation. A pamphlet of 1727 refers to the disputation he had advertised with Mr. Marcus, a converted Jew, on the question of the Messiah and the Law of Moses, and claims that Mr. Marcus was only a 'personated Jew' hired for the occasion which was in fact a rowdy and undignified affair, 'Your wretched Crew of Followers, (not Admirers of your self, as you vainly imagine, but of your unparallel'd Impudence) laughing all the while at both'.[2] Another such occasion is recorded in much greater detail. It claims to be partly from the writing and partly from the mouths of several persons present, and has the circumstantial ring of authenticity about it. It deserves fuller consideration, for the way in which it re-creates for us the course of an evening at the Oratory, and the machinations behind, as well as in front of, the scenes. Henley had advertised a disputation for 27 November 1737 on the questions '1. Whether Men or Women are most constant? 2. Whether the Prophecy of the Woman in the revelations be this Year fulfilled? 3. Whether there be a just Schism among the Gregorians in London?'. The questions combining the ever-popular themes of the war of the sexes, prophecy, and contemporary gossip, drew a large audience which was outraged when Henley failed to proceed with the advertised entertainment. He gave reasons for this before he retired, but it is most likely that he sensed a dangerous mood in his congregation. 'His Clark said, among other things, in the passage to the Oratory, That his Master saw from the beginning, that there were a set of Gentlemen, who came on purpose to raise a disturbance; and he himself thought so, since some of them cried out, "*Black your shoes, your Honour?*"' Henley's premonition was correct, for his departure produced a riot which is vividly described.

[1] *G.S.J.*, 18 Dec. 1732.
[2] *A Letter to the celebrated Orator etc.*, p. 5.

The Audience, highly enraged at Mr. H's abrupt departure, expressed their resentment by hissing, and loud demands of a return of their money. To appease which, the Clark at last mounted the *rostrum*; and thus elevated made a very diverting appearance. His aspect was very pale and meagre; and his eyes seemed very proper to observe a large audience, as looking directly forward, and to the right and left, at the same time. The paleness and thinness of his visage were very much heightened by a light, bushy, powdered ornament; which, in its curling days had, no doubt, decorated the same rostrum, tho' not fixed on the same block. Thus accoutred, he began to defend his Master's absence, insisting, That what they had already heard was worth more than a shilling pay'd by each, and that it was very indecent and unjust to raise such disturbances &c; so that he was on a sudden unwigg'd, un-rostrum'd, buffetted, and forc'd to retire with greater precipitation than his Master.

Henley advertised the disputation for the following Sunday and this time, having lectured the numerous congregation on the text 'love as brethren . . . be courteous', he fulfilled the under-taking.

Then came on the Disputation, in which the 2d. Question was proposed first, 'Whether the Prophecy of the Woman in the Wilderness be this year fulfilled.' On which occasion, Mr. C. the Disputant put on his spectacles, and read, in a very low tone, the greatest part of Rev. XVII with some old *Notes* upon it, a little new-vamp'd; which it had been very proper for the Disputant himself to have been. . . . He was some-times interrupted by the archness of Mr. H. and sometimes by that of particular auditors: and so the Dispute ended.

On the 1st Question which was postponed to the second place, 'Whether Man or Woman be more constant?' Mr. C. to prove the former so, alledged Eccles. vii. 28. *One Man among a thousand have I found, but a woman among all those have I not found.*—Mr. H. answered, that SOLOMON did not there speak with respect to *inconstancy* but to *deceitfulness*; that He could not with any grace complain of the *inconstancy of women*, who by his own confession had *known a thousand*; and that in proof of *Female Constancy* a very strong line might be produced from *Martial*. He then exspatiated in an harangue in praise of the Fair Sex; which, tho' acknowledged by all to be very seasonable, after his having been a widower for a week, seemed very fulsome, grew tire-some, and occasion'd them to call for the last Question, *viz*. 'Whether the *reported* Schism among the Gregorians be Just?' which he had altered from the first State of the Question, as it stood in several

Advertisements, 'Whether there be a just Schism among the Gregorians?'

Mr. H. then call'd upon Mr. C. by the name of Mr. Brown, (C. in the Oratorical Alphabet standing for B) and demanded What he had to say against the *Gregorians*? He answered That he had nothing to say at all against them. But being further urged by Mr. H. he said, That by their behaviour the last Sunday, they seem'd to be like gall'd Horses that wince and kick. Upon which Mr. H. required him to prove first, That they were like *Horses*; secondly That they were like Gall'd Horses; Mr. BROWN replied, that he would not undertake either.

A Gentleman ask'd Mr. H. How he came to advertise a Dispute on that Question? His answer was That it had been desired in a letter— With what name was it subscribed?—It had none.—Can you produce it?—I can't tell, I have received a thousand such.—How came you to advertise a Dispute, and have no one to oppose?—Mr. BROWNE promised to oppose, and to prove that the *Gregorians* were Papists, and derived their name from *Pope* Gregory.—This Mr. BROWN denied, affirming that it was at Mr. H's insistence that he appeared there, and that he had received his *Notes* for the Disputation from him.—Which Mr. H. absolutely denied.

The Gentleman then asked Mr. H. How he could undertake to defend the *Gregorians*, since he was not of the Order, and consequently knew nothing at all of their Constitutions? Mr. H. answered, That he was a *Gregorian* in the properest sense of the word, it being derived from the Greek Γρυγορεω, which signifies *vigilo*, to *watch*. That *vigilance*, comprehending *study*, he had a juster title to the name of a *Gregorian* than any man in the kingdom, having studied more than any one man, and more than any seven Clergy-men of the Church of England. Having spoken to this effect, he retreated without waiting for an answer; and left Mr. BROWN to be ridiculed, hissed, and buffetted by the bubbled Audience.

And so, even with a disputation, the evening ended as before— with a riot.

We learn more of the unfortunate Mr. Brown the following week, and something also of Henley's methods of arranging his disputations, in a letter purporting to come from the said Brown. He had been associated with Henley on previous occasions and he claimed that Henley was 'many times beaten off the Stage by me In all his Arguments well known to several Gentlemen that have been present'. Despite this, Henley approached him to act as a disputant, providing him with his material so that, as a useful Aunt Sally, he could be spectacularly knocked down by the Orator. In his somewhat incoherent prose, Brown tells how

the Questions of the Constancy of Men and Women and Concerning the Gregorians were Intirely Mr. H's one Projections and propositions to me and at his request I promised to speak to them with no other view than to say I knew no Order of Gregorians but Popes and Papists wherefore the question defined was what the Modern Gregorians were and did profess which is Evident was no Reflection on them but an oppertunity to defend themselves against all popular Reflections that might accrue from their own Publick advertisements. . . .

He duly attended on the night when the disputation was cancelled and, though he said nothing himself, came in for some of the rough treatment meted out to Henley's clerk, whereupon he duly complained to him:

. . . when I discoursed with him about the treatment the 27th. of Nov. he gave me 3 shillings for satisfaction that time I replied that was poor pay for the abuse I had received yet he Incisted on my appearing the next Sunday on the same questions which I Declined but upon him promising me Protection of 3 Cunstables and others to Defend me I promised to be there for which he agreed to give me six shillings and artfully puts himself In the advertisements for the Gregorians with a Desire as I suspect to screen himself and demolish me by the Insults of that freternity and thereby Retreave himself from Reflections. . . .

So it was that Brown appeared again that second Sunday and put up his strange and unrehearsed performance which forced Henley to improvise and prematurely close the proceedings, leaving Mr. Brown to suffer 'violence and an attempt to murder me betwixt the Dore and side of the Rostra by squesing me to death however I had Curage to tell them I was not born in a wood to be afraid of a nest of —'. After all this, Henley evaded seeing or speaking to him and, as Brown sadly closed his story, 'shames me by leaving me 4 shillings for the six he Promised me as he has used me at other times'.[1] Henley, even in his fury, should not have exulted over the fact that 'Mad Browne' should have had to take advantage of the Insolvent Debtor's Act.[2] How different is this muddle of dissimulation and petty fraud, rowdiness and riot and nonsense from that rule for the disputations which Henley had laid down ten years before:

[1] The account of this evening and its planning is reconstructed from *G.S.J.*s for 8, 15, and 22 Dec. 1737.
[2] *London Post*, 16 Dec. 1737.

No digression from the point propos'd, no personal reflexion, no calumny, nothing indirect, captious, unfair, insidious, or ensnaring; nothing that is prejudic'd or passionate, ill-bred, malicious, sophistical, or equivocating; no jests, puns, turns of wit, drollery, ridicule; nothing but what belongs strictly to the point, shall be allow'd or answer'd.[1]

The scenes on these two evenings remind us that the assault on the Oratory was not just a paper war, an affair of pamphlets and lampoons. From the beginning the Oratory had suffered from rowdy disturbances and its services had been interrupted by heckling and argument, but it is not until the late '30s that we find a sufficient body of evidence to show that this was becoming a regular and dangerous feature of the place, and that Henley was becoming increasingly enraged and troubled. On 1 September 1742 he saw fit to publish a general warning reminding all and sundry that the Oratory was part of his dwelling-house, properly taxed and legally licensed and therefore doubly protected against intruders and violence.

I do hereby admonish all and each Person, not to come thither, not to pay there, not to stay there, but on my own Terms:— Which in part, are as follows, viz. That each Person, by coming or paying, does make that his own express, voluntary, solemn, authentic Act and Deed, of Covenant with me, to pay me the sum of One Hundred Pounds, (over and above all other Damages, thereby also by him acknowledg'd due to me, and in my Favour) if he does not behave perfectly well according to the Rules of the Place . . .[2]

In the following year there are constant references to disturbances, warnings to all those attending to keep quiet, to keep in their places, not to question or interrupt the Orator, not to threaten him or start arguments. A long advertisement on 4 March 1743 blames Pope and the *Grub Street Journal*'s attacks for encouraging these disturbances, and offers for the first time rewards for information leading to the prosecution of these nuisances.

Bills of Indictment being found against several Disturbers of the Oratory, beginning Disorders by putting on their Hats, . . . continuing those Disorders by speaking aloud, against Order, to the Preacher in the Pulpit and Desk, asking Questions, talking scurrilously, abusing and assaulting the Servants, entering rudely about Seven o'Clock from

[1] *The Laws of the Conferences of the Oratory*, p. vi, in *Oratory Transactions No. 1.*
[2] Lysons 113.

certain Taverns and Coffee-Houses &c. on Sunday Evenings, by Concert, and by several other injurious Practices, occasion'd much by the abusive writings of Mr. Pope, and others, misrepresenting the Affair and the Preacher; and by the clandestine Arts of a Church-Director, whose Perfidy, in some measure, brought it on: Notice is hereby given, that if any Person will discover the Combination of these Disturbers from the year 1726, when the Undertaking commenced, till now, he shall receive One Hundred Pounds, on their Conviction: and on the like discovery of any Party of them, and its leader, particularly on Feb 6, and Nov 14 last, and in March and February 1741 and 1742, and in 1737 and 1739, or the like hereafter, some being employ'd to trace and know them, Ten Pounds, from me.[1]

These disturbances varied from noisy interruption to downright physical violence, and resulted in the whole congregation joining in the argument or scuffle. We hear that 'one in the 6d. Places . . . in a Blue Surtout Cape Coat, tall and slender, with a thin Stick in his Hand, encourag'd some, by speaking aloud, against the Rules of the Place, to interrupt my Preaching',[2] or of a concerted effort when

lately five Rogues, five Times advertis'd, swore and curs'd, Price 40s. and bleated and brayed, like stray Calves or Jack-Asses, at a Door, where they said, was a Place of Worship, consequently no Place for them: for Convicts from the Indians, to worship the Devil in: The Chief, Capt. Tagrag was a short, thick, black, fresh-look'd Punchinello, a new-painted Signpost: A Champion, he had beaten enough on a wooden Anvil for Cravats, to last their Lives; but his Dudgeon can't parry a Constable's Battoon, or a Parchment Scrip: Beasts go home, or be pounded.[3]

Another evening 'two brace of Bugbears, Subverters of the King's Peace . . . sought whom to devour . . . and after some Acts and Menaces, which render them Malefactors, Prisoners at Large, and Debtors to him, whirl'd to the F. Tavern, in C. Street, where, at N 7, they proferr'd a Bottle.'[4] More violent was the action of 'one Poplar or Stoplar' who attempted to rush the protective spikes around the pulpit, but found them too hard for him, or of Joseph Watton, the servant of a certain Mr. Wildey a deceased toy-shop proprietor, who had been angered by the advertisement

[1] Advertisement for 4 Mar. 1743 (Lysons 115).
[2] Advertisement for 21 Feb. 1755 (Lysons 192).
[3] Advertisement for 13 Nov. 1751 (Lysons 170).
[4] Advertisement for 9 Feb. 1751 (Lysons 167).

of what looked like a satirical funeral sermon on his dead master.
He turned up at the Oratory in his brown coat with brass buttons,
in a short wig, threatened the Orator and started a disturbance in
which the fighters, complained Henley, 'push'd down a Partition
of my Tenement'.[1] His reaction to this noise and violence was
various. He was no mean hand at dealing with simple hecklers, and
his repartee was part of the Oratory's attraction. A writer of 1727
recorded some of the Henleian responses to interruptions, as
from the height of his pulpit he attempted to unite his congregation with him in laughing them into silence. In response to general
rowdiness:

'Methinks this Meeting looks like the *Bear-Garden* at *Hockley in
the Hole*. . . .'
'You will hear the Devil at any time, and therefore you may
as well hear me for once.'

To a heckler pressing too close to the pulpit:

'Prithee *Pastry-Cook* stand farther off. . . . I do not know but
thou mayst make as good Mutton-pies as any Body, but I
would not have thee take me for a Piece of Dough. . . .'

To a solitary interruptor:

'Now here stands an Honest Friend before me. . . . I have
heard him call'd . . . But I bar all such Reflections, I bear my
Testimony against them. . . . I say, Friends, I have heard him
call'd by the Name of *Death's Head upon a Mop-Stick*.'[2]

When Henley failed to silence the noise, he was occasionally
helped by faithful supporters (though their help must have produced even rowdier scenes) and he publicly thanked such supporters for their assistance. At one time he thanks his friends for
their help in 'quelling and driving out the Knights of the Pump-
kin',[3] or a 'young Gentleman, who dislodg'd a Lincolnshire
Barbarian from the Oratory'.[4] At another he writes to 'intreat
the worthy Gentlemen who, on Sunday last went from the
Standing Place in the Oratory Chapel to the Gallery, and did

---

[1] Advertisements for 26 July 1748 (Lysons 153).
[2] *Punchinello's Sermon*, pp. 14, 8, and 15.
[3] *Daily Advertiser*, 4 Jan. 1744.
[4] Advertisement for 14 Feb. 1755 (Lysons 191).

justice to themselves and to all, to accept of my personal ac-
knowledgments'.[1] Though the result was a successful one, the
clattering of his supporters up the stairs, the tussle in the gallery
and the hustling of the interruptors downstairs and out, must
have made a considerable rough house! More quietly efficient
must have been the ministrations of two constables who, by
1749, he always had in attendance.[2] He often knew his adversaries
by name, warning 'William Thistleton and his, never to come
here, or any like them',[3] and he finally prosecuted George
Alexander Stevens who was a perpetual annoyance to him.[4]
When he knew no names he took steps to discover them, and
offered rewards for information, publishing details of any successful investigation when he had 'discover'd the Name, Abode, and
some Atchievements of that Heroic Compound of Don Quixote,
and Orlando Furioso, who led up a Rabble of Bedlamites lately . . .',[5] or that 'The B**ps last Mum-Huffins are discover'd,
and Justice is effectuating her Demands on them.'[6] He did not
always go to the full length of prosecution. At times he was
satisfied with a letter of apology which, duly published, appeased
his anger and incidentally gave the Oratory publicity. A certain
servant, Samuel Eustace, refused entry by Henley's servants,
forced his way in and caused a disturbance. An infuriated Henley
waited personally on the family in whose service Eustace was,
and also sent an attorney to them. The result was a published
letter. 'Having behav'd in an unjust Manner towards the Rev.
Mr. Henley and his People on Sunday Evening last, I ask his
Pardon for the same; and will not incur the like Behavior
for the future.'[7] The furious Joseph Watton, having defended
the memory of his master by pushing down a partition, duly
apologized, accepting responsibility for the damage and undertaking to make a public confession and ask for pardon at the
next Oratory meeting. One 'S.I.' whose full name Henley spared
'in Concern for his Character', wrote in equally abject terms.

[1] Advertisement for 14 Dec. 1753 (Lysons 184).
[2] B.M. MSS.Add. 10349.
[3] Advertisement for 1 Mar. 1755 (Lysons 192).
[4] Samuel Ireland, *Graphic Illustrations of Hogarth* (1794), vol. i, p. 141. The figure directly under the pulpit, in the print, with the hand raised and stick under his arm, is probably intended for him.
[5] Advertisement for 28 Feb. 1755 (Lysons 192).
[6] *Daily Advertiser*, 7 Jan. 1744.
[7] *Daily Advertiser*, 10 Dec. 1743.

'Whereas, I did lately disturb the Congregation at the Rd. Mr. Henley's Oratory Chapel, interrupted him in the Discharge of his Duty, and assaulted his Servants, I do hereby declare my sincere Thanks to him, for his kindness in not prosecuting me at law, for my Offence, which must have ended in my ruin.'[1] Henley was not always so easily satisfied, and unlike 'S.I.' his disturbers were often prosecuted for disturbing the peace, trespass and damage and violation of the Toleration Act. Warrants and Bills of Indictment are often mentioned in his advertisements, and successful prosecutions, when 'it has cost some young Fellows lately 6o£ &c.', were contentedly recorded. Despite these moments of revenge, however, in successful charges and forced apologies, this possibility of violence and turbulence facing him every time he entered the pulpit must have been one of the most exhausting and harassing aspects of the whole assault on the Oratory. Pamphlet and newspaper squib could be ignored or answered at leisure, but the shouts and jeers and scuffles were inescapable and had to be dealt with on the spot. The last ten years of the Oratory's history, increasingly filled with noise and violence, were privately a great strain on a man who was not, as we shall see, without other things to tire and worry him.

Publicly, Henley roared defiance to the end. In newspaper letters and advertisements, in challenges to disputations, he answered his attackers and defended his position. In the '30s he thundered back from the pulpit at the *Grub Street Journal* in his 'General Defence against Objections, from the beginning of the Oratory till now, especially against the Atheistical obscene Reflections of some Enemies',[2] and for some weeks under the general title of 'The History of Ninnies' he continued to pillory his enemies and to offer 'Grubbism display'd, or ten Monsters upon one Canvas'.[3] It was a solitary struggle, an 'undertaking', as he said, 'during so many Years, of one Man, to so numerous an Opposition',[4] and hardly a voice can be found raised on Henley's behalf. A solitary poem in Henley's praise, signed 'Robinson', proclaimed:

[1] Advertisement for 28 Feb. 1753 (Lysons 179).
[2] Advertisement for 17 Apr. 1731 (Lysons 53).
[3] Advertisement for 29 May 1731 (ibid.).
[4] Advertisement for 2 Oct. 1746 (Lysons 145).

> Let Bigots scorn, let envious *Prelates* rail,
> Henley, nor Scorn, nor Envy shall prevail;
> Thy Truth, thy learning never shall submit
> To *Priestly* Vengeance, or to *Grubstreet* Wit.[1]

And in fact, Henley did *not* submit and *did* prevail. Despite all the writings and schemings and rowdyism, the Oratory went on year after year and the enemies fell away. As the birthdays of the undertaking came round, the Founder took stock of past and present and published a birthday message. Let the last voice in this chapter of hostile voices raised against him, be Henley's— boastful, defiant, and not at all cast down, as he celebrated the twentieth birthday of the Oratory:

My Character, and that of the Oratory, having been misrepresented and depreciated by many, who neither know that, nor me, I beg leave to intimate that the Oratory this Day enters into its twentieth Year. I have hitherto only labour'd under three Misfortunes, Want of a proper Genius for Knavery, Laziness and Insignificancy: Relief of a Bishop: and an ardent Desire to excell in my Profession, preferring that to Preferment, otherwise the ten thousandth Part of my Application to the Oratory, my Delight, would have procur'd me long ago a Cardinal-Grenadier's Cap in the Church: As to my Circumstances, I shou'd have been easy, if I had never begun it, and shou'd be so, was it to end tomorrow: But in Regard to my Right of holding it, and my Duty in Conscience to be and do Good to the utmost of my Capacity, if my Property in the Case should be violated, it would be indifferent to me, if the chief Pastor of the Codex, even the Devil, in his own proper Person, was to rule the Roast in Great Britain: I am not vain in saying, that I have studied to be useful in setting a Pattern of a Design, and an Execution of it, an equal to which no Adversary has ever invented or produc'd, tho' some have stole and murder'd it: None of an opposite Religion can defend it against ruin: No Objection can be advanced against me, or the Oratory, which I cannot answer: Where I have undertaken, and have had the Concurrence of Principle and Inclination, Time and Means to excell, I can stand the Test, and where I have been defective, it has been owing to the Want of some of these Particulars: To such as have called the Oratory, a Nuisance, I reply, that if all Affairs were conferred and Managed as I have done that, there would not be one Nuisance nor Grievance in England: I pretend to nothing, which I do not perform, and assert nothing, which I cannot prove: So that the Christian Appelatives of—Puff—Quack—Nonsense—Impu-

---

[1] *London Evening Post*, 19 Nov. 1737.

dent, &c. I kick back to the Billingsgate Fellows at Foot-ball: I most humbly thank GOD, the Head of the Rationalists, and those my Friends, and am at this present Writing, more than twenty Years younger and merrier, at His Devotion and their Service.[1]

[1] Advertisement for 3 July 1745 (Lysons 139).

CHAPTER VII

Controversies and Crises

THE WHOLE OF THE ORATORY'S HISTORY was, then, one long controversy as it weathered one crisis after another. The story of the continual assault mounted against it captures the general babble of the snip-snap of attack and retaliation as Henley zestfully took the opportunity to 'kick back to the Billingsgate Fellows at Foot-ball'. There are, however, in this running battle, certain passages of arms which are of particular interest, either because of the combatants involved or because of the principles at stake. Like many a minor figure in this century he became involved with the great and famous, and his involvement adds detail to our knowledge of them. Similarly his taking part in the religious and political controversies of his time helps us to see what happens to the lofty theorizing of bishops and divines when it is re-handled and often distorted at the popular level, to see the workaday side and the smaller man's view of the great events and movements which the history books record on a grander scale.

I. LITERARY CONTROVERSY

Henley's literary quarrels were not primarily literary: they were quarrels with personal or political enemies who happened to be men of letters. Though Henley was by no means unread in literature—as his frequent references and quotations show—and though he often lectured on the great names in English literature, he was nothing more than a workaday critic and a rather hack popularizer. He needed the stimulus of party fervour and above all the excitement of personal animosity before he could launch with any real feeling and interest into literary controversy. In his long labours as a Whig journalist he felt moved to defend the cause not only against political pamphleteers, election-riggers, and crypto-Jacobites, but against the poets and writers who haunted the Tory Parnassus. Glover's *Leonidas* received a bantering and destructive review mainly because the Tory writers of *Commonsense* has praised it and read it as an anti-administration allegory of the times.[1] Richard Savage's *Progress of a Divine* was attacked as second-hand, uninventive, ill-tempered, and dishonest.[2] Even harmless Stephen Duck, perhaps because he had been encouraged by Pope and his friends, came in for such quips as 'Richmond [boasts] of that sweet Swan, Stephen Duck's Singing in Metre, with a Flail, to catch Lady-Birds with the Chaff',[3] and his ordination produced the scandalized abuse of 'the Revd. Mr. Stephen Duck's being admitted into ye Sanctum Sanctorum, without scholastic and university course of preparation, which cost me about £1000—ye said Duck being fitter for ye Ducking-pond at May-fair, to cry, Queck, for a Queck-Doctor of Divinity'.[4] Eustace Budgell, another of the protégés, was continually insulted with such disparaging greetings as 'Friend Budge' and 'Prithee Eustace'.[5] Henley was even willing to let party loyalty get the better of critical judgement by defending with much scholarly reference Laureate Cibber's New Year odes, simply because the *Grub Street Journal* had attacked them, and by demanding of one of the authors of that paper 'Why does Mr. Russell expose his Monkey Tail by climbing so high a Tree as Antiquity, in the *Classics*, and sputter about *Pastorals*?'[6] Fortunately he overcame that same loyalty, to join Pope in his condemnation of 'Slashing Bentley', and produced a pleasant quip on that learned man's edition of Milton, from which we learn 'that *Milton's* Paradise has been *Lost* over again, till Dr. *Bentley* found it in the *Saxon* Manuscript, that was *Lost* under his Custody: Mr. T———n says, the Doctor shall make it Paradise RE-GAIN'D to himself when the D——l's *blind* as *Milton* was, and there is no *forbidden* Fruit in the Poem.'[7] These are all passing blows which never developed into a battle where Henley's blood was seriously roused.

One might have expected more dust and heat when great Opposition figures were engaged, but Henley's relations with Fielding were comparatively controlled, and with Swift, the greatest Tory writer, curiously distant. Henley's period of political journalism coincided with Fielding's activity as an anti-Government dramatist, at a time when the theatre at Lincoln's Inn Fields and 'Mr. Fielding's Scandal Shop' at the Haymarket

---

[1] *Hyp Doctor*, 12 Apr. 1737.   [2] *Hyp Doctor*, 29 Apr. 1735.
[3] Henley, *The Lord Mayor's Shew: or The City in its Glory* (n.d.), p. 5.
[4] Discourse for 28 June 1752 (B.M. MSS.Add. 11784).
[5] *Hyp Doctor*, 23 Feb. 1731.   [6] *Hyp Doctor*, 16 Jan. 1733.
[7] *Hyp Doctor*, 11 Jan. 1731.

drew enthusiastic Tory audiences to applaud the variously veiled attacks on Walpole and his administration, and yet the pages of the *Hyp Doctor* show very little interest in this noisy and notorious centre of dissension. Some plays which the Government had taken exception to were dealt with in his columns. *The Fall of Mortimer* at the Haymarket in 1731 was criticized for piracy and plagiarism, its adaptor being stigmatized as an out-of-work upholsterer.[1] *Edward and Eleonora* and *Gustavus Vasa* (the banning of which stimulated Dr. Johnson's rage) were also criticized for their shocking style and treasonable content;[2] but, beyond these few occasions, Henley appears uninterested in the theatrical scene. His support of the Government's Stage Licensing Bill in 1737, the direct outcome of the excesses of Fielding's theatre, was a general and impersonal effort. Such reticence is all the more surprising because Fielding had not refrained from satirizing Henley in his first successful comedy *The Author's Farce* which was produced at the Haymarket in March 1730. In the second part of that play, *The Pleasures of the Town*, Henley, as Dr. Orator, had been presented in a tub, discoursing before the Goddess Nonsense on 'The History of a fiddle and a fiddlestick . . . being particularly desired in a letter from a certain querist on that point', his explosive punning style tellingly parodied, desperately trying to woo the Goddess but defeated in the end by Opera, and mocked out of court by Punch's song,

> No tricks shall save your bacon
> Orator, Orator, you are mistaken.

Years later, in *The True Patriot*, Fielding struck passing blows, such as his including Henley as a large black man among the assembled ghosts, who 'talked for a Whole hour what none of his hearers understood'. But despite this, Henley appears to have liked him and admired much of his work. When Fielding died in 1754, Henley spoke a funeral oration on him, approving him as a private man, as a magistrate, and as a novelist, and mentioning 'His talk to me and satirizing me'.[3] We have no record of what must have been an interesting meeting, nor any proof that Henley had not missed some Fieldingesque irony when he asked 'Pardon

---

[1] *Hyp Doctor*, 25 May–1 June 1731.
[2] *Hyp Doctor*, 5 June 1739.
[3] Advertisement for 2 Nov. 1754 (Lysons 189).

for the seeming Vanity of hinting, that the late Mr. Fielding, often, publickly, said, one was the Greatest Man in the World'.[1] Had Henley not, we wonder, read *Jonathan Wild*?

His attitude to Swift shows this same confusion of literary admiration and necessary attack on him as a party writer. In the early days of the Oratory, Henley had lectured on 'The Genius and Departure of Dr. Swift, and the History and Principles of Ridicule',[2] and he appears to have admired above all Swift's *Tale of a Tub*, constantly referring to it or taking hints from it for his own satiric invention. The Dedication to Prince Posterity, Peter's proving that a bread-crust was mutton, and his letter to all Emperors, Jack's begging for a good blow about the ears, and the coat of the three brothers, are all quoted and improved upon, while Swift's hint of a proposed *General History of Ears* gave him the idea of a Swiftian fantasy on the restricted hearing of the *Craftsman's* readers, and the performing of necessary ear operations on them.[3] He admired, too, *The Battle of the Books*, and produced his own *Battle of the Birds* with the King as the Eagle, Walpole as the Phoenix, and the Tories as the Scarecrow party, imitating Swift's mock-heroic simile and tone. He even copied in detail the closing action of the book, with 'Three *Raw* Squires, *Caleb, Fog* and *Budge*, all in a Row, pinion'd together, to be roasted'.[4] At other times he referred to and used the *Contests in Athens and Rome*, the *Use of Madness in the Commonwealth*, and what he called *The History of Farting explain'd*.[5] Swift was however a Tory who had packed cards with Harley and still consorted with the arch-enemy, Pope, and as such he had to receive his quota of punishment. Even though 'the merry Dean', as he often called him, 'had been hurry'd so hastily off the scene'[6] he was still a distant menace. He had 'coalesced with *Pope*, a Protestant with a Popish *Rabbet*, and often imports from Dublin a Remnant of *Irish Manufacture*, to mend and patch the Old Suit of the Patriot Cause',[7] and so Henley claimed the right to 'take the Advantage to treat him ... on Occasion with the same

---

[1] Advertisement for 1 Nov. 1754 (ibid.).
[2] Advertisement for 27 Jan. 1728 (Lysons 19).
[3] *Hyp Doctor*, 6 Apr. 1731; 12 June 1733; 6 Apr. 1731; 19 Jan. 1731; 20 Apr. 1731.
[4] *Hyp Doctor*, 30 Mar. 1731 and 27 Apr. 1731.
[5] *Hyp Doctor*, 27 Apr. 1731; 11 Feb. 1735; 21 Dec. 1731.
[6] *Hyp Doctor*, 6 Apr. 1731.
[7] *Hyp Doctor*, 29 Jan. 1740.

Freedom, as my Name-sake, Isaac Bickerstaff once serv'd honest Dr. Partridge'.[1] He took the advantage on surprisingly few occasions, perhaps because that very distance between England and Ireland seemed to lessen Swift as a party power. His influence was something of the past, something to be mocked in the past tense of these verses of 1736, from the *Hyp Doctor*:

> You once could dance and make a leg,
> Could fetch and carry, cringe and beg,
> At evening late and Morning early,
> E'er made a *Dublin Dean* by *Harley*.[2]

Only once did he descend to crude personal attack when he referred to 'Dean Swift, who likes *Eating* more than *Praying* or *Preaching* so far, that he thinks even a *Grace before Meats* hinders good Company',;[3] and, in a discussion of the Place Bill that same year, he took the opportunity for a little word play to assert that 'the famous *Dean* and *Pope* themselves are only Common-Placemen and Pilferers of Wit, in their most celebrated performances.'[4] The famous Dean had never taken any notice of Henley who, without the need to defend his own character and actions, could not work himself up into the fury which prolonged controversy and added more lurid colour to his writing. Far otherwise was his relationship with the 'Popish Rabbet', Alexander Pope.

Here personal attack and party animosity combined to produce an uninterrupted flow of mingled critical abuse and unqualified personal abuse. Henley claimed that he was not the first to antagonize Pope and that an examination of his orations and advertisements and conversation would prove that Pope was the first offender.[5] He is right. There is no evidence to prove that Henley had attacked or provoked Pope personally before the appearance in 1728 of the scarifying portrait of Henley among the dunces of *The Dunciad*, but once that poem was published Henley's contribution to the ensuing slanging match was almost entirely one-sided. Except for retaining the portrait of Henley in the later versions of *The Dunciad* and allowing an extended abusive footnote to it and except for minor passing references, Pope did

[1] *Hyp Doctor*, 14 Dec. 1731.　　　[2] *Hyp Doctor*, 11 May 1736.
[3] *Hyp Doctor*, 29 Apr. 1740.　　　[4] *Hyp Doctor*, 22 Jan. 1740.
[5] *Why how now, Gossip POPE?*, p. 5.

not enter into a literary confrontation. There exist, however, two tantalizingly brief hints of a personal confrontation between the two. In an advertisement for 8 June 1751 Henley referred to 'My Talk with Pope', and two years later, in another letter-advertisement, recalled how

Mr. Pope, pale and trembling, told me, that he did not write the Prose Notes of his Dunciad on me, but had them, with the rest of his Verses, from Mr. Savage, call'd half-hang'd Savage (of whom I had preach'd, that, by Law, he could not be pardon'd for murdering Mr. Sinclair); the Jackalls for his Dunciad were the first of the Dunces.

Where or when this memorable meeting took place, it is impossible to say. Henley had indeed preached on Mr. Sinclair's murder on 14 January 1728, but this is the only fact in the story which we can substantiate. We know that Pope often turned pale and trembled when he read the attacks on himself: it would be fascinating to know for certain that those same symptoms appeared through fear of the furious and explanation-demanding Orator. But for want of further certainties, this must remain one of the Imaginary Conversations of the century. In Pope's whole extensive correspondence there is no reference to this meeting, nor even to his inveterate enemy by name, yet Henley alleged that 'I never published⎫ a lecture but his beck was up. His ill nature work'd advertised⎭ like a Mole within, and threw up a Hillock in ye rear of him.'[1] The only other possible rival in persecution is the *Grub Street Journal* which, as we have seen, included repeated harrying attacks on Henley throughout its existence, and Henley knew that 'the Contrivance of the GRUBSTREET Journal [was] encourag'd by Mr. Pope', attributing many of the attacks against him to Pope or suspecting his inspiration behind the rest. In the years up to 1741 there was the added motive of political opposition to keep warm Henley's hatred of Pope. In answering the Tory propaganda of the *Craftsman* and *Fog's Journal*, it was necessary to attack the Tory poets, and Pope came in for his share along with the politicians and great men out of power who resorted to his grotto at Twickenham. He was abused along with other Tory pensioners who 'rail at *Smithfield*, like broken Horse-coursers,

---

[1] Henley's lecture, 'The Gypsiad' (Guildhall MSS. 252, vol. 6).

or as Pope would banter, the *Smithfield Muses*, when some of his Verses have *sold his Readers a Bargain*, and *himself a better*, tho' the *Criticks* say, they deserv'd to be immortaliz'd by a *Smithfield* Faggot'.[1] Pope's part in Tory journalism drew down the *Hyp Doctor*'s wrath on his head. He was 'the Beginner of the Grub Paper', and 'we are told that Mr. P–pe wrote the Poem call'd *The Dawley Farm* and the *Norfolk Steward* besides several letters in *Fog* and the *Craftsman*',[2] an accusation repeated with much the same detail five years later: 'A. POPE is known to be an odd kind of Monster, a *Republican Papist*, and that he has written ten *Fogs*, and *Craftsmen*, is not to be doubted, by those who remember the *Norfolk Steward* in Fog &c.'[3] As Pope's later satires started to deal with social and political rather than literary themes, this 'sweet singer of our Israel'[4] was treated more and more as a party writer, the suspected confederate of Atterbury and Bolingbroke, infuriated, like all his powerless friends, at being out of place and favour. A *Hyp Doctor* poem 'From a Phoenix at Court to a Screech-owl at Twickenham', suggests a possible grievance:

> Though now on loftier *Themes* he sings,
> Than to bestow a Word on *Kings*,
> For *Kings* he is resolv'd to hate,
> 'Till a *King* makes him *Laureate*.[5]

He was 'Mr. *Pope*, a *Minstrel* to the Gang, a smooth Fiddler to the Brotherhood', 'the great Oracle and *Diana* of the Party', and, in his willingness to treat general rumour as fact and use real names in his attacks, 'that third-hand Bard is Hangman General to the Opposition'.[6] Pope might proudly claim his independence of party and that

> Tories call me Whig; and Whigs a Tory.

Henley was in no doubt as to who was right, and this certainty, combined with self-defence, gave him a twofold reason for never letting up in his pursuit of this 'cur that barks, but never bites'.[7]

He produced only one substantial pamphlet against Pope, published in 1736 and reprinted in 1743 when *The Dunciad in*

[1] *Hyp Doctor*, 16 Feb. 1731.   [2] *Hyp Doctor*, 2–9 Nov. 1731.
[3] *Hyp Doctor*, 17 June 1736.   [4] *Hyp Doctor*, 1 Jan. 1740.
[5] *Hyp Doctor*, 11 May 1736.   [6] *Hyp Doctor*, 15 Jan. 1740.
[7] *Hyp Doctor*, 11 May 1736.

Four Books brought his portrait afresh before the public, a pamphlet engagingly entitled *Why How now, Gossip POPE? or, The sweet Singing-Bird of Parnassus taken out of its pretty Cage to be roasted: In one short Epistle (Preparatory to a Criticism on his Writings) to that Darling of the Demy-wits, and Minion of the Minor Criticks. Exposing the Malice, Wickedness and Vanity of his Aspersions on J. H. in that Monument of his own misery and spleen, the Dunciad.* It is a mixture of autobiographical detail offered to disprove the various accusations of Pope and the *Grub Street Journal*, and of retaliation in such violent and picturesquely abusive prose as this:

You shrewdly call *the Orator this Person*, and this *extraordinary Person*: any *Spectator* may judge, whose *Person* is more EXTRAORDINARY, Mr. HENLEY'S or Mr. POPE'S: and who is fitter for that Country you speak of—*where* MONKEYS are the *Gods*—that is, where PERSONS, like a certain *Ape of Poetry*, are *Idolised*: If there be such another *grinning Lover of Mischief in the World*, in whom Nature has *mimicked and mocked* the *Species*: the MONKEY's *Paw* of a Low Faction, one that can only use *the Old Woman's Weapon of malicious Gossiping, venomous Scandal*, and *lying Chit-chat, like* a TRUE SON of an Impudent WHORE of BABYLON, famous these 1700 Years for *bespattering, stripping*, and *murdering*, with her slanting stolen Dress, *like your Verse*, her hypocritical rebuking Face, *like your Satire*, and a rotten Constitution, for ever infecting all she wickedly and unfortunately charms, *like your Numbers* and *your Laelius*.

This was a style Henley—like many other lampooners of Pope—favoured when he attacked 'Tomtit Pope' and 'pluck'd his *Giblets*, and flung his rhyming Gizzard, and *Gall bitter'd liver* for a Prey to the Dogs'.[1] One more example, this time from the *Hyp Doctor*, should sate any appetite for more of this strong but coarse meat:

The Mind that inhabits his little Glass-case is like Assa foetida in a Thumb-bottle, or flat Vinegar in a broken Crewet; ill within, and worse without Doors: it gnaws and preys upon his Body, which causes him to fret and gnaw upon every Character he meets with; a public Worm by his own private one; his life is a Corrosive, that eats first on itself, then on other people; it is that which shrivels up his Understanding, his good Humour, and his Carcase; when Nature infus'd the vital Principle into him, she went no farther than Still-life, and only etch'd

---

[1] *Hyp Doctor*, 30 Mar. 1731.

a rusty Copper-Plate and coarse Wax with *Aqua Fortis*: His Bow, as his Back informs you, is too weak, and his Arrows too short and blunt for Execution, therefore he tips them with the Native *Arsenic* of his own Malice. What he calls writing is his poisoning Paper and Reader; he lives on Scandal, like a Maggot on Putrefaction, or a Fly on Excrement; he is a small hand-grenado, charg'd with Feathers, that burst, fly about, give Offence, and do no harm, whatever is intended.[1]

The remainder of his controversial material is various in form and scattered in many different places. The pages of the *Hyp Doctor* are full of such squibs as 'It was by a glorious Fit of the Spleen, that the Greek Alexander became *Great*, and *Poetical Alexander* so very little!'; 'It has been a bad Season for Verses imported from Tw———m this Year; they will not keep', or 'Mr. P–pe is admitted to some Ladies, because in his Capacity as a *Druid*, he knows how to *cast their Water*'[2] (apparently a reference to an early poem which Pope regretted and wished to disown). Throughout the Oratory's history, also, Pope was the frequent subject of discussions and dissections of varying degrees of seriousness and savagery. It must have been a constant source of annoyance to his apprehensive nature to read in the daily papers of such promised subjects on the Oratory's agenda as:

The Wednesday's Subject will be particular, and Advertis'd in the Daily Journal, with the History of the NINNIES continued, or Henley's Tee hee at that genuine Successor of F. Quarles, A. POPE, his FICTIONS of Mr. Orator by Poetic License, taken out from the Hawkers and Pedlars Office.[3]

The Year of Monsters . . . monstrous Apparitions: a monstrous Leg that fell from a broken wheel of Apollo's Coach at Twickenham, and split into two living Legs.[4]

Pope (a sorry Poet) His Prayer, God mend me, not answer'd.[5]

A new edition of the Psalm, with my Dog and I, by Mr. Pope.[6]

Alliance of Church and State. i.e. Pope and Warburton; and Service for a Funeral Sermon on the Death of Mr. Pope's Reputation.[7]

Pope's soliloquies near Bath.[8]

[1] *Hyp Doctor*, 11 May 1731.   [2] *Hyp Doctor*, 5 Jan., 24 Aug., 14 Dec. 1731.
[3] Advertisement for 1 May 1731 (Lysons 53).
[4] Advertisement for 5 Jan. 1731 (Lysons 47).
[5] Advertisement for 3 July 1742 (Lysons 112).
[6] Advertisement for 10 July 1742 (ibid.).
[7] Advertisement for 4 Sept. 1742 (Lysons 113).
[8] Advertisement for 15 Jan. 1743 (Lysons 114).

Pope's new Hero, and verses on his Den.[1]

Mr. Pope's new Diarrhoea.[2]

Dunciad lying in State?[3]

Mr. P* and W*b* married?[4]

Mr. P–pe's Disease, and Cruelty to Mr. S––ge.[5]

And in addition to including items such as these in address and oration, Henley also submitted Pope's works to trial by disputation, when he doubtless ensured that any question of their worth was resoundingly decided against Pope. On the whole Henley was satisfied that, despite all the efforts of Pope's supporters, on all these occasions truth had prevailed—or rather that his own opinions had been triumphantly upheld! He tells Pope:

Pretty Beaux have ever been rude and mobb'd, and lively *Petit-Maitres* have drawn their terrible Blades for you, in want of Sense. *Whites*, the *Bedford, Tom's, Nando's, George's*, and the *Crown*, &c. have pour'd forth their well-dress'd Auxiliaries, Lace, Bag, Sword, Toupee and Snuff-box, all the *Rival Modes* in support of Mr. POPE'S Right to be esteem'd the first of the Age: but their Apologies have been *murder'd, hack'd* and *maul'd*, even *butcher'd* in the *Priestly Stall*, and your exemplary Wit hung up in *Effigy* as only fit for a *Scare-Crow like yourself*.[6]

The results of this hacking and mauling, the reasons for refusing to recognize Pope's claim to greatness, throw an interesting and often odd light on his contemporary reputation, shaped as they are by ideas and emphases so different from our own.

The Dunciad with its violent provocation was the work which first received Henley's close attention, but in his angry reactions to it he sometimes looked to Pope's earlier works to find targets for satire. The *Pastorals* were a subject for an Oratory disputation but we have no record of the arguments which led to their condemnation. The edition of Shakespeare and the translation of Homer were condemned for reasons which were frequently given by Pope's other critics, and one of Henley's earliest gibes at Pope snipes at these works. 'Mr. *Pope* grows witty', he wrote in the year following the publication of *The Dunciad*, 'like *Bays* in the

[1] *Daily Advertiser*, 15 Oct. 1743.   [2] *Daily Advertiser*, 5 Nov. 1743.
[3] *Daily Advertiser*, 12 Nov. 1743.
[4] *Daily Advertiser*, 31 Dec. 1743.
[5] Advertisement for 21 May 1743 (Lysons 116).
[6] *Why how now, Gossip POPE?*, p. 13.

Rehearsal, by selling Bargains, praising himself, laughing at his Joke, and making his own Works the Test of every Man's Criticism; but he seems to be in some Jeopardy, for the Ghost of *Homer* has lately spoke to him in *Greek*, and *Shakespear* resolves to bring him, as he has brought *Shakespear*, to a Tragical Conclusion.'[1] The Shakespeare, admittedly one of the least defensible of Pope's labours, was frequently subjected to such incidental jibes as 'now I think of it, I had *Pope's* Shakespear brought to my Shop t'other Day among other Waste Paper...'[2] The translation of Homer was dismissed as dull and also as a fraud, a passing off of the labours of employed hacks as the work of the master. He sneered at 'Mr. Broome and Mr. Pope, who were rather Undertakers of Homer, to bury him over again, than Translators';[3] and when, in a journalistic fantasy, he examined the houses of his enemies with his 'optic-acoustic-stentero-phonic telescope' which could discover stolen goods, he commented as he viewed Pope's house at Twickenham, 'They paid him their Subscriptions for *his own Works*, and what he brought them in was done by *Undertakers* and *Jobbers of Rhymes*, at so much the great hundred.'[4] But all these were backward shots in a battle where the real enemy was close at hand, the monstrous and insulting bulk of 'Mr. *Pope's* History of *his own Times*, very gravely intitul'd by him, *The Dunciad*'.[5]

Henley had no doubts about the cause and the motive of the poem, and would simply not have understood much modern criticism of it as a noble defence of moral and cultural standards. For him the cause was a specific personal resentment and the motive was to labour, 'tho' impotently, which is the Defect of his *Genius*, not of his Inclination, to deride a large Number of Persons'.[6] This is his version of the poem's genesis:

... the Dunciad was written by that sweet singing Bird of *Athens*, Mr. Pope, to abuse certain Gentlemen on a parallel Motive, as the *Craftsman* traduces the Government. Mr. *Theobald*, in his *Shakespear Restor'd*, convicted Mr. *Pope* of Ignorance, both of Shakespear, which he pretended to publish, and of the *English Tongue*, in numerous Instances. Mr. Pope's little Bag of Choler burst within him on his sinking in

---

[1] *A Dissertation upon Nonsense*, p. 29, in *Oratory Transactions No. 2* (1729).
[2] *Hyp Doctor*, 16 Nov. 1731.   [3] *Hyp Doctor*, 12 Apr. 1737.
[4] *Hyp Doctor*, 18 July 1732.   [5] *Hyp Doctor*, 17 July 1733.
[6] Henley, *An Oration on Grave Conundrums and Serious Buffoons etc.* (1729), p. 14.

Reputation, by that attack of Mr. Theobald, & he wrote a *Dunciad* to blacken all that knew he was prov'd an *Ignoramus*, that is, all Mankind. . . .[1]

Henley's peculiar contribution to *Dunciad* criticism is his insistence that, once the decision was taken to write the poem, Pope employed Richard Savage as his collector of material.

Mr. Pope, [he wrote,] piqu'd by some, resolv'd like his brother *Lyrick* in the Play, to go Home, and *write a Satire* on *all Mankind*: The Brat was like the Father, Dad's known Phyz to a Tittle: Sheer-Poetry, for *all* was Fiction . . . Richard Savage, Esq. was the *Jack*-all of *that Ass* in a *Lyon's Skin*, he was his *Provider*: like *Montmaur*, the *Parasite of Paris*, he rambled about to gather up *Scraps of Scandal*, as a Price for his *Twickenham Ordinary*; no Purchase no Pay; no Tittle-Tattle, no Dinner: Hence arose those *Utopian* Tales of Persons, Characters and Things, that rais'd by the clean Hands of this Heliconian Scavenger, the Dunghill of the Dunciad.[2]

A year later he repeated the charge in almost the same words: 'But that same Mr. *Savage*, chiefly, was entertain'd by you to give you Tittle-Tattle for Bread, of my self and others.'[3] Henley blamed Pope for never troubling to find out whether his scraps of tittle-tattle were true, but of using them indiscriminately with no regard for fairness nor accuracy. Because of this, and because of the violence and bad temper of the poem, he excluded it from the body of great satire, dismissing it as '*Catholic Invective*, but not true, nor Poetry; nothing is Poetry, that offends Reason, Fact, Probability, Good Nature, Virtue, Decency, Good Manners, or Contradicts the Attributes of God.'[4] What made *The Dunciad* even more dangerous—and Henley was honest enough to say this—was that it was wonderfully written. Though it had its crudities when 'Mr. P. adds the dirty Dialect to that of the Water, and is in Love with the Nymphs of *Fleet-Ditch*',[5] its general technical brilliance was treacherously seductive, as he admitted in couplets of his own in a *Hyp Doctor* poem:

> Delicious P——! how ravishing thy Art!
> O! charming Numbers, will but Fools take Part!

---

[1] *Hyp Doctor*, 22 June 1731.   [2] *Hyp Doctor*, 29 Apr. 1735.
[3] *Why how now, Gossip POPE?*, p. 6.   [4] *Hyp Doctor*, 25 Nov. 1735.
[5] *Oratory Transactions No. 2*, p. 18.

> Produc'd false lights the vulgar to mislead,
> Which made them from the Path of Reason tread;[1]

The perfection of the poetry became in itself an evil, as the instrument of persuasion in establishing falsehood as truth.

Mr. Pope in his Dunciad [he wrote] has told numerous lyes, the belief of which has prevailed above ten years, and, by Virtue of Prejudice, and his Way of telling those Lyes, may be believed much longer: how many false facts have I (and could again) convicted him of, in that dirty, scandalous Chronicle, which, like a Harlot, that paints, dresses and sings tolerably, pleases and poisons at the same time.[2]

Certainly because one of those 'numerous lyes, the Belief of which has prevailed above ten years' concerned himself, he was understandably indefatigable in his attack on the poem. It is as well that he could not know that the lie was to prevail for over two hundred years, and almost be posterity's only knowledge of him.

The attempt to undermine *The Dunciad* in his journalism and orations was augmented by Disputations at the Oratory and, although the *Grub Street Journal* alleged that Henley was defeated despite his attempts to secure a supporting clique over drinks in a tavern before the meeting, Henley claimed victory. He reported that 'After the Question on Mr. Pope's Dunciad, in which, tho' above 30 Persons spoke, Mr. Henley vindicated himself so clearly, ... Mr. Pope's friends gave him up, and the Orator's enemies became his Friends.'[3] Twelve years after this event Henley hinted again that there had taken place an even closer confrontation— that he had met Pope and discussed the poem. We have already seen this picture of Pope 'pale and trembling' and attempting to shift the blame: now he adds another detail to the picture. 'I once had the Pleasure of being known to the learned Mr. Warburton, when he and I were younger,' he wrote, no doubt referring to their school-days at the same school; 'I envy not, that I am in my Oratory-Church-Militant, and he is in his Coach-Church-Triumphant: I wish he had known that Mr. Pope promis'd me to omit me in his next Edition, because some think ill of me without Grounds on that Score.'[4] All we can say of this story is that Pope failed to keep his promise, and by that time had passed

---

[1] *Hyp Doctor*, 17 Sept. 1737.   [2] *Hyp Doctor*, 6 Jan. 1741.
[3] *G.S.J.*, 5 Jan. 1738.   [4] Advertisement for 20 Apr. 1750 (Lysons 163).

beyond being able to confirm or deny its truth. Henley remained forever pilloried in *The Dunciad* and, for the rest of his life, waited like an angry spider to rush out on any poem of Pope's which buzzed its way into the world.

The *Moral Essays* and the *Essay on Man* were no more exempt from this attention than the satires, and were denounced for their complacency, hypocrisy, and muddled thinking. The *Epistle on Taste* infuriated Henley by its bland assertion of infallibility in judgement, when 'His Works are, it seems, the Test of every Man's Probity, as puny Pope insists that his verses are the Standard of every Man's TASTE',[1] and this word TASTE, often in distinguishing capitals to prevent our missing the reference, occurred over and over again in the '30s as he laid into those Tory pamphleteers and lampooners whose 'Leader has a *soft* and *agreeable Pavillion* at *Twickenham*, and their Watchword is *Taste*'.[2] How far Henley saw this TASTE as a false assumption of superiority concealing an inner baseness is clear in these extracts from an imaginary epitaph on Pope, 'occasion'd by his Poem of Taste in Building':

> His TASTE of Judgment in making verses upon Building,
> When nothing was ever so *sorrily Built as himself*;
> His TASTE of History, in calling a Meal a *Sacrifice*,
> When at Sacrifices Dogs are whip't out, and he stay'd,
> His TASTE of Honour in dining with Lords to Lampoon them,
> As he expos'd his Friend, Mr. Addison, in Satire.

N.B. The Poem and Poet are both register'd in the History of INSIPIDS.[3]

The *Epistle to Bathurst, Of the Use of Riches*, was greeted with an equally hostile review when it appeared in 1733,[4] a review which is of interest in its insistence on the political purpose of the poem, seeing it not as a general moral disquisition, nor even as a general lament on the corruption of the modern age by wealth, but as a very specific attack on the Ministry, and timed to appear before the town at a very carefully calculated moment. 'Mr. Pope', said Henley, 'sallies out of Twickenham like *La Mancha*'s Knight in his *Essay upon Criticism* with Mr. Budgell's fifth Edition of HIS *Liberty and Property*, (no other Person's) before him, for

---

[1] *Hyp Doctor*, 18 Jan. 1732. [2] *Hyp Doctor*, 8 Feb. 1732.
[3] *Hyp Doctor*, 21 Dec. 1731. [4] *Hyp Doctor*, 23 Jan. 1733.

Arms, the Day before the meeting of Parliament', and he asserted that of all persons unqualified to write against riches and the corrupt amassing of riches, Pope was surely in the forefront.

Mr. Pope has written a Satire upon *Riches* . . . Riches acquir'd by false Friendship, false Principles, false Religion, false Scandal, false Poetry, to all which this Gentleman has been True: had this been publish'd before the Subscription to his *Homer*, they who lavish'd *their Riches* upon it might have been wiser in their use of them. For what has a Poet to do with *Riches*? Or, with what Truth can he decry Corruption, Venality, and the Misapplication of Riches, who owes his House at Twickenham, and his Fortune to the CORRUPT TASTE of some, that could not separate the *Poetical Buffoon* from the *Real Friend*?

He accused Pope of lack of invention, using commonplaces and of continually writing out of humour, but his final blow was political. He dismissed Pope as a cat's-paw of Bolingbroke and his clique of out-of-place Tories, bringing out into the firing line all the old Whig artillery of the scandal of Utrecht, the years of Tory misrule, and the threat of Popery–Jacobitism—

But we are properly to consider Mr. POPE, as a *short* DRY COW, or *small Syringe*, wherewith my L–d B––l––ke *froths* his Venom to *squirt* it at the Ministry: Therefore Mr. POPE, Mr. BUDGEL, the EXCISE, the ARMY &c. all push'd out at once before this Sessions: Tho' as this Poet exposes his Patrons, he has play'd his GAMBOLS with HIM in speaking of

> . . . France reveng'd by Anne's and Edward's *Arms*;

which fulfill'd his Wizzard's Prophecy to Sir J. Bl––t at the Treaty of *Utrecht* with a Vengeance, when the *Use of Riches* was so well known, that Mr. POPE'S Darling Minister (now) sacrific'd all the Treasure and Battles of Ten Years to *France*.

Romish as well as Tory sympathies were found in the poem, and Henley wrote at length to prove that the Papists were indeed the originators of the Fire of London, as the inscription on the Monument asserted and which Pope dismissed as a lie. Ten years later he returned to the point with added bitterness and physical abuse of Pope who

a Small Member of a very *Hot Church*, accustom'd to *Roasting Cookry*, to *burn Hereticks*, had this Distich on ye Fire of *London*, or rather ye Inscription on ye Monument,

There *London's Column*, pointing to ye skies,
Like a Tall Bully, lifts her head & lies.

But *Pope*, a *Short Bully*, may lye, as well as a *Tall one*: only being a *Shrub*, and a *crooked Billet of Knee-Timber*, he envy'd ye Monument for its *Height & Straightness*.[1]

The *Essay on Man* also faced its trial at the hands of Oratory disputations and, though we have no record of the prosecution or defence pleadings, the inevitable verdict was publicly and triumphantly recorded. The Sunday subject on 31 October 1736 was 'Whether Mr. Pope's Philosophy in his Ethical Epistles or Essay on Man, be just?'[2] and we hear that there was such 'great stickling for the reputation of Mr. Pope'[3] that night that the subject was to be pursued on the following Sunday when the assembled company would hear 'Mr Pope's Philosophy examin'd by Reason, Wit, Poetry, Criticism, the Gospel, Milton, &c. shewing his ethical Epistles to be a Dunciad on all Mankind, the Creation, the Whole Church &c.'.[4] As a result of this inquisition, 'Mr. Pope, in the Capacity of a man of Sense and Philosophy, fell on *Sunday* last, at a fair Disputation, managed by two of his Advocates.'[5] Some hint is afforded of the manner and tone of these proceedings from the account of an eyewitness in the *Grub Street Journal* who reported that in a disputation on 'Whether Mr. Pope be a man of sense in one Argument' Henley had taken the phrase which aroused so much religious and philosophical disquiet—'Whatever is, is right'—and from it deduced that he, Henley, must therefore be right, and therefore not a proper object of satire![6] This account seems dependable, despite its source, because, in an issue of the *Hyp Doctor* of the same week, we find Henley using the same bantering methods to expose the dangerous inadequacy of Pope's general foundations. He depicted a gang of thieves discussing the *Essay on Man* and finding, in its misinterpretation, justification for their thieving activities. 'This Pope', they agree, 'is a fine Fellow: prithee, who is he, does he belong to our Gang?' The offending 'Whatever is, is right' provokes the conclusion that 'it is *right* for us to take a Purse, there is *Reason* for it and it is *Pride* that makes *Authority punish us*' and, after studying the couplet

[1] Discourse for 28 Aug. 1743 (B.M. MSS.Add. 11920).
[2] *Hyp Doctor*, 26 Oct. 1736.   [3] *Hyp Doctor*, 2 Nov. 1736.
[4] *Hyp Doctor*, 6 Nov. 1736.   [5] *Hyp Doctor*, 9 Nov. 1736.
[6] *G.S.J.*, 15 Dec. 1737.

All Discord, Harmony not understood;
All partial Evil, universal Good,

they agree heartily—'True; when we and the People we meet on
the Road are at Discord, it is Harmony, but ill understood at
the Old Bailey.'[1] Such was the popular handling of the accusations
of an inherent fatalism in the poem which in the following year
Crousaz was to present in such a serious way as to give Pope
much more concern than these first Oratory rumblings, and require the urgent aid of the Orator's old schoolfellow Warburton.

In that year, however, Henley had turned his attack onto a new
poem, Pope's imitation of the *Fourth Satire of Dr. John Donne*,
or *The Impudent*, which, as a loyal Government journalist, Henley
saw as a slight on the Court and the Court party. As the poem
also contained a reference to himself he had double cause to be
angry. Disputation and journal were again his weapons, and our
first account of the 'disputation' comes, unusually enough, not
from Henley but from the *St. James's Evening Post*:

A publick Disputation was intended to be held at the Oratory on
Sunday last in the evening, upon the Question, Whether Mr. Pope's
Impertinent, or Visit to the Court, be a *truly witty*, *satirical Poem*; but no
antagonist appearing, Mr. Orator took upon himself to prove the
Negative; and after divers wide, logical Inferences, rambling criticisms,
low Quibbles, and some harsh Reflections on Mr. Pope and his
Religion, (being very essential to the Topick he was upon) was going
off triumphantly, but not without an attack from a Gentleman, then
present, who informed him he should take an other Opportunity to
disprove his Assertion . . . and prove that Mr. Pope's Poem is quite
the Reverse of what he had endeavour'd to make it appear; however
it cannot much be wonder'd at that Mr. Orator shou'd endeavour to
damn Mr. Pope, as a Poet, in this Performance (tho' in the main he
allow'd him to be a good one) when it is consider'd, that Mr. Pope had
long ago so justly damn'd him for an *Orator* in the *Dunciad*.[2]

The angry gentleman was as good as his promise and obviously
brought along his supporters, for Henley, well satisfied with the
result, recorded that 'A Body of Gentlemen having agreed to
Dispute at the Oratory on Sunday last, for a Public Good, their
own Reputation, and Improvement, attack'd the exposition and

[1] *Hyp Doctor*, 9 Nov. 1736.
[2] *St. James's Evening Post*, 3–6 Sept. 1737.

Oration then deliver'd, and were regularly reply'd to.'[1] The critical line Henley took in oration and disputation can be surmised from the *Hyp Doctor* attacks on the poem which he kept up for three weeks in September of '37. In the main his charge was one of plagiarism and lack of invention, a charge he had often brought against Pope—

Mr. Pope deals sometimes in *Plagiarism* of a higher Class, or rather, is a better Furbisher and Trimmer of Second-hand Wares, as his *Rape of the Lock, Pastorals, Windsor Forest*, and *Descriptions and Notes of the Dunciad* abundantly testify; for there is not one Poem which can be called Invention (the main Constituent of a Poem) in his whole Collection.[2]

It is interesting in the light of much modern criticism of Pope's use of allusion and the enriching of his work by layers of reference, to read a not-uninformed contemporary critic who appears to know nothing of all this or even to have grasped the theory of the Imitation which had been developing since the late seventeenth century. In an open letter to Pope, Henley wrote, 'It is, Sir, I think, most generally agreed that your Numbers and Versification, Images and Diction are pleasing: But we must go deeper to be *justly pleased in Poetry*.'[3] To go deeper, the poet must be a *maker*, and here Pope had failed. He had merely copied Donne, and Henley printed lengthy quotations from Donne's satire to prove his point. It is difficult to see why Henley tried to make critical capital in this way, for Pope had printed the Donne text alongside his own in the 1735 collected works, thereby inviting readers to judge and enjoy his poem as an imitation. Perhaps Henley had only seen the anonymously published 1733 edition, but this seems highly unlikely for a man who took such a watchful interest in all Pope's doings. Whether the cause was ignorance or stupidity, he continued to hammer away at the Donne source which invalidated the poem not only as original poetry but as a comment on the Court. He took up a quibbling and often stupid line-by-line analysis, either missing the point or deliberately misinterpreting; but, in the midst of this, dropped another clue in the mystery of his personal meeting with Pope. On the line, 'Henley himself I've heard' he comments: 'Right. That was, when Henley pronounced his Dissertation concerning *Nonsense*, and gave Mr.

---

[1] *Hyp Doctor*, 13 Sept. 1737.   [2] *Hyp Doctor*, 24 Feb. 1736.
[3] *Hyp Doctor,* 13 Sept. 1737

Pope the Precedence in it: Who by the Way, at the end of the Oration, was mortify'd at a *Great Person's* declared Approbation of that Discourse, on his asking his Opinion, and endeavouring to decry it.'[1] This discourse was spoken on 29 May, 1728, just over a week after the first appearance of *The Dunciad*. If Pope and—as Henley surely suggests—Walpole were in the audience, it was indeed a memorable occasion. It could not have been the meeting when the angry Pope, 'pale and trembling', waited for the Orator after the audience had dispersed and explained away the *Dunciad* prose-notes, for those notes did not appear until the following year. For the rest, these papers merely yield examples of abuse, critical in part, but still in the Billingsgate tradition of Popeana:

Mr. Pope is no Satirist, no Philosopher, no Critic, he is not a Man of Sense, but a mere Bundle of Ignorance, Folly and Contradiction: What Lord Rochester says, is fulfilled in thee, O *Alexander!*
   ... We plainly see,
   That Satire's of Divine Authority,
   For God made one on Man, when he made thee.[2]

and even more violent:

Mr. Pope is a baby ... Mr. Pope, by being always malicious, must be always disorder'd ... Is not Mr. P. a huffing, puft Braggart, when he calls himself a Terror of the Town? ... Mr. Pope who is an Ape, an Imitator, a meer Mimic; Dr. *Donne's Ape* confess'd, *Horace's Ape*, *Dryden's Ape*, and an *Ape* to all the Poets: for is there *one Original* written by this *Jackanapes* of *Parnassus*? Had H--ley been the *Priest* when he was baptiz'd, he would, in *Decency*, have christen'd him PUG POPE, instead of SAWNEY.[3]

A similar outburst had greeted the publication of another attack on the Court in the middle of the year, the *Epistle to Augustus*, and again the party journalist had rushed to the defence of the King and that party of peace which Pope had attacked, motivated, according to Henley, by pique and spleen at not being made Poet Laureate. 'The Sword of Augustus', he wrote, 'and Thousands to second it, will be ready to defend his *Sceptre*, and trim the Pens of these Poets.' As for Pope, he wrote him off in the nicely cadenced concentration of 'His *Poetry* like his *Religion*, is professedly built on Hear-say; his *Fame*, like his *Verse*, is all *Fiction*; and what *befringes* the *Rails* of *Bedlam* is his proper *Bays*.'[4]

[1] *Hyp Doctor*, 13 Sept. 1737.   [2] *Hyp Doctor*, 20 Sept. 1737.
[3] *Hyp Doctor*, 27 Sept. 1737.   [4] *Hyp Doctor*, 31 May 1737.

Pope died on 30 May 1744, and all there was left for Henley to do was to speak ill of the dead. The Oratory advertisements for the summer of this year show that he found frequent opportunity. Pope's last days were celebrated by an oration item which drew together the *Dunciad* collaborators in 'Mr. P's Extreme Unction from Mr. W–rb–n',[1] and his death provoked inevitably a funeral oration:

Friend Pope's Funeral Sermon, the fifth Dunciad. Mr. P*pe's Obsequy, or a Farewell Lecture to the Arch-Poetist and Executioner General of his Age; who never dedicated one Poem to the 10th of June, nor an Epic to our Glorious Edward I or III or to the Black Prince, or Richard I, or Henry V. nor wrote one Satire on M*M; but was more fond of hanging up in Effigie little Fools than great R*s, and had been the woful Ruin of many a pretty Gentleman's Judgment and Honesty.[2]

Henley participated, too, in the reading of the will with a 'commentary on that Part of Mr. P*pe's Last Will, in which he resigns his Soul to God, enquiring whether he did not die in—Tindal's, Toland's and in Woolston's—Religion, &c.'.[3] Henley continued that summer to cast pebbles on the grave from the Oratory pulpit—'Pope no peerless Bard',[4] 'sobs in verse on Pope's Death',[5] and to examine 'Mr. *Pope's unexceptionable Epitaph*, written by an *Undeniable Friend,—his own dear Self*—so that none will censure it',[6] but his hatred of Pope did not long survive his enemy's death. It was now the critics who came to bury Pope as much as to praise him, and Henley's interest had been personal and political and only partly critical. Moreover the rebellion of '45 and his dangerous involvement in it gave him more immediate cause for concern than the insulting over an enemy who could no longer harm him. It was not until the '50s that he found a new literary opponent of any repute, in the strange person whose veneration for the memory of Pope was as strong as Henley's detestation—Christopher Smart.

Smart's first appearance in London, after leaving Cambridge, had not been as a poet and not in his own person. Disguised as

[1] Advertisement for 28 Apr. 1744 (Lysons 127).
[2] Advertisement in the *Daily Advertiser*, 9 June 1744.
[3] Advertisement in the *Daily Advertiser*, 23 June 1744.
[4] Advertisement for 14 July 1744 (Lysons 130).
[5] Advertisement for 18 Aug. 1744 (Lysons 131).
[6] Discourse for 10 July 1744 (B.M. MSS.Add. 11921).

'Mrs. Mary Midnight', he offered to the town in 1751 the first volume of a miscellany of poems and essays, *The Midwife, or the Old Woman's Magazine*; but it was not until Mrs. Midnight launched out into theatrical production that Henley was drawn in. An advertisement on 3 December 1751 gives some idea of the curious entertainment offered at the Castle Tavern, and the reasons for Henley's interest and disquiet.

This Day, being Tuesday the 3rd. instant; at seven in the evening, Paternoster-Row, a grand Concert of Vocal and Instrumental Musick, by Gentlemen who are eminent Performers. And at the same time will be open'd, and given gratis, THE OLD WOMAN'S ORATORY; or *Henley in Petticoats*. To be conducted by Mrs. Mary Midnight, Author of the Midwife, and her Family. There will be four Orations. After the first of which Signor Antonio Amaticiano, from Naples, will perform a Concerto on the Cremona Staccato, vulgarly call'd the Salt-Box. After the second will be presented a Great Creature, on a very uncommon Instrument. After the third, a Solo on the Viol d'Amore, and another Piece by the Great Creature. Then the Candles will be snuff'd to soft Musick by Signor Claudio Molepitano for his Diversion, being the first time of any Gentleman's appearing in that Character. And the whole will conclude with an Oration by Old Time, in Favour of Matrimony; a Solo on the Violoncello by Cupid in *propria Persona*; and a Song to the Tune of *the Roast Beef of Old England*, to which all the good Company are desired to join in Chorus. Note, No Admittance without Tickets, which are to be had at the Bedford Coffee-House, Covent Garden, and at the Place of Performance, at 2s,6d, each. The Room will be lighted with Wax Candles. The Publication of the next Number of Mrs. Midnight's Magazine will be deferr'd until the 16th. instant, and will contain the Orations deliver'd at the Oratory.[1]

Henley had apparently been forewarned of this new threat to his reputation and, three days before the first performance, fired a warning shot, drawing scandalous conclusions from Smart's fondness for feminine pseudonyms and the donning of petti-coats—'Ah Molly Smart!... Pimlico Molly Midnight translated to Rump-Castle: Hum-buggers-bougre.'[2] Once it was certain that he was being uproariously parodied in Mrs. Midnight's orations he filled the Oratory with his furious replies, the advertisements

---

[1] Advertisement for 3 Dec. 1751 (Lysons 170).
[2] Advertisement for 30 Nov. 1751 (Lysons 171). Moira Dearnley, in *The Poetry of Christopher Smart* (1969), pp. 25–6, discusses the possible sexual abnormality behind these disguises of Smart and his circle. Henley, clearly, was in no doubt.

for them being often almost incoherent in their abuse and innuendo. He harped on the disreputable poverty of the participants—

Ah! Kitty Smart dead?... the Religion, a Plan so envy'd, that the mimicking it last Tuesday for a *'s Benefit, sav'd a broken Fellow of a College, his Hedge-Tavern Fiddlers, Booksellers, Printers, Bunters, Rogues, Mollies, and Vagabonds, from starving. . . . Prayer, that false Pleasures and false Law, may not make our two Cities Sodom and Gomorrah.[1]

The following week came even darker hints of a plot against him by this gang of mercenary hacks:

Mother Midnight's Pettycoat Plot has no Secrets: J. Wild's Hydra of 5 or 6 Heads of the Rappers, (as among the Garnanites,) should be knock'd down by Hercules's Club. They are beaten out of the Castle to Mortimer's Hole in Westmr. Those Macheaths have hir'd a poor-Smart-ill-paid Author, and a shivering Bookseller, for Music, and Saltbox, and to make the Old Woman sell 4d: and to swear all into Places: as Gregg by Harley, so Henley: a Treasonable Packet was sent to his House yesterday, to be found by a Messenger. The old Play.[2]

The town, however, did not share Henley's disapproval, and the show was such a success that it was announced that it would move from the Castle Tavern to the theatre in the Haymarket, a promotion which Henley greeted with shocked anger. To mount such a production at a time of public mourning for the Queen of Denmark! Surely now that a licensed theatre was being used, the Stage Licensing law should be enforced—

The Religion of the Oratory is, in the Face of the Court, Justices, Licenser of the Stage, and C. of the University, advertis'd to be expos'd on the Hay Market Stage, by such as were driven from College, and from the City: and just on the Mourning for the Q. of D. Courtiers may punish this Indignity to them, by serving the Vagrants: Otherwise the Mourners and Actors may be thought Good Company, and the Stage Act useful for Christmas Pies.[3]

This appeal to law and decency went unheeded and the show went on at the Haymarket where its success continued. One member of

---

[1] Advertisement for 7 Dec. 1751 (Lysons 171).
[2] Advertisement for 11 Dec. 1751 (ibid. 171).
[3] Advertisement of no date (ibid. 171).

the audience in May 1752 was Horace Walpole who some days later wrote to George Montagu, 'I was t'other night to see what is now grown the fashion, Mother Midnight's Oratory—it appeared the lowest buffoonery in the world even to me who am used to my uncle Horace. There is a bad oration to ridicule, what it is too like, Orator Henley: all the rest is perverted music.'[1] A report on the day following its first performance gave a more glowing report and taunted Henley with its success.

Yesterday Noon was perform'd, at the New Theatre in the Hay-Market, Mrs. Midnight's Oratory, which was conducted with the utmost Decency, and receiv'd with most extraordinary Applause, not-withstanding the many Artifices made use of to depreciate it in the Eyes of the Publick; ... There was a most excellent Band of Musick, consisting of thirty Hands, among whom were several Persons of Fortune and Distinction, on whose Account all the Performers were dress'd in Masquerade; and it was universally acknowledg'd, that there was more real Casuistry, in the Jew's-Harp, and more sterling Sense in the Salt-Box, than ever came from the Tub, at the Slaughter-House of Sense, Wit, and Reason, near Clare-Market.[2]

The entertainment was a curious medley of music, sketch, and recitation, slap-stick, and circus turns. The overture to *Ariadne*, the march from *Judas Maccabeus*, the *Water Music*, alternated with solos on the Jew's harp, appearances of Cupid, 'a man who plays so nimbly on the kettle drum, that he has reduced that noisy instrument to be an object of sight ... another plays on a violin and trumpet together ... another mimics a bagpipe with a German flute ... the last fellow imitates farting and curtseying to a French horn. ...'[3] In the midst of all this came the orations which so angered Henley, and which were so popular.[4] Their popularity is evidenced by the proposal to mount another such production, recorded in a curious document entitled *Fun: A Parodi-tragi-comical Satire. As it was to have been perform'd at the Castle Tavern, Pater-noster Row, on Thursday Feb. 13th. 1752, but Suppressed by a special Order from the Lord Mayor and Court of*

---

[1] Letter of 12 May 1752, Yale edition of the correspondence, ed. Lewis and Brown, vol. ix, p. 131.
[2] Advertisement for 28 Dec. 1751 (Lysons 170).
[3] Walpole's letter of 12 May 1752. See note 1.
[4] For further details of these, see the advertisement of 30 Dec. 1751 (Lysons 170).

Aldermen. The piece has been attributed to William Kenrick, Smart's friend and sometime collaborator in the Mrs. Midnight jokes, and Henley clearly considered it as part of the general Smart assault on him. He welcomed its suppression with an Oratory item 'Midnight Screech-Owls Flight from a ruin'd Castle'.[1] We may take it, I think, that in the fourth scene of this strange piece we have an example of the type of parodic satire which Mrs. Midnight sandwiched between the other acts of her variety show, and well understand why Henley was infuriated by this distorted imitation of his oratorical manner:

SCENE IV
The BRAZEN HEAD
A *Specimen of* TRUE ORATORY

Old Women the Pests of Creation—what constitutes them? Ignorance and a College Education—University itself an old Woman—Want of Impudence want of Senses—no Man beside myself e'er dar'd to say so—Nonsense—Puns—Quibbles—Conundrums—*Smart* Sayings—St. *Paul's Church-yard* and Grub Street the same Place—Puffs—*Horses,* the Consumers of Oats, gone to draw *Asses* to *Mother Midnight's Oratory*—Long Ears best to taste the Music of the Salt-box—In my humble Opinion they are got on the wrong side of the Post there—*Mary Midnight* not herself—See the *Old Woman's Dunciad*—what signifies her pretending to stand up for her own Existence? She don't exist at all—I can prove it.

Roxana Termagent, an old Apple Woman, who is she? Who's afraid? Not I—I don't screen myself under Petticoats—none but Fools and Villains oppose *Justice*—Who's a Favourite at Court?—I am—they can't persuade me to be a Bishop for all that—*Subsidies subside*—Who's King then?—I shall write my own memoirs soon—or set up a Daily-paper—the *Clare-Market Journal*—who'll smoke then? Protestants—who?—Pope a Pop—who says so?—No honest Man—I am an honest Man—Nobody'l deny that—whoever could prove me a rogue.

It is necessary Women should have masculine Epithets when Men creep into Petticoats—why should not a Woman be call'd a Rogue, Rascal, Scoundrel, Villain—no Proof to the contrary—Sauce for Goose Sauce for Gander—I say it—prove it—*New* Astronomy *no* Astronomy; *Gresham College* an *Old Woman*—Man in the Moon set up there by *Moses.* *Moses* a much greater Man than Sir Isaac Newton—a Comet, what?—Neither a *Catherine Pear* nor a *Cheshire Cheese.*

[1] Advertisement for 22 Feb. 1752 (Lysons 171).

Mother Midnight made use of unfair Weapons—Salt-boxes! why does a Salt-box make her a better *Man*? Why I can get five Salt-boxes and then I am five times as good as she—Solo on a Broom-stick—did you ever hear a Dog sing—Signor *Canini* from *Bologna*—come forth—now trust your Ears—

Here a Song by a Dog

There's the masterly—the grand Coup—the ev'ry Thing—Music itself no more than Sound. Sound no more than Noise—I myself a good Musician—perhaps a little harsh to old Women or so—but come—Signor *Canini* renew the Strain—

Dog sings again.

—Conviction! Now who's Conqueror? *Epaminondas* a great Man—I much like him—have been up long enough since I go down unconquer'd.

We may agree with a contemporary review in the *Inspector* that this stuff is 'the most absurd and most contemptible of all Performances that have disgraced a Theatre',[1] but the public thought otherwise and eagerly patronized them for the next year or so. Henley frequently retaliated in the Oratory by demanding 'That the Ministry will suppress Vagabond Stage-Pulpits in Westmr. as London did',[2] and by exposing, with some justification, the inadequate crudity of the means employed to devalue him, as he suggests in this conversation between a Lawyer and a Parson:

L. What, no Receipt to confute Mr. Henley?
P. Yes, by F. Kit's Mother, the Preaching Midwife, to bring B's to Bed.
L. And how answer the Coup de Grace?
P. By fencing with a Salt-Box, and nothing in't.
L. And how reply to the Plan of the Oratory?
P. By a Jew's-Trump twang-dillo'd, by Mother Church.
L. And how get rid of his Arguments, Learning and Wit?
P. By Fiddle and Broomstick, and the Cov.Gard.Journal, No.3. calling Judges and Justices Old Women.
L. Ha, ha, ha, you have him there, egad. Ha, ha, ha![3]

The last exchange with Smart was poetical rather than theatrical. On 3 July 1752 Smart's *Poems on Several Occasions* was published and Henley greeted it with a letter to the press, asserting

---

[1] The *Inspector*, 7 Dec. 1752.
[2] Advertisement for 21 Mar. 1752 (Lysons 172).
[3] Advertisement for 17 Apr. 1752 (Lysons 173).

that, if a Smart Rag-Fair Collection of Poems (not one Poem in them) on several Occasions, i.e. those of the Jobber and Manufacturer, with Royal Paper, and Pack thread, and Cuts, George o'Horschak and lac'd Gingerbread, claims 10*s*. 6*d*. of the Cullies that buy it, I am intitled to twenty Guineas a Head, every Oratory: I will lay 1000 Guineas on it. My Esther, written at 15, is a Diamond to it.[1]

Smart was able to accept even such criticism without rage, and reply with exuberant banter. He bided his time until the following year when his satire on John Hill, *The Hilliad*, appeared with mock-learned footnotes compiled by his collaborator Arthur Murphy, and there Henley was attacked with devastatingly accurate parodies of his style. To Line 101, 'But boldly versify without a Muse', is appended the note:

No! the devil a bit! I am the only person that can do that! My Poems, written at fifteen, were done without the assistance of My Muse, and better than all Smart's poetry—The Muses are Strumpets—they frequently give an intellectual *Gonorrhoea*—Court debt not paid—I'll never be poet Laureate—Coup de Grace unanswerable—our foes shall knuckle, and buckle, and truckle, and all our friends shall checkle and chuckle—five pounds to any bishop that will equal this—*Gum Guiacum* Latin for *lignum vitae*—Adam the first Dutchman—victorious stroke for Old England—Tweedle-dum and Tweedle-dee.
Oratory-Right-Reason-Chapel, Saturday 13th
of January, and old-stile for ever.

Later in the poem, at lines 105–8,

> He said—and Clamour of Commotion born,
> Rear'd to the skies her ear-afflicting horn;
> While JARGON grav'd his titles on a block,
> And styl'd him M.D. Acad. Budig. Soc.

the Orator is allowed further comment:

JARGON is here properley introduced graving our hero's titles, which are admirably brought into verse, but the gentleman who wrote the last note, Mr. Orator H--ley, takes umbrage at this passage, and exclaimeth to the following effect. 'Jargon is meant for me. There is more music in a peal of marrowbones and cleavers than in these verses. —I am a logician upon fundamentals.—A rationalist,—a lover of

---

[1] Advertisement for 4 July 1752 (Lysons 174).

mankande, Glastonbury thorn, huzza, boys.—Wit a vivacious command of all objects and ideas.—I am the only wit in Great Britain. See
Oratory Tracts &c. 10036.'

The spelling 'mankande' is interesting, and is repeated in another
satire of the period, making it very likely that here in this phonetic
representation of one of Henley's favourite words we have one
authentic note of the famous voice.

After this exchange, Henley appears to have lost interest in
Smart. The last three years of his life were frequently interrupted
by illness, and there were, anyhow, other more active enemies
to keep at bay. In 1756 Henley died, and Smart's first complete
mental breakdown removed him, if not so permanently, from the
world of controversy. It is perhaps as well that Henley never
knew of his adversary's madness, for his triumphant use of it as a
final insult would have been as painful as it would have been
inevitable.

II. RELIGIOUS CONTROVERSY

It might seem inaccurate to speak of Henley's religious controversies, for it is almost impossible to find any opponents who, after
the first few years of the Oratory, took specific issue with him,
or attacked with reasoned arguments any of the positions he took
up. His beliefs and pronouncements were either ignored as
beneath contempt, or were treated merely with contempt, general
and unargued, such as that of Dr. Delaune, President of St.
John's College, Oxford, and Lady Margaret Professor of Divinity,
who, in dedicating a volume of Twelve Sermons in 1728, spoke
of the heresy and infidelity abroad in the nation,

which the very Defenders of the Faith themselves, though armed with
Regal Power, have not been able to give a check to. They have long
since stole up into the Pulpit, and prostituted that sacred place to so
prophane a use, as from thence to publish the vain Inventions of Men,
instead of the pure Word of God, and very often in direct contradiction
to it. Nay; to make mirth with these enormous impieties, they have at
last found a way to make merchantable goods of them; there being one
great market, *Newport* I think it is called, where they may by wholesale
or retail be had every week in the year.[1]

---

[1] William Delaune, *Twelve Sermons upon Several Subjects and Occasions* (1728), The
Dedication.

Equally typical is this contemptuous dismissal of Henley later in his life, as 'By Profession a *Druid*, by Practice an affected *Dissenter* to the utmost Extent of Affectation of *dissenting*, so as to have tried and quarter'd the whole Circle of Religions, and to shelter himself at last in *Superstition*'.[1] Both the contempt and the refusal to take him seriously infuriated Henley, and produced in all his writings a belligerent controversial tone, as he defined his beliefs and shouted his defiance at a world he knew was hostile but which never seriously took up his challenge. The only answer was the repeated echo of his own voice, year after year, asserting, denouncing and demanding the serious attention which never came.

Such attention was given to more distinguished men whose names appear now in any history of the religious thought of the century, men such as Hoadly who, in his famous sermon of 1717, started the furious Bangorian controversy over the nature of the Church and Church authority; Samuel Clarke, whose *Discourse Concerning the Being and Attributes of God* influenced the beliefs and imaginations of many men in shaping their near-Deistic beliefs or colouring their more orthodox ones; the many famous divines involved in the Reason and Revelation controversy which split the century, or in the steady growth of latitudinarian thinking. Yet many of these lines of thought and the influence of many of these more famous men are, as we shall see, found in Henley, often popularized, often rather crudely simplified, and often developed to those logical conclusions which the caution or the ecclesiastical eminence of their originators had inhibited them from reaching. To examine Henley's religious thought, then, is not, as his enemies would have us believe, merely to wander from eccentricity to lunacy, but to see a phenomenon not unknown to us at this present time—the end-product in the popular mind of the higher theorizing of eminent divines, crude certainties for their qualified suggestions, loss of faith for their tentative questionings, an actual change in behaviour from their academic moral re-examinations. It might well be suggested that, in examining such minor popular teachers as Henley, rather than the more learned pamphlets of bishops and divines, we approach more closely the climate of belief in the century, as it affected the man in the pew and in the street.

[1] *A Comparison between Orator H--- & Orator P---*, p. 4.

The start of Henley's religious thinking was, as we have seen,[1] connected with his break with the Established Church, and motivated very much by his desire to justify that step and protect himself against possible resulting ecclesiastical discipline. Influenced by William Whiston's writings and example, he had embraced the idea of a primitive Church whilst rejecting the idea of a primitive Church discipline, denying, on grounds of history and practice, the Apostolic authority of the Church, her orders and her sacraments, preaching and, as he believed, establishing a congregation based on Scripture and the earliest records of belief and worship. Beyond this, his early statements and sermons showed little unorthodoxy in subject or treatment. He avoided any theological involvement in Whiston's Arianism, and preached perfectly respectable sermons on Christian living, the saving work of Christ, grace, repentance and forgiveness, death and judgement. But the seeds of his future development were there in this questioning of authority, a questioning at first—and no doubt partly on self-interested and prudential grounds—only of the authority of the Church and the basis of that authority, but a questioning destined to extend beyond the Church to the other great pillar of authority, the Scriptures themselves. In the end, the rejection of authority and the assertion of complete freedom of personal interpretation produced the belief which Henley called 'Rationalism', which others might call a form of Deism, and which many called the impiety of an unbeliever.

The attack on the Church and her authority which had been the main theme of his early thought, occupied him for the rest of his life, growing in intensity with his personal sufferings—real or imagined—at the hands of the episcopacy, and his increasing anger at the general inhumanity and callousness of the hierarchy and administration. In the early days he had been willing to deny any disrespect to the Church of England in so far as her principles were primitive; but by 1737, even though forced to speak as an official news-writer for the Administration, he stressed only the legal validity of the Anglican Establishment, and managed not to be dishonest about his own disbelief in its spiritual validity. The official spokesman agreed that

the Glorious Original Compact between Church and State, in the Commission of King Ethelbert to Augustin, first Arch-bishop of

[1] See Chapter III above.

Canterbury, *nulla coactione*, as Bede records it, proves this to be the Constitutional Religion of *England*, and therefore the Statutes and Canons concerning Religion are declarative of it, as the Genuine Intention of the Legislature.

but the private man added, 'The Sentiments of Bishop Taylor, Dr. Clarke, Bishop Hoadley etc. are here espoused, that God alone being the legislator of the Conscience, as he only is the Judge of the Heart, Subscription to the *Articles of the Church* is discretionary, political, judicial, in *Foro* exteriori.'[1] In a sermon in 1750 he was more explicit: 'I can subscribe to ye Church of England, as a political system, by Law established; wch. is all I can make of it.'[2] He could, in fact, make quite a lot more of it. The Church of England, like the Church of Rome and every other organized church with a law and a government, was the creation of man and not of God. 'The Difference of Clergy and Laiety', he claimed, 'has no Foundation in the Gospel . . . the Clergy's assuming to themselves a Difference from the Laiety was the Source of Popery',[3] and he insisted above all that the Scriptures offered no grounds for episcopal government. He alleged that the texts 'All Power is given unto me' and 'Go and teach all nations' were put into the mouth of Christ by party interest, and that 'The Bishop's Commission for Peter, Christ and God, was never shown, nor is it extant in the World.'[4] From the bishops came the whole paraphernalia of Canon Law and, they being false, it must be false too. It was especially Bishop Gibson, his personal enemy, whom he saw as the arch-imposer of this rule of unfounded law in his *Codex*, that 'notorious System of Protestant Popery',[5] and against whom he continually lectured and wrote. Typical is an attack in the *Hyp Doctor* of 12 August 1740 where we read that 'under the Divine Sun-shine, in that Hot-bed of pious Hypocrisy, G----n's Codex grew up, in which the Canon Law of *Rome* and the Authorities of . . . Popish Bishops . . . are made and avowed to be the Legal Foundation of that Nursery of Rebellion, Contention, and Inhumanity, the Ch—.' As he grew older, the aspect of the Church's inhumanity on which he dwelt with growing insistence was the grievous disparity between the reward of

[1] *Hyp Doctor*, 10 May 1737.
[2] Sermon for 1 July 1750 (B.M. MSS.Add. 11778).
[3] Henley, *The Coup de Grâce: Mr. Bayle's Prophecy fulfilled etc.* (1745), p. 38.
[4] Ibid., p. 29.
[5] Advertisement letter of 3 Aug. 1743 (Lysons 117).

the higher and the lower clergy, and the mismanagement and misuse of the Church's temporal possessions which were, moreover, another mark of her ungodly nature. In his last major pamphlet on these topics, *The Coup de Grâce* of 1745, he insisted that legal grounds could be found for the return of church lands to their rightful owners, for 'they glibly took them from the Papists, and what is Sauce for a Goose is Sauce for a Gander.' He reviewed the growing holding of land by the Church with 'What a RUN has it had! What a long Tail our Cat has got!' and he attacked the huge number of Church officers, 'this *Army*, or Church Militant'. The only excuse for retaining these possessions could be that they should be used, not to increase the wealth and pomp of bishops and deans, but for charity and to improve the lot of the humble parish priest and curate. How far before his time did Henley demand what the Church Commissioners have but recently enacted—

they and the Dignitaries, and over-grown Rectors, &c. (as of *Winnick*, *Wigan*, and the like,) ought to augment the small Livings, and soon bring them all, at an Average, to at least 100£ *per Annum*. . . . The poor Livings are not discharged from Tenths payable to the Bishops, though they are eased of the First-Fruits payable to the Crown: How shocking is that Difference, that the Crown is more generous and charitable to the Clergy, than the Bishops are to their own Brethren? Is this Christianity?

As late as 1753 he was still hammering away at this, suggesting the foundation of a society for the defence of the inferior clergy.[1]

All this is what Henley rejected—the claims of Apostolicity, the organized clergy, and the ruling episcopacy, the creeds and canons and articles of the Church, the obedience and discipline enforced by them, temporal power and possessions. All this was the mark of Popery and 'If *Popery* is to be turn'd out, let it *all go*; Arch-Bps, Bishops, Priests, Deacons, Cathedrals, Churches, Presbyters, Baptists, Independents, Quakers, Methodists, & so on. They all have it more or less.'[2] By 1745 he was denouncing Whiston's primitive Christianity as Popery, as his own ideas on the true belief and worship moved ever farther from any form of organized religion, developing but never quite deserting those

[1] Sermon for 13 May 1753 (B.M. MSS.Add. 11789).
[2] Sermon for 10 Sept., no year marked (B.M. MSS.Add. 11776).

principles he had laid down in the first months of the Oratory's existence:

The fundamental authority of it as a Church, will be the same (to speak no higher at present) with that of all the modern Churches, i.e. a legal liberty of private judgment in religion; that is the very principle of the reformation, the basis of all the protestant interest, and is thought the most valuable branch of the freedom of our constitution. . . . Its principles are 1. In belief, a liberty of conscience from all secular restraints. 2. In morality, the religion of nature, of which revelation, in this respect, is only declarative. 3. In historical or reveal'd religion, that of the primitive church, in the first ages. Its view is, impartially to examine the pleas of all religions, proposing them as the truest Standard and Center of Union.[1]

His views on the nature and use of revelation were to become more radical and he was to desert, with all other tradition, even that of the primitive Church, to emphasize increasingly the supremacy of the individual judgement and conscience in matters of faith, when 'The Blessing, Grace of Salvation of God, may be obtained without any external hierarchy, or established form of instituted Religion'.[2] The only Church he admitted was 'a visible congregation where the word is preached and the sacraments administered. It is Gospel pattern that there should be no further organisation, or rule or law, (V. Hoadley).'[3] In such a Church, the Oratory being the unique example, he claimed his full liberty to preach as he wished, 'the ONLY PROTESTANT who not admitting Tradition and Church-Authority, is not bound to be a Papist'.[4]

The 'V. Hoadley' which ends Henley's description of the Gospel Church clearly establishes the direct influence of that Bishop's writings on Henley's thought, and a brief glance at their central teachings confirms this. In his *A Preservative against the Principles and Practices of the Non-Jurors both in Church and State* Hoadly denied that it was necessary for men to belong to one external Church in order to gain salvation and, as Henley was so often to repeat, claimed that the Roman Catholic Church alone could, because of its claim to be infallible, pretend that divine authority

---

[1] *The Plan of the Oratory*, p. i, in *Oratory Transactions No. 1*.
[2] Sermon for 14 June 1741 (Guildhall MSS. 252, vol. 2).
[3] Sermon for 22 Mar. 1735 (B.M. MSS.Add. 11769).
[4] *The Victorious Stroke for Old England*, p. 25.

had been delegated to it. His own belief was that the liberty of private judgement and not the dictates of an authoritarian Church was the essence of Christianity. 'Every one may find it, in his own Conduct to be true,' he wrote, 'that his Title to God's favour cannot depend upon his actual being, or continuing, in any particular Method, but upon his *Real sincerity* in the conduct of his Conscience and of His own Actions, under it.'[1] His sermon on 31 March 1717 on the text 'My Kingdom is not of this world', spelt out even more clearly these startling suggestions. In an attempt to rescue the notion of 'the Church' from what he considered confused and misleading ideas, he identified the Church with the Kingdom of Christ and proceeded to describe the Church as Christ had described his Kingdom. There, Christ 'is Himself the sole *Lawgiver* to his *Subjects*; and himself the sole *Judge* of their *Behaviour*, in the Affairs of *Conscience* and *Eternal Salvation*',[2] but in the Church 'He hath, in these *Points*, left behind Him, no visible, humane *Authority*; no *Vicegerents*, who can be said properly to supply his Place; no *Interpreters* upon whom his Subjects are absolutely to depend; no *Judges* over the Consciences or Religion of his People.'[3] He went on to make his meaning inescapably clear:

For if this were so, that any such absolute *Vicegerent Authority*, either for the making of *new Laws* or interpreting *Old Ones*, or *judging* his *Subjects*, in Religious Matters, were lodged in any Men upon Earth; the Consequence would be, that what still retains the Name of the *Church* of *Christ*, would not be the *Kingdom of Christ*, but the *Kingdom* of those Men, vested with such *Authority*. For, whoever hath such an *Authority* of making Laws is so far a *King*; and whoever can add new Laws to those of *Christ*, equally obligatory, is as truly a *King* as *Christ* himself is; Nay, whoever hath an *absolute* Authority to *interpret* any written, or spoken Laws; it is *He* who is truly the *Lawgiver*, to all Intents and Purposes; and not the Person who first wrote, or spoke them.[4]

From this followed inevitably a declaration of freedom and equal standing to all Christians and, by clear implication, to all Dissenting believers, for

[1] Hoadly, *A Preservative etc.* (1716), p. 90.
[2] Hoadly, *A sermon Preach'd before the King. The Nature of the Kingdom, or Church, of Christ* (1717), p. 11.
[3] Ibid., p. 11.
[4] Ibid., p. 12.

All His *Subjects* in what Station soever they may be, are equally *Subjects* to *Him*; and ... No One of them, any more than Another, hath Authority, either to make *New Laws* for *Christ's* Subjects; or to impose a sense upon the Old ones, which is the same thing; or to *Judge*, censure, or Punish the Servants of *Another Master* in matters relating purely to *Conscience*, or *Salvation*.[1]

So the Church was reduced to 'the Number of Men, whether Small or Great, whether Dispersed or united, who truly and sincerely are Subjects to *Jesus Christ* alone, as their *Lawgiver* and *Judge*, in matters relating to the Favour of God, and their *Eternal Salvation*,'[2] whose guide was a private reading and interpretation of the New Testament, the record of their King, and whose assurance and authority was sincerity of belief.

Such were Hoadly's pronouncements which produced the 'Bangorian controversy' and so profoundly affected Henley. In Professor Norman Sykes's words, 'It was evident from the tenor of this sermon that Hoadly had reduced the visible church to ruins, and enthroned in its place the principle of unlimited private judgement,'[3] but he did not so evidently as Henley put those principles into practice. It was Henley himself, much later in his life, who spoke scornfully of 'those, who affirm, ye *Kingdom of Christ alone* not of *this World*, (who yet are willing to enjoy *Christian Revenues* in *this World*)'.[4] Henley's secession from the Establishment, his constant attacks on episcopal government and possessions, authority, man-made ordinances and traditions, appear a far more honest reaction to the sermon and the logical outcome of a sincere acceptance of its tenets.

Equally so was his broad and generous toleration of other communions, especially the Dissenters, a toleration which even extended to Rome, a Church which above all exemplified all he disbelieved in but which he saw as consistent and honest in its beliefs. Admittedly during his period as *Hyp Doctor*, he allowed himself to toe the line of the party which was hiring his pen and, on political grounds, defended the penal laws and the double taxing of Papists who 'detract from, and abuse the Ministry in all Places and on all Occasions ... they write against

[1] Ibid., p. 16.   [2] Ibid., p. 17.
[3] Norman Sykes, op. cit., p. 293.
[4] Sermon for 29 July 1753 (B.M. MSS.Add. 19924).

the Government. . . . They sap and undermine the very Foundation of Government.'[1] He lamented that it was not possible, in
order to face the effective unity of Rome, to 'contrive a General
Council of Protestants'.[2] When, however, he spoke without
such inhibitions, his tone was different. In 1745, when fears of
Popery and Jacobitism were reaching a new extreme, he preached
repeatedly on the Papists, defending them from unfair and
ungrounded charges and showing them to be no worse than
their Protestant brethren. Four advertised discourses of 1745
amply illustrate his attitude:

A Genuine Declaration of a Catholic on their Sufferings, and on the
Enquiry whether they be good Subjects.   [February 8]

A large Discourse on Protestant Inquisition, Persecution, and Penal
Laws against Papists; Stocks and Credit lower'd by such Causes;
Instances of Protestant Cruelty and Sin, worse than the worst of the
most cruel Inquisition.   [February 22]

An Argument to Protestants, to afford the Roman Catholic Priests,
and others, kinder Usage, from the Falsehood of those Commonplace
Objections, which their Adversaries use against them.   [April 11]

defending, on Protestant Principles, F. Gothair, and the Ch. of R.
against [the] charge, that Popery opposes Civil Society, and that
Papists are bad Subjects.   [April 19]

In the '50s he continued this tolerant appeal to remove misunder-
standings over Rome and to give her her due. He announced
that the Pope 'is ye honestest believer on ye Globe of Earth, &
if he be wrong all believing Xendom is wrong;'[3] and argued that
if the Church of England insisted on preserving all its Popish
elements, then the Roman Catholics 'Have a right to a Slice, at
least, of their own loaf'.[4] In an advertisement in 1753 he assured
a Roman lady,

Madam, My Zeal for you exceeds that of some for a Roman King: you
call me Infidel, yet I am a Rational Believer; in Benevolent Unity with
all. I pull off my Hat to a Cross, and to every Place and Minister of
Public Religion: Say Mass by myself, and all your Worship and all of all

---

[1] *Hyp Doctor*, 30 Dec. 1740.   [2] *Hyp Doctor*, 13 Aug. 1734.
[3] Sermon for 11 July 1751 (B.M. MSS.Add. 11781).
[4] Sermon for 13 Oct. 1751 (B.M. MSS.Add. 11782).

Religions: as far as I can: But yours most: for either the Pope or I (as I have proved) ought to be Primate of the World.[1]

He refused to subscribe to the contemporary bogy-man idea of the Pope and the Popish threat, asking in one of his sermons, 'Who is this monster, this bugbear, so much talked of, the Pope? Why a man! Pope is derived from *Papa*, and papa signifieth father; that is, the Pope is father and head of his church. Is there anything so mighty frightful in all this?'[2] Small wonder that his opponents, ignoring his line of argument and hearing only his conclusions, should suspect him of being a crypto-Papist and a Jacobite, or find it impossible to reconcile his attitude to Rome with his equally warm defence of the rights of Dissenters. A typical reaction is that of a correspondent in the *Gentleman's Magazine* who records how Henley 'once fell into company with a Roman Catholic gentleman, who he gave a hearty squeeze by the hand, and said, emphatically, 'God bless you, I love you all, I love you all!' Whether this expression proceeded from universal philanthropy, or from a bias towards Popery, his own heart best knew.'[3] It proceeded certainly from the universal philanthropy of all sincere believers, which he had learnt from Hoadly, as did his belief that

without a *free Pen*, as well as a *free Tongue*, no Grievances can be well known nor stated: Therefore *free Pulpits*, within the bounds of Property and Right, are everywhere necessary: And if one should be confined and put down, let the People make another, in every House, both publick and private; and every Man to be a *Whitfield* and a *Wesley*, in all Places to *speak* for his Country.[4]

He lamented the fact that England 'packs off Whitefield, and his poor Methodists, for a Doctrine which the first *Protestants* thought the best guard against Popery',[5] was angered by the sending of missionaries to the Dissenting churches of New England, which he saw as a move by the High Churchmen of the Establishment to impose a hierarchy and a notion of holy orders which was un-Protestant,[6] and in 1744 preached on Mr. Wesley who

---

[1] Advertisement for 23 Mar. 1753 (Lysons 179).
[2] Nichols, *Leicestershire*, vol. ii, pt. i, p. 260, footnote 4.
[3] *Gentleman's Magazine*, vol. lvi, p. 294.   [4] *The Coup de Grâce*, p. 44.
[5] *Hyp Doctor*, 18 Sept. 1739.   [6] *Hyp Doctor*, 20 May 1735.

has given ye *devils their dues*, in a Sermon at *Oxford*—in wch. he has nobly perform'd *ye office of an Evangelical Preacher*, to reprove, rebuke, exhort, with all long-suffering and doctrine . . . to tell ye House of Christ Church their Transgressions, & ye House of Maudlin their sins. . . . Was every preacher in *England* to be as free & righteous as that Gentleman . . . ye people wd. be more able to right themselves, by knowing their Strength . . . Was Mr. Wesley to preach at Court against all ye sins there Committed—& in ye *Convocation*—& before ye Houses of Lords and Commons—& on Fast-Days—& other public occasions—& every Pulpit echo to his sound, it wd. be ye *finest Concert of Music* that was ever heard in England—& lead up a country dance beyond Sacheverel.[1]

In 1752 he was still preaching sympathetically on Wesley and Methodist preaching in London, and prophesying that persecution would only strengthen and extend the movement's influence.[2] The Quakers too were embraced, and throughout his life he preached in their defence, praising their sincerity and admiring their courage under persecution and suffering.[3] Around 1730 he had, we are told,

offered himself as a candidate for Church Communion with some of the Independents. His character, however, weighed against his zeal; the *triers* of the conventicle rejected his application. When he was informed of this, he entered into the vestry belonging to the meeting-house, where the matter had been solemnly debated, and, assuming a very grave countenance, made a most reverend bow, and departed with the apostolical Valediction, 'Finally, brethren, farewell.'[4]

There is no reason to believe that he did not use that word 'brethren' with full conviction, accepting and practising the dictum of Hoadly's that 'All His *Subjects* in what Situation soever they may be, are equally *Subjects* to *Him*; and that No One of them, any more than Another, hath *Authority* . . . to Judge, Censure, or Punish, the Servants of *Another Master* in matters relating purely to *Conscience*, or *Salvation*.'

The other key to Henley's religious development may also be

---

[1] Sermon for 2 Sept. 1744 (B.M. MSS.Add. 19922).

[2] B.M. MSS.Add. 12200.

[3] See, for example, the sermon for 12 Sept. 1736 (B.M. MSS.Add. 11770); advertisement for 31 May 1754 (Lysons 187); sermon for 2 June 1754 (Guildhall MSS. 252, vol. 5).

[4] *Gentleman's Magazine*, vol. lv, p. 359.

found in Hoadly's writings—the insistence on personal reading and interpretation of the Scriptures as the only way of discovering the laws of the Kingdom. As Henley questioned and denied the authority of any visible Church or Church tradition, so he increasingly questioned the absolute authority of that other source of authority beloved by Protestants, the Bible. His questioning of the exact nature of the 'inspiration' of the Scriptures widened out into an examination of the whole idea of 'revelation' and led him ultimately to the faith which he described as 'Rationalism'. In this line of exploration, too, he reflected another of the controversies which engaged the divines of the century, and again produced his own peculiar and extreme solution.

The early years of the Oratory found Henley apparently perfectly orthodox in his views on Holy Writ. The Bible was still the ultimate source of truth, more important than the traditions of even the primitive Church, for 'If an opposition should be proved between the voice of the primitive church, in that whole compass of time, and that of the scripture, we should disregard that primitive consent, and espouse, as in duty bound, the word of God.'[1] In 1729 he preached in opposition to Woolston, defending the historicity of Christ's miracles and insisting on his Resurrection as a real and historic event;[2] and in a sermon published in the same year, *Samuel sleeping in the Tabernacle*, in words which form a startling contrast to his later beliefs, he deprecated philosophic, rationalist sermons which hardly mentioned Christ. Such preaching was a dangerous thing when 'at this juncture . . . human reason, the law of nature, and good works, apart from faith in Christ, are so much dwelt upon . . .'. Rather, he insisted,

We are always to see what Christ and his apostles and prophets, have said, or give foundation to reason, about a subject: to consider, that salvation comes from, and by him only; to observe what he has said, and done, when we examine the state and objections of unbelievers, to build upon his excellency and dignity: his divinity, manhood, priesthood; to consider all morality as his act, his sanctification, his justification; to encounter and answer infidels and hereticks, as his enemies, enemies to *his truth and person*; to receive and propose doctrines, as

---

[1] *The First Sermon etc.*, p. 30, in *Oratory Transactions No. 1.*
[2] B.M. MSS.Add. 11768.

from his instruction; not to mention any virtues as entitling men to GOD's favour, but thro' him; and when we urge their fitness and righteousness, to shew that, as regarding him, as well as other respects, directly and immediately, 'He is the beloved Son, in whom God is well pleas'd . . .'

In the '30s he still maintained a generally orthodox view, repeating his defence of the miracles and Resurrection of Christ in a sermon on 16 May 1736, and declaring that he accepted the Bible, not from the Church, but, as did the first Christians,

from Christ and the Apostles; and I, for instance, examine what Bible Christ and his Apostles gave the first Christians, and left the World, and I take the same; not because the first Christians, or those whom any will call the Church, took it; but because they were bound to take it, and because I see myself bound to take it, on the original Evidence of its Proposal, whether they had taken it or no.[1]

By the early '40s, however, his views began to change and doubts over the historical truth and accuracy of the Scriptures started to appear. The former defender of the historical Resurrection, in replying to a pamphlet *The Trial of the Witnesses*, now displayed grave doubts as to its provability in any legal or evidenced way. In an open letter to the Bishop of London he wrote:

The Author of the Trial of the Witnesses has justified a Separation from your Lp . . . making himself Judge, Jury, Witnesses etc. secundum Usum Sarum: A Common-Law-Witness is an Eye-Witness of the Fact in Question, duly qualified, producible in Court, or on Record in a Court of Record; not a constructive Witness of appearing accidental Consequences of the Fact: Our Saviour is no such Witness at Common-Law, for there none is Witness for himself, Magdalen and the Disciples did not see Christ rise, are not Eye-Witnesses, not therefore Witnesses. . . . there are no consistent Witnesses of that, if none at all.[2]

A second letter brought his doubts even more into the open:

The Apparition of Christ after Death, not upon Record, to unknown, unbelieving, deceiv'd, ignorant, doubting, or incompetent Witnesses, in uncertain Authors, suspected varying Histories. And Scriptures . . . not canonical, not inspired, not therefore Law to our Courts,—these are not legal Evidence to a Jury, that he rose again with the identical natural human Body, that was in the Tomb. If it was a supernatural

---

[1] Henley, *A Lecture on High Fits of Zeal, or, Mrs. Cadière's Raptures* (1732), pp. 6–7.
[2] Letter in the *Daily Advertiser*, 4 Feb. 1744.

Body, it is not cognizable to a Jury, and God could not rise again. Histories relate Apparitions of the Dead performing all the Functions of Animal Bodies, when the very Bodies were or might be, elsewhere: as Samuel to Saul: and the Point would be not what but why, they believ'd: in the first was a Deceit, Magdalen was deceiv'd, she no Witness, she took him to be the Gardener, and was not believed by the Disciples themselves: the 2nd. was in another Form, not of Christ, to two Disciples not nam'd, so no Witnesses: the 3rd. to eleven Disciples not named, so no witnesses; and Disciples might not be Apostles; they wondered, were ignorant, terrified, thought him a Spirit; the 4th to Thomas, he did not say he believ'd, nor put his hand to his Side, is no Witness; the 5th to the 500 Brethren, not named, nor therefore Witnesses: The 6th to Paul, who, how, when or where, uncertain, no Witness: not one Witness in Law of his rising, or having risen.[1]

From now onwards he continually questioned the accuracy, authenticity, and alleged authorship of parts of the Scriptures, with such disputations as 'The Greek Testament spurious ?',[2] and such assertions in sermons as 'There are *more false Translations* in ye *English Bible*, than there are *Chapters in it*',[3] or 'The author of the Epistle to the Hebrews (what *that was* wants another Epistle in ye *St. James Evening Post* to inform us'.[4] His summing up of his position in *The Coup de Grâce* is sober and on the whole true, neither marked by the panic of the frightened believer who sees the ground of his belief crumbling, nor the exulting of the unbeliever who finds more evidence for his unbelief:

Scriptures, Writings, Manuscripts, are the same, written by Men; alter'd, forged, interpolated, corrupted, diminished, augmented, translated, commented, preached or written upon, at Pleasure, by Party-views, or as Governors dictated: some sunk, others trumpt up; never uniform . . . So that was this *holy History as true* as any other, it would not be *true*, much less obligatory from God on the Conscience, since *Christ*, who came on Purpose for Revelation, never wrote nor promised Inspiration to any Writers at all; and his, and the Apostles Discourses, were occasional, to those Persons, Times and Places, not a perpetual Law to all Times and Places.[5]

[1] Letter in the *Daily Advertiser*, 24 Feb. 1744.
[2] Advertisement for 6 Apr. 1745 (Lysons 138).
[3] Sermon for 15 Apr. 1753 (B.M. MSS.Add. 11788).
[4] Sermon for 8 June 1755 (Guildhall MSS. 252, vol. 6).
[5] *The Coup de Grâce*, pp. 29-30.

This acceptance of the idea that contemporary theology, historical settings, and limitations of knowledge in the writers of Scripture, shaped and coloured their work, was not common in the century. It has been said that

Both critics and defenders of orthodoxy were hampered by their bondage to a literal theory of Biblical interpretation, which allowed no possibility of error of detail in the Sacred Writings, and by consequence reduced Deists to attacking the moral probity of their authors and church men into defences of their integrity ... To an age lacking the magic key of an evolutionary conception of the development of religious dogma, the idea that a tertium quid might be established between the absolute inerrancy of the Scriptures and deliberate forgery on the part of their authors was as uncongenial as revolutionary.[1]

If Norman Sykes is right, then Henley must be placed among the revolutionaries, for he found it not in the least uncongenial, having realized the special conditions of the making of the Scriptures, to establish that *tertium quid*, a *quid* which, it hardly needs saying, was highly personal and unorthodox. He rejected as irrational and superstitious the acceptance of the Scriptures as true and infallible in every detail. Only a Roman Catholic who accepted in a similar way the laws and traditions of his Church could logically do this, and 'Scripturists are bound to be Roman Catholics, or to throw away the Bible.'[2] This paradox, as we shall see, was one he was to develop on a much wider front. In 1750 he asserted that 'That Preacher is an Imposter, who imposes on the People the Word of Man for the Word of God, by preaching Reveal'd Religion from Manuscripts, of which he, bound to the Proof, has not, nor can, prove one true Original Copy, nor version, from God.'[3] The alternative was to accept the varied nature of the scriptural content, and to select only part as a divine guide to belief and action, guided by the inspiration and revelation which God puts into the reason and understanding of men. For Henley, inspiration was 'the Faculty of Right Reason given to Man with the Breath of Life inspir'd into him by God',[4] and this power was at work not only in the

---

[1] Norman Sykes, op. cit., p. 421.
[2] Advertisement for 21 June 1746 (Lysons 143).
[3] Advertisement for 31 Oct. 1750 (Lysons 166).
[4] *Sermon III*, p. 45, in *The Oratory Magazine No. III*.

writers of the Scriptures but in the minds of the readers. Revelation was not only, therefore, something given and fixed in the words of Scripture: it was vouchsafed through the power of God working as Right Reason in a man reading and interpreting the Scriptures and contemplating the phenomena and pattern of created things. Henley rejected the opposition of Reason and Revelation which exercised the minds and pens of so many polemical theologians of the time, uniting what he considered wrongly limited notions of the sphere and activities of reason and revelation in a wider definition of revelation.

God spoke in divers Manners [he wrote] *and* therefore *all* are some kind of *Revelation. Reason* itself is a Degree of *his Voice in the Soul*: The *Works of God reveal something more of him; the Word of God more still: the Spirit of God* adds to *all* these Methods of *Revelation*, and these Parts together, make the *whole* of it; to argue, therefore, whether *Reason* or *Revelation* be sufficient, is to argue, whether a *Part* of Revelation be the *whole*: This is the short State and *Solution of this Problem*; in which concise Light I do not find that any Disputant on either Hand has put it.[1]

Guided by these principles he proceeded to deal with the Scriptures in his own peculiar way, in an intensifying process of demythologizing, of rejecting the supernatural and miraculous, and the nature and work of Christ as it related to man's eternal salvation. The Scriptures, interpreted by Right Reason, became little more than a record of words and deeds on which man might base his moral and political life. 'The Truth of the Gospel', he wrote in 1741, 'is in its *Spirit* and *Moral*, its *practical Graces*: the rest is, in Comparison, as sounding Brass, or as a tinkling Cymbal',[2] and a year later we find him debating the proposition 'All the Scripture, except the moral Part, apocryphal'.[3] This line of thought remained unchanged, and ten years later he was still preaching it. In a sermon of 1751 he declared:

It is false that ye Rationalists do not believe Reveal'd Religion. They believe all that is Rational and Moral in ye Bible, all that proceeds from God's Moral Government of ye World . . . reveal'd from God to ye Mind of Man, by that Reason, wch. is ye Word of God, is God Himself in ye Soul . . . & if they can apply what is *Mystical, Consistent, and*

[1] Henley, *Deism defeated, and Christianity Defended etc.* (1731), p. 18.
[2] *Hyp Doctor*, 20 Jan. 1741.
[3] Advertisement for 9 Jan. 1742 (Lysons 110).

Supernatural to a morally political use, they believe *that* to be inspir'd: for there is a Spirit in Men, and ye Inspiration of ye Allmighty giveth him Understanding.[1]

In this application, as he exercised his right to make allegorical, moral use of Scripture as his Reason directed, and as he demonstrated his belief that the Bible could be the source for discussion of *all* topics, he displayed that growing eccentricity which shocked the orthodox but whetted the curiosity of his congregations. Biblical texts became the starting-point not so much for a disquisition on moral behaviour, but on the behaviour of ministers and the Board of Trade, King William and the Dutch, the state of taxation and the scandals of naval administration. When Joseph's coat of many colours became the text for an attack on the Plaid Act, and the words of Ezekiel 40:16—'And there were narrow Windows to the little chambers, and to their posts within the gate round about, and likewise to the arches'—legitimized an attack on the '*Arch*-bishops' and their luxurious living, it is understandable that many judged his principles by his practice, and rejected both as irreligious and insincere. Certainly his general discussion is more impressive than his practical application, and though he never ceased 'to find *lively Texts* (for, as to ye *flatter Commonplace kind*, I leave *to ye Prelates*, who are bound in Duty to be as *dull*; as *those, who promoted them*)',[2] his violence of twisting the text, via pun, parallel, and imagery, rendered them mere pretexts for political commentary and topical journalism. In the end the not entirely unreasonable principles of Biblical interpretation which he had propounded, reduced his Scriptures to a mere storehouse of epigraphs for his political, social, and diminishingly moral discourses, and there was little of the religious to be found in these embodiments of that wider idea so closely connected with these principles, the Religion of Right Reason, or in Henley's special sense, Rationalism.

Henley's Rationalism was the total expression of the ideas which were separately at work in his approach to scriptural revelation and Church authority, a rejection of what he considered man-made ideas and laws, and an absolute dependence on personal interpretation and sincerity of belief. The progressive demythologizing

---

[1] Sermon for 20 Oct. 1751 (B.M. MSS.Add. 11782).
[2] Sermon for 21 Oct. 1753 (B.M. MSS.Add. 11793).

and 'moralising' of the Scriptures was paralleled by a progressive rejecting of most of the supernatural doctrinal tenets of the faith. The Virgin Birth, the Atonement, the self-purposed sacrifice of the Cross, the Resurrection, and the last Judgement—all these were rejected or reinterpreted in a way which removed their supernatural implications. An early sermon of 1731, *The Original of Pain and Evil*, contained many of the great arguments on the theme popular in the age—that the whole must be viewed before judgements of 'good' or 'evil' can be made, that man, being by definition a creature below perfection, is necessarily subject to imperfections, and that the apparent disproportion of good and evil in the world will be compensated in the world hereafter. Belief in the world hereafter was based on a twofold revelation which either a Deist or a Christian could accept—'The Being of a God, and a future State of Rewards and Punishments are the Pillars of all Religion. They are known, either by God's Works, or his reveal'd Will; hence we infer his Being, his Nature and the final Equity of his Proceedings.'[1] There is a noticeable absence, however, of any reference to Christ and the place and significance of his life and death in the problem of human suffering, a silence especially remarkable in the sermon of a man who but two years before had attacked any preaching not based on Christ, as dangerous, when 'human reason, the laws of nature, and good works, apart from faith in Christ, are so much dwelt upon'. The early '40s saw, once more, the sudden acceleration in his radical development, and in *The Coup de Grâce* we find him proving that the terms of the Old and New Testaments had special meanings in their time, upon which false doctrines quite at variance with those meanings have been built. One by one he reduced doctrines from a supernatural and eternal to a natural and temporal level, to a sphere of moral activity rather than divine salvation.

For *Salvation* meant Deliverance from such Evils as God threatened to the *Jews* for their Sins against the Law which were Temporal, implying a *Temporal Messiah*. *Wrath to come* meant those Evils to come in this life. *The World to come* the World under the Messiah, to come in this Life. *Heaven* meant either the Air, or any Place where God favourably is, or promised to be. The *Kingdom of Heaven* meant the Time and Place of the Kingdom or Reign of the *Messiah* in this Life; supposed to be promised

[1] Henley, *The Original of Pain and Evil* (1731), p. 2.

by God. *Eternal life* meant the State of *continual Living* free from the temporal Punishment of Sin in this life, threatened by God to the *Jews* in the Law of *Moses*. *Damned* meant *condemn'd* by the Law of those Punishments. *Judgment* meant God inflicting such Punishments here, and calling Men to Account. *Day of Judgment* meant the Time when that was to be; *Christ* said, as suppos'd, the Father only knew it; that is *God knows when*, which any might *reveal*. *Resurrection* was *Pharisaism* from *Pagan* philosophy, preach'd by *Paul*, from the *Pharisees*. *Hell* meant any dark Place, Prison, Dungeon, Grave, or the Valley of *Hinnom* . . . This is Scripture. Lord *Herbert* and others have prov'd that God, Repentance, and a future State, were known by Reason. They are suppos'd in the Bible, not *reveal'd* there: and Immortality meant, that the Bodies of those, who were alive at the Coming of the *Messiah*, in this World, should be preserved free from Dissolution by Fire, or the same as Eternal Life, or never punished by Fire here &c.[1]

The citing of Lord Herbert and his insistence that reason rather than scriptural revelation establishes the main basis of belief, indicates a movement towards what might well be called deism, a description he sometimes accepted with qualifications. The Resurrection which *The Coup de Grâce* rejected as 'Pharisaism from Pagan philosophy' he elsewhere defined as 'rising to a better understanding, a clearer Judgment, a more correct Reason and Conduct',[2] and by the '50s the general rejection of the supernatural content of the Scriptures, which we have already examined, resulted in a corresponding rejection of the other doctrines based on that content. The death of Christ he saw as the man-sacrifice of evil men similar to the human sacrifices of pagans, rather than the self-sacrifice of Christ to the Father in a divinely ordered plan. 'God is good', he wrote, 'willeth not the death of a Sinner: but of one who had no sin! It pleased him: Meer Will is Arbitrary: is he so?'[3] The life of Christ was to him an example of moral living and of a national saviour who was the pattern for the true patriot. The divine nature of Christ was redefined in terms of the Right Reason he believed ruled the universe and was incarnate in all men—'I am not an infidel,' he asserted, 'because I believe that *Christ, God, and ye Spirit of God* & Infinite Right Reason are ye *Same*. 3 in one. I do not deny any other explanation, but sus-

---

[1] *The Coup de Grâce*, pp. 61–2.
[2] Sermon for 27 Nov. 1743 (B.M. MSS.Add. 10578).
[3] Advertisement for 20 Apr. 1753 (Lysons 180).

pend my Faith, or assent, till it is prov'd to convince me.'[1] This was the new Trinity of Right Reason which he preached and defended to his death, branding all those who thought otherwise, not as infidels and heretics, but as Papists.

This description of his orthodox opponents in doctrine was of a piece with his description of those who opposed him on the nature and authority of the Church and the infallible inspiration of the Scriptures—all depended on fallible man-made laws, records, and traditions rather than divine truth apprehended by Right Reason. He constantly repeated this argument in the pulpit, in advertisements, and in pamphlets.

Supernaturally revealed Religion and Faith, are founded on Popish Vouchers and Witnesses of Tradition and Church Authority . . . those Protestants who hold a Canon of Scripture, Sacraments, Christian Obligation to them, or to Church-Assemblies . . . are bound in Conscience and Honesty to be and profess to be, Papists . . . we are the only Protestants in the World. . . . We interpret and quote the Scripture, only as Rational, otherwise *ad hominem*.[2]

The Protestant cry, 'Scripture, not Tradition', was branded as illogical, for 'Such Protestants as are against Tradition must be Rationalists: if they be Traditionists as to Scripture, they must be so, as to Popery, from the same traditional Witnesses, in the Main, for both.'[3] *The Coup de Grâce* extended the range of those acceptances which 'infer Obligation to Communion with the Church of Rome', to include 'Church Authority, Implicit Faith, Traditional Religion, Infant-baptism, Canon of Scripture, Synods, Trinity, Sacraments, Schism, Heresy, Church-Union, visible Communion, Creeds, Necessity and Fact of Reveal'd Religion to Society'.[4] The sermons in the *Oratory Magazine No. 3* of 1748 apply this to specific articles of doctrine: 'I conclude, with affirming, that none can prove the Divinity of Positive Reveal'd Christianity, or any Article of it, as the Resurrection, &c. but a Papist, or on Popish Principles'; and again,

He must go to the Church of *Rome*, to prove, we are RELIGIOUSLY, DIVINELY OBLIGED to believe his Conception by the Holy Ghost

---

[1] Sermon for 1 Oct. 1752 (B.M. MSS.Add. 11785).
[2] *Sermon II*, p. 26, in *The Oratory Magazine No. III*.
[3] Advertisement for 25 Feb. 1746 (Lysons 142).
[4] Advertisement for 1 Aug. 1746 (Lysons 144).

of the Virgin *Mary*, or one Word about him; if the *Roman* Catholick can't prove it, he can't . . . No Protestant can, as such, impose IMPLI-CITE FAITH, or entertain it . . . Protestants must be Rationalists, or Papists: no Medium.[1]

What, then, finally, *was* the '*only Protestant-Religion in the World* . . . Rational Faith in Christ and the Scriptures . . . *New Rational Lights* . . . its Principles everlasting and unchangeable: This truest, greatest, best original Design . . . which is the Distinction of the Author, and of his Religion'?[2] Henley defined God as Eternal Reason and accepted with approbation Jean Leclerc's version of John 1:1, which he Englished as 'In the beginning was Reason. Reason was with God, and God was Reason. .'.[3] Christ he accepted as 'a Teacher of *Right Reason*'[4] in his words and actions, rejecting as superstition and traditional accretions the supernatural claims of the Scriptures. Man's necessary response to the Father and the Teacher of Right Reason was to use his own Reason, in examination and argument, to reach the truth, for, as he put it, 'I am bound in Conscience to be governed by that Reason, God has given me, adequately us'd; i.e. to self-evidence in every argument.'[5] Nor was he ashamed or disconcerted to be accompanied by the pagans in such a search. 'We must recur to Philosophy,' he asserted, 'to *Plato*, *Epictetus*, *Pythagoras*, *Socrates*; &c. who pretended to no Church-Powers or Revenues, or to impose a Revelation and Creeds as from God, on Men . . . The Philosophers were honester Men than the pretended Saints, and love of Wisdom, which is Philosophy, is love of *Christ*, who was called, *Wisdom*.'[6] It was on these grounds that he defended the discussions and disputations of the Oratory, for 'The greatest Sign of the Truth of any Religion, is the being permitted to ask Questions concerning it, and suffering the *Tenets to be examined and disputed upon*.'[7] On the basis of such inquiry, with private judgement and with liberty of conscience, the Rationalist moved to a position where he could say with Henley, 'I'll prove my Religion only to be Reveal'd; i.e. defin'd,

[1] *Sermons III* and *IV*, pp. 63 and 81.
[2] *Second St. Paul in Equity Hall etc.*, p. 22.
[3] Advertisement for 7 Mar. 1755 (Lysons 192).
[4] *The Coup de Grâce*, p. 33.
[5] Sermon for 28 June 1752 (B.M. MSS.Add. 11784).
[6] *The Coup de Grâce*, p. 41.   [7] *Hyp Doctor*, 30 Dec. 1735.

demonstrated, felt evidently',[1] curiously echoing an early statement of John Wesley to his mother—'faith is a species of belief;
and belief is defined as "an assertion to a proposition on rational
grounds"; without rational grounds there is therefore no belief,
and consequently no faith; faith must necessarily at length be
resolved into reason.'[2] It was a position Wesley moved away
from as Henley moved towards it, to proclaim it for the last twenty
years of his life as the true belief. The old images were not rejected
as vehicles to express the new faith: 'Truth alone is the Church
that is built on the Rock of Ages, against which the Gates of
Hades, that is, the Incidents of Mortality, shall not prevail:
Right Reason is the only Guide to Truth; therefore they are the
Church, they are the infallible everlasting Gospel, they are
Christianity, and Revelation';[3] and again,

... Right Reason is the last Resort of all Mankind, Test and Centre of
Communion, Life of God in the Soul of Man, Essence of all Religions,
Law, Science, Humanity; a perpetual Prayer, Sacrament, Mass,
Liturgy, Primitive Church, Martyrdom, on the Rock of Immutable
Truths, the Gospel of Perfection of all that is excellent, Sublime,
Beautiful; equitably compar'd in the whole; Each improving Exercise
of it is Religion ...[4]

The rhapsodic enthusiasm of such proclamations is undeniable
but still leaves more than a little vague the exact nature of 'the
Gospel of Perfection' or what exactly 'each improving Exercise'
of the believer was.

An answer, still very general, but somewhat more specific,
can be pieced together from Henley's occasional hints and from
the predominant preoccupations of his sermons. The aim of the
search of human Reason was to discover, through the works of
God and the rationally acceptable parts of the Scriptures, the
attributes of God, Eternal Right Reason. These attributes were
'Knowledge, Truth, Wisdom, Justice, Goodness &c',[5] to which
he added '*Infinite Happiness* & Benevolence',[6] and once these
were discovered and accepted, it was the duty and aim of the

[1] Advertisement for 13 Apr. 1753 (Lysons 179).
[2] Letter of 29 July 1725, in *Letters*, ed. J. Telford (1931), vol. i, p. 22.
[3] *The Coup de Grâce*, p. 61.
[4] Advertisement for 27 July 1753 (Lysons 182).
[5] Advertisement for 6 Nov. 1754 (Lysons 189).
[6] Sermon for 14 Apr. 1751 (B.M. MSS.Add. 12200).

Rationalist to reproduce them as far as possible in his own life. Henley's rationalism was, in the end, a code of moral behaviour, for, 'all, except Morality, is Superstition: Morality, or Conformity to God's Attributes being the whole of Divinity and Religion that is requisite';[1] and with equally unequivocating simplicity: 'The RELIGION of a Rationalist, is the Obligation of Man, to his Power, considering the Attributes of God, or Godlike Attributes, to resemble them, by the Practice of Universal Right Reason.'[2] His innumerable discourses and lectures, based, no matter how precariously, on Biblical texts, filled with historical and scientific examples, and using—though often in a questionable way—the processes of logic, dealt with countless of the broader and some surprisingly particular aspects of moral, social and political matters, and were Henley's sincere even though sometimes bizarre attempt to put into practice these ideas which he had been so long and painfully developing. If the later statements of his belief appear too often wild and enthusiastic and his performances far inferior to his pretensions, we cannot deny him a consistency of argument on his own premises and a loyalty to the system he had created. When, in 1732, he made one of his earliest statements on the theme of the true love of God, his ideas strike one as serious and sober:

It is not an Unthinking, unreasonable, *maudlin* Delight: the Love of God is Judgment, not Dotage; if it be more than flows from Judgment it is not religious Joy; if it flows from the Spirits only, so far again it is Animal, not religious: if it be from a wrong Thought, it is an Erroneous Joy, if from absence of Thought, foolish; if from a disorderly Thought, frantic, if from a sinful Thought, not at all religious, but totally wicked and Diabolical, if from a religious persuasion and disproportion'd to the Truth of that persuasion, it is Enthusiasm. It is, to be Christian, and good, a pleasure from a just Conscience of known Duties done, a judicious Intellectual pleasure only, any other falls under some article above-mentioned.

The Love of God is an Act of Judgment and Understanding, with the will fix'd on the Sovreign Good: Not a blind irrational mechanical love, or an Animal fondness: It is an esteam, and a desire to have God's Favor and Presence above all Things, and a delight in him with all the Heart, reasonable, not delirious: founded on a distinct Thought of God's Attributes and Actions.[3]

[1] *The Coup de Grâce*, p. 39.
[2] *Sermon II*, p. 18, in *The Oratory Magazine No. III*.
[3] *A Lecture on High Fits of Zeal etc.*, p. 9.

Exactly twenty years later his ideas were basically unchanged as he requested permission from his congregation 'to congratulate with you, and myself, on the encrease of my Converts, that now, the Majority of Clergy, Teachers, Professions, and People, are turn'd Rationalists, and struggling to appear so';[1] and four years after that, his dying assertion to the world as he made his last will and testament was 'Tell my notorious Enemies I dye a Rationalist in Perfect Communion and such only.' We cannot, certainly, reproach him with inconsistency in a scheme of belief which, though often odd and often curiously argued, was well this side of the impious lunacy his enemies would damn him with.

III. POLITICAL CONTROVERSY

Involvement with politics was, as we have seen, an inevitable corollary of Henley's entering the struggle for clerical preferment, in an age when advancement and honours in the Church were the jealously guarded gifts and rewards of the ruling party. His arrival in London in 1721 coincided with Walpole's firm establishment in power. In the previous year Walpole had returned from his period in opposition and, in the discrediting of so many statesmen at the bursting of the South Sea Bubble, had emerged with his own reputation unstained, to become First Lord of the Treasury and Chancellor of the Exchequer. For the next twenty-two years he was to be the unchallenged master of the Administration. So it was that Henley, giving his allegiance whence preferment might come, threw in his lot with the Whigs, with Walpole and Gibson as the twin sources of honour. He published his *Apotheosis* in 1722 with its fulsome references to 'The DARLING Figure of WALPOLE' and to Gibson as one of the 'ANGELS OF THE CHURCHES': he poetically dedicated his edition of Addison's miscellanies to Walpole, 'The Help, the Guide, the Guardian of *Mankind*': and, in association with Curll, was active in literary secret service on behalf of the administration, even though, in 1728, he suffered at the hands of the very Messengers and the informers whose work against other seditious libellers he was secretly assisting. Despite this and despite Gibson's rejecting his claims for preferment, his allegiance to the Whigs remained

[1] Advertisement for 22 Dec. 1752 (Lysons 177).

firm. His hatred of Gibson was naked and unashamed, and on the episcopal head he poured all his wrath and invective, exonerating Walpole and the administration from any part in those perfidious treacheries. Even if ecclesiastical preferment was for ever closed to him, the protection and favour he needed in his new role as Independent Orator could only come from those in power. He gave them his support and, as a mark of his party loyalty, shortly hired out his pen on their behalf.

This was the great age of political journals and newspapers. There were daily and weekly papers printed in London, as well as many which appeared three times a week, and the number of ephemeral productions lasting but a short while produced from Pope the not-unjustified gibe—'These are,—ah no!—these were, the Gazeteers!'[1] In the absence of any printed records of Parliamentary proceedings, and with the jealously guarded and widely interpreted notion of Parliamentary privilege, these journals were the main channel through which the Opposition and the Ministry could communicate their ideas and criticism. A speaker in 1738 was of the opinion that 'The people of Great Britain are governed by a power that never was heard of as a supreme authority in any age or country before. . . . It is the government of the press. The stuff which our weekly newspapers are filled with is received with greater reverence than Acts of Parliament, and the sentiments of one of these scribblers have more weight with the multitude than the opinion of the best politician in the Kingdom.'[2] Chief among the Opposition papers was the *Craftsman*, set up by Bolingbroke and Pulteney, which is said to have attained at its peak a circulation of 10,000. At its heels followed such papers as *Mist's Weekly Journal*, *The Bee*, and a host of others. It was therefore a necessary activity of government to support a press capable of answering such attack and criticism, and Walpole was keenly aware of this necessity. The inquiry after his downfall from office discovered that of the £1,453,400 spent in ten years as Secret Service money, £50,000 had been paid to writers for their defending the policy and actions of the Government, and of this huge sum an insignificant but no doubt useful amount had found its way into the pocket of Henley who, from 1730 to 1741, regularly each Tuesday, explained, excused, and defended the Ministry

---

[1] *Dunciad* (1743), Book ii, l. 313.
[2] *The Parliamentary History of England* (Hansard), vol. x, p. 448.

and exposed the dishonesty and stupidity of the Opposition and their literary hacks, in his paper, the *Hyp Doctor*.

We know nothing of the negotiations which led up to Henley's employment in this work, and only a little more of the terms of that employment. He was known personally to Walpole as an agent of the Ministry, and it is quite possible that, with his own boisterous and even coarse manners, Walpole might have found him a not uncongenial character. Henley had, according to his enemies, previously 'offered the services of his pen, in one morning, to two great men of opinions and interests directly opposite'[1] and been rejected by both, but Henley violently denied these aspersions. In his second approach—if second it in fact was —when, he claims, 'HE laid the first Plan, and communicated the Hint and Projects of *that Paper*, as he did of another',[2] he was more successful, and, according to Pope—the sole evidence for the fact—'had a hundred pounds a year given him for a weekly paper of unintelligible nonsense, called the Hyp Doctor'.[3] Evidence of other remuneration is equally slender, but it was rumoured in 1738 that, in addition to this salary,

a Gentleman who has been known to the World under various Names and Characters, he is sometimes *Alexander Ratcliffe of Elbow Lane*, sometimes the *Hyp Doctor*, and sometimes the renowned Orator of *Clare-Market*; this Gentleman, in Consideration of his Modesty, Piety, and other good Qualities which shine both in his Face and his Conduct, had the good fortune to have a Pension of 200£ *per Annum* conferr'd upon him by a certain great Man . . .

The same newspaper even asserted that, when Henley's wife willed away £100 from him, Henley himself let it be known 'that this Hundred Pound is also order'd for him by the same Person who procur'd him the Pension—were it even out of the Publick Money, who would grudge to pay Taxes when they are so well bestow'd?'[4] Henley himself, however, in 1742, vehemently stated that 'he never had Place or Pension to lose, that he never was a favourite of the last Ministry.'[5] We are left with the conflicting evidence of two very interested parties; and the undocumented secrecy of the Secret Service Accounts, which not

[1] *Dunciad* (1729), Book iii, l. 195, footnote.
[2] *Hyp Doctor*, 2 Dec. 1740.
[3] *Dunciad* (1743), Book iii, l. 199, footnote.
[4] *Englishman's Journal*, 13 Mar. 1738.
[5] Advertisement for 19 Feb. 1742 (Lysons 111).

even a Parliamentary inquiry could penetrate, prevents our discovery of the objective facts and figures. One thing is surely certain: that it was not without some worthwhile remuneration that Henley undertook the oppressive labour of writing—single-handed as far as we can discover—a weekly paper in addition to all his other activities, and for eleven years, Tuesday by Tuesday, never failed to produce his copy.

It was on Tuesday, 15 December 1730, that the first number appeared, a single sheet decently printed on comparatively good paper for this sort of production. It sold for twopence and, at this price and in this format, remained unchanged until the last number we possess appeared on 20 January 1741.[1] The paper took its curious name from the 'author' Dr. Isaac Ratcliffe of Elbow Lane, 'Physician in Ordinary & Extraordinary to a fine island, that has a very ailing and *splenetic* Constitution'.[2] His aim was to cure the 'hyp' of the land, that curious lowness of spirits, a vaporous depression, by instruction and laughter, and the early numbers have such sub-titles as 'Ingredients of this Dose' and 'The Ingredients of this Pill'. In a few weeks, however, this conceit was quietly dropped, as was another intention of making this a 'Club' paper on the lines of the *Spectator*, with contributions from Mr. Queer, a Country Gentleman: Mr. Bramble, a critic: Mr. Air-pump, an F. R. S: Mr. Killrhyme, a poet: Dr. Dolittle, a divine: Mr. Woolhead, a city merchant: Lord Protest who hates Dissenters: Beau Pigtail, a fine gent: Mr. Laetitat, a Temple Bencher.[3] The fiction of Dr. Ratcliffe was maintained much longer: a hearty seventy-three-year-old despite his sharp and pale face, his tufts and his pimple, happily married to Rebecca, open and good-natured, taking odd trips into the country now and again, and once to Paris for a few weeks while substitutes such as 'Monsieur Colbert', 'Jack Ripley', 'Inigo Jones', and 'Roger Hodgskins' held the fort until the return of the Doctor, informed and polished, to keep his eye on the health of the nation.[4] Henley obviously enjoyed the pretence and the denial of his own authorship (which was universally accepted by

[1] The collection of this paper, in the Nichols and Hope collections of newspapers in the Bodleian Library, has no number later than this, nor has the collection in the British Museum.

[2] *Hyp Doctor*, 15 Dec. 1730.   [3] Ibid.

[4] These papers by so-called substitutes are nos. 156-70, from 13 Nov. 1733 to 19 Feb. 1734.

friend and enemy alike), lamenting 'that he has liv'd to see his Works attributed by some Modern Writers to the renown'd Orator (as the *Craftsman* calls him) of Clare Market',[1] and, with a double bluff, claiming that 'The Bolt which the Craftsman shoots at the Clare-Market Orator is a Puff, for the Orator, as he is not concern'd, so ought not to be involv'd with the Hyp-Doctor.'[2] Henley did not, in fact, ever explicitly acknowledge his authorship of the paper, but the general belief is reinforced by the large amount of Oratory material in it. References to the Oratory first appeared in 1733 with three letters from delighted visitors there. In 1734 there were only two short advertisements for the Oratory published, but in the following year these increased to nine, including letters sent by Henley to the editor and from defenders of the Oratory and its proceedings. In 1736 the *Hyp Doctor* became closely identified with the Oratory and a main source of our knowledge of it, having forty-five advertisements and reports of what was promised or accomplished there. There was a falling off in 1737, with only eighteen references and, after the total absence of extant copies for 1738, there is no Oratory material in 1739 at all, only two short advertisements in 1740, and the final furious letter of John Guess, alias Henley, to Bishop Gibson on 20 January 1741. This material in itself is no more proof that Henley wrote the *Hyp Doctor* than that he wrote the *Daily Gazetteer* where so many Oratory advertisements and puffs appeared, but taken with the general acceptance of the time, and reinforced by the unmistakable presence of Henley's various styles, there seems no reason to doubt his authorship. Whether it was a sole authorship, or whether he used the help and contributions of others, we do not know. When he speaks of the survival of his paper through 142 copies, unaided by advertisements, news, or a junto of supporting booksellers, it sounds like the voice of a single writer proud of his achievement 'that a Paper should exist, subsist, and not desist till after the Age of 142, older than *Aminadab*'.[3] Lacking any evidence to the contrary and with our knowledge of his amazing industry, we must take it that it was his own pen, guided very possibly by occasional official hand-outs of information and arguments,

---

[1] *Hyp Doctor*, 14 Sept. 1731.   [2] *Hyp Doctor*, 21 Dec. 1731.
[3] *Hyp Doctor*, 7 Aug. 1733.

which produced the weekly copy on time, fulfilled his duty to the Ministry, and justified his £100 annual retainer.

His duty as Hyp Doctor was a dual one: positively, to present and defend Government policy and action, and, negatively, to destroy the propaganda of the Opposition journals by argument, mockery, and abuse. The *Craftsman* appeared every Saturday and Henley's slap-stick humour depicts the effect on its readers: 'The Babes that get their lessons in the *Craftsman* expect he will be ever *feeding them with the* same Spoon-meat; they take their prattle from him, like *Daws*: he says every Saturday, Caw-Jack, they open their Bills, *and soft Cheese or Maggots*, it's all one to them; they talk by rote after him.'[1] He summed up his duty succinctly in 'The Corruptions of the State are the Theme of the Craftsman, and the Corruptions of the Craftsman are my theme';[2] and often in the few days between Saturday and Tuesday, despite the Sunday demands of the Oratory, he managed to mount a reply to his antagonist, to answer letters in the *Craftsman*, to expose the falseness of some historical analogy, to argue point by point against some argument. Sometimes time was too short and a week elapsed before the answer came and the damage of the Saturday's dose of sedition and falsehood could be made good. Meanwhile he filled the gap with the picturesque abuse at which he was so skilled, and assured his readers, in amazingly varied ways, that 'As a dead Ass produces Maggots, even so a putrify'd Whig, Fly-blown by a corrupt Tory, breeds Craftsmen.'[3] The 'putrify'd Whig' and the 'corrupt Tory' were Pulteney and Bolingbroke respectively, and when he was not demolishing the previous *Craftsman's* arguments, he was defaming its founders and inspirers. Bolingbroke, now returned from France and living in retirement at Dawley, figured as the principal villain, sometimes as 'Lord Belchingbroke', sometimes as 'Harry Bellows-broke', often treated in pastoral terms mocking his rural retirement, when 'Lord B——e cries, O the Country:—O the charming Curds and Cream; charming, charming Curds and Cream',[4] or figures in 'A new Prospect of Dawley Farm, or the Jolly Sheep-shearing',[5] or, in a special Michaelmas number, appears as a keeper of geese.[6] Dawley Farm, like Pope's Twickenham retreat, is seen

---

[1] *Hyp Doctor*, 6 Apr. 1731.   [2] *Hyp Doctor*, 8 Aug. 1732.
[3] *Hyp Doctor*, 27 July 1731.   [4] *Hyp Doctor*, 26 Apr. 1737.
[5] *Hyp Doctor*, 13 July 1731.   [6] *Hyp Doctor*, 21 Sept. 1731.

as a rural centre of Opposition plotting, and the Hyp Doctor informs his readers that 'If any Gardener would be furnish'd with a Parcel of right good Sedition-seeds, Caleb Roots, State-slips, and Grafts of Court-Scandal to innoculate upon Patriot Stocks in the Gardens of some Country Gentlemen, let him repair to the Nursery open'd at Dawley-Farm, where he may be supply'd at reasonable Rates. *Caveat Emptor.*'[1] Even when Bolingbroke left England for France he was not forgotten nor forgiven, but pursued with the irony of 'that Lover of his Country, that Patriot, that *Craftsman*, that *innocent uncorrupt Minister*, that Upright Dis-interested Man, that Declaimer against all Projects and all Excises and Taxes and Debts, the Angelical, Pious, Bright, Precious L——B——'.[2]

It was not enough however to give his weekly 'Answer to the Insolencies of these Curs'.[3] His readers had to be informed and instructed until the excellence of their leaders and the rightness of their principles were accepted articles of belief. Walpole himself was the subject of constant appraisal and approval, and slurs against him were rejected with spirit and often with justified anger. His innocency in the affair of the South Sea Company and the investing of national money in that ill-fated venture, was asserted again and again,[4] and the praises of the Great Man, the 'SHIELD TO GREAT BRITAIN', 'The Delegate of Caesar and of God', are too innumerable to catalogue. As the country approached the General Election of 1740, whole articles and all the stressings of typography were given over to present him as the only possible saviour of the nation, for 'In a WALPOLE we have a RICHELIEU, a XIMENEZ, a COLBERT, all that *true Liberty, fine Genius*, and the Blessings of all the *Muses* can inspire.'[5] As well as Caesar's delegate, Caesar himself and his family received their share of praise, for the theory of government Henley was defending saw the power of government centred in the King, his Minister, and the supporting Parliament.[6] Royal marriages were celebrated, the death of Queen Caroline lamented, and the King's much-criticized absences in Hanover

---

[1] *Hyp Doctor*, 7 Sept. 1731.
[2] *Hyp Doctor*, 22 June, 1731.   [3] *Hyp Doctor*, 26 July 1737.
[4] See the *Hyp Doctor*, nos. 39, 244, 256, 264-6, for example.
[5] *Hyp Doctor*, 13 May 1740.
[6] See the *Hyp Doctor* for 4 May 1736, 29 Nov. 1737, 7 Dec. 1736, respectively.

defended. 'The Laws of England', he wrote, 'give a sacred Sanction to the King',[1] and he was in no doubt where, for a true Whig,
that sacred sanction was bestowed. There could only be one
'who can challenge the Name, a Whig, in General, in Opposition
to a *Jacobite*, that is FOR or AGAINST the House of *Hanover*,
and the Protestant Succession'.[2] The King's support must be
given to that party which supports him, and this joint power of
King and party is the power of government, assisted by a Parliament the support of which, rightly and reasonably, is maintained
by rewards and favours from the Administration. It is in the
King, his ministers, and the Parliament, and *not* in the people at
large, that government is vested, and Henley never tired of
warning the nation that Parliament was not and never had been
responsible to the people at large; that true liberty was willing
obedience to the law, and that the Opposition cries of 'Liberty',
'the People', unbridled freedom of criticism, could only lead to
the breakdown of government, to a 'democracy', to the rule of
the mob. This was a time when, as Lecky wrote, 'Political agita-
tion grew to new dimensions, and doctrines about the duty of
representatives subordinating their judgments to those of their
electors, which had scarcely been heard in England since the
Commonwealth, were freely expressed.'[3] Against all such doctrines, against riot and disorder over Parliamentary decisions,
against 'Instructions to Parliament', the *Hyp Doctor* maintained
a steady attack, for

when a Controversy arises, whether a certain Law be serviceable or
hurtfull to the Public, and the Legislature is the Judge of the Question,
the interposal of Violence is irregular, not self-defense, but self-
destruction, for the legislature is *themselves*, and there cannot be a more
unreasonable Frolick, than for the People to judge their own elected
Judges.[4]

Paper after paper maintained this central principle,[5] but even
though it might indeed be 'an unreasonable Frolick for the People
to judge their own elected Judges', the *Hyp Doctor* obviously saw
no harm in informing the people of the rightness of laws and
decisions taken by their masters, not to produce judgement but

[1] *Hyp Doctor*, 1 Oct. 1734.   [2] *Hyp Doctor*, 24 July 1733.
[3] Lecky, *History of England in the Eighteenth Century*, vol. i, p. 396.
[4] *Hyp Doctor*, 1 May 1733.
[5] Representative papers on this topic are nos. 6, 128, 140, 187, 190, 196, 198, 202,
207, 221, 238, 251.

to induce acquiescence, and expose the ignorance and folly of those who would presume to judgement.

Week by week the *Hyp Doctor* gives a political weather report of the period, when the history books have only time and space to record larger changes in climate. The Riot Act, the Septennial Parliament Act, the controversy over the standing army, press censorship and control, imprisonment for debt, the reduction of the land-tax, the naturalization of foreign Protestants, the Act for the control of spirituous liquors, the stage censorship Act of 1737, the troubles over the Porteous riots in Edinburgh—these were all the subject of detailed exposition and explanation.[1] When Walpole was in greater difficulty there was a correspondingly increased coverage of the problematical proposal. His excise scheme which aroused such violent opposition in Parliament and eventually in the country at large, was the subject of no fewer than seventeen papers in 1732 and 1733. Despite their reasonable arguments they fell on deaf ears and, though Parliament was won over, Walpole had in this instance to yield to the clamours of Lady Mob and withdraw the measure. His dilemma over the move to exempt Dissenters from the Test Act is similarly reflected in a number of papers which, in a tone of sweet reasonableness, exhort the Dissenters to support the Government as their best friend, but not as yet to press their claims until the time is ripe. The argument of the unripe time was Walpole's constant argument in the House and to every deputation, and the *Hyp Doctor* faithfully echoes it, whether or not it knew the truth which Walpole is said imprudently to have revealed when pressed to say *when* the time would come: 'If you require a specific answer, I will give it to you in a word—never.' The number of papers given over to the defence of places and pensions as rightful methods of maintaining the King's friends in Parliament and the Ministry's friends in the electorate, and to opposing demands for inquiry into such rewards and retainers, is again an indication of the importance of such a system to the Government, and of the vociferous accusations of 'Corruption' kept up by the Opposition.[2] Foreign as well as domestic matters received their share of attention, sometimes in general defences of Walpole's pacific

[1] See nos. 2; 174, 184, 487, 491; 14, 60, 277, 283; 19, 47; 62; 74; 274; 302; 14 and 28 June 1737; 21 Sept. 1736; 17 and 31 May 1737.
[2] See nos. 298, 469, 472, 477, 479, 481, 483, 529, for example.

policy in the face of popular warlike feeling, sometimes in detailed explanation of specific events, to show that the changing alliances and re-allotment of territory in Europe could not harm Britain and should not influence her against maintaining neutrality. When finally popular outrage drove Walpole into war with Spain the *Hyp Doctor* turned its attention to enthusiastic support of the naval strategy of the war. The Government could do no wrong, at home or abroad, and until the end the *Hyp Doctor* maintained the line it took in 1733: 'It is a Distinguishing Honour to this Administration that more Various and brighter Efforts for Universal liberty have appear'd in the Space of five Years, under its Influence than four times the Period hath produc'd in any Administration recorded in *English History*.'[1]

Though the voice of the people was not the source of government, the vote of the limited electorate was the source of Parliamentary representatives, and their careful wooing by place, pension, or straightforward bribery was an accepted part of maintaining the King's Government. The *Hyp Doctor* did not lag behind in adding the voice of persuasion and argument, when these important occasions called. The election of 1734 brought the Doctor to the hustings, exhorting the electors of Leicestershire to support a Whig candidate, producing manifestoes for the Whigs and exposures of the perfidy and corruption of the Tories, and finally rejoicing over the Whig victory in heroic couplets to Walpole:

> Still let thy Mind Britannia's Nerves pervade,
> The sound Majority demands thy Aid,
> Exert that Genius which of old withstood
> The Madness of the Raging Multitude.[2]

The next election was more crucial and uncertain. Opposition to Walpole had been growing. He had lost a great ally by the death of Queen Caroline; the Prince of Wales steadily opposed him; his slowness to declare war on Spain had displeased the nation; feeling in Scotland over the aftermath of the Porteous riots ran high, and at home his use of troops to quell election riots in Westminster had been eagerly misinterpreted by the Opposition press. The *Hyp Doctor* began its electioneering at the end of 1739 with number upon number addressed to the electors, detailed

---

[1] *Hyp Doctor*, 8 May 1733.   [2] *Hyp Doctor*, 4 June 1734.

defences of the Ministry's record at home and abroad, and four
addresses to the electors of Scotland who were obviously felt
to be uncertain in their loyalty.[1] All this effort was in vain.
Scotland produced an Opposition majority and, in the Parliament
which met in December 1741, Walpole had only a bare majority.
In the following year he was defeated over an election petition
and resigned, ending an uninterrupted and undefeated rule of
two and twenty years. As far as we can tell, the *Hyp Doctor*
fell with him and ended its vociferous and varied career of eleven
years, leaving what must have seemed a great but welcome gap
in Henley's life.

Variety, indeed, had been the spice of the *Hyp Doctor's* life,
and its weekly production had demanded wit and invention as
well as knowledge. In an early number Henley put into the con-
gratulatory letter of a 'correspondent' what was his own idea
of the special feature of his journalism:

Your Paper is distinguished for taking in a large Extent of Subjects, a
great Variety of Turns given to them and a peculiar Choice of them . . .
you do not roll on in the same heavy Strain of endless Tautology and
Repetition, but are always for launching some new Topick that is
properly diversify'd by its mixture of Solidity and Entertainment.[2]

The 'Variety of Turns' is certainly great, and a full survey of the
many different ways in which Henley sought to make his propaganda palatable would take a whole chapter. He devised fables;
he produced dialogues and disputations between such significantly
named characters as Whipt Cream, Junior, B.A., Fellow of All
Souls, and the Revd. Mr. Sour Buttermilk, Fellow of B.N.C.,
or Mr. Justice and Captain Mohock, or Mr. Free-booter and
Mr. Free-holder; he wrote mock catechisms; printed innumerable
letters; he preached sermons in Scots dialect or the quaint
language of the Quakers; he dreamed fantastic but meaningful
dreams; he worked out historical parallels; he printed woodcuts
and interpreted them like an old-fashioned emblem writer—and
he also produced serious and straightforward essays, filled with
statistics and solemn phrases. Word play, pun, witty turn of
phrase and conceit were his delight, and sometimes his downfall.
He was especially fond of taking a simple simile from such things as

[1] See nos. 468, 469, 475, 476, 509, 514, 517, 518, 519, 526, 528 for papers on this
election.
[2] *Hyp Doctor*, 2 Nov. 1731.

geese, a fever, worms, horse-racing, a country dance, and working them out at length and in detail. He could range from the highly coloured figurative abuse of 'inanimate son of Salopian Cheese-curd' and 'this *unhumaniz'd Chip* of misty *Cadwallader*' to the solemn and serious prose of discussions on political morality or foreign policy, when one suspects that the details of the official intelligence have suffered little imaginative transformation by a tired journalist, and appeared, for instance, as

A Political Dissertation, in which the Natural Right of his Royal Highness the Prince of *Orange* in the Marquisate of *Ten Veer* and *Flushing*, claim'd by the States of Zealand, and his Stadtholdership, are vindicated, in favour of the Pretensions of the Prince of *Orange*, and the King's letter on that Subject, undersign'd by his Excellency *Horatio Walpole*, Esq., justify'd by Law and History, in a new Argument.[1]

At times the suppressed poet in Henley was allowed his fling, producing a wide variety of verses, from the comic ode on the funeral of the *Craftsman*:

> Stream thousand Eyes,
> Here *Caleb* lies,
> That learned Man of *Gray's Inn*;
> Whose Projects bright
> Gave *Europe* light,
> Profound! and all amazing![2]

to an epigram on 'The Craftsman's Love of his Country':

> The Patriot writes his Country to embroil,
> Yet pleads Affection to his native Soil;
> Thus a Town-Rake pursues a vitious Flame,
> And cries, he loves the Spot from whence he came.[3]

He can turn his notes to more solemn couplet strains in praise of Walpole:

> Confusion heard thy Voice—the CHAOS ceas'd,
> And in new Smiles thy Gracious Power confess'd:
> Again Distinction rose with Native Grace
> And Order reassum'd her Antient Place;
> The System thus reform'd with Splendor glow'd,
> While all the Master-strokes of Wisdom shew'd
> The Delegate of *Caesar* and of GOD.[4]

[1] *Hyp Doctor*, 12 Oct. 1736. [2] *Hyp Doctor*, 1 June, 1731.
[3] *Hyp Doctor*, 15 Aug. 1732. [4] *Hyp Doctor*, 4 June 1734.

to the light-hearted quatrains on the end of the newspaper *The Bee*:

> Ye insects all that fly or creep
>   Assist my Doleful Ditty,
> The Fate of Bee defunct to weep,
>   Of Bee so humming Witty . . .
>
> . . . Squeez'd at a Press this *Humble* Bee
>   Can now no longer sing;
> Thus pointless ends my Elegy,
>   My Wasp has lost her Sting.[1]

or to the jogging octosyllabics beloved by so many writers of poems on affairs of state:

> When my merry Days were younger,
> E'er I was a *Journal-Monger*:
> When I had a little Leisure,
> And I took a little Pleasure:
> E'er I fell to peevish Writing,
> And all Parties were delighting:
> E'er I curs'd the Name of Party,
> None were hollow, all were hearty. . . .[2]

The *Hyp Doctor*, inevitably, suffered not only from the attacks of its rivals in the political trade, but from the general hostility which Henley was always heir to. The *Grub Street Journal* voiced the typical line of derision:

> Preach on, Great Orator, but Printing dread:
> Thy Jargon spoke seems sense; 'tis nonsense read.[3]

and 'Sometimes he has had convulsions in such a manner, that you could not understand one word he said in a whole packet or paper . . . he is at present afflicted with a sort of lunacy, that he has not spoke a sensible word this fortnight.'[4] The inescapable result, it was alleged, was that 'Hardly anybody reads it; and those few that do, don't understand it',[5]—a good example of the wishful thinking and unfair criticism which so often marked the controversies of the time. As Henley frequently pointed out, no paper lasted without a reading public, and his lasted for eleven years and outlasted many rivals. Nor was its quality so poor or

[1] *Hyp Doctor*, 17 June 1735.   [2] *Hyp Doctor*, 16 Sept. 1735.
[3] *G.S.J.*, 18 Mar. 1731.   [4] *G.S.J.*, 30 Sept. 1731.
[5] *G.S.J.*, 9 Mar. 1732.

its style so incoherent. Admittedly there are numerous papers
where the allusiveness, the secret jokes, the over-exuberant
word play and invention make him difficult and sometimes
impossible to follow: at other times he is solemnly and intolerably
dull: at others vague and puffy, saying very little under a cloud
of seemingly lofty verbiage; but, on the other hand, there are
hundreds of papers which are interesting and often entertaining
and amusing. The reading of a complete run of a political journal
for these years is not a form of entertainment one would recommend to any but the most ardent student of the period, but if
there be such an adventurer, looking for the common man's
view of the Walpole era and the instruction mingled with a
rather odd form of pleasure, he could be worse advised than to
turn the pages of old Dr. Ratcliffe, the Hyp Doctor of Great
Britain.

The fall of Walpole marked the end of an era in English history
and the end of a phase in Henley's political life. For eleven
years he had been tied to the Ministry, loyally bound to support
its activity, and this he had done week by week in his paper and
in the increasingly political content of his orations and discourses.
Now all that was changed. He was a free agent and turned from
being a party to being a free-lance non-party commentator on the
affairs of the nation. Walpole had been not only his employer but,
it must be admitted, his hero. After Walpole's downfall and death
three years later, Henley looked back with increasing nostalgia
to the good days under his sway. Around him he saw a growing
political degeneracy. 'To *Bob* Walpole succeeds yee-bob and
nay-bob'[1] he cried from his pulpit, and in his varied and often
violent criticisms of this new scene it is not surprising that he
often assumed the attitudes of the Great Man. What is surprising,
and not a little ironic, is that in his general disillusion with the
post-Walpolian world he began to sound like his old enemy
Pope who had inveighed against that very world in his later
political satires.

In 1742 Henley proclaimed his new independence, denying
that he was ever a favourite of the last ministry and certainly
denying any allegiance to the present. 'His Principles', he
advertised, 'are those of Reason, Truth and Honesty; he is for

---

[1] Sermon for 24 Sept. 1752 (B.M. MSS.Add. 11785).

or against any Ministry as they are for or against them And he is independent, and does not want, tho' he is not above, the Favour of the Ministry.'[1] There is however a certain amount of evidence to show that he was by no means above the favour of a ministry, and that the sort of secret service activity he had learned with Curll years before, still continued. The evidence is scrappy and the picture which emerges is blurred in outline, but the general pattern can be discerned. Bound up in a volume of his manuscript sermons for 1745, there is what appears to be the rough draft of a letter to the magistrate Sir Thomas de Veil— with whom he elsewhere claims to have been on friendly terms— dated 8 October, and arising from a recent disturbance at the Oratory over what must have been his comments on the '45 rebellion. He tells Sir Thomas that he had written to Mr. Pelham, asking him to communicate to the Duke of Newcastle and Lord Harrington that this disturbance was caused by a piqued clergy-man. He had played gentle and taken no action, adding, 'If I seem to byass another way sometimes, it is to hit the jack & make discoveries & be more effectually qualify'd by some stratagem to serve them.' He speaks of a Captain T. who has been to see him—obviously another disturber of the Oratory's peace—for whom he has a warrant which he did not serve, because 'I shall, by that very incident learn something. I hear he was in the French service at Dettingen & now has a French Pension, perhaps as a spy.' He asks Sir Thomas not to mention his name in the affair, to be pretty rigorous with Captain T. if the Messengers bring him in, and ends with a promise to learn more and be of service. The next draft letter, dated 17 October, was addressed to P–l—m and referred to this same case, advising great secrecy in their proceedings and requesting that only the Duke of Newcastle and Lord Harrington should be privy to them. He desired 'it to be taken as a proof that seeming to be against you is being for you—when ye Principles and Interest of ye Person are ye same with yr. own'. He lists a number of things to be found out about one whose name in the letter is illegible but appears to be the Captain T. of the previous letter—whether he is in the service of France or Spain, or receiving payment from them, to find out details of his way of life, the number of Irish Catholics in town, their plans, and whether any of them are also in the service of

[1] Advertisement for 29 Feb. 1742 (Lysons 111).

France.[1] A letter of 2 June 1746 recorded that 'my last vote was for Mr. Pelham's Interest: he knows it',[2] and when Pelham died in 1754, Henley preached a glowing funeral eulogium on him, 'whom I had ye Honour to know Personally in a particular Manner above 30 years'.[3] A letter survives from the following year addressed to Lord Chancellor Hardwicke, in which Henley seeks to attach himself to a new master in the old 'particular Manner':

I most humbly ask Pardon for informing your Lordship that one proof of my serving his Majesty, and the ministry, is, that I gain intelligence by them of the *real* enemies of the court; and the Rt. Hon. Mr. Pelham engaged it should not be known but to the royal family, first ministers, and judges. And Mr. Pelham, some months before his death, gave me ten guineas for one piece of intelligence about certain elections, which, with others, I could not have obtained but by such advertisements and discourses. I received sixty guineas from him, in the whole, for various services of that kind on severall occasions; and I allways invariably devoted my oratory, and do to ye like intention in several shapes; and shall be proud of every opportunity to be of any service to yr. Lordship and ye noble family.[4]

One other scrap of evidence suggests that Henley's relationships with his masters were not so friendly or easy, but nevertheless repeats that such relationships existed. Samuel Ireland, in 1794, records 'an anecdote mentioned of the late Duke of Newcastle; who, when Secretary of State, was applied to by the Orator to render him a service; which not being complied with, he, in a petulant way, replied, "*Remember I have a pen*:" to which the Duke retorted, "and my brother (meaning Harry Pelham) *shall mend that pen for you.*"'[5] The claim seems to be that during these years after the downfall of Walpole, when Henley appeared to be a frequent and fierce critic of the Administration and the Court, he was in fact a secret supporter of the Government, acting as an *agent provocateur*, spreading his provocative and near-seditious advertisements and discourses only as a bait to draw out and expose those who might agree with him. If any unsuspecting listener rose to the bait he was noted and reported, and the Secret Service disbursed the rewarding guineas. It is a claim which

---

[1] B.M. MSS.Add. 10346, pp. 216 and 219.
[2] Manuscript letter in Bath Public Library (AL.2327).
[3] Sermon for March 1754 (B.M. MSS.Add. 11797).
[4] Quoted in an article signed 'A.L.' in *Notes and Queries*, xii, p. 45, 1855.
[5] Samuel Ireland, op. cit., vol. i, p. 141.

it is difficult to accept entirely. It seems hardly credible that the whole political comment of fourteen years was a completely false front created and maintained for what—even by Henley's account—were neither frequent nor generous rewards. The most likely explanation, and one not inconsistent with Henley's character, is that his independent criticism of administration and current affairs was perfectly sincere though often irresponsible, and yet he was not above turning the dishonest guinea when opinions were exposed in the resultant Oratory disturbances and were of the sort in which the Government might take a paying interest. In such activity he could settle scores with those who annoyed him and disturbed his meetings, make a little money which was always welcome in these later years, and—very importantly—maintain useful relations with the powers that be, even deceiving them for long periods into a mistaken belief in the loyalty of his motives, while he continued to preach freely what he felt in his heart.

One person, in 1746, was under no illusion about Henley's political attitudes. It had certainly never crossed the mind of the author of *An Epistle to Orator Henley*[1] that the Oratory was anything more than the home of 'Discourses calculated chiefly to keep up a Spirit of *Sedition* in a superstitious Sect of People, your Neighbours, against the Government, and Abhorrence of our Holy *Religion*, happily established in these Kingdoms'. He presented his bill of indictment against Henley's '*indecent, libertine*, and *obscene* Expressions', under the heads:

First, Of gross and insolent Misrepresentations of the King's Government.

Secondly, Virulent Invectives against the Ministry, and all other Officers of State, both Civil and Military.

Thirdly, Misrepresentations of the Protestant Religion as established in these Kingdoms, Defences of the *Romish* Church, its Superstition and Members, and their Encouragers, during the late National Troubles.

Henley denied frequently that he had ever preached sedition or treason, though he insisted that 'A preacher is bound sometimes to be *Plain* and *Blunt*',[2] and that 'Free Speaking on Trustees of

---

[1] Anon., *An Epistle to O----r H–nl–y; containing some remarks on the Discourses set forth at the Conventicle etc.* (1746), pp. 4, 5, 7–8.

[2] *The Victorious Stroke for Old England*, p. 21.

Government [is] no Sedition, but one Criterion between a free *English Protestant* Sway, and a *French Popish* Authority.' He claimed the people's right to be informed and, when properly informed, to criticize the actions of the Government, though not to *do* as they please;[1] and it was in this role of independent political teacher of the people that the later Orator cast himself.

A critic, some years after Henley's death, asserted that 'As to any fix'd Principles with respect to political Notions, he had none, but employ'd all his Talents to laugh at, and make all Government appear a mere Joke;'[2] but a study of the advertisements and the surviving manuscript sermons of these years suggests that his pronouncements were not so unprincipled nor his attacks so irresponsible. True enough, many of his discourses were on specific events, his adverse judgements were *ad hoc*, and might well give the impression of a trigger-happy political sniper rather than a grand strategist. He exposed the conditions of sailors at sea and the plight of their families at home, and criticized the minister and the naval administration responsible; he attacked the Board of Trade and the customs policy, comparing it with what he considered the enlightened policy of France; he accused the Government of mishandling charitable trusts; he denounced the growth of the standing Army; he repeatedly deplored the Government's weak attitude towards the Dutch poaching in our fishing grounds, demanding stronger measures and bemoaning the neglect of the Navy; he viewed with distrust the growth of Parliamentary power and privilege, suggesting a dangerous similarity between 1751 and 1641; he warned his countrymen against untrustworthy foreign refugees and all imported foreigners, even Italian opera singers; and violently opposed any use of troops to keep civil order, declaiming 'Alass! Troops and Force of Arms will not support a *Free Protestant Empire*. Nothing *violent* can be of *long Continuance*: a *King of England is only such*, by ye *affection*, ye *free Equitable Consent* of ye *People*.'[3] All these and many more such variegated topics could be assembled to show him as nothing more than the eighteenth-century equivalent of our unprincipled laugh-catching political satirists, but such an

---

[1] Ibid., pp. 44–54.   [2] *The History of the Robin Hood Society*, p. 135.
[3] See the sermons for 17, 24, and 31 Jan. 1748 (B.M. MSS.Add. 11773); 1 and 8 Apr. 1750 (B.M. MSS.Add. 11777); 8 and 15 July, 30 Sept. 1750 (B.M. MSS.Add. 11779); 7 and 28 July 1751 (B.M. MSS.Add. 11781); 28 Oct. 1753 (B.M. MSS.Add. 11793); 8 July 1753 (B.M. MSS.Add. 11791).

interpretation would ignore more constant and recurring themes in Henley's discourses.

He inherited many ideas from Walpole, admitting in a sermon of 1748 that 'There were two Principles of a late Minister, in which I defended him, and ye Court with them, keeping out of Foreign Broils & diminishing ye Debts of ye Nation. I am consistent to these points.'[1] He coupled with this hatred of foreign involvement a distrust of the Hanoverians—which had been another mark of the younger Walpole—seeing their European possessions as potential inducement to unwelcome European interest and expense, and the presence of Germans in England as a hateful alien threat to true Old English interests. 'It is really a misfortune to *English-men*', he thundered in 1744, 'that they are anyway oblig'd to go thro these mean and beggerly Sovereignties of *Germany*, whose people are Slaves . . . and most of their Princes sharpers—Falstaff and his Regiment, two shirts and a half, in ye whole body of them, are their Picture.'[2] For some reason this year 1744 saw Henley returning again and again to attacks on the Hanoverians and their European connections, defending his loyalty as well as justifying his criticism with the formula 'to ye King our loyalty is due, but ye Elector is a stranger to our Constitution.'[3] This would hardly seem to cover such insults as '—our Royal Race is more exalted—lose none of their Stature—High German—Cock & Strut—a couple of them, joyn'd at top, might go towards a Stuart';[4] or the new Athanasian statement of the Hanoverian Faith:

To *believe* one Monarch, *Elector, King & Captain*, Cap, Crown & Hat with a Feather; not *confounding them*, nor dividing ye Substance,—wch is ten millions per annum . . . & it is also necessary to believe ye *Son*—Westphalian of ye substance of ye Father, begotten, before he came hither, and *English* of our substance, born of 100,000 a year—Perfect something, and perfect nothing, of an unreasonable Soul, & inhuman Flesh subsisting.[5]

By 1752 his language and accusations were becoming fiercer: 'Old England is to *pay* ye Py'd Piper, for dancing ye *Hanover*

[1] Sermon for 17 Jan. 1748 (B.M. MSS.Add. 11773).
[2] Sermon for 23 Sept. 1744 (B.M. MSS.Add. 11771).
[3] Discourse for 1 Apr. 1744 (B.M. MSS.Add. 10578).
[4] Discourse for 29 Jan. 1744 (B.M. MSS.Add. 11921).
[5] Discourse for 20 May 1744 (B.M. MSS.Add. 11921).

Rats out of *ye Ditch*, as he once led them into it';[1] and, inspired by his old hero, he bemoaned the fate of the overtaxed Briton who 'can't, by his honest Diligence, get ten shillings, but, some *beggerly German Prince*, as Sir R. W. call'd them, mumps for 5*d.* of it'.[2] The virulence increased. In the following year he summarized the post-Stuart era when '*Pumpernickles* (call'd by some, *Hanoverians*) *invaded ye Country; ravish'd away her Fortune;* scourg'd and afflicted her',[3] and by 1754 he was describing England as a 'Hanoverian Pig-stye'.[4] Small wonder that, despite his denials, he should be regarded as anything but a friend of the King's Government, especially as his attack on the ruling dynasty was reinforced with an increasingly vocal adulation of the House of Stuart in the years after 1745, when such an attitude inevitably suggested treasonable longings for the old days.

'It has become a fashionable Topic', he said, 'to rail at the *Stuarts*; which is, without doubt, ye *first and best Family* in Europe, none excepted';[5] and he set his face to be as unfashionable as possible, defending the characters and the actions of the Stuarts in a stream of discourses about them or in side references in other discourses, and in a steadily maintained abuse of their supplanters, William III and all things Dutch. 'King Wully was puny', he mocked, 'of ye Family of ye dutch Tadpoles, ye Newts in Ditches',[6] and he crudely rejoiced in his childless marriage— 'The other *Mary* was *quarter marry'd* to a *low Dutch Frog*, as dead as a Herring in a Fishmonger's Basket—thank heaven, none remain of *ye Breed*—to make monsters—in ye House of Lords between Flesh and Fish.'[7] Charles I was presented as a cruelly murdered father of his country;[8] Charles II was defended as a learned and charitable man;[9] James II was described as 'ye Greatest Oeconomist of his age—for ye Good of *England*',[10] and even his disastrous alienation of Oxford over the Magdalen fellow-

---

[1] Sermon for 31 May 1752 (B.M. MSS.Add. 11784).
[2] Sermon for 12 Nov. 1752 (B.M. MSS.Add. 11786).
[3] Sermon for 9 Dec. 1753 (B.M. MSS.Add. 11794).
[4] Sermon for 13 Jan. 1754 (B.M. MSS.Add. 11795).
[5] Sermon for Sept. 1750 (B.M. MSS.Add. 11780).
[6] Sermon for 6 Nov. 1743 (B.M. MSS.Add. 10578).
[7] Sermon for 29 Jan. 1744 (B.M. MSS.Add. 11921).
[8] Sermon for 8 Mar. 1752 (B.M. MSS.Add. 11783).
[9] Sermon for 8 Jan. 1748 (B.M. MSS.Add. 11776).
[10] Sermon for 21 July 1754 (B.M. MSS.Add. 11798).

ships is defended;[1] Queen Anne, he asserted, 'was inclin'd to be a *Stuart*, in *her heart* as well *as Blood*:—but ye *World*, ye *Flesh*, and ye *Devil*, something contradicted it.'[2] He praised the Stuarts for keeping the nation out of foreign broils[3] and for their strong support of the Navy,[4] and he constantly reinforced the claim of the Stuarts to be the best of princes by contrasting the present sorry state of things with their golden days, when there were 'In Stuart Times, fewer and lesser Crimes',[5] when 'Stuarts never put London in Mourning on my Ld. Mr.'s Day',[6] when the 'Stuarts had no GottingEN to starve us Cambridge MEN'.[7] One can understand the outrage of the loyalist who, hearing such utterances, wrote, 'It must make an honest Man's Ears tingle to hear *a Spirit of Jacobitism* advanced to a publick Audience',[8] though one can equally sympathize with Henley who was heartily sick of the slack use of this scare-word 'Jacobitism' to describe any criticism of the Court or the Ministry and which he thought was used as a convenient bogy-man to frighten the people into acquiescence, the word, 'if it intends anything—for in reality it is void of sense—being *personal*'.[9] He pooh-poohed the prevalent Jacobite alarmism and mocked the frequent occurrence of Jacobite scares: 'It is expedient, that a Plot or Two, should grow up before, or in, ye Spring Season.'[10] A man could praise the past—even if the kings of the past *were* Stuarts; he could deny the dangers of Popery and defend Rome against unwarrantable aspersions; he could criticize the present Government and satirize the Established Church—not because he was a Jacobite, plotting to restore a Pretender, but because he was an honest man seeking after Truth with Right Reason. To us there is something admirable in Henley's attempts at tolerance and moderation in an age of bigotry and irrational prejudice, his refusal to use the unthinking cant of political parties which fixes crudely simplified labels to the most varied

---

[1] Sermon for 13 Oct. 1751 (B.M. MSS.Add. 11782).
[2] Sermon for 31 Oct. 1753 (B.M. MSS.Add. 11793).
[3] Sermon for 10 Jan. 1748 (B.M. MSS.Add. 11772).
[4] Sermon for Sept. 1750 (B.M. MSS.Add. 11779).
[5] Advertisement for 9 Nov. 1751 (Lysons 170).
[6] Advertisement for 26 Oct. 1751 (ibid.).
[7] Advertisement for 12 Oct. 1751 (ibid.).
[8] *An Epistle to O————r H–nl–y etc.*, p. 17.
[9] Discourse for 20 May 1753 (B.M. MSS.Add. 11789).
[10] Discourse for 8 Apr. 1753 (B.M. MSS.Add. 11788).

and complicated beliefs. Equally there should be no surprise
that the details and motives of his arguments were ignored, and
the conclusions firmly stamped as 'the spirit of Sedition' and 'the
Spirit of Jacobitism'.

Beneath all his detailed comment on policy and action, and
springing from his admiration of a past age, there is a continuous
lament over the degeneracy of the times. Henley, seeing a general
decay from the time of the 'Deformation',[1] laments that 'we
seem to be retiring backwards to ye antedeluvian age'.[2] From
top to bottom the nation was corrupt and 'Lords, Commons, &
even Bishops, are a most astonishing Collection of Spiritual and
Temporal Rakes and Fornicators.'[3] As for the nation's Government, 'Moll Flanders & her history is ye history of our Politicks',[4]
rent with savage and increasingly meaningless party divisions so
that it became her fate 'to be *divided* & therefore, weaken'd &
betray'd by Parties'.[5] Corruption was rampant and all was to be
bought and sold in London, where 'A back-door has introduced
many to a Perk, & ye greatest Persons are ye Masters of ye
Ceremonies, of ye BackStairs',[6] where 'Top People and fine
folks are Bullies, Sharpers, & Catch-Poles'.[7] Every Corner was
filled with some pensioner or placeman, contemptible because
'What a *Machine*, or a Puppet is, by necessity, he must acquire
by Habit';[8] and he did not stop at false etymologies to enrol
in the attack the Biblical prophecy that 'The Locusts, that is,
Placemen, (from *Locus*, a *Place*) shall consume thy Field'.[9]
Small wonder that we were the scorn and derision of Europe
when 'Our very allies despise and laugh at us: an Englishman
is a *Jest* in Holland, Germany, Italy and France; our Taxes send
our Workmen, starving there, to seek their Bread, and carry
our Trade abroad.'[10] The good simple days of Old England had
passed away, and chaos had come again.

Whiggify Tories, & Torify Whiggs, Dutchify English, & anglicise
Dutch: Spaniardise, Russianise, King-Romanise, Germanise, Hanover-

[1] Discourse for 2 Dec. 1753 (B.M. MSS.Add. 11794).
[2] Discourse for 24 Feb. 1754 (B.M. MSS.Add. 11796).
[3] Discourse for 4 Sept. 1748 (B.M. MSS.Add. 11774).
[4] Discourse for 25 Sept. 1748 (B.M. MSS.Add. 11775).   [5] Ibid.
[6] Discourse for 7 Oct. 1753 (B.M. MSS.Add. 11792).
[7] Discourse for 8 Jan. 1748 (B.M. MSS.Add. 11776).
[8] Discourse for 22 Mar. 1752 (B.M. MSS.Add. 11783).
[9] Discourse for 24 Oct. 1754 (B.M. MSS.Add. 11799).
[10] Discourse for 8 Jan. 1748 (B.M. MSS.Add. 11776).

ise, Naturalise, Brutalise, till no Mortal can tell whether his Face be
before him, or his back behind him, or whether he was born 11 days
on one side, or 11 days o' t'other, or born at all, or be here, or there,
or any where, or no where: This is a most *admirable Constitution*; and an
Establishment wch. I defy all *ye Jacobites upon Earth* to unestablish.[1]

In the midst of this degeneracy and corruption, Henley saw himself as the Jeremiah of his time. If that great prophet of denuncia-
tion and doom had returned to London, there was but one pulpit
he could have preached from—the pulpit of the Oratory—[2] and,
to complete the similitude, Henley not only assumed that prophet's
mantle: he once suffered, though not so grievously, part of that
prophet's fate.

On 25 July 1745 the Pretender landed. There is little need to
recount the details of this often-chronicled débâcle. By October
Prince Charles was prepared to invade England. Carlisle was
captured on 15 November and the rebel forces moved south as
far as Derby. Their retreat began on 6 December and their
demoralized forces were decisively and terribly defeated at Culloden on 16 April 1746. The subsequent 'pacification' of the High-
lands was carried through with a savage thoroughness. It was in
this crisis, when passions and suspicions were violently inflamed,
that Henley spoke out boldly and defiantly, and suffered accordingly. It was in the September of 1745 that he first started to
advertise orations on the rebellion—'The Pr**r! Popery! Murder!
Fire! where, where?' and 'The Seeds of the Plot may rise, tho'
the Leaves fall', but it was not until the last Sunday in September
that the trouble really broke out with his discourse on 'A General
salted at Preston-Pans', in which he had commented on the
battle of Preston and the behaviour of the generals in charge
there, adding satirical comments on Herring, the militant Archbishop of York who was so active in raising money and soldiers
and even riding out to review the troops. There is no extant
copy of this discourse and the only evidence of its content is in a
letter to the papers purporting to come from an ear-witness at the
Oratory that night.

I was very lately present at the Indecencies thrown on the Person of
his Majesy; I heard his Troops ridicul'd for the late bad success in the
North, and could scarce contain myself when he emblazon'd the

---

[1] Discourse for 16 Dec. 1751 (B.M. MSS.Add. 11794).
[2] Discourse for 6 Oct. 1751 (B.M. MSS.Add. 11782).

character of the Pretender with all Colours of Honour and Respect; he prophesy'd that this Invader of our Rights would prosper; he lavish'd reproaches on the French for not sending Succour to him; and declar'd that we should soon be call'd back from the Desertion (his own phrase) of the Chevalier's Father . . .[1]

The immediate reaction to this oration was an attempt to organize a counter-attack. On 30 September there appeared in the press a letter:

Those Gentlemen who disapprove the scurrilous and treasonable Discourse made last Night to a numerous Audience, are desired to give some Gentlemen a Meeting, who intend to shew their Abhorrence and Detestation of that audacious, insolent, and dangerous abuse of Liberty, and from a Principle of Gratitude for the Security they enjoy under the present happy Establishment, intend heartily to concur in their Endeavours to put a stop to the licentiousness of that insolent Firebrand, who in defiance of our Laws, and contempt of that Government, by whose Lenity alone he has hithertoo escaped Punishment, dares openly applaud, and endeavour to justify the present Rebellion; any Gentleman or Gentlemen so inclin'd, may advertise a Meeting in this Paper; or direct a letter to P.L. at Peel's Coffee House, Fleet Street.[2]

This unleashed a furious newspaper controversy, Henley thundering his full range of abuse—'bullying Regiment of Raggamuffins', 'Bellowing drumhead Hottentots, that holy scold, that spiritual Gossip, that roaring Bull of Basan, Parson Funk'—denying the charges, and claiming that he had explained himself to the Ministry.[3] The explanation—no doubt on the lines of the two letters to Sir Thomas de Veil and Pelham which have been discussed, and which belong exactly to this time—must have been accepted, for there was no punitive reaction from the Government and the worst which happened was continued uproar and violence at the Oratory. Henley was by no means frightened off the subject, and the next advertisement for his discourses, headed 'To squirt at a Red-Herring is High Treason', promised what was obviously an unrepentant defence of his preaching in 'A Discourse asserting the Liberty of Preaching, of Rebuking, and ridiculing Political Follies and Vices boldly . . . against such Bishops and their

---

[1] Lysons 140.   [2] Ibid.
[3] For Henley's letters to the press and replies to him, see Lysons 140.

Implements, who would ensnare the Ministry to be their Tools, and make a Rebellion serve their private Passions against particular Persons.'[1] So the year ended, Henley still discoursing on the rebellion, as the Pretender withdrew northwards, and still unable to resist punning attacks against Archbishop Herring.

The year 1746 saw the defeat of the Pretender and the savage reprisals against the rebels. Henley had maintained his interest in the rebellion and often devoted his discourses to it. In February he lectured on Anglo-Scots relations with the provocative title of 'The King of the North shall return',[2] and three days before Culloden he spoke of the Highland regiments, giving 'Reasons against banishing or marinating the R* Sc*s and the H* Reg*; Memoirs of these brave Forces'.[3] The treatment of the Scots at Culloden and afterwards genuinely outraged Henley, who denounced it as inhumane and stupid. In June he delivered 'A very curious Dissertation on the treatment of Rebels'[4] and returned in discourse after discourse to the fates of the Scots lords executed for treason, being especially moved by the bravery and dignity of Lord Balmerino, and later defending the aged Lord Lovat as he hopelessly and without assistance stood trial for his life. It was his preaching on Lord Lovat which brought matters to a head and enabled his enemies to succeed where they had failed in '45.

Sunday 30 November was the fateful day, coming after a week of disturbance. On the previous Sunday his house had been broken into by an unknown person, and manuscripts had been taken away, whilst five or six conspirators—one a tall slender young man, fair, round-visag'd, in a whitish coat with brass buttons—raised a hullabaloo in the Oratory to divert attention. It seems highly likely that this was the first step in the plot against him—an attempt to obtain documentary evidence.[5] On the 30th he preached on Lord Lovat and prayed for the deliverance of Scotland. The Oratory was in an uproar and scuffles took place between his supporters and servants and his opponents in the congregation. Those opponents lost no time in putting into action

[1] Advertisement for Oct. 1745 (Lysons 140).
[2] Advertisement for 1 Feb. 1746 (Lysons 142).
[3] Advertisement for 12 Apr. 1746 (Lysons 143).
[4] Advertisement for 21 June 1746 (ibid.).
[5] Advertisement for 27 Nov. 1746 (Lysons 145).

what must have been a prearranged plan. The very next day they and Henley appeared before a magistrate, and in the morning paper of that day was printed an advertisement appealing for witnesses, which must have been handed in on the previous night, announcing,

Whereas some Gentlemen who were at the Oratory in Lincoln's Inn Fields Yesterday, are to wait on Thomas Burdus, Esq., at his House in Bow Street, at eleven o'clock this Morning; this is therefore to desire all Gentlemen who are Well-Wishers to the illustrious House of Hanover, and Lovers of the Country, who were present at the said Oratory, to give their Attendance at the said Justice's.[1]

The machinery of justice moved surprisingly—even suspiciously—swiftly. Later that day all the interested parties were assembled and the examination took place. The newspapers reported next morning that

Yesterday the famous O----r H---y was examin'd by Thomas Burdus, Esq., and several other of His Majesty's Justices of the Peace, then sitting at the Vestry-Room in Covent-Garden, and after four hours Examination was committed by the said Justices to the Custody of the High Constable of Westminster, charg'd on the oaths of George Garnon, Esq.; the Rev. Dr. Clark, and several Gentlemen then present, for many expressions deliver'd at his O--y in L--n's I-- F--ds last Sunday Evening, tending to alienate his Majesty's Subjects from their Duty and Allegiance; and at the same Time two of his Door-Keepers were also committed for a violent Assault on the said Gentlemen.[2]

The town hummed with the news, and Horace Walpole did not fail to report that 'The famous Orator Henley is taken up for treasonable flippancies', when he wrote to bring Mann up to date with the latest gossip soon after the arrest.[3] Later Henley was to add the names of Moor, Cope, Coates, and Mawd to the list of his successful accusers[4] and subsequently described them as 'one a pious Church-Clergyman, another, a Counsellor, two Military Officers, a Yorkshire Surgeon, who mistook the Right Vein; and a Custom Officer, who robb'd ye King of something towards 15,000 £'.[5]

[1] Advertisement for 1 Dec. 1746 (Lysons 145).
[2] News item for 2 Dec. 1746 (ibid.).
[3] Letter of 5 Dec. 1746, Yale edition of the correspondence, ed. Lewis, Smith, and Lam, vol. xix, p. 341.
[4] Advertisement for 29 Aug. 1747 (Lysons 150).
[5] Sermon for March 1754 (B.M. MSS.Add. 11797).

With Henley safely in custody, there appeared a sudden rash of anti-Henley propaganda, so extensive and so exactly ready for the critical moment, that it becomes quite clear that a careful and long-prepared plan was being put into operation. On 5 December two pamphlets appeared. The first—*An Epistle to O--r H-n-y; containing some remarks on the Discourses set forth at the Conventicle, the Corner of Lincoln's-Inn-Field*—was a serious and not unreasonable attempt to list his alleged treasonable statements, and advising him to give up a life spent in 'endeavouring to support unprofitable and dangerous Principles'. The second was *The Puffer Puff'd, or O-r H****ly an Overmatch for the Devil; a Vision. In an Epistle to a Friend, by Phantasius Teratopaeus.* The author, fallen into a profound sleep as he thinks of the Orator and *The Coup de Grâce*, dreams that Henley is dead and is being brought to judgement. His Temple is cleansed of 'Treason and Rebellion, Atheism and Blasphemy, Infidelity and Ignorance, False-testimony, Deceit, Perjury', but Henley's fate is harder to settle. The Devil sends a deputation to plead for his not being sent to Hell: he has enough with Oates and Sacheverell, and fears that Henley's 'turbulent Disposition and restless Spirit' would make 'an Addition to Hell's wild uproar'. Pope Alexander VI makes a similar plea for Purgatory where Henley's 'pestilential and contagious Blasts' might undo much of the cleansing work of the fires. At last, with a rather weak collapse of the fiction, Henley is sent to the Tower amid the loud applause of the multitude. These verbal assaults were reinforced by pictorial satire, two prints appearing on the bookstalls, *The Brazen Faced Popish Incendiary in the Temple of Rebellion* on 12 December, and *Orator Henley in the Suds* on 17 December. The town had also been diverted by what the *General Evening Post* reported as 'a Whimsical Procession, on Account of O-H-y's being confin'd, at which the Butchers in Mourning attended with Marrow Bones and Cleavers',[1] and a new 'Orator' advertised that in the unavoidable absence of his learned friend, he himself would mount the rostrum and endeavour 'to puzzle your Understandings, confound your Judgments, poison your Minds, and pick your Pockets, at the small Price of a Turnip or a rotten Egg'.[2]

Meanwhile, away from all this excitement, Henley was still in

[1] *General Evening Post*, 6 Dec. 1746.
[2] Advertisement for 10 Dec. 1746 (Lysons 146).

custody. Reports that he had been moved to Newgate to await execution and promises of the future publication of his dying speech were satirically printed and soberly denied.[1] In fact, two days after his being committed into the custody of the High Constable of Westminster, he was delivered over to a Messenger by a warrant from the Earl of Chesterfield,[2] and on 15 December he was still in the Messengers' hands, awaiting the examination before the Lords of the Privy Council. One account survives of this occasion in a curious collection of odds and ends published by John Miller in 1855—*Flyleaves: or Scraps and Sketches*. No authorities are quoted for the anecdote, but as it is our only one, and has an air of authenticity, it cannot be rejected. It runs,

In one of his orations during the year of the rebellion in Scotland he uttered some expressions which were thought seditious, and he was cited before the Privy Council. He was asked why he turned the exertions of good citizens into ridicule, and especially why he tried to inflame the minds of the people, by his satires against Archbishop Herring? . . . Henley's reply excited great laughter. 'I thought there was no great harm, my Lords,' said he, 'in cracking a joke upon a Red Herring!'
In reply to several questions, and why he meddled with affairs of state at all, he replied to the Earl of Chesterfield, 'My Lord, I must live.' The Earl rejoined, 'I see no kind of reason for that;' at which the other Lords were observed to laugh. Henley appeared irritated, and then said—'That is a very good thing, my Lord, but it has been said before.' He was detained in custody for a few days, and then dismissed as an impudent fellow, without sufficient reason in him to be dangerous.[3]

The memory of this gibe seems to have been short lived for when Henley preached a funeral sermon on the Earl of Chesterfield four years later, he asked a blessing on the man who

when false Witnesses rose up against us, and laid to our charge, Things we knew not, had Justice and Humanity not to push ye Power with which Courts are invested, but first preferr'd an Equitable Lenity, to ye more Rigorous & peremptory Method of proceeding, &, on a Judicial Proof of ye Falsehood & Inconsistency, Malice & Baseness of ye Agents, & Evidence, dismiss'd ye Cause.[4]

---

[1] See Advertisements for 9 Dec. 1746 (Lysons 144) and 15 Dec. 1746 (Lysons 146).
[2] Samuel Ireland, op. cit., vol. i, p. 145, and the *Gentleman's Magazine*, vol. xvi, p. 666.
[3] pp. 96–7.   [4] Sermon for 1–3 July 1750 (B.M. MSS.Add. 11797).

4. Orator Henley versus Culloden

5. Orator Henley in the suds

According to Henley, Henry Pelham was also one of the examiners who 'affirmed, after my and my Servants' Innocence was demonstrated against six Oaths, "that he would nothing against me"',[1] and had previously 'declar'd in ye House of Commons, there was no law against ye Oratory'.[2] Again, according to Henley, his examination aroused interest in a wider circle than his immediate accusers, and 'The Coaches of 16 Eminent Directors of ye Church were at ye Doors of ye Ministers during that most Religious Negotiation.'[3] It seems to have been the general verdict that Henley was a noisy but not dangerous nuisance, certainly not dangerous enough to treat seriously with the full rigour of the law, and after a fortnight in custody he was admitted to bail on 20 December.

Once free, Henley took care not to offend again. Though he continued to deny all the charges brought against him and pertly regretted that he could not 'furnish some that hear me with Brains to understand me right, or Honesty to own it',[4] he did not preach again until 1 March and he made two public confessions of his possible errors which are so unlike his normal performances that one suspects that they, as well as his temporary pulpit silence, might have been demanded as conditions of his release. His denial that he had been prohibited from preaching increases our suspicions.[5] The first 'confession' is just a little too contrite to be true, and it is difficult not to believe that the Orator smiled as he wrote it:

I am not conscious of any Immoral Practice or Intention; I may have been guilty of Error in Judgment, and Impudence in Conduct, not, that I know, of Depravity of Will; if, in my Advertisements, Orations, and Deportment, I have been thought to have given Offence to any Body of Men or Individuals, I ask their Pardon; I forgive all my Enemies without Exception; and I will employ my utmost Caution to avoid all Occasion of Distaste for the Future; particularly on Sunday Feb. 1st., when I propose, God willing, to begin new Discourses, till I can perfect my Design of a Political Academy for the highest Service, glory and Grandeur of our Gracious Sovereign, His Most Sacred Majesty King George, and all the Branches of his Royal and Illustrious

---

[1] Advertisement for 8 Mar. 1754 (Lysons 186).
[2] Sermon for March 1754 (B.M. MSS.Add. 11797).   [3] Ibid.
[4] Advertisement for 19 Dec. 1746 (Lysons 146).
[5] Advertisement for 31 Jan. 1747 (ibid.).

Family; and the Honour and Interest of the Administration, the Bishops and Clergy, and my Brethren the Dissenters, of all Denominations.[1]

More like his own voice was his appeal to the public to 'Tolerate one English Cervantes in the Pulpit'.[2] Nevertheless, his oration subjects for the next month or so were calmer and less political, and at times the loyalty of his addresses was so complete that they could well have been ironical performances. What can we make of this report on Henley's honouring of Butcher Cumberland?

On Sunday Evening last, the new Military Prayer, adoring and invoking the God of Battle, in the most sublime language, in honour of the approaching Birthday of his Royal Highness the Duke of Cumberland, and the Elogium on his Royal Higness, then pronounced, was peculiarly and universally approv'd by a numerous Congregation at the Oratory, and were, each of them, by some Auditors, call'd a Master-Piece.[3]

Such pledges of loyalty and dutiful performances must have been accepted however, and supported the opinion of his official examiners. When he appeared with his bail in the Court of King's Bench on 19 June 1747, he was discharged, and his last serious clash with authority ended.[4]

In the years which followed he returned, as we have seen, to weekly criticism and satire of the Government in often more virulent terms. He never forgot the cruelties of Culloden nor ceased to oppose the military and legal reprisals against the Scots, 'the cruelties and desolations in Scotland',[5] 'When ye Innocents were slaughter'd, by King *Herring*, I mean, Herod',[6] and when he likened Culloden to Newmarket Races, because '*they set out in a Battle of Beasts* and *Men*, for ye *Prize*'.[7] He attacked the Plaid Act and with gruesome details exposed the atrocities committed in its enforcement.[8] It is difficult not to see seditious incitement in his reaction to the activities of the Army in Scotland when he suggested that

---

[1] Advertisement for 24 Jan. 1747 (ibid.).
[2] Advertisement for 28 Mar. 1747 (ibid.).
[3] Advertisement for 14 Apr. 1747 (Lysons 147).
[4] *Daily Advertiser*, 20 June 1747.
[5] Sermon for 3 June 1753 (B.M. MSS.Add. 11790).
[6] Sermon for 31 May 1752 (B.M. MSS.Add. 11784).
[7] Sermon for 29 Apr. 1753 (B.M. MSS.Add. 11788).
[8] Sermon for 9 Sept. 1750 (B.M. MSS.Add. 19924).

Every Man, Woman & Child in Britain ought to kill a soldier & those that order them, till not one is left in ye Country . . . We will not be Dragoon'd: & if one falls, let Thousands rise to maintain ye Quarrel: it would be no Rebellion, but a more lawfull Resistance, than at ye Revolution . . . Popery & ye Inquisition, to this, are Paradise.[1]

But the panic atmosphere of the late '40s, which had no doubt helped his enemies to bring him into custody, had changed. In the years ahead he was attacked and mobbed, and faced repeated riots in his Oratory, but never again the Magistrates or the Privy Council. Authority obviously remained of the opinion that he was but 'an impudent fellow, without sufficient reason in him to be dangerous', and acquiesced in tolerance of this 'one English Cervantes of the Pulpit' as, like the great creation of that satirist, he tilted at any windmill in sight—especially Dutch ones!

[1] Sermon for 23 Sept. 1750 (ibid.).

CHAPTER VIII
The Private Man

SOME MEN LIVE entirely in their public acts. The story of their lives is a recounting of policies, controversies, and publications, and there is little in them and less outside them to help us to know the man himself, to discover the feelings, the weaknesses, and the idiosyncrasies which make him a unique personality. Dryden was such a man. Henley was most certainly not. Though so far our story of the London Henley has told of the man the public knew, of his work at the Oratory, of his ideas and his involvement in public controversy, a very definite outline of a personality has emerged, a personality driven by high ambition, proud and self-sufficient and supremely self-confident, given to violence in word and action, a curious mixture of learning and nonsense, of common sense and eccentricity, of high ideals and petty actions. He reveals so much of himself, even though in public actions, because of his complete lack of objectivity in all he said and did, his inability to cloak his personal involvement or disguise his voice. In seeking Henley, the private man, therefore, we shall often be merely adding detail, lights and shades, to the outlines already publicly revealed, but we might add something new, something of the life which went on outside the Oratory and the world of pamphlets, when he had disappeared through the door behind the rostrum and, having completed his next advertisement or latest pamphlet, laid aside his pen for a while.

The many prints of the period devoted to Henley give us a full, and, from their consistency in detail, an accurate record of what he looked like. In his early years in London, he was by no means an unhandsome man and even the addition of fox's ears in the Reynard-Parson print do not disguise the fact. The eyes are large and bold and, as the years went by, became more protuberant. The nose is long and prominent and the mouth full with a marked bow of the upper lip and a tendency, increased with years, to set in a downward almost sneering expression.

In middle years he grew plumper and rounder in the face, but age and illness towards the end of his life gave him a more haggard look, the cheeks fallen, the large somewhat insolent eyes sunken, and the long nose more prominent above the down-turned mouth. One thing the prints cannot show is his complexion, but there is a mass of evidence agreeing on this. The *Grub Street Journal* constantly returned to the subject. 'Was that steddy face of his,' it asked, 'that goodly Bronze, that more than English or Welch Copper, in his dun and dusky countenance, given him for nothing?'[1] In its description of him as a jolly nag it added 'His colour was a dark brown',[2] and a letter from 'Nicholas Stentor' confirms this detail of complexion while adding a reference to the Orator's nose, when the writer, about to take up the Orator's challenge to a public disputation, added 'and [I] doubt not to convince the by-standers, that I've a phyz of as good colour and gristle as this cartilaginous hero's . . .'[3] An independent eye-witness wrote to the *Weekly Journal* about his visit to the Oratory and recorded that 'I eyed the person of the Orator thoroughly, and could point out in every lineament of his face the features and muscles of a Jew, with a strong tincture of the Turk.'[4] This dusky complexion, so conveniently 'brazen' for the satirists, was invariably bewigged, and was no doubt accentuated by the white preaching bands he always appeared in. Despite his secession from the Established Church he never discarded her canonical habit, of which he appears to have been very fond, and not only in the pulpit but in the streets and coffee-houses he appeared in cassock, gown, scarf, and bands. A year before his death he recorded how, though now unfashionable, he retained the custom: 'The Canonical Habit', he wrote, 'is not now worn by the Clergy: what they wore, I frequently do, and always in the Pulpit.'[5] That there was something of defiance in his insisting on this dress is suggested by a curious reference in a sermon of 1750 to 'a Group of Bishops, who met many Times at *Lambeth*, to enquire, whether I ought to wear a Gown and Cassock'.[6] His appearance in the pulpit in these venerable robes had shocked and scandalized many auditors who found them so

[1] *G.S.J.*, 13 May 1731.   [2] *G.S.J.*, 9 Nov. 1732.
[3] *G.S.J.*, 18 Oct. 1733.   [4] Quoted in J. P. Malcolm, op. cit., p. 238.
[5] Advertisement for 4 Apr. 1755 (Lysons 193).
[6] Sermon for 20 Oct. 1751 (B.M. MSS.Add. 11782).

at variance with the sentiments expressed there and the language of their expositor. Even more incongruous must they have seemed when Henley descended from the pulpit and, in places less reverend even than the Oratory, behaved without the inhibition of Christianity however primitive, or the control of Elocution.

There is a striking unanimity amongst all contemporary witnesses and in all later memories of the man, on his temper and manners which were boisterous and often violent. He had, we are told, 'a strong voice, fluent language, an imposing magisterial air, and a countenance, which no violation of propriety, reproach or self-correction, was ever known to embarrass or discompose'.[1] This strong voice and fluent language were frequently in use, not only in the pulpit, but in the streets and taverns, in argument and abuse. Samuel Paterson the bookseller, who knew Henley personally, told Nichols that 'His manners were indeed, rough and unpolished as the very Butchers among whom he chose to set up his first and last Conventicles'.[2] Another contemporary described him as 'Vindictive in his Temper, and profligate in his Manners',[3] while the author of *A Letter to the Celebrated Orator*, as early as 1727, explained that his letter would have reached Henley earlier but he

could not find a Messenger who had Courage enough to Approach you with it, for fear of that *Porter-like Discipline*, with the feeling of which you have Threatened Mr. *Whiston*. Nor indeed, tho' that fearless Man cannot be perswaded by his Friends, to beware of being Drubb'd or Assassinated, does your present Adviser think it consistent with common prudence that he should let himself be known by you; Not only for fear of your *Porterlike* but *Billingsgate Discipline*, of which also you have given an ample Specimen, in your Treatment of the same Mr. Whiston.[4]

This treatment of Mr. Whiston has already been examined and it was indeed marked by violence of word and action. Even more so was another such quarrel from the early years which has been preserved for us in all its rowdy liveliness in a pamphlet entitled *The Duelling Orator Delineated*.[5] The letters published in that

[1] *The Lounger's Common-place Book*, p. 138.
[2] Nichols, *Literary Anecdotes etc.*, Addition to vol. iii, in vol. viii, p. 484.
[3] *A Comparison between Orator H——— and Orator P———*, p. 5.
[4] *A Letter to the celebrated Orator*, 'The Advertisement'.
[5] *The Dueling Orator Delineated*, p. 13.

pamphlet, unstylish and unpremeditated, undoubtedly capture the speaking voice of the enraged and obstreperous Orator. His opponent was a certain William Wood, who describes himself 'of Christ Church, Oxford', and who admitted that for a brief period he had helped Henley at a time when Henley was in ill health and 'lame in his hands', by collecting for him some references to elocution and action out of Cicero. He had even considered becoming a Reader at the Oratory but, on advice, had decided against it. Henley's remarks on the deficiencies of the Universities had turned his erstwhile assistant into a public opponent and Henley, enraged by this, rushed round to Wood's house, as he had once rushed round to Whiston's. Wood wisely refused to see him and demanded a letter instead. By noon the letter had arrived written on a filthy scrap of paper and left by a Porter, unsealed, at Wood's lodgings. It is a remarkable piece of colloquial prose:

Mr. WOOD, I thought, having parted friendly, you and I had nothing to say to one another in any other Way: You remember you offered to be Reader to the *Oratory*, which you so much write against, and not only so, but to collect *materials* for something, I *forget what*. However, you shou'd have let me know you intended to write against it, and I might have clear'd the Point to you, unless all that Design be, the *Penny*: And you shou'd have managed the Argument with Fairness, Reason and Learning, not with Personal Reflections and scurrilous language, which are nothing to the Purpose, and are in you, to whom I have been Civil, highly *villainous and ungrateful*. I wou'd know, whether your Continuation is to be as scurrilous, and full of personal Invective; and whether you be dispos'd to meet about this Matter any Time and *private Place*, you propose.

I will not be insulted *tamely*. Learning and Reason are always welcome, but not ill Language.

Before this Matter goes farther, you would do handsomely to let me see you,

Who am Yours,
J. HENLEY.

Mr. Wood wrote his reply and sent it round to a coffee-house where he knew Henley often visited. It was not a rude letter, but it was firm. He refused to stop writing until Henley stopped satirizing the Universities, and dropped a hint that Henley's private character was 'a Thing too tender to be touched on' and 'had

been more often vindicated than attacked by him'. Henley flew
into a rage at this and, with his usual precipitate action, made his
way to the house of Mr. Wiger who kept a private school and
where Wood had sometimes stayed. Here he pumped Mr. Wiger
for information on Wood's private character and, armed with
new facts, rushed round to confront his enemy. Wood's account
is highly picturesque.

He, like a famish'd Tyger in quest of his *Prey*, came to the Place of my
abode, highly inflam'd with Indignation and Revenge; and not meeting
with me, the Passion increased for want of full Satisfaction of his
Spight, till he had at length play'd the Part of a *Madman and a Fury, or a
Counterfeit of both*, with as much *Perfection* as ever any *Actor* did on the
Stage. But perceiving his Auditors were *partial* Judges, shewing little
or no Regard to his Performance, he abruptly made his *Exit*. . . .

Now in high fury he sought the nearest pen and paper at Wilson's
coffee-house in Bell Court, Gray's Inn, and wrote a challenge
which deserves inclusion in any anthology of invective prose, a
letter almost incoherent with concentrated insult and frustrated
rage:

MR WOOD,
     You know me, where I live: You dare not meet me *fairly*:
You was suspected of *Sodomy* at Mr. Wiger's, and your Debts in *Oxford*
will ever hinder your appearing there. You have *pawn'd* Books of
Wiger's Scholars, and 10000 Things. In short, I will HEW you down,
or you shall me. Meet me *privately*: you are a *Coward* and a *Villain*.
Appoint the Time, Place and Manner.
        J. HENLEY.
Write to my House, and I'll meet You. What I remark on the *Universities*
is *true* . . . and I will continue it. You will never get a *Farthing* by the
Universities. What have You to do with me, mind yourself, and beware:
I will take Care to *watch* you, and be *up with you, where I* see *You*.

No duel ever took place, and Wood placed as epigraph on his
title-page

    Tutius est . . . igitur contendere verbis,
    Quam pugnare Manu.

It was a motto Henley might well have adopted as, through the
years, he engaged in verbal combat in the Oratory or in private
and in the columns of the daily papers. He was easily aroused,

quick to take offence, and fluent in his use of invective whether
it was controlled, violent, or downright vulgar. Even his warmest
advocate could not deny the facts, though he might modify
the conclusion of a verdict on Henley later in the century:

He was of an over-bearing Temper, insolent to his Inferiors, and
unmannerly to his Superiors. His Pride, which was excessive, taught
him to despise everyone with whom he conversed; and his Self-Love,
which was inordinate, and reign'd over him with a despotic Sway led
him to suppose, that every one was inferior to himself in Point of
Judgment. Hence that ridiculous Vanity which was visible in his every
Action, and prompted him to enforce his own Arguments with the
most indecent Noise and violent Gesticulations, to disregard the
Sentiments of others and to be continually interrupting them in the
Course of their Reasoning. As a Companion, therefore, he was odious;
as a Clergyman, indecent; as an Orator, reprehensible; as a Christian,
culpable; and as a Man, contemptible.[1]

The writer has seen an important truth about Henley—that
whatever else he was, he was consistent as a character. His public
and private personality are the same. In public disputation or
private discussion, in open opposition or private quarrel, in the
pulpit or the coffee-house, these characteristic traits of pride,
self-sufficiency, and violent temper guided his action and utter-
ance, justifying too often those charges of Billingsgate and
Butchers' Champion made against him. It was a character already
starting to reveal itself in his Cambridge days when he first came
up against authority and felt able to challenge it. Thwarted ambition increased his resentments without diminishing his pride
and self-confidence, and the years of savage and not always justified
assault hardened and exacerbated his weaknesses. We know so
little of his father and family, but what little we know suggests
that environment and not heredity shaped his character, and that
he might have been a very different man if, instead of fighting
his battles in the London world of cut-throat ambition and scandal
and satire, he had remained content to study and teach at Melton
Mowbray, as his father did happily for so many years.

Melton Mowbray and his family have almost been forgotten
in the tumultuous story of these London years. Henley, too, seems
to have had little to do with his family once he cut the cord and

---

[1] *The History of the Robin Hood Society*, pp. 136–7.

came up to town. He wrote of his father with admiration in the *Narrative* of 1728, and fifteen years after his father's death prepared for the press, as we have seen, his devotional tract; but there is little evidence to show that Henley revisited Melton Mowbray after he had left, or maintained any intimate contact with his family. His brother Simon entered his life once. He too had left Melton Mowbray and come to London, establishing himself as an apothecary in Holborn, a fact revealed to us by his coming forward to stand £100 bail when his brother John was arrested in 1728. That arrest affected his father in a far different way. There can be little doubt that this faithful pastor of the Established Church must have been troubled by the strange activities of a son to whom he had given the best possible education to fit him for a career in the Church like his own. The story of the founding of the Oratory and its early troubles must have reached his ears and worried him: the arrest and imprisonment of his son brought public scandal and shame which obviously deeply affected him. In the November of the year of the arrest, he sat down to make his will and, in his own hand, began: 'Imprimis. I give to my Son John one shilling. Item. I give to my Son John my Library.' In other words, he disinherited John, making it quite clear by the recognized bequest of a shilling, that he had not merely overlooked his claim on the estate.[1] The use of this formula may have been, in Blackstone's words, a 'vulgar error',[2] but the Revd. Simon Henley's intentions are clear. Let John have his library, for there was no one else in the family who might use it, but not a penny would he get to support his indecorous life in London. In an undated codicil to the will he relented to the extent of giving a guinea to his erring son to buy a mourning ring and also a guinea to his daughter-in-law, Henley's wife, that she might wear one too. Perhaps some slight reconciliation had taken place: perhaps it was a touch of conscience. We do not know. But Henley still got nothing of his father's not inconsiderable estate, whereas his brother Simon was left £5 and his sister Elizabeth, obviously the favourite, received 'two hundred pounds including Bowden-land'. After small bequests to charity, the

---

[1] On this aspect of testamentary law in the eighteenth century, see Plucknett, *A Concise History of the Common Law*, 5th ed., pp. 745–6. Also *O.E.D.* entries under CUT, V.55.(i).

[2] Blackstone, *Commentaries*, 2, p. 503.

bulk of the estate was left to Mrs. Henley.[1] Of all this Henley was ignorant until his father died on 5 June 1731, when any hopes he had of some inheritance were dashed. Had 'Philo-Grubaeus' in a letter to the *Grub Street Journal* that month any inside information to add extra nastiness to his remark, 'I hope your Orator's Father lately deceased has left him some estate; otherwise he may be obliged in a little time to take an opposite corner to that which the Blind Orator possesses in Lincoln's Inn Fields'?[2] Henley was not inactive about his father's death, for the *Daily Advertiser* announced that '. . . the Rev. Mr. Henley discontinues his Week-days orations for this Summer, except the contrary be advertised, 'till September next, on affairs occasion'd by his Father's death; and that the Sunday's attendance proceeds, as usual, at the Oratory.'[3] It is difficult to know what he was doing. The will was not contested and was proved on 14 June 1731. Perhaps he was arranging the removal of the library to the Oratory lodgings.

Henley's mother followed her husband three years later, and though her will contains no formal phrase of disinheritance, her son 'John Henley of the City of London, Clerk' received again only a guinea to buy another mourning ring. Simon was more favoured with £15, but again it was to the unmarried younger daughter Elizabeth that the bulk of the estate was bequeathed.[4] Six years later, at the age of nineteen, she too died, and the Orator finally lost any hope of touching the family fortune. Her lands and tenements at Little Bowden and the bulk of her estate she left to her sister Mary and her heirs for ever. She left £10 so that the poor of the parish might be given a gift each Christmas Day, and she bequeathed the considerable sum of £100 to Thomas Cave, clerk of Melton Mowbray, who had witnessed both her father's and her mother's will.[5] Perhaps the young girl had fallen in love with the curate, as her mother had done so many years before. Certainly her bequest to him, with not even a mourning ring for her brother John, must have completed Henley's knowledge of his alienation from his family and home. After the journey to London only his brother Simon ever entered

[1] Will of Simon Henley, proved 14 June 1731 (Leicestershire Record Office).
[2] *G.S.J.*, 1 July 1731.
[3] Quoted in *G.S.J.*, 1 July 1731.
[4] Will of Arabella Henley, proved 14 Apr. 1735 (Leicestershire Record Office).
[5] Will of Elizabeth Henley, proved 20 Apr. 1741 (Leicestershire Record Office).

his life to do anything more than show, positively or by omission, disapproval of an erring son and brother.

The loss of his family's friendship and support did not however leave him alone, for on coming to London and leaving father and mother, he had taken to himself a wife. In 1725 he married Mary Philips about whom we know very little except that she appears to have come of a respectable City family, her brother Clifford William Philips being a Justice of the Peace in Goodman's Fields and subsequently knighted.[1] There is very little to be learned of their domestic life together. Henley never referred to her and, until her death, his enemies never mentioned her. In *A Short Essay on the Lady's Choice: or, a Touchstone of a Marriage-Ring* Henley commented on the married state, and, because of this lack of direct evidence, one is tempted to see a generalization on his own experience when his violent spirits found vent—or opposition—in the home rather than in the Oratory. '. . . the Jars of Wedlock', he suggested, 'are no Fault; Variety is diverting, and Contrasts set off and relish each other: Family Pictures must have Shades to the Lights to be valuable . . . He or she that is in a Passion, is the patient distemper'd: let a Funnel be put up near a Chimney, talk thro' that half an Hour a Day, and all's done.'[2] A similar praise of silence in a wife is voiced in a much later description of the perfect happiness which comes from being 'a skillful, prudent, reputable, charming Wife, that, with him, will fulfill ye view of Matrimony, be dumb . . . when he desires, and never make him a cuckold.'[3] A fuller and more detailed account, signed 'R.S.', appeared in *Common Sense* a month after Mary Henley died at the age of forty-eight in November 1737. Its malice and irony make it not entirely trustworthy, and it is difficult to know how far we must reverse the praise to find the truth. It adds, however, one or two facts to our knowledge:

In this Time of Melancholy and Mourning it may not be improper to put the Publick in Mind of a Loss little noticed, but of great Consequence to the Town. The Wife of *Orator Henley* is dead! She is fallen amid the Sighs and Tears of all the Poulterers and Fishmongers in *Clare-Market*, even Butchers weep; and we may say with *Macbeth*,

---

[1] Nichols, *Leicestershire*, vol. ii, pt. 1, p. **261.
[2] Henley, *The Orator's Miscellany: No. I* (1731), Essay I. *A Short Essay on the Lady's Choice: or, Touchstone of a Marriage-ring.*
[3] Discourse for 10 June 1753 (B.M. MSS.Add. 11790).

She should have died hereafter.

She was a Woman whose understanding and whose Person both combined to make the *Orator* happy. She was captivated with his Manly Countenance during the most melancholy days of her Widowhood. She no sooner saw him labouring on his *Rostrum*, but the Air and Mien of so great a Man struck her at once with Love and Surprize; and upon her Return home, as she was un-pinning her Hood, she cried out, (being a perfect Mistress of Virgil)

Agnosco veteris Vestigia Flammae.

The *Orator* had the Dart within him as well as the Lady: He view'd her from his Pulpit, with no less Emotion than *David* view'd *Bath Sheba* from the Roof of his House. The Consequence of Love, among virtuous People is Marriage; and their Nuptials were celebrated with great Oratorical Pomp and Gaiety: The Orator himself dancing, with surprising Nimbleness, *Parson upon Dorothy*.

It will be needless to point out her Merit and Perfections: In general I may say, that her Piety, her good Nature, her Sincerity, and her Affability, were remarkable even to a Proverb in the Market where she lived. As many went to see the Wife as to hear the Husband. She smiled upon them all, and generally said something in Praise of the Orator and his Learning. She always had a hand in his most elaborate Discourses: and those Orations which appear to have the most Fire, and to be the least intelligible to vulgar Understandings, were the Redundancies of her Pen.—But she is gone! and we are to look forward to the Consequences of her Death, rather than spend our Time in fruitless Tears and inharmonious Sighs.

The Orator has many Enemies. Envy and Malice follow Merit throughout the Universe: and the Orator's Tenderness on this late unhappy Occasion has betray'd him into a kind of Frenzy: He is, as Mauxalinda says, *non se ipse*, and grieves beyond the Power of his Oratory to describe.—His Enemies take advantage of his Misery, and already begin to form Schemes for his Ruin. New Orators arise; the Daily Papers are filled with their Advertisements: what can this end in? Is it not time for the Orator to rouse himself, and break from his Grief? etc.

I have administered to my Oratorical Friend *Seneca* and *Cicero* in vain, and the only Remedy now left for him is Common Sense, but he seems to scorn that.[1]

His wife was indeed a widow, the relict of William Clifford, Gentleman, of St. Paul's, Covent Garden, but the romantic

---

[1] *Common Sense,* 31 Dec. 1738.

story of Cupid's darts flying from pulpit to entranced auditor is, alas, apocryphal. The marriage settlement was dated 29 January 1726,[1] months before the first Oratory opened its doors, and if a pulpit figured at all in the courtship it would have been that of St. Mary Abchurch. We only catch one brief glimpse of her during her married life when Whiston, recounting Henley's angry visit to him, recorded that 'About two Hours afterwards he came, with his Wife, as I suppose she was, in a Coach to my House to speak with me.'[2] On this occasion, at least, she was supporting her husband. Henley's emotion at her death, though maliciously reported by 'R.S.', was sufficient to throw him out of his stride. The day of his wife's death was the day on which the riot in the Oratory took place over the cancelled disputation on the Gregorians. Henley was obviously under great strain, his wife on the point of death in his house, and a hostile evening congregation waiting for him next door. He had prayed for his wife at the morning service and in the evening, having finished his lecture on the death of the Queen, he 'desired them to excuse his not proceeding to the Disputations, because his Wife was then lying at the point of death; and then immediately retir'd'.[3] Though his enemies disbelieved him and gave other reasons for his retreat, there is little reason to doubt that Henley spoke truly, and that he spent the last minutes at his wife's deathbed with the noise of the rioters shouting and attacking his clerk echoing from the Oratory. His enemies would not even allow him to be capable of honest human grief at the loss of a loved one for, shortly after his wife's death, the *Englishman's Journal* callously informed its readers that

... the Publick has already been acquainted that the Wife of his Bosom is no more, yes, Saints and Angels have her ... but one Circumstance in Relation to her Death went to the Orator's Heart ... whether she had lost her Senses towards her latter End, or to what it was owing is hard to say, but having a Power by a Settlement to make a Will, she left a Hundred Pounds from the Orator: this was a killing Stroke: If the Orator loved the Widow much, he loved her Money more.[4]

---

[1] Mary Henley's Will (Guildhall MSS. 9172/142).
[2] *Mr. Henley's Letters and Advertisements which concern Mr. Whiston, etc.*, p. 9.
[3] *G.S.J.*, 8 Dec. 1737.
[4] *Englishman's Journal.* Report dated 4 Mar. 1738 (Lysons 92).

By whatever means the newspaper had obtained such information, it was true. In her marriage settlement it was set down that she had the right to 'give or devise the sum of One Hundred pounds to such Person or Persons and in such manner and form as I by my said last will or other writing shall order and appoint', and in her last days, a week before her death, with the signature to the will extremely unsteady, the hand of a dying woman—she revoked all former wills and exercised her right, leaving the money to her brother and sister and £5 to her friend Christiana Horne, the wife of a peruke-maker. She ordered her husband to pay over this money, appointing her brother and sister as executors to see all this was done. No doubt this came as a blow to Henley who, at this stage of his career, could well have used an extra £100. Less certain is what we can infer from Mary's action. Perhaps the marriage had not been a happy one; perhaps she became more and more convinced that Henley had only married her for her money; perhaps she was only exercising a right she had always intended to from the time of the marriage settlement. Without further evidence our conjectures are as uncertain as those of the *Englishman's Journal*. What is certain is that from that day in November 1737, with no children of the marriage and no second wife, Henley lived alone in his house adjoining the Oratory or in Milman Street.

When the work of the Oratory did not keep him at his desk or in the pulpit, he left the loneliness of the house to find company, conversation, food, and stronger stimulants to keep his spirit up. There are a surprisingly large number of casual references to his being seen in coffee-houses of which he was obviously a regular *habitué*. He was that 'very facetious Gentleman, well known for his great Skill as an Orator, and his vast Propensity for Eating in every Publick House about London. . . ."[1] William Wood addressed his letter to Henley to 'Squires, Where, as I was then told, he was constantly either in the Morning or Evening', and after Henley's furious visit to Mr. Wiger's in search of evidence against Wood, 'he abruptly made his *Exit*, to *Wilson's Coffee-House* in Bell Court.'[2] In these coffee-houses he not only took refreshment: he indulged that irrepressible urge to talk,

---

[1] Advertisement for 9 Aug. 1754 (Lysons 188).
[2] *The Dueling Orator Delineated etc.*, p. 12.

argue, and harangue which even the outlet of the Oratory was insufficient to drain. Under his Hyp Doctor persona of Dr. Ratcliffe he makes what is surely a truly personal confession when he describes how on entering a coffee-house,

I laid down my Gloves and Cane in Form, repair'd to a Table where a numerous Company were in Conversation, and took leave to make an Addition to them. It is observed that *Englishmen* are shy of talking to Strangers, my Temper is the Reverse, if none accosts me, I always break through the natural Taciturnity of my Country, and let it be Man or Woman, as much endeavour to converse, as I struggle to eat a Dinner, though it be against my Appetite.[1]

Subjects he had orated about at the Oratory he continued to discuss in these less formal surroundings. We read that when Toland's *Philosopher's Prayer* first appeared, 'no man exclaim'd more loudly against it than the ORATOR; he deafen'd all the company at a certain Coffee-house with endeavouring to shew them the horrid impiety of this *detestable Prayer*, as he was *then* pleased to call it. . . .'[2] Henley denied this discussion 'unless it had been with a Roman priest I knew'[3] and this circumstantial qualification suggests the basic truth of the story. And when his audience was but one, he still talked and argued—and lost his temper. One snatch of such conversation has been preserved for us by someone who in 1786 remembered dining some thirty years before at a chop-house opposite the end of Palsgrave-head Court in the Strand and, finding no other company there but the Orator and an Attorney, could not help overhearing their conversation. He set it down, and we can still hear the dialogue over the chop-house partition:

Attorney: I remember the man well, but I don't know what became of him. I think they say he went to the West-Indies, and settled at Ceylon, or somewhere thereabouts: in one of our islands however.
Orator: In the first place, Ceylon is no island of ours; and, in the second place, it is not in the West Indies, but in the East.
Attorney: I deny that.
Orator: The more shame for you. I'll bring you a boy ten years old who shall prove it to you.

[1] *Hyp Doctor*, 27 Jan. 1736.   [2] *G.S.J.*, 4 Dec. 1735.
[3] *Hyp Doctor*, 23 Dec. 1735.

The Revd M.^r H—n—y Orator, grown lean.

6. Orator Henley grown lean

Attorney: Well, I thank God, I know nothing about East or West either. I am no great Geographer.

Orator: So, then, you thank God for your ignorance, do you?

Attorney: (Looking very angry) Yes, I do, Sir.

Orator: (making him a low bow) Then, Sir, you have much to be thankful for.[1]

He rapidly gained a reputation as a heavy drinker in his frequent visits to these taverns and public houses and, facing his accusers, he did not deny the charge outright. 'Here stands one ready to tell ye, that he has seen me drunk. Well, it may be so, we have all been transgressors.'[2] William Ayre speaks of drink as 'the God he oft'nest bows before, tho' he should pray twenty Times a-day',[3] and Pope immortalized his weakness in the couplet:

> . . . Henley lay inspir'd beside a sink,
> And to mere mortals seem'd a Priest in drink.[4]

It was no doubt on his way home from such an evening, but in better control than Pope depicts, that Henley was attacked by a street robber, 'but he made so brave a defence, that the rogues thought fit to make off.'[5] The scandals over womanizing which dogged his early career in London do not often reappear in these later years, when male company and the bottle appear to have satisfied him. Once he accused his enemies of having 'fetched Whores out of Bridewell to swear other sort of Things against me',[6] but that was in early days when the scandal of Mrs. Tolson was being stirred up; and from these later years, amid all the other grounds for abuse there is one solitary reference to this weakness for women, in verses below a print of Henley baptizing a baby:

> The pamper'd priest, on whose extended arms
> The female infant lies: with budding charms,
> Seeming to ask the name, e'er he'll baptise,
> Casts at the *handsome wife* his wanton eyes . . .
> One guest enquires the parson's name—says Friendly,
> Why don't you know, Sir? 'tis Hyp-Doctor Henly.[7]

---

[1] Letter from W.C. to Mr. Urban, *Gentleman's Magazine*, July 1786, vol. lvi, pt. 2, p. 572.

[2] *Punchinello's Sermon*, p. 9.   [3] William Ayre, op. cit., vol. i, p. 277.

[4] *Dunciad* (1743), Book ii, ll. 425–6.   [5] *Daily Journal*, 30 Aug. 1731.

[6] *Punchinello's Sermon*, p. 10.   [7] Samuel Ireland, op. cit., vol. i, pp. 134–6.

It is extremely doubtful whether Henley in 1745, believing as he
did, would ever baptize anyone, and the accusation is of as doubtful authenticity as the setting. The silence on this score—for his
detractors would most gleefully have exploited it if they could—
suggests that only the conversation and wine of coffee-house
and tavern were his main pleasure and his outstanding weakness.

In other company, too, he found the society his empty house
denied him, and the opportunity for talk and argument. He was
a 'clubbable' man, fond of meetings and social dinners, and it is
no surprise to find him entering the Antient and Honourable
Order of Free Masons. It is equally no surprise to find this fact—
like so many other facts in Henley's life—questioned. A later
Masonic historian, W. B. Hextall, believed that 'The question
"was Henley himself a Freemason?" should probably, upon such
information as we have, be answered in the negative,'[1] but the
case he puts forward for such disbelief is not a strong one. It is true
that no mention of Henley appears in any official records of the
Craft, but records at this period were few and incomplete, and the
absence of a name from a Lodge list or minute proves nothing.
Hextall admits that his other arguments may tell either way, or
they are based on interpretations of Henley's character permissible
as opinion but not as proof. One suspects that a desire to disown
a disreputable brother influenced the historian to reject as untrustworthy the body of positive evidence in the public press and
in Henley's advertised activities and in his writings. The *Leeds
Mercury* for 9–16 June 1730 announced the Orator's initiation in a
news item from London: 'London 11 June. On Monday last the
celebrated Mr. Orator Henley was admitted a Free and Accepted
Mason at the Prince William Lodge, Charing Cross, several
Noblemen and Persons of Distinction being present at the
Ceremony.' The news was also published across the Atlantic when
that enthusiastic Mason, Dr. Benjamin Franklin, reprinted the
item in his newspaper the *Pennsylvania Gazette* for 20 August.[2]
There was no delay in Henley's enthusiastic participation in
masonic activity and talk. In the month of his initiation he announced, 'On Wednesday, to entertain the Right Worshipful

---

[1] *Transactions of the Quatuor Coronati Lodge*, vol. xxix, p. 370.

[2] *Early newspaper accounts of Freemasonry in Pennsylvania, England, Ireland, and Scotland
from 1730 to 1750, reprinted from Franklin's 'Pennsylvania Gazette' with illustrative comments by C. P. McCalla* (Philadelphia, 1886).

the Deputy Grand Master (in the Absence of the Grand Master)
the Grand Wardens, and the most ancient and honourable
Fraternity of Free and Accepted Masons, will be an Elogium on
MASONRY, and a Gentleman will be ready to dispute on
Gormogonism.'[1] This was obviously an official attendance by
the Officers of Grand Lodge drawn most expeditiously into the
sphere of their new Brother. In a collection of songs and anti-
masonic satires published in 1730, Henley is mentioned as
Master of the Lodge—an impossibly speedy exaltation even for
Henley—in a section of the book called 'Second Degree, or
Fellow-Crafts Part', and this oration is described in the dedication,
which is a general satire against Henley, as 'that curious Dissertation of yours, intitled, *The Free Mason's Triumph; or Hod and
Trowel beat the whole Field*. Malicious people say, you borrowed
these Redundancies from *Pool's Parnassus*.'[2] In November 1731
another oration was on 'ALL SIGNS IN THE WORLD, or
a learned Charge to the HONORARY FREE-MASONS, jocose;
the first Attempt of the Kind',[3] and in an August edition of the
Hyp Doctor in 1732, proving that the *Craftsman* was no true Mason,
he wrote in the character of a Freemason, vowing that 'I shall
here write nothing but what long ago has been publish'd by their
own authentick Orders, for I honour my Brethren inviolably.'
He shows a detailed knowledge of Masonic mythology,
instruments, and ceremonial language—aprons, gloves, trowels,
handshakes, and the Song of the Entered Apprentice.[4] This story
of Henley's progress in the craft is, however, somewhat confused
by an announcement in the *Grub Street Journal* for 8 March 1733,
reprinting an announcement from the *London Evening Post*:
'Last Saturday Eustace Budgell Esq., was admitted a freemason,
at the Sun tavern in Fleet Street: as was on Sunday last in the
evening, Mr. Orator Henley, at the bear and harrow in the Butcher
Row without Temple Bar', and the *Journal* commented:

As the gentleman of the law was initiated into the mysteries of Masonry
on the Jewish Sabbath, the burlesque orator of the gospel was initiated
on the Christian: But the place and the sign, in the latter case, had the

---

[1] Advertisement for 13 June 1730.
[2] Peter Farmer, *A New Model for the Rebuilding of Masonry etc.* (1730), p. iv.
[3] Advertisement for 13 Nov. 1731 (Lysons 59).
[4] *Hyp Doctor*, 8 Aug. 1732.

greatest propriety, the butcher-row, bear and harrow, being lively emblems of his usual auditory, action and elocution.[1]

The circumstantial details of place and date suggest a Masonic event, though, in the light of earlier evidence, it could not have been initiation. It may have been merely a meeting of Henley's Lodge coupled inaccurately with Budgell's initiation for satiric ends; it may have been Henley's raising to the degree of Master Mason rather than his initiation. Certainly, after this date, he took office in his Lodge. On 7 June 1733, at the grand anniversary feast of Masons at Mercers' Hall, with the Grand Master, Lord Strathmore, presiding, the brethren chose Henley as their Chaplain and, almost inevitably, he 'gave them an extempore harangue proper to the occasion, which was received with universal applause'.[2] The Grand Master must have joined in that applause and found Henley's oratory to his liking for, in the *Daily Journal* of 21 June, there appeared this announcement:

By Command of the Right Honourable and right worshipful the Grand Master of the Antient and Honourable Society of Free and Accepted Masons, at the last General Assembly at Mercer's Hall, and for the Entertainment of the Brethren. At the ORATORY, the Corner of Lincoln's-Inn-Fields, near Clare Market, this present Thursday, being the 28th. June, at Six in the Evening, will be delivered An ELOGIUM upon FREE-MASONRY. The first ORATION on that Subject. N.B. At the Feast, the Brethren were desired by the Grand Officers to come cloathed to this Oration: It will be spoken in the proper Habiliments. Price of the Seats to all Persons whatsoever, Masons and others, Two Shillings.

One cannot help wondering how much Henley's suggestion and how much the Grand Master's initiative was responsible, at the festive board, for ensuring a large audience at a raised entry fee, at a time when a heat wave was doubtless cutting down his regular attendance. The occasion, as we have seen, did not pass off without trouble at the cash-box from disgruntled non-masonic customers. On 30 March 1743 he was elected Chaplain of the Grand Lodge,[3] but after this there are fewer and fewer Masonic

[1] *G.S.J.*, 8 Mar. 1733.

[2] *Read's Weekly Journal*, 9 June 1733, and the *Daily Advertiser*, quoted in *G.S.J.*, 21 June 1733.

[3] *St. James's Evening Post*, quoted in E. H. Dring's *A Bibliography of English Masonic Literature before 1751*, in *Transactions of the Quatuor Coronati Lodge*, vol. xxv, p. 370, item 133. There is no official record of Grand Chaplains before 1775.

references to Henley or in Henley, which may reflect a fading
of interest and participation. From 13 November 1733 to 19
February 1734, he changed the name of fifteen *Hyp Doctors* to
the *Free Mason*, addressing some of his articles to the Grand
Master and exploiting some of the notions and language of
Masonry. We find him in 1737 defending the Freemasons against
an attack made on them by the *Craftsman*,[1] and in the same year
one of the orations in an advertised publication *Select Orations on
Various Subjects* was *On the Divinity and Sublime of Masonry, as
display'd in the Sacred Oracles, inscrib'd to the Right Worshipful the
Grand Master of the antient and honourable Society of Free-Masons*.[2]
After this the Masonic subjects are very few and far between.
From his remaining oratory advertisements over a period of
nineteen years, only six such subjects are announced,[3] and the
last cryptic phrase for an item on 29 February 1752—'Masons
bad'—makes us wonder whether Henley long continued to
assist in the business of the Lodge or enjoy the dinners which
followed, whether in his increasingly turbulent career he continued
to be an acceptable Brother to that strange cross-section of society
which eighteenth-century Masonry embraced, or whether he
turned elsewhere for the fulfilment of his social gregariousness.

There was certainly no lack of clubs and orders and debating
societies for him to choose from, and from them he elected to
become a member of the Robin Hood Society. *A History of the
Robin Hood Society* published in 1764 purports to give a true
chronicle of its origins and activities. The writer claims that the
club went back to 1613, when his grandfather founded it; and his
father continued it as 'A Society for free and candid Enquiry'.
It had an original constitution and a roster of different meeting
places. Since 1747 it had met at the Robin Hood and Little John
in Butcher Row—the same street where Henley's Masonic Lodge
was held—in a room where new benches had been set up, il-
luminated by a splendid new eighteen-branched candelabra, with
a large 'curiously gilt' chair for the President. The entry ticket
cost 6*d.* and out of this 4*d.* provided lemonade or porter for

[1] *Hyp Doctor*, 19 Apr. 1737, replying to the *Craftsman*, 16 Apr. 1737.
[2] Neither the British Museum nor the Bodleian has a copy of this. The advertisement is in the *London Evening Post*, 14/16 June 1737.
[3] Advertisements for 7 Nov. 1741 (Lysons 109); 24 Apr. 1742 (Lysons 112);
4 May, 15 and 29 June 1745 (Lysons 138); 29 Feb. 1752 (Lysons 172).

incidental refreshment, and 1½d. went to charity. Mr. Jeacocke
was appointed permanent President, and the society met nightly.
This history is highly suspect as the idealizing work of an interested member, and another pamphlet paints a far less dignified
picture.¹ It denies the ancient origins of the Society, claiming that
it is the new creation of Mr. Jeacocke the Baker, and that its
members are 'the most contemptible Sett of Mortals that ever
existed: Their Impieties first drew upon them the Notice and
Observation of the World, as their repeated Blasphemies still
do the equal Pity and Indignation of the Candid and Charitable.'
It alleges that 'This illustrious Assembly is composed of Bakers,
Shoemakers, Journeymen-Barbers, *Fleet* Parsons, Psalm-singing
Clerks, and Apprentice Boys, who every *Monday* Night make no
inconsiderable Figure on the side of Infidelity.' As a member of
this 'Society for free and candid Enquiry' or as one of this
'most contemptible Sett of Mortals' sat Orator Henley. The
History tells us that he was a member at its first opening, and he
appears in action there in a satirical account of the Society's
proceedings in The *Gray's Inn Journal*.² The general picture of
these is one of nonsense, cant, and a ridiculous hotchpotch of
pseudo-learning. The assembly is continually interrupted by
cries for porter or demands for lemonade, while the President,
pathetically out of control and suffering from a very bad cold,
bangs his hammer and calls in vain for silence. We hear various
speakers in the debate, Cantwell, Dr. Talmud, Wiseacre, and
Broadbrim, and then Henley rises to his feet:

Orator Bronze: I am pleased to see this Assembly; You're a Twig from
 me: a Chip of the Old Block at *Clare-Market*;—I am the Old Block,
 invincible;—*Coup de Grâce* as yet unanswered;—We are Brother
 Rationalists;—Logicians upon Fundamentals; I love ye all; I love
 Mankande in general—Give me some of that Porter.
President: Pray, Gentlemen, don't laugh;—Gentlemen, I have a very
 bad Cold.
Orator Bronze: I am glad to see you joyous;—the Deity is a joyous Being.
President: Time, Sir.
Orator Bronze: Do you know who you stop? I'll never come here again
 —no the Devil a bit.

¹ *Genuine and Authentick Memoirs of the Stated Speakers of the Robin Hood Society, with
specimens of several of their Speeches* (1751).
² *Gray's Inn Journal*, No. 18, Saturday, 17 Feb. 1752.

The satirist Arthur Murphy has caught something of the peculiar exclamatory note of Henley's orations as well as sprinkling the dialogue with those phrases and ideas which were his favourites at the time and often figured in the advertisements of the period. He has noticed too that favourite word of Henley's—'Mankind'—and, as when he wrote the notes to *The Hilliad*, attempted to capture in his spelling a peculiarity of Henley's accent. Has he too, in the opening speech he gives to Henley, unconsciously revealed what drew him to the Robin Hood Society? Perhaps he found here indeed a 'chip of the old block' where, without the responsibility of the rostrum, he could indulge in the disputation and argument which he loved so much, and give vent to his ideas on religion and politics in a congenial atmosphere of free thinking. Whatever his motives for attending, he was faithful to his club when it was attacked. We are told that 'the Pulpits everywhere display'd its evil Tendency, and resounded with its Infamy',[1] but from Henley's pulpit in 1752 resounded orations in its defence—'R. Hood's Sign and Defense: E. of Hn. The Rationalist Baker's Honour',[2] 'Arguments for Robin Hoods',[3] and 'Robin Hoodians honestest Prot*ts, and this no Christian Countrey'.[4] The *History* gives us a résumé of the Oratorical defence:

Dr. HENLEY vindicated it from his Rostrum, and comparing it to some of the famed Assemblies of Yore, where a CICERO, or a DEMOSTHENES harangued, he affirm'd it to be of the most Eminent Service to Mankind, by mending their Morals, enlarging their Knowledge, and refining their Taste; that it was infinitely preferable, consider'd as a School of Oratory, to the Bar, or the Senate; and that it excell'd the Pulpit, both with Respect to the Advancement of TRUE RELIGION, and the spreading of Human Knowledge. Nay, he affirm'd it to be the Sun of the intellectual and moral World, that with its radiant Beams enlighten'd, chear'd, and vivified the Spiritual System, as the Firmamental Sun doth the Natural.—In short, he undertook to vindicate it from his Rostrum in *Lincoln's-Inn Fields*, from all the Calumnies and Aspersions, that ever had been, or could be raised

---

[1] *The History of the Robin Hood Society*, p. 123.
[2] Advertisement for 8 Feb. 1752 (Lysons 172).
[3] Advertisement for 29 Feb. 1752 (ibid.).
[4] Advertisement for 11 Apr. 1752 (Lysons 173).

against it, and insisted on its being the most perfect human Institution that was ever form'd, except—his own Oratory.[1]

Though this is reported speech, it is typical of Henley, full of his enthusiastic support of causes and persons which vanished as quickly as it developed, full of rhetorical exaggeration which often—and certainly in this case—misrepresented the truth; and ending as it began where all Henley's real life and thought began— in the Oratory.

Here he worked, and he worked hard, reading and preparing for his public appearances, making notes and plans for his orations, transforming those notes into mystifying advertisements, answering attacks, preparing new ones. And in between and after all these activities came what he himself described as an important part of a 'Rationalist's Daily Office'—'Intermediate Exercise, corporeal and ingenious; Relaxation, Refreshment, Pleasure, and Repose'.[2] The methods and results of his working life are fully chronicled: the more private scenes of his relaxation, refreshment, and pleasure have been sketched in, though less sharply and in sparser detail. The inner man beneath the private man is still elusive, and in the end his obituary will have to be written from our own interpretation: the inner stresses will have to be inferred from the surface. He left no diary, no intimate journal, no self-revealing letters to intimate friends, which are the usual key to a man's inner life. We are left with the more doubtful evidence of public testimony, uncertain how far rhetoric rather than personal belief and feeling shaped the words. What are we to make of these words in a sermon he preached in 1730 against the sin of suicide, full of good advice which he himself followed, and other advice which he so obviously did not?

The Means to secure ourselves against this Temptation, are, to maintain on our Spirits a constant Sense of the crying Sin of Murder itself: to love nothing in this World so much, as that the loss of it should throw us off our Guard; to keep a strict Watch on all the ruffling and disquieting Passions of human Nature; to be temperate, sober, and virtuous; to beware of such Sins as may provoke GOD to leave us to this Evil, as Pride, Self-confidence, a worldly Mind, Unbelief, all

[1] *The History of the Robin Hood Society*, p. 123.
[2] *Sermon III*, p. 66, in *The Oratory Magazine No. III*.

heinous Crimes, and Backsliding from GOD and Goodness; to repel
Melancholy, endeavour to be always employ'd; discover to others the
Temptations we are under, and resist them; be frequent in Prayer to
GOD; but to avoid too much Solitude, and to rectify the animal
Constitution.[1]

Are they the words of a consummate hypocrite? Of a person
completely self-deceived? Or is it truer as well as more charitable
to see them as the advice of a man who would have admitted to
understanding only too well those words of St. Paul, 'For that
which I do I allow not: for what I would, that do I not; but what
I hate, that do I . . . For the good that I would, I do not: but
the evil which I would not, that I do'? The obituarist must
choose, or admit that, after all this exploration, Henley still remains an enigma. There are still a few years through which we
must follow this life to its end, before we face the questions
and bring him to his earthly judgement.

[1] Henley, *Cato Condemn'd: or, the Case & History of Self-Murder* (1730), pp. 30–1.

CHAPTER IX
The Closing Years

THE LAST YEARS of Henley's life repeated very much the pattern
of what had gone before, but a new element enters the story.
Whatever we have thought of Henley in his early years and in
his prime—rogue, charlatan, misunderstood innovator—one
thing we have never been able to call him is pathetic. His ebul-
lience, his ability to fight back, his obvious enjoyment of a fight,
never flagged. Only on very rare occasions, as on the night of
his wife's death, was there a hint of the possible sadness and
despair which might have existed behind the defiant public
front. In these later years, perhaps because we find more of these
personal glimpses behind the scenes, we are able to see the
front very much as a façade concealing something different
from the confidence and defiance which he still shouted at the
town, and that difference is at the same time courageous and sad.

The assault which had been mounted against the Oratory from
the day on which it opened its doors, and which had increased in
violence and riot in the troublesome '40s, continued to the end.
It would be unnecessarily repetitious to recount the details, for
the old accusations were levelled again and again, and the old
answers shouted back. One comparatively new form of attack,
however, was especially prevalent at the close of Henley's
career—attack by parody and imitation. Parody is only possible
when the style and ideas of the victim are well enough known
for the distorted imitation to be immediately recognizable, and
so perhaps it is not surprising that this sort of satire should be a
late arrival, when Henley and his ways and words had become
commonplaces in the gossip and conversation of London. And
so, alongside the genuine Oratory advertisements, mocking
them by their lunacy and yet their likeness, there began to appear
in the newspapers such entries as:

Friar Bacon's brazen Head at the Oratory spitting Fire and bursting in
Pieces. Miracle upon Miracle, or St. McH———y's Head first liquifying,

then chang'd into a solid Blunderbuss. The Heads on Temple-Bar bowing to it. Popelings indebted to him, Ten thousand Asses. The Magazine of Folly proves nothing.[1]

At the Oratory British Chapel, the one corner of the new Gaol, South-wark, on Monday next; the religion, a new Curse upon the Old Ham. . . . Priest-Craft no Gentle-Craft; no Faith in Verbo Sacerdotis; The Glorious Stroke for the Mint, and the Borough of Guzzledown here.[2]

Right Rev. Admonitions! Right Rev. Fiddle-Sticks. Epistles to the Living! Sermons to the Dead. Mr. Royston wrong! My good L--d of ---- wrong. Spirits for Scribblers. No Pen, Ink and Paper in t'other World. Bolingbroke right! Hume righter! My Friend M----- rightest! His L---p and Mrs. Oldfield old Acquaintance! well it's no worse! . . . Right Reason only here! Admonitions against all Reason![3]

This parody was not confined to the newspapers. It became also a theatrical entertainment. We have already examined the most famous and developed of these—Smart's *Old Woman's Oratory*— and it was doubtless the success of this strange piece which encouraged imitation. Before Smart's performance, the actor and mimic, Samuel Foote, had already suggested the mode in an odd presentation at the Haymarket, which he advertised on 27 April, 1748: 'This Day (being the Ninth Day's Sale) At his Auction Room, late the New Theatre in the Haymarket, Mr. Foote will exhibit, for the Satisfaction of the Curious, a choice Collection of Pictures, all warranted Originals, and entirely new. The Auction to begin exactly at Twelve . . . '[4] Henley learnt that one of the 'pictures' to be auctioned was a portrait of himself, and his fury burst into print:

Whoever attacks my reputation and livlyhood is a mad bull to me, and ought to be knock'd down, prosecuted &c. &c. I live by my Oratory, he that attacks me there by stage exposing, is a Robber. I hear I am to be hung up on Wednesday, at the Haymarket by one Foote, a Fool. But it is hoped all Gentlemen or Lovers of Gentility will treat him as an Invader of Property, a scandalizer or Robber . . .[5]

[1] Advertisement for 28 Oct. 1749 (Lysons 160).
[2] Advertisement for 26 May 1750 (Lysons 162).
[3] Advertisement for 7 Mar. 1754 (Lysons 184).
[4] Advertisement for 27 Apr. 1748 (Lysons 151).
[5] Advertisement in *Love at first sight*, a collection of comic advertisements quoted in Lysons 151.

Foote attempted to defend himself and plead 'not guilty', but
Henley's blood was up. If Foote used the stage to attack him, he
would reply from his pulpit. Accordingly, with heavy pun,
he announced that on the following Sunday he would preach on
Phut, the son of Ham,

His Funeral Sermon, or the H*ym*ket Hobglobin . . . the Mimick an
Enemy to all, to Conversation, Friendship, Charity, Modesty, Truth,
Business, Pleasure, Honour, Families, Posterity; that he gives to each
mimick'd a Right and Duty to end him, the worst Murderer, his
Accessaries, Principals; Picture of him to be added to the Catalogue:
Statute against Rogues and Vagabonds, and non-execution of it.[1]

He also dashed off a pamphlet against Foote entitled *The Jackanapes
Journal, or the Stage Distemper* which was a 'Box of Pills for
Cibber the 2*d*. and those infected by him'. This he read to Samuel
Paterson, the publisher, but quarrelled with him and took away
his manuscript in a huff. It remained in manuscript until his
death and, ironically enough, Paterson found it when he took
charge of the auction of Henley's papers.[2] He continued to press
for legal action against Foote well on into the summer, reminding
the Lord Chamberlain in a discourse that he was 'oblig'd by the
Statute . . . to prohibit the exposing and mimicking of living
Characters, especially any Preacher, on the Stage . . .'.[3] The
Lord Chamberlain failed to respond, and the controversy fizzled
out to be replaced three years later by Smart's mimicry, equally
undeterred by the statute.

The year before Henley's death, the Haymarket was the setting
for yet another such performance, with a different star, George
Alexander Stevens, who announced that he would open a course
of comic lectures at the Little Theatre and that at them 'An
Orator's Head will be dissected secundum Artem. The Orator
will be shewn lying in State. The Question will be, Whether they
shall be allow'd Christian Burial? If it is granted, a Funeral
Oration will be spoke on them by Martinus Scriblerus . . .'[4] The
parody was obviously a much closer one of the Oratory's proceedings, and this mixture of fun and malice found a setting much more

---

[1] Advertisement for 23 Apr. 1748 (Lysons 152).
[2] Letter from Samuel Paterson to Nichols, *Literary Anecdotes*, Additions to vol. iii,
in vol. viii, pp. 483-4, and item 383 in Paterson's catalogue of Henley's MSS.
[3] Advertisement for 4 June 1748 (Lysons 153).
[4] Advertisement for 2 Jan. 1755 (Lysons 189).

like the Oratory itself when it moved away from the theatre and set up in 'Mr. Macklin's Great Room in Hart Street', offering to the public 'The British Inquisition. The Lecture will be upon Impudence; the Advantage of it in an Orator, Actor, Author, Courtier, Lawyer and Physician ... The Inquisition will be held on Mondays, Wednesdays and Fridays, the Doors will be open'd exactly at Six o'clock, and the Inquisitor take the Chair at Seven.'[1] Here we have an imitation of the Oratory, half-serious, half-parody; and the serious taking up of the idea and the method of the Oratory in these years suggests a public demand for such forms of teaching and discussion. The Robin Hood Society itself was one such body which Henley supported and defended, but he angrily saw danger and competition in another Philosophical Society which sprang up in 1751, too closely modelled on his own inimitable foundation. An advertisement appeared in January 1751 announcing 'To all candid Enquirers and Philosophers, That in the Oratory-Room at the Red Hart in Shoe Lane, every Sunday Evening at Seven, are delivered, lectures of Natural Philosophy, Natural Religion, and Rational Christianity. Every Man to pay Threepence at entering the room, which is upstairs through the Entry.'[2] Henley might well have been angry. Not only did this upstart society offer much the same bill of fare: it met at the same time as he performed and, even worse, undercut his entry fee severely. He lost no time in mounting his attack when the following Sunday he included in his oration the item, 'An Oratory-Room-Ape unlicens'd shews a Room in his Head unfurnish'd'.[3] But the Society showed itself as capable as Henley of rebuffing criticism and continuing its work, replying to Henley that

This is to give Notice, That the Philosophical Society meet at the Red-Hart in Shoe-Lane, henceforwards at Six every Sunday Evening; where a Course of Lectures on Dr. Clarke's Divine Attributes are begun, by Mr. Annet. We do not usurp the Priest's Office and Authority, nor deprive him of his Dues; No Devotion or Worship being perform'd in this Place. We only philosophize, Therefore Mr. H——might have spared his Reflections last Saturday. It is the Part of a

[1] Advertisement for 14 Jan. 1755 (Lysons 190).
[2] Advertisement for 12 Jan. 1751 (Lysons 166).
[3] Advertisement for 19 Jan. 1751 (Lysons 167).

Philosopher to bear Reflections, but not to make them on any Man's Person.[1]

It is doubtful whether Henley was deeply concerned whether the Philosophical Society was usurping the priest's office and authority or not. He cared more that it was usurping the mono-poly of the Oratory, lecturing on his own particular speciality of the Divine Attributes, and persisting in drawing away his potential congregation which, for all its love of Right Reason, could not be in two places at 6.0 o'clock on a Sunday evening.

This was a very real problem in the last years of the Oratory, which were years of decline. In its early days it had indeed flourished and drawn considerable crowds: in the middle years through the '40s it had found steady support and provided Henley with an adequate income: in these last years his congre-gation and prosperity dwindled. A correspondent in the *Gentle-man's Magazine* wrote to say that 'I heard him once in the decline of his popularity; his auditors (exclusive of the Clare-market butchers then under pay) were few in number',[2] and a similar story is told in another late-eighteenth-century account:

The Orator, with various Success, still kept up his ORATORY KING GEORGE'S or CHARLES'S CHAPEL, as he differently term'd it, till the year 1759 [sic], when he died. . . . But for some years before its Author's Death, it dwindled away so much, and fell into such an hectic State, that the few Friends of it fear'd its Decease was very near. The Doctor, indeed, kept it up to the last, determin'd it should live as long as he did, and actually exhibited many Evenings to empty Benches. Finding no one at length would attend, he admitted the Acquaintances of his Door-Keeper, Runner, Mouthpiece, and some others of his Followers *gratis*.[3]

There are, however, references in Henley's advertisements of the period to disturbances and rowdiness at the Oratory which suggest that this general decline had occasional hectic reversals, but, for the most part, we see Henley having to resort to almost press-gang methods to ensure at least an embryo congregation. The only other alternative was to stop holding forth, and of this he seems to have been constitutionally incapable, even though

[1] Advertisement for 26 Jan. 1751 (Lysons 166).
[2] *Gentleman's Magazine*, vol. lvii, pt. 2, p. 875.
[3] *The History of the Robin Hood Society*, p. 138.

the financial reward was becoming smaller every week. In the
'50s we find him attempting to supplement his income through
the sale of the manuscripts of his orations. 'The Price of a
Manuscript Argument is from 5s. to 5 Guineas, or more, paid
ready,' he advertises, 'and a Day taken to revise and correct
each: the Argument to put all out of Dispute, in 5 Pages, is
5 Guineas.'[1] And it is in this period that he started again, rather
desperately, to make those proposals for establishing the Oratory
on a new footing, with subscribed capital, which we have discussed in an earlier chapter.[2] In this time of general economic
uncertainty, he was also worried by insecurity of tenure of the
very Oratory building itself. He did not own but rented the
premises in Clare-Market where he held sway for thirty years,
and from certain cryptic references in his advertisements it would
appear that his landlord or some hostile group was attempting
to get rid of a no doubt troublesome tenant. In June 1753 he
announced in a public letter to the press:

My Lords, Notwithstanding the Cannibal Attacks on me in a happy
Establishment, I owe nothing, thank God, to any Man; my Oratory
Chapel is indebted to me some 100ds. of Pounds, Surplus, of what I
have punctually paid, above Rent, in Repairs, Taxes, Damages, &c.
I have a Covenant signed by an imaginary, not acknowledg'd Owner,
to possess it during his Hypothetical Claim. It is in many Ways
incumber'd, not on my Part, but between Him, Groundlandlord, Title,
Assessments, Co-tenants &c. I proposed, Years ago, another Chapel,
and caution the Printers not to advertise any pretended Proprietor to
lett or sell it, without my Direction. J. Henley.[3]

In the March of the following year he reasserted that 'The Place
cannot be lett, but by such as have prov'd a Legal Right to lett
it; not any Combination to impose or extort Money J. H.'[4]
Whatever the truth behind this legal tangle, it is clear that here
we have another anxiety to add to all the others—uncertainty
of congregations, uncertainty of income, and now uncertainty
even of a house and Oratory.

Despite all this, the defiant and even triumphant public front

---

[1] Advertisement for 10 Jan. 1755 (Lysons 191).
[2] See Chapter IV above.
[3] Advertisement for 13 June 1753 (Lysons 181).
[4] Advertisement for 29 Mar. 1754 (Lysons 186).

was maintained with the old exuberance. In advertisement and public letter he defied his enemies and defended the Oratory. Increasingly he looked back to his earlier years and reminded his readers of his respectable family, high academic qualifications, and exalted patrons. He exhorted his supporters with such battle cries as

To True Britons. Country-men, Your only Pulpit-Defender summons you, whenever he preaches, from the Slave-shops to the Standard of Right. We set out well, last Time: I was, what, in myself, I am, For-tunate. Vincam aut peribo, the Word. Persevere, multiply: Each proselyte, and bring more. Extirpate the Piratical Nests of Barbarian Robbers, whose lives and whose All, are our Forfeits. If any be against us, make them tell, why: as I will, next Sunday, why, how, and who are bound to repay what they have robb'd us of, and pay our Debts and Taxes. We, the Regiment of Life, will hush the Regiment of Death. J. Henley.[1]

His last full-scale self-defence was published in the year before his death—*Second St. Paul, in Equity Hall, to Felix, Caesar, and All*—when, casting himself in the role of Paul before his judges, he took as his texts, 'As he reasoned of Righteousness (Right Reason) Felix (His Judge) TREMBLED', 'Judge not according to Appearance, but judge Righteous Judgment', and 'Why is my liberty judged of another Man's Conscience? He that judgeth is the Lord.' His aim was 'that the prejudiced, the enemies to Reason and to God, may be eternally self-condemned and self-exposed, for misconstruing and misrepresenting the Advertise-ments and Discourses; asking no Favour any where, but to be rightly understood and fairly treated'. The pamphlet is not entirely undignified or ineffective, although it has its occasional outbursts of Henleian wildness and incoherence. It is the work of a man looking back over a long life of effort and opposition, defending and explaining once again and for the last time, his ideas and actions, and turning over for a last examination the successes, the disappointments and the treacheries of those years. This habit of taking stock, of looking backwards and then to the future, grew on him, and the birthdays and anniversaries of the Oratory, which he had always celebrated, became increas-ingly important to him. As Henley's life draws to an end we

---

[1] Advertisement for 14 Aug. 1752 (Lysons 175).

shall hear little more of his public voice and more of the private voice behind the scenes, so let his last public words, filled with the external confidence and boasting he always maintained, be his proclamation of the Silver Jubilee of the Oratory:

This day, July 3, 1751, closes the first Jubilee, or twenty-five years, of the Oratory: I was not disappointed by the late * of L. or his Black Guards: I have carried my Point: which was, to have a Town-Pulpit of my own for a Quarter of a Century, excelling confuting, on my own perfect Plan, without one Lie, i.e. Puff (one private inferior English-man, against at least 70 Fools and Knaves in 100) Beating, all the World, past, present, and to come. Veni, dixi, vici. I am gay and easy, what may now befal me; it can't rob me of this Triumph. Advance on, is the Word, and to God all the Glory. J. O. C. Henley.[1]

'I am gay and easy' was a courageous lie, but it was still a lie. Not only were Henley's congregations and income falling off: his health was failing too. A friend of Nichols, who recollected seeing him in Fleet Street at this time, looking at a print shop, described him as 'dressed in a brown coat, his legs much swelled, and with a cadaverous countenance',[2] and this description is confirmed, as far as the countenance goes, in a contemporary print of 'The Revd. Mr. H–n––y Orator, grown lean', where, although the hands are extended in the old gesture, the once round and proud face is drawn and fallen. In August 1754 he fell ill and had to cancel the Oratory performance that evening, not knowing at the time that he would not be able to appear in the pulpit again until October. The *Connoisseur* for 10 October 1754 noted with ironical regret 'that the Orator has of late discontinued to oblige the public with his Sunday evening lectures', and feared that, if Christianity were abolished during his absence, he would miss certain preferment for 'he would probably then hold some honourable station equal to our present Archbishop of Canterbury.'[3] From those months of sickness two letters have survived which give a unique picture of Henley completely hidden from the public eye, writing without anyone to persuade

[1] Advertisement for 3 July 1751 (Lysons 169).
[2] Nichols, *Leicestershire*, vol. ii, pt. i, p. **261.
[3] The *Connoisseur*, no. 37, for 10 Oct. 1754, and also no. 126, for 24 June 1756, contain interesting late references to Henley, no. 37 containing a letter alleged to be from Henley to the editors, dated 26 July 1754. Nothing new in them of fact or opinion is, however, worthy of note.

or attack, revealing his life at home, with his old servant woman to
care for him, vainly reading his medical books and trying to
cure himself. By this time he had been ill for over a month, when
there called on him Dr. William Stukeley. We know nothing of
their acquaintance before this, though they might well have found
each other acceptable company if Warburton is correct in his
description of this antiquary, physician, and amateur scientist
as a strange compound of 'simplicity, drollery, absurdity,
ingenuity, superstition, and antiquarianism'.[1] Henley would
have warmed to a man who, preaching his first sermon in spectacles, chose as his text 'Now we see through a glass darkly'!
He wrote to Dr. Stukeley from his sick-bed:

Sept.21.1754.
Very Reverend, and (what is better)
          very good Sir,
   This is the first moment of ability I have had, to thank you for the
very great honour and favour of your calling on me. In you, the *Priest*
excels the *Samaritan*: your humanity and benevolence shine, not only
in your aspect and words, but your actions; as your learning and
erudition are not ostentatious, but genuine and solidly useful.—When
you called, I was at my repose; and feared also that one who attends me
(I wish, you *had*, were it not for *the trouble*) would meet you.
   I have been ill these eight weeks. My disease was from an atrabilious,
hot, saline acrimony in my blood. I am liable to a cachexy, scorbutic,
and jaundiced; with eruptions in my face and head, and a Saint
Anthony's fire. I wish the Saint had kept his fire to himself; the flames
of Saints are more mischievous than the wicked—I have been purifying
my blood by some mixture of *flores sulphuris* &c. &c. My skin is generally smooth, and myself, thank God, healthful. I have a good stomach,
but cannot rest well. I am very sure, *an honest Aesculapius would cure me
soon, and no* relapse. I have been reading Dr. Turner, Quincy, Fuller and
Surgey, about it: but I will not use the least mercury. I know the cause
was internal, and it is in the acrimonious humours, and that proper
phisic would help; but I am a Rationalist, and love to enquire into
ingredients, and no Doctor will talk reason with me. They are like
Popish priests, and *demand implicit faith*. I beg, dear Doctor, you would
consider well this, and take my health under your guardianship. And,
I have a servant, who has lived with me sixteen years, who, from an old
contusion in her leg, is almost lame. Surgeons make only jobs of these

----

[1] Warburton, quoted in the *D.N.B.* article on Stukeley.

things, as physicians do. She has cost me a great deal of money; but, I doubt, she must go into an Infirmary, if she cannot come into a more summary cure, internal and external, without relapse. I wish you would be so kind and compassionate to her as to write for her. (Christ was a servant, and a physician; and, I think, he lived upon physic. The word, in the *Acts*, nor is there *salvation* in any other, is, in the *Greek*, ἴασις, *healing*; and forgiving sins, was curing distempers, which were God's penalties for sins, executed by evil demons; and the word *soul* means the *life*, the *person*; nay, sometimes it signifies a *dead man*.—This is the bye) I wish I could wait on you, but my eruptions in my face are the only things that hinder my coming abroad, or into my Oratory; which always was, is, and shall be, at your service.

I could send a message to receive what you *write*, if you condescend to do it for *me* and *my servant*. I pray God keep your *most valuable health and life, and your good family*. I wish you would make this (asking pardon for interrupting you so long) the object of some mature practical reflections. I wish I was in the Church to preach for you now and then, being, with the truest veneration, Sir, your most devoted and hearty friend and servant,

J. HENLEY.[1]

Henley's cry for help did not go unanswered. Stukeley must have replied by return, for the next day we find Henley writing to thank him and at the same time, characteristically, proving to be a difficult patient. He presumes to advise and correct his new consultant and, obsessed with the need to study and to preach in his Oratory from which he had too long been banished, asks for new treatment:

Good Sir,

I humbly thank you for your kind prescription, but please not to be offended, that I acquaint you, that having often ye Gravel, I am used to drink daily or nightly, warm whitewine whey: & no Mineral Water ever agreed with me, of any kind:

Could you not be so good as to direct me a *Purge*, instead of a *Vomit*? wch. has a Violence, that hurts Faculty of Speaking.

If you could send by ye Penny post, it wd be best: I'll pay ye postage:

I wd. know, what Regime is proper for me, as a Very Great Student,

---

[1] Letter printed in Nichols, *Illustrations*, vol. ii, p. 808. The symptoms described in this and the next letter have been examined by Dr. Bruno Gans and Dr. John Macleod, who think that Henley was suffering from systemic *lupus erythematosus*, an uncommon form of jaundice, and normally fatal.

not too low—for works of Wit, Spirit, & fancy require being above
Par, a little.

> I am, with great Respect,
> Very Worthy Sir,
> Your most obliged humble
> Servt.
> J. Henley.

Is there no method to get away a few scabby Pimples, from *ye Face*—
without hurting ye Body—[1]

Whether it was the white wine whey or the purge which helped
Henley to a recovery, we do not know. Another month of
confinement passed by before he announced his reappearance to
the world, and, still bearing the marks of his illness, asserted his
undaunted energy. He advertised that 'Being recovered in the
Main, I thank God, from my late illness, and most of its Appearances, I intend to resume the Oratory on Sunday next at Six;
with the same Spirit, Vigor, Argument, Erudition and Vivacity
as ever.'[2] His undoubted spirit kept him at work to the very
end in the Oratory which had become a necessary part of his
way of life. In December 1755 he jokingly announced that 'ye
way to end the Oratory, would be to give me a Mitre, for a Night-
cap, to make my skull as thick as those that have it.'[3] The
manuscripts of his discourses in 1755 fill ninety-three volumes,
and he preached on until the summer of 1756. Only death was
able to close the mouth of the Orator or stop him working. His
last illness confined him again to his room. The benches of the
silent and deserted Oratory were hung with old caps and aprons
set out to dry.[4] On the night of 13 October 1756 he gave up
the struggle, as he met the Disputant which even he could not
defeat.

The only evidence we have from these closing days is Henley's
Last Will and Testament. From it we can reconstruct something
of the final scene and discover, though not solve, the mystery of a
person whose presence prevented him from being completely
lonely and desolate. His will[5] is in his own handwriting, even

---

[1] Manuscript letter in the Bodleian Library (MS. Eng.Misc.c.113, No. 243 in the
Stukeley collection).

[2] Advertisement for 18 Oct. 1754 (Lysons 189).

[3] Sermon for 7 Dec. 1755 (B.M. MSS.Add. 11800).

[4] *Gentleman's Magazine*, vol. xxvii, p. 181.

[5] Somerset House (pcc.Glazier.274).

more untidy and uncertain than usual, and often difficult to read. The endorsement on the outside 'Not to be opened or read till six days after the decease of the party enclosed' was obviously ignored for it had been opened on the day after his death, and revealed not only his last wishes, but the last defiant cry of its writer as he remembered the many enemies and detractors who had been part of his life for so long:

I, John Henley, of sound mind & memory, make this my last will and Testament. Give and bequeath to Sarah Brown all I have or that may come to me my House in Millman Street if not sold or disposed of before. So [?] All my goods apparel utensils & copies lectures Manu-scripts about 6000 more or less which I value at a Guinea a piece more or less with another, Provided she does not give to her housband or relations any part of it for then it shall go to my right heirs. I or [?] Give her my Books, Parchments, papers writings especially those under the broad Seal and Seals in Chancery and Common Law to be speedily and effectually served as directed especially on Sandys Jones, William Whitaker and his fellows, Charles a Berry William Thistleton and his Agents, Tell my notorious Enemies I dye a Rationalist in Perfect Communion and such only. Witness my hand—John Henley—Witnesses Joseph Rodbard—Wm. Shergold John Freeman.

The will is endorsed:

On the fourteenth day of October in the year of our Lord one thousand seven hundred and fifty six, administration (with the will annexed) of the Goods Chattels and credits of John Henley late of the parish of Saint Giles in the Fields in the County of Middlesex, Clerk deceased was granted to Sarah Brown (wife of Ralph Brown now belonging to the East India Ship Chesterfield—at sea) the reinversal [?] legatee named in the said Will (for that no executor is named therein) having been first sworn duly to administer.

All did not go smoothly for Sarah Brown. It would appear that the 'right heirs' mentioned by Henley challenged the will's validity, for its execution was postponed on 24 November and it was not until 7 February in the following year that sentence was promulgated for the validity of the will and it was registered and executed. Who were these 'right heirs'? Were they nephews and nieces from the family which had neglected and disowned him, who now gathered like vultures around the corpse? Even more intriguing, who was Sarah Brown and what was her relationship with Henley? Her husband, Ralph, had sailed from Spithead aboard the *Chesterfield* on 13 March 1756, making the long voyage to Madras and not returning to Deptford until 17 July 1757.[1] Had Henley taken this lonely wife of an absent seaman to live with him and alleviate his own loneliness, ending his life in London, as his enemies alleged he had started it, with a kept woman? A more charitable explanation would be that she was a kindly neighbour or member of his congregation who came to look after him in his last illness, but Henley's express exclusion of Ralph Brown from any share in his estate suggests that his relationship with Sarah was of such a nature that the husband was a disliked and distrusted part of it. Whatever the truth may be which is hidden behind these scanty clues, one thing is certain— that in those last days of illness and approaching death, she remained the one person towards whom he felt any love and gratitude, one of the very few in his whole life, and we know hardly anything of her. Henley's was a life where enemies had figured more largely than lovers, and as it was in his life, so it was in his death. The *Evening Advertiser* marked the occasion with the same heartless cruelty as that with which the press, years before, had treated the death of Henley's wife, by printing a suggested EPITAPH:

> Here
> Rots unregretted
> The Residium of J. Henley,
> A Man
> Below all Character.[2]

and in the following year the elegiac Muse inspired this poetic obituary in the *Gentleman's Magazine:*

> *On the Death of Orator* HENLEY.
> Unblushing *Henley* unlamented dies:
> No *Grub-street* scribbler lifts him to the skies!
> Is all he writ forgot, and all he spoke,
> The antick gesture, and unmeaning joke?
> Unmatch'd in impudence he reign'd alone,
> Supreme on folly's everlasting throne.

[1] The Log of the Chesterfield (India Office Records, 507 D & N).
[2] *Evening Advertiser*, 27 Oct. 1756.

Fearless alike of pillory and rod,
He laugh'd at justice, and he libel'd God.
This truth *Claremarket*, echo'd thro' the *Strand*,
The *devil* and *orator* went hand in hand;
No equal, this, nor future times shall see,
'Midst all the *Quixots* of divinity.
   Touch'd for his fame, shall none by special grace,
On mimic brass, revive his mimic face?
Shall no congenial butchers, say, 'farewel',
No mournful cleavers ring his passing bell?
His pulpit only, sheds the drops of woe,
And humble rags, adorn the seats below;
This verse ev'n *Henley's* memory may claim,
He had no morals, and he felt no shame.[1]

It was in a similar mood that the town cleared away the rest of the material remains of John Henley. The Oratory itself which for thirty years had echoed with his elocution and disputation and been an unfailing source of interest and scandal, fell from glory. Though the *Evening Advertiser* followed up its savage epitaph by reporting that 'DR. SANGRADO is making interest to succeed to that noted Lyceum of depravity ignorance and sedition (Nicknamed the ORATORY) near Clare-Market',[2] the truth was less picturesque. A later enemy records that 'no one having Iniquity or Impudence sufficient to continue it on . . . it is turned into a Tradesman's Warehouse.'[3] One wonders whether the tradesman stripped the place before he moved in, or whether the gold and velvet pulpit still looked down on the piles of bales and packing cases, a fading and decaying reminder of better days.

There was left one further remnant of the Oratory for the public to dispose of, the results of innumerable hours of study and labour, the record of innumerable hours in that same pulpit— Henley's manuscripts. He had set a high value on these discourses and orations and academic notes, a value on which he dwelt more and more as he grew older. 'I value my manuscripts', he had written, '(which have more and better Curiosities than Sir H's or Dr. M's) at 2000£.'[4] He counted them as one of his most

---

[1] *Gentleman's Magazine*, vol. xxvii, p. 181 (April 1757).
[2] *Evening Advertiser*, 27 Oct. 1756.
[3] *The History of the Robin Hood Society*, p. 138.
[4] Advertisement for 1 Mar. 1754 (Lysons 185).

valuable assets, the disposal of which was a weighty problem. 'Having been frequently asked', he said in a letter-advertisement, 'how I intend to dispose of my Books and Manuscripts, I answer, sell them, if I can, or give them to a Friend, who will obtain me Right, in my Pretensions.'[1] In the end the friend proved to be Sarah Brown and those 6,000-odd manuscripts were, in Henley's opinion, worth over £6,000. It was as well that Henley never knew the fate of his much-valued writings, when, nearly three years after his death, they were put up for auction. Samuel Paterson undertook the sale at Essex House in Essex Street in the Strand, and on 21 June and the three following evenings, offered to the public these literary curiosities. He produced an elaborate forty-one-page catalogue for the sale[2] arranging items under their year of composition, with quite a full descriptive note on the contents of each volume. His care and labour were, alas, in vain, and he later told Nichols of the commercial disappointment: 'His MSS which I am told he valued at 10,000£ fell very, very short of 100£. I am sure my commission upon the sale, independent of the immense trouble I took with them, did not pay for the Catalogues.'[3] Evening after evening these miscellaneous volumes came under the hammer amidst scenes reminiscent of the Oratory itself at its most rowdy. Those who had mocked him when he was alive and insulted him when he was dead, gathered again to jeer at his memory and his work. A later account tells us:

The sale of ORATOR HENLEY'S books followed hard upon that of Richard Rawlinson's: and if the spirit of their owner could, from his 'gilt tub' have witnessed the grimaces and jokes which marked the sale—with the distorted countenances and boisterous laughter which were to be seen on every side—how it must have writhed under the smart of general ridicule, or have groaned under the torture of contemptuous indignation! Peace to Henley's vexed *manes*! and similar contempt await the efforts of all literary quacks and philosophical knaves.[4]

So with 'boisterous laughter' and 'contemptuous indignation' the Town dismissed Henley from the stage, and soon forgot him.

---

[1] Advertisement for 22 Mar. 1754 (Lysons 186).
[2] There is a copy in the Bodleian Library (Mus.Bibl.III.8°.64).
[3] Nichols, *Literary Anecdotes*, vol. viii, pp. 483–4.
[4] T. F. Dibdin, *Bibliomania: or Book Madness*, new and improved edition (1876), pp. 371–2.

A few months before these uproarious auctions, a lonely voice had been heard which was neither contemptuous nor indignant, perhaps the voice of some faithful remnant of his congregation, perhaps even the voice of Sarah Brown, which announced anonymously that

Forty Shillings, in Bread, will be given to the poor of any parish, as far as the money left will go, to let the following lines be painted against the inside wall of churches: 'In Memory of John Henley, M.A. Late of St. John's College, Cambridge, Author of the Universal Grammar, and a great Orator, that contradicted all Religious Sentiments contrary to Reason; he was a Rationalist, but few of his opinion in his time. Departed this life, aged 60, in the year 1756, and 29th of the reign of King George the Second.' Direct to Robert Robinson, Mason, at Dock-head.[1]

But there is no evidence that any parish gave Robert Robinson the chance to display his skill and honour the Orator's memory. London turned to other novelties and notorieties, and Henley, who had infuriated and entertained that fickle mistress for so long, was soon overshadowed by them. Except in the notes and queries of curiosity-collecting scholars, he became as if he had hardly been, and would have joined the innumerable company of those who have left no memorial, if Pope had not fashioned the portrait which still hangs, stark and unfaded, in the gallery of Dunces.

[1] From the *Daily Advertiser*, reprinted in the *General Evening Post*, 27 Jan. 1759.

Obituary

THIS SEARCH FOR HENLEY began and ends with Pope. Its first aim was to try to discover the real man behind the caricature, to fill out the crude selectiveness of a satiric portrait, and to suggest the motives and passions which formed his personality and directed the strange course of his life. A complex and fascinating man emerges in place of the twitching puppet of *The Dunciad*, but a man still enigmatic and difficult to judge.

The many and varied incidents of his life have been chronicled, and in the course of the history some of the shaping forces have been felt and some pattern discovered. It was a life filled with promise of success and repeated hints of good, but continually thwarted and frustrated from within and without. He was a man of not inconsiderable learning, widely and curiously read, often witty and inventive in conversation and writing, often shrewd and acute in his grasp of a problem, capable of sustained and energetic industry, and with ideas far more respectable and interesting than the lunatic rhapsodies with which alone his enemies credit him. In many of them—on education, training for the priesthood, preaching and liturgy, religious and political toleration—he was in advance of his day; and in our own time of adult education and open universities, theological colleges, witty and humorous preaching embracing all social and political problems, liturgical reform and ecumenical zeal, we must admit even more certainly the truth which Isaac Disraeli in 1812 grudgingly expressed, that 'in all his charlatanerie and his knavery, he indulged the reveries of genius; many of which have been realised since; and, if we continue to laugh at HENLEY, it will indeed be cruel, for we shall be laughing at ourselves.'[1] In his own day, however, he could not avoid hostility, opposition, and misunderstanding, and his personality was such that he could not bear opposition and must return violence for violence. He was a man of high passions and temper, without decorum and smooth manners, and lacking the coolness and self-control which alone

[1] Disraeli, *The Calamities of Authors*, i.170.

could have steadied him in the face of the lies and cruel mockeries which were heaped on his head. At the same time he had a pride and a self-assurance which refused to be beaten down, and kept him fighting courageously, shouting defiance to the end despite illness and loneliness and increasing poverty. The life which results is a vicious spiral of frustrating opposition, violent reaction producing even more violent attack and savage reply. Added to this was a repeated history of thwarted ambition, haunting memories of many 'might-have-beens'. He might have been a fellow of his college like many of his contemporaries but was passed over; he might have advanced far in clerical preferment but his protector resigned from office and his episcopal hope turned traitor; he might have prospered farther as a Government journalist but the Great Man, his sponsor, fell from power. In the end this life of uninterrupted frustration and dispute, the certainty that few would even try to understand him and that most would misrepresent his every word and action, drove him to ever-increasing outrageousness in thought and word.

To read the surviving Oratory performances of the last ten years of his life is to experience an ever-increasing gap between the idea he had of his own aims and purposes, and their actual fulfilment in sermon and lecture. Only when he speaks of his general ideas and beliefs—the following of the Divine Attributes, the universal relevance of religion to all human affairs however small and ordinary, the holiness of laughter, the necessity to unite all knowledge and science in the search for and the expression of truth—does he retain our interest and respect. The actual performances are, more often than not, shallow in their learning, crude and clumsy in their humour, rambling and incoherent in their structure.

Herein, I think, is the final cause and explanation of the enigma of this man, who was neither knave, mercenary, nor hypocritical drunkard. His inborn hatred of authority, whether in university life, scriptural and dogmatic tradition, or ecclesiastical government, forced him into a life of solitary independence, but he lacked the powers of self-criticism and self-discipline which were needed to replace the rejected authority. He was a projector without the power to fulfil his projects, who showed touches of genius in his plans and purposes, sudden insights beyond the abilities of many of his contemporaries, but lacked the intellectual equipment to put them into practice, to embody the great idea in effective action and convincing detail. The ideas of Primitive Christianity, the Plan for the Oratory, the Disputations, the academic schemes and the Gentleman's Own University, the theories of preaching, the theology of Right Reason, were, as we have seen, often original, exciting, and ahead of their time. Their actual results too often deserved the mockery and savagery with which his enemies greeted them, not because of the motives and principles behind them, but because, as was too often the case, of the ludicrous gap between promise and fulfilment, theory and practice, a gap which he became increasingly incapable of closing as continuing persecution, riot, and satire weakened his intellectual powers and emotional self-control.

So, after all our inquiry, we come to accept some of the epitaph which a former explorer along our ways wrote for Henley. Isaac Disraeli concluded:

Such was 'Orator HENLEY'. A scholar of great acquirements, and of no mean genius; hardy and inventive, eloquent and witty; he might have been an ornament to literature, which he made ridiculous; and the pride of the pulpit, which he so egregiously disgraced; but having blunted and worn out that interior feeling, which is the instinct of the good man, and the wisdom of the wise, there was no balance in his passions, and the decorum of his life was sacrificed to its selfishness. He condescended to live on the follies of the people and his sordid nature had changed him till he crept, 'licking the dust with the serpent'.[1]

We would temper some of its judgements with more mercy, and lay some of the blame on others as well as Henley. We would remember too something which Disraeli ignores but which, to someone bringing to a conclusion a long acquaintance with the man and his works, is undeniable—that Henley was an exciting, funny, and often attractive man. For all his failings and weakness, his wildness and humbug—perhaps often because of them—one cannot resist an admiration, even a fondness for the man. I find myself echoing with sympathy the words of an anonymous gentleman who, at that uproarious auction of Henley's manuscripts in 1759, had purchased *The Lord Mayor's Shew: or the City in its Glory*, and later published this performance of 'the

---

[1] Ibid., i.183-4.

late ingenious and facetious Orator' with these gentle words of introduction:

... so now, perhaps, that by Time and the Interposition of the awful Conqueror of all Men, Opposition, Malevolence, Party Spirit, and private Resentment (howsoever incurred) to the less-shining Qualities of the Author of the following Piece, are subsided; Remembrance of his Wit, of the Hours of Entertainment many have received from it, and Reflection on the impossibility to be further aggrieved or entertained by it, may stamp a Value on this first-published Oration; may excite in those who read it a chearful Smile and inoffensive Laugh; and induce them to *forgive the* Follies, and *admire* the *Parts* of *him* who wrote it; and, perhaps, even to say, with a regretful Sigh for his loss, in the Words of Hamlet;

'Where be his Gibes now? his Gambols? his Songs? His Flashes of Merriment, that were wont to set the Audience in a Roar?'[1]

'Alas, poor Yorick' is reserved inalienably for the black tomb of another eccentric clergyman, but let the rest of Hamlet's words remain as epitaph for the Reverend John Henley, Master of Arts, Independent Minister of the Oratory, the 'Harlequin Divine' of his age.[2]

[1] *The Lord Mayor's Shew: or the City in its Glory*, Introduction.
[2] *G.S.J.*, 20 Oct. 1737.

Appendix
A LIST OF HENLEY'S WRITINGS

I. MANUSCRIPTS

The British Museum possesses fifty-one volumes of Henley's autograph writings, with the following MSS.Add. press marks and contents:

10346. 11 lectures and discourses from 1729, 1731, 1733, 1742, 1743
10347. 2 discourses of 1743, and Occasional Thoughts on Government and Idolatry, 1750
10348. 5 discourses, January 1744–November 1744
10349. 5 discourses, 1745, and drafts for advertisements and letters
11768. 2 discourses, 1729 and 1736
11769. 4 discourses, 1735
11770. 2 discourses, 1735 and 1736
11771. 8 discourses, 1740, 1742, and 1744
11772. 4 discourses, 1747 and 1748
11773. 6 discourses, 1748
11774. Prayers, 1747 and 1748
11775. 4 discourses, 1748
11776. 4 discourses, 1748 and 1749
11777. 6 discourses, 1750
11778. 6 discourses, 1750
11779. 5 discourses, 1750, and Prayers
11780. 3 lectures, 1751
11781. 5 discourses, 1751
11782. 5 discourses, 1751
11783. 6 discourses, 1752
11784. 5 discourses, 1752
11785. 7 discourses, 1752
11786. 5 discourses, 1752
11787. 7 discourses, 1753
11788. 6 discourses, 1753
11789. 7 discourses, 1753
11790. 6 discourses, 1753
11791. 2 discourses, 1753, and Prayers, 1753
11792. 4 discourses, 1753
11793. 5 lectures, 1753
11794. 7 lectures, 1753
11795. 6 lectures, 1754
11796. 5 lectures, 1754

11797. 7 lectures, 1754
11798. 7 lectures, 1754
11799. 5 discourses, 1754
11800. 4 discourses, 1755
11801. 5 discourses, 1756
10576. 4 discourses, 1737, 1745, 1747, 1751
10577. 4 discourses, 1743
10578. 4 discourses, 1743 and 1744
  7118. 1 discourse, 1753
12199. 5 discourses, 1750
12200. 5 discourses, 1751, 1752, and 1756
19919. 4 discourses, 1728 and 1742
19920. 4 discourses, 1731 and 1743
19921. 4 discourses, 1744
19922. 4 discourses, 1744
19923. 2 discourses, 1744
19924. 5 discourses, 1750 and 1753
19925. 13 Academical Orations, 1726 and n.d.

The Guildhall Library in the City of London possesses seven volumes of Henley's autograph writings, with the following press marks and contents:

252.1. 10 discourses, 1728, 1730, 1731, 1732, 1733
252.2. 5 discourses, 1733, 1736, 1741, 1743
252.3. 5 discourses, 1741, 1747, 1750
252.4. 5 discourses, 1750
252.5. 5 discourses, 1750 and 1754
252.6. 5 discourses, 1754 and 1755
253.   A sermon on Nehemiah 8:18, 1750

Bodleian Library (Douce MS. 254), 'A Lecture for March 26, 1755'; (MS. Eng.misc.e.1), 'A Lecture for March 8, 1750, on the recent earthquakes'

The Library of King's College, Aberdeen (MS. 118, dated 15 Jan. 1748/9), Two sermons of 1749, 'On Second Chronicles X.16' and 'One Reason to give up Gibraltar'

The Library of the University of Birmingham (MS. 6/ii/8), two volumes of sermon notes for 1754-5

The following manuscript letters are preserved:

Bath Public Library (MSS. AL.2327), Henley to an unknown trouble-maker
Bodleian Library (MS. Eng.misc.c.113), Henley to Dr. Stukeley; (MS. Eng.Th.c.29, ff. 143-4), Henley to Dr. Brett

British Museum (MSS. Add. 32709, ff. 296-7), Henley to Pelham
Public Record Office (SP. Domestic 36, vol. 5.101), to Lord Townshend (?); (SP. Domestic 36, vol. 7.23), to the Duke of Newcastle

II. PRINTED BOOKS

1712. Letters signed Peter de Quir and Tom Tweer, in the *Spectator*,
nos. 94 and 578

1714. *Esther Queen of Persia. An historical poem in four books*

1719. 'On a Lady that could not help laughing at Nothing, and another
taking the laugh from her', in the *Court Miscellany*, No. II

1719-23. *The Compleat Linguist, or an universal grammar of all the considerable tongues in being*
    1719, August: *A Grammar of the Spanish Tongue*
    1719, September: *A Grammar of the Italian Tongue*
    1719, October: *A Grammar of the French Tongue*
    1719, November: *A Grammar of the Greek Tongue*
    1720, January: *A Grammar of the Latin Tongue*
    1720, March: *A Grammar of the Hebrew Tongue*
    1721: *A Grammar of the Chaldee Tongue*
    1722: *A Grammar of the Arabic Tongue*
    1723: *A Grammar of the Syriac Tongue*

1720. *Oratio habita in Schola Meltoniensi, ad Comitia Cleri, Calata, Maii
16, 1720*

1721. (Editor) *The Works of the Most Noble John Sheffield, late Duke of
Buckingham, etc.*

1722. (Translation) *A Critical History of the Establishment of the Bretons
among the Gauls etc.*, by Aubert de Vertot d'Aubeuf

1722. *Apotheosis. A funeral oration, sacred to the memory of John Duke of
Marlborough*

1723. *The History of Sweden; from the Most Early and Authentick Accounts
of that Kingdom, etc.*

1724. (Editor and Translator) *Pliny's Epistles and Panegyrick Translated
by several hands, With the life of Pliny*, 2 vols.

1725. (Editor) *The Works of the Honourable Sr. Philip Sidney, Kt. In Prose
and Verse, in Three Volumes*

1725. *The History and advantages of Divine Revelation, with the honour that
is due to the Word of God*

1725. (Translation) *The Antiquities of Italy*, by B. de Montfaucon

1726. *The primitive Liturgy for the use of the Oratory etc.*, third edition,
1727, fourth edition, 1727

1726. *An Introduction to an English Grammar . . . being number x. of the
Complete Linguist*

1726. *The first Sermon preach'd at the opening of the Oratory, etc.*

1726-7(?) *A guide to the Oratory; or, an historical account of the new sect of the Henleyarians*

1727. *The Appeal of the Oratory to the first ages of Christianity*

1728. *Oratory Transactions No. I*

1729. *Oratory Transactions No. II*

1729. *The Child's Guide for the Reverend Mr. T. Harrison, etc.*

1729. *The Conflicts of the Death Bed, or, The Javelin of the King of Terrors*

1729. *The Butcher's Lecture . . . being no. IV of Oratory Transactions*

1729. *Milk for Babes: or, a Hornbook for That Able Divine, Eminent Lawyer, and Honest Politician, Mr. H--s, etc. being no. V of Oratory Transactions*

1729. *An Oration on grave conundrums and serious buffoons, etc. being no. VI of Oratory Transactions*

1730. *The Lord he is God: or the Atheist tormented by sure prognostics of Hell-Fire*

1730. *Cato condemn'd: or, the case and history of self-murder, etc.*

1730. *The Reed of Egypt piercing the Hand that leans upon it etc.*, by 'Simon Croxeall, D.D.'

1730. *Light in a Candlestick, to all that are in the House: or, the Impartial Churchman*

1730. *The Pangs of Expiring Penitents*

1730. *Samuel sleeping in the Tabernacle: or, the model of Christian preaching asserted, etc.*

1730. *Sion in perfect beauty; or, the Heaven of Heavens*

1730 (15 December)-1741 (20 January). The *Hyp Doctor*, in weekly numbers

1731. *The Orator's Miscellany: Numb. I*

1731. *A Course of Lectures on Various Subjects*

1731. *Deism defeated, and Christianity defended*

1731. *The Original of Pain and Evil, etc.*

1732. *Miscellaneous tracts on several subjects*

1732. *A Lecture on high fits of zeal; or Mrs. Cadière's Raptures*

1732. *The Sermon that shou'd have been preach'd before the Societies for Reformation of Manners, etc.*

1736. *Why how now, Gossip POPE? etc.* (reprinted 1743)

1745. *The Coup de Grâce; Mr. Bayle's prophesy fulfilled, etc.*

1748(?). *The Oratory Magazine: Numb. III*

1748. *The Victorious Stroke for Old England, etc.*

1750(?). *Law and arguments in vindication of the University of Oxford, etc.*

1755. *Second St. Paul, in Equity-Hall, to Felix, Caesar and all, etc.*

1756. *A dissertation on University learning, deliver'd at the Oratory*

Index

This index is selective, confining itself to the main personalities, ideas, literary works, and events of the narrative. It has omitted single passing references to persons and events of no special importance. It does not record, under the references to Henley's own works, the occasion of every quotation from those works, the sources of which are always given in the footnotes of the text. It does not include references to all the secondary authorities from whom quotations are made, and which are acknowledged in full detail in the footnotes.